The Best of
OUTDOOR LIFE

THE SPORTSMAN'S AUTHORITY SINCE 1898

One Hundred Years of Classic Stories

From Outdoor Life's Finest Writers

COWLES
Creative Publishing

The Best of Outdoor Life
One Hundred Years of Classic Stories

Introduction by Todd W. Smith, *Outdoor Life* Editor-in-Chief

President: Iain Macfarlane
Group Director, Book Development: Zoe Graul
Creative Director: Lisa Rosenthal
Senior Managing Editor: Elaine Perry

Executive Editor, Outdoor Group: Don Oster
Editor and Project Leader: David R. Maas
Managing Editor: Denise Bornhausen
Associate Creative Director: Brad Springer
Art Director: Amy S. Mules
Photographers: Chuck Nields and Greg Wallace
Copy Editor: Janice Cauley
Desktop Publishing Specialists: Eileen Bovard and Laurie Kristensen
Publishing Production Manager: Kim Gerber

Specials thanks to: Jason E. Klein, President, *Outdoor Life*; Camille Cozzone Rankin, Bob Brown, Ed Scheff and the staff of *Outdoor Life* magazine; Judith Bowman; Bobbette Destiche; Guy Chambers; John Fletcher; Tom Heck; Highwood Book Shop; Iowa State University Library; Pete Press; the photo studio staff of Cowles Creative Publishing; Southdale Hennepin (Co. MN) Area Library; Tracy Stanley; Dave Tieszen; and the University of Minnesota Entomology, Fisheries, and Wildlife Library

Printed on American Paper by: R. R. Donnelley & Sons Co.
02 01 00 99 98 / 5 4 3 2 1

The Library of Congress Cataloging-in-Publication Data
The best of Outdoor life : one hundred years of classic stories / from Outdoor life's finest writers.
     p. cm.
   ISBN 0-86573-076-8 (hardcover)
    1. Hunting--West (U.S.)--Anecdotes. 2. Fishing--West (U.S.)--Anecdotes.
  3. Outdoor life--West (U.S.)--Anecdotes. I. Outdoor life (Denver, Colo.)
  SK45.B47 1998
  799.2--dc21   97-44258

TABLE OF CONTENTS

INTRODUCTION by Todd W. Smith

It is interesting, though not surprising, that the first storytellers were hunter-gatherers. Long before the Dead Sea Scrolls or Virgil's *Aeneid*, men gathered around fires in smoky caves to hear the telling of great hunts.

Just as we feel the need to strike out into the wilderness to stalk a deer or cast upon some faraway stream in search of trout, the importance of coming home to tell the story of that experience is as old as man himself. As contemporary sportsmen, the need to share stories from the field is in our blood just as surely as it flowed through the veins of our Neanderthal forebearers. And I can't help but believe that somewhere, in some cave painting perhaps not yet scrutinized by scholars and anthropologists, we'll find evidence that on a particular day an ancient group of hunters sat spellbound by a crackling blaze as the master bard of the clan told the story of the great saber-toothed cat that got away.

J.A. McGuire, *Outdoor Life's* founding editor, understood the fundamental importance of storytelling to outdoorsmen. He set out to attract the greatest writers of the day and, in so doing, set the

standard of writing excellence for every editor that followed. Instructional stories that make us better hunters and fishermen. Humorous pieces that make us laugh. Boldly written editorials that take controversial subjects head on. Stories that herald the need to conserve our fish and game resources so that future generations might enjoy the same outdoor experience we hold so dear. That's what has kept sportsmen subscribing to *Outdoor Life* all these years. And it is that same honest, straightforward writing that keeps readers satisfied today.

Over the course of its 100-year history, *Outdoor Life* has been a showcase for many of the 20th century's most famous hunting and fishing writers—authors like Zane Grey, Archibald Rutledge, Townsend Whelen, Russell Annabel and Jack O'Connor.

Born in a small Denver office in 1898, *Outdoor Life* chronicled the final taming of the West. And on each page there was the underlying sense of adventure that comes with challenging Nature on her own terms with rod or rifle. To that end, *Outdoor Life* has featured dozens of stories in which sportsmen were attacked by grizzlies, charged by lions and stalked

by cougars who, in the end, managed to turn the hunter into the hunted.

Over the years the magazine has attracted a number of famous personalities to its pages—all of whom were proud of their skills as outdoorsmen. Among them are men such as Ernest Hemingway, Theodore Roosevelt, Grancel Fitz and Fred Bear. Their tales of high adventure have always served to balance the strong conservation message played out in the pages of *Outdoor Life* by such notable authors as Aldo Leopold, Dall DeWeese and Ben East. It is through their writing that readers today will come to understand the pivotal role *Outdoor Life* played in getting such important conservation legislation as the Lacey Act passed.

Finally, there are a number of authors who simply fall into the category of "classic" *Outdoor Life* authors, many of whom, like Charles Elliott, Jim Carmichel, Jim Zumbo and Jerry Gibbs, comprise the backbone of today's editorial staff.

What follows is a compendium of the "best of the best" stories that have ever graced the pages of *Outdoor Life*. Having to narrow the field of

possible inclusions has taken the editors at Cowles Creative Publishing months of hard research. And I know just how difficult the decision to cut certain candidates must have been.

What they have created, however, is a wonderful glimpse into the rich written history that has built the *Outdoor Life* legacy. So find a comfortable chair by the fire, top off your glass and prepare to feast on the wonderful storytelling that is *The Best of* Outdoor Life—*100 Years of Classic Stories.*

Todd W. Smith

Todd W. Smith, Editor-in-Chief
November 16, 1997
Rye, New York

HUNTING

A MOOSE HUNT
IN ALASKA by Dall DeWeese

The following story is the revised copy of a letter written by Mr. DeWeese from Alaska to a coterie of sportsmen friends residing in his Colorado home, Canon City, relating the experiences of an Alaska hunt on which the largest moose ever recorded was killed. As the story is best told in the great hunter's simple language to his friends, we reprint it verbatim at his request.—The Editor (1898)

COOK'S INLET, HEAD OF KUSILOFF RIVER, MOOSE CAMP, SEPT. 9, 1897. Consistent as I am with human nature, boys, I wanted one more moose and I don't believe you will say, "game hog," for you must remember that I am a long way from home and where these animals seem plenty and I am saving the skins and antlers to be mounted for my museum. Up to this time I could have killed two other moose with small heads (about 45 to 50 inches) and two cows and one calf moose, but I did not want them. After I secured my first bull it was then a good one or none. If you give this letter to our home paper and it should fall into the hands of some of the "would-be sportsmen," I will hear them yell "hog," but I should dread to see them have the opportunities for slaughter that I have been surrounded with on this trip.

The next day or two we looked up a better route through the timber to the lake and succeeded by following a well-worn bear trail which led in that direction. Mr. Berg still continued to pack my trophies to the lower camp and did not return that night, so I was alone in these far-away wilds some eighty miles from all but one living man, and he twelve miles away. As night came on I had a good fire going in front of the "lean to" and sat down on some fir boughs. Had you been with me, I know how you would have enjoyed your pipe and tobacco, but as I don't use it I sat there long into the night gazing into the fire; yes, all alone, high up on the rolling timbered table lands at the head of Kusiloff River, and my friend alone down at the lake. With lightning rapidity I recalled all your faces and reminiscences of our grand old times in former years, when I lived in Troy, and we made our camp fires on the Ausable, Manistee and Fife Lake Michigan;

camps on the Au Plain, Menomonee and Spread Eagle Lake, Wisconsin; Swan River and head waters of the Mississippi in Minnesota; Devil's Lake, Dakota; camps on Black and White River, Arkansas (where we had those turkey roasts and duck bakes in our "clay ditch oven"); then, dear Jim, the camps on the Savogle and Marinuchi in New Brunswick; camps in Wyoming, Utah, Montana, Mexico and all the streams that head in the big game country of our Colorado from North Park south to head of the Bear, Williams, both forks of the White, the Grand, Eagle, Piney, Gunnison and southward to the San Juan. In the burning embers of my campfire, I could in my fancy see all your faces, and how gratifying to know that those of you who were with me were true sportsmen and never a thing occurred to mar the pleasure of our outing, for the good and bad side of man or woman will be revealed in camp. How I wished you all with me that night and tonight for I am having too much sport on this trip to enjoy it alone.

As my fire burned low I rolled up my blankets and crawled under the "lean to" upon a caribou skin thrown on some spruce feathers and then with a thought of the dear ones at home, what tomorrow's luck would be, and with weary body I was soon in dreamland. Daylight next morning found me preparing a hurried breakfast of moose steak, boiled rice, tor-te-os (fry pan bread) and tea. I ate heartily, for I intended to make in a new direction that day. I had a birch horn with me and had tried the "call" one evening for three hours without success and thought I would take it with me this morning. About 7 I tried the "call" more out of curiosity than otherwise; first, the "short call," then the "long call," and repeated several times. An hour passed and finally my patience was rewarded by a light crackling behind me. I listened—then a thud behind the alders. I then made a "low call" and soon his mooseship waded through the patch of alders and stood in open ground (other than the tall grass) not more than sixty yards from me. Oh, for a camera. He would swing his big head to and fro, sniffing the air; then lowering it with muzzle extended stood silently working his ears forward, then back. I had detected a slight puff of air and noticed it to be in his favor. Suddenly he raised his head high and sniffed loudly and slowly swung around and made for the low timber; not rapidly, but simply as if he had made a mistake. He was a big brute but his antlers were much inferior to those I had. My curiosity being satisfied, I again moved cautiously along much amused; how plainly I can recall his every move, and I want to tell you I don't like that kind of moose hunting. I was dressed for "still hunting," and as I moved silently along how little I dreamed that I would be rewarded in not killing this last animal by having in my path a much better specimen of moose than I had yet seen.

About 10, while still hunting through rolling ground with patches of spruce and tall grass, I sighted a cow lying down within eighty yards. I looked carefully, knowing the velvet was now off and a bull might be near, and after crawling a rod or so I saw the wide white blade of a bull between the trees close to the edge of the timber. I put my glasses on him to look at his horns but it seems he had sniffed me and a startled glance showed his big horns. The cow ran to my left the bull to my right quartering and a little downhill. My first ball caught him in the short ribs on the right side and stopped at the skin in front of the left shoulder; he stopped and swung around broadside. I sent another clean through him. He headed off again and I pitched another one into him. He again stopped broadside and coughed hard and when his great sides would heave I saw the blood spout from the wounds. I knew he was done for, and while he stood there with lowered head I ran around and below him as I had heard a terrible rolling through the tall grass (four feet high) below him, and thought it must be a bear making off. I could see nothing and returned to the moose expecting to find him down and dead; but imagine my surprise when on coming up a little raise I found myself within thirty yards of that great brute on his feet and coming toward me with his head lowered, shaking those massive antlers. I can't tell how I did it but as I afterwards found I sent a ball at his head

which caught him in the brisket. Still he came and my next ball was better aimed and struck between the eyes. That stopped him and he sank down upon his limbs but did not roll over. Boys, I am frank to acknowledge that I was startled. I am cold yet never have I had even a grizzly give me such a feeling. As he came through that tall grass breathing the blood and tossing those wicked antlers, truly he looked like an old McCormick self-binder.

I was carrying my new Manlicher that day and right there saw an advantage in smokeless powder as well as once more before the day closed. However, I have used the Winchester for twenty-four years; in fact, my first hunt for deer in Henry County, O., when but 16 years old, was with the old rim fire Henry rifle and when the King's model of 73 Winchester came out, I got that and have used all models since and had them made specially to fit me. I have now in camp my special made 40-70-330 metal patched soft-nose, black powder 86 model Winchester, which I have used for the past four years. I brought both my guns on this hunt for fear something might go wrong with one or the other. Boys, you wanted me to report on this Manlicher and I must say that it is the most deadly gun I ever carried. Its great velocity of 2000 feet per second and its extreme flat trajectory makes it very desirable for long range shooting. At three to four hundred yards if held on the game the ball is into it almost the instant you touch the trigger. I was using the metal patch soft nose which will mushroom on flesh and the patch seems to be slightly cut with the lands of the barrel when fired and expands by the pressure of the soft nose when it strikes and then goes through the animal like a buzz-saw. The sheep when struck drop as limp as a rag, and the moose no matter in what part of the body he was struck seemed paralyzed from the first shot. Again, the gun is very light, which is a great advantage when you pack your loads on your back. You know I am not an agent for the Manlicher works, but let honor fall where it is due. There is, however,

A mighty spread.

an object to the close range between sights, for you must hold very carefully or you miss. This can be remedied by a peep on the rear of the hammer. I don't think they have any of these small calibres quite perfected; a few years more experiment will doubtless make a great improvement in them.

Well, there I stood by the side of my giant moose, without a camera or a friend with me to admire my prize. Oh, what a carcass. I had my steel tape with me and commenced his measurements and now give them to you as I put them down in my diary. Of course, the first measurement was the spread of his antlers which is sixty-nine inches; length of beam, forty-eight inches; palmations fifteen inches; circumference of beam burr at head fourteen and one half inches; circumference of beams at smallest place ten inches; antlers have thirty-two points. His great body measured sixteen feet four inches from lip to point of rear hoof; seven feet eight inches from front hoof to top of nithers; girted eight feet nine inches, and six feet seven inches around the neck at shoulders; thirty-three and one-half inches from tip to tip of ears; ears seven inches wide and forty-four

inches around the lips of the open mouth. What a match he will be when mounted for my big elk. Boys, I know that I hew close enough to the line of "true sportsmanship" not to be overcome by selfishness and will say that all points considered, size, massiveness, etc., I believe I have a world beater; but be this as it may, I will be satisfied when I get it packed out and home. Some hunters saw the heads through the skull and then when being mounted by some they are given more spread; I know of a moose head whose spread was eight inches more when mounted than it was before it was sawed apart and an elk head that is seventeen inches more than it was naturally. I haven't a sawed head in my collection and would not take one as a gift for mounting. This method doesn't belong to true sportsmanship, and it makes the animal look very unnatural. They say it was necessary to saw them apart to get them out of the terrible country. I say that a big game animal doesn't exist in such a country that makes it impossible to get the antlers out whole. I don't believe there has been game killed in a worse country of access than this. For many miles there is a mass of down timber, criss-crossed and covered with slippery moss, and intergrown with tall grass and bushes; then canons and ice cold streams to cross, but I intend to take those antlers down and out without sawing them if it takes all winter.

But back to the moose. It took me till 1 p.m. to dress him and I then started towards camp in the rain with the neck skin which was all I could carry, and content in mind that Alaska is the home of the largest moose in the world, and why not when this country affords such wonderful growth for food, and he lives to get age, which he must have to grow large horns; then his healthy condition does the rest. About 3 p.m., drenched, tired and hungry I was at the edge of the heavy spruce and thick willows six to ten feet in height and heard a cracking near me— thought 'twas a moose—then saw the willows shake near me, and stepping upon a rotten log and looking about, there, within twenty-five feet, on his hind legs, looking at me over the willows, stood one of those fighting Alaskan grizzlies. I had this neck skin of moose, shot pouch fashion, over my neck with left arm free; but in an instant I cocked my Manlicher while bringing it in position and plugged him through the neck just under the head. He dropped and I stepped from the log that I could see better under the willows and sent another ball through his shoulders while he was roaring and fighting the willows and ground. I used lead and gave him another through the neck which settled him. I still kept the neck skin on, thinking to use it for a shield if he charged me. He had evidently scented the skin and was coming right after it. This was some sport. He is a monster, has claws four inches long, head twenty-two inches from nose to ears, measures ten feet seven inches stretch; foot eight by twelve inches and has a good coat of hair. It took me till dark to skin him and after it was off I could not lift it. I dragged it over the willows and left it and got in camp after dark thinking Alaska had bears of uncomfortable size and numbers for night travelling while alone.

As I approached camp I gave my usual shrill whistle and was answered by Mr. Berg through his gun barrel. Boys, how glad I was to hear it and when he came out to meet me, gave me a hearty handshake and then relieved me of my heavy load. As I neared the fire how appetizing was the smell of his good supper already prepared, and I might add that my day's work without food had something to do with my appetite. I was drenched to the skin and after a partial change of footgear we were soon drying, eating and talking of my "red letter day" which pleased my big hardy companion seemingly as much as myself; yet we knew that we had both taken great risks in being alone in these wilds. This ended my hunt in Alaska. I have killed two specimens hard to duplicate, and of the class of animals of which I have had such a desire to add to my collection. I am more than pleased and wish all my hunting friends were here now, to take a look and a shake. Mr. Berg says they are more massive and heavier than the record head he killed two years ago which was mentioned in Forest and Stream, of March 6th, 1897.

It has been raining and snowing all day. We will now pack every thing down to the lake and I will care for my heads and skins and work homeward as fast as possible, for truly I feel that I am well paid for my long and tiresome journey of 8000 miles, round trip, on land and sea. I am compelled to travel 185 miles from here on foot and log canoe to reach the steamboat landing. It is now too dark to write and will finish at lower camp. We will make supper of moose steak, boiled rice, wild red current sauce and tea.

Dall DeWeese

CONQUEST OF THE
KING OF THE GRIZZLIES by Jack Bell

"Old Mose," the most dreaded grizzly bear in the entire United States, met a death befitting his long life of murder and outrage at 4 o'clock Saturday evening, April 30th. His last stand was made in a quaking asp draw within the confines of his home among the broken rocks at the northwest corner of Black Mountain near Canon City, Colo. He died befitting his rank and lay down in his last sleep with imposing grandeur. Just think, after being shot through and through times without number, baited with every device and cunning known to the trapper; chased by demon posses of cowboys and ranchers bent upon his extermination, and in all this he has met them with superior generalship, cunning unexcelled, knowledge supreme, and for thirty-five years by actual record of the cattlemen of this middle Southern Colorado country. (It is estimated that he was five years old when he first gave evidence of his presence in that section.) His taking away is due solely to the years of training of a pack of incomparable bear dogs, who know their quarry, his habits, mode of attack, retreat, as well as this magnificent animal himself. He was handicapped by this band of intelligent trainers and knew not their circling, pinching, running away tactics. All this was new to the old monarch—the talk of the dogs brought him to a standstill with wonder and amazement. He did not even strike at them, but sat still and seemed to ponder and try to unravel their unknown and untried quality that he had never before been called upon to meet. So he sat and looked and looked, without a growl or even a passing of the murderous paws. J. W. Anthony knew the language of his pack with wonderment, this hunter with over forty bear

pelts to his credit, and his amazement grew as he watched the unusual action of the monstrous grizzly.

"Now, what in thunder is that old fellow figuring on? Never in my life did I see such an attitude of utter indifference by any bear towards my dogs," muttered Anthony.

"I'll just take a shot—lemme see—about eighty yards."

Bang! went the carbine carrying a softnosed .30-40. Old Mose ignored the shot, although it went through his jowl and cut a quaking asp on the other side. "Too low—darn that dog that was in the way."

The bleeding wound did not even interest the massive animal, and he did not as much as look toward the man with the gun. His interest was centered upon the four dogs snapping around his immense bulk. Very likely he said to himself, "You are not the first that has put bullets in me. I'll attend to you later—at present I must investigate these funny acting little dogs." The second shot went into the left shoulder and passed clear through, and still he stood speculating upon the very little fighters— merely glancing at the man who was firing the death-dealing missiles into his body. The third shot brought the seeming inanimate body into lightning activity. The bullet struck a quaking asp and threw splinters into his face. A sweep of his mighty paw directed at one of the dogs cost him a claw, and, missing the dogs, he uprooted an aspen that was six inches in diameter. But never a snarl or a growl from this king of all grizzlies. He, however, in a leisurely manner, without even condescending to notice the

Supposed to be the father of Old Mose, killed on 39-Mile Mountain, by J. J. Pike, in 1894. Weight, 997 pounds.

dogs, started at a slow walk toward Anthony. The hunter fired his fourth shot, which went a bit high through the shoulders, and "Old Mose" turned and went back to the point where the dogs had stopped him and sat up for a moment, apparently surveying the country, and acted as though there was neither man nor dogs within a thousand miles. The fifth and sixth shots were hurled into the carcass, both taking effect through the shoulders, and never a howl, growl or snarl did he make. He took his medicine in the same manner as he had administered his power for thirty-five years—neither giving nor asking quarter. The sixth shot did not bring forth the expected, the awful death cry of the bear, neither did he by sign or symptom show cowardice or anger.

Looking steadfastly at the man refilling the magazine of his rifle for a few seconds, he at last made up his mind that it would be policy to first kill him and then pursue his uninterrupted analysis of these strange dogs that had had the courage to snap at him and tear bunches of his fur from his incomparable coat. Slowly he started toward the hunter, never leaving the awkward, slow walk of his species. His eyes burned as with fire, and his coming was terrorizing to any but the seasoned bear killer. When at about sixty-two feet away he lowered his head with an unsounded challenge, and as his head was bending low, the hunter drew bead at the point between the ears, and, taking a long breath, gently began pressing the trigger. Slowly, as the mountain pine begins to fall under the woodman's ax, Old Mose, the terror of all, man and beast alike, began to settle down. Slowly, slowly, with neither sound nor quiver, the massive king gave up his life as he had lived it, in blood and violence. He met his death with honor, willing to the last to measure his great strength and cunning in mortal combat with that of the hunter, who dared to stand before him and dispute his reign.

Beyond any reasonable doubt, Old Mose has cost the cattlemen thousands of dollars by his depredations. He was seen by a cowboy to run down a three-year-old bull, slap it over the withers, and, while down and struggling, turn it over and sink his wicked teeth through the neck, instantly killing him. Another stunt much in vogue with the old fellow was to spy upon lonely prospectors in the hills, appear before them suddenly, sit up, and let out an unearthly growl, and seemingly enjoy the fright and stampede of the nearly-scared-to-death man.

Jack Ratcliffe, an old-time bear hunter, camped on his trail for years and years. In 1886, with a party of hunters, he got on Old Mose's trail. For ten days they followed his fresh signs all the time. Up in a rough gulch on Tallahassee Mountain Ratcliffe found his den, and while peering down into the box gulch,

fell. In a second Old Mose came out of the rocks, twenty-five feet away, and charged the intruder. Ratcliffe fired his Old Henry. He was unable to load and fire again. The bear took one fell swoop of his iron arm and paw, and Ratcliffe fell to the ground, scalp torn completely from his head and cut five gashes entirely down his back, stripping the flesh from the bones. He fell fainting, and Old Mose walked away. When he revived he began to call and his companions heard him, but, unfortunately, so did the bear, and with another rush he was upon his victim and began his murder. He cuffed and bit him until he was a mass of broken bones and mutilated flesh. Old Mose hit the trail, and when the hunters found their friend they gave up all thought of the bear. He was tenderly carried to Stirrup ranch, and the boys started to Fairplay with the suffering man to obtain the services of the nearest doctor. He died on the way, and the last words he uttered were: "Boys, don't hunt that bear."

James Asher, an old-time hunter, met the same fate as Ratcliffe several years later and in almost the identical manner.

On Cameron Mountain, over in the Glenwood country, a skeleton was found with a rusty rifle beside it. The gun was identified as the one made by Pap Rudolph of Canon City, and Old Mose was credited with the death. Last summer a skeleton was found on Thirty-Nine-Mile mountain, that of a cowboy, the boots and spurs were beside the bones, and as this was the stamping ground of this mammoth, he was duly credited with the murder.

J. W. Anthony came to Canon City from Idaho, where he has hunted bear for years. Last year he took sixteen hides. For years he has read of Old Mose, and came here to take a try at him. With him he brought thirty well-trained bear dogs. W. H. Pigg of Stirrup ranch fame, invited him to his ranch for the purpose of hunting the king. For two months they have scoured the country, and found his trail on the 26th of April, the day he had come out of his winter's sleep. They trailed him faithfully and well. When the dogs gave tongue to the fresh tracks, part of the pack back-trailed and Pigg took his bunch. Anthony was behind and followed the dogs that barked at bay.

Among the well-known hunters who have trailed Old Mose are D. F. Waterhouse, Dall DeWeese, Ira Carrier, Dan Hall, Joe Hall, C. W. Talbot, H. N. Beecher and scores of others.

William Stout and M. B. Waterhouse, two of the oldest pioneers of the Arkansas Valley, have both suffered the loss of over a score of cattle from the depredations of Old Mose, and to one of these men is given the credit of giving the old desperado the name by which he has been known for so many

The rocky, narrow pass that led across the Sangre de Cristo Mountains, near Alta Rita Peak, used by Old Mose.

years. What prompted the appellation was the manner in which the bear moseyed toward men he would happen upon—his slowness in leaving a carcass when fired upon, and his general habit of just plain "mosey." He has caused Mr. Stout no small amount of trouble, and many are the partly eaten steers bearing his brand that this bear has pulled down—of course he was always known by the missing toes of the left hind foot, and could be easily identified. A rather strange thing comes to light with the passing of the king. There has been following in his wake of murder a cinnamon bear that measured from the reach on their several rubbing posts, showing but a difference of eight inches in this cinnamon's height and that of the dead bear. This bear has never consorted with the old bandit, but has carefully followed him and taken the leavings that he has left—but never have their trails crossed. Mr. cinnamon has invariably been in the rear. Mr. Anthony has noticed this remarkable thing, as well as the foregoing old-timers.

C. W. Talbot, one of the old-timers in his country, gives the following about Old Mose: "Some fifteen years ago I was down in the Antelope country prospecting. At this time there was a reward of $500 offered for the carcass of Old Mose. The stockmen and the ranchers in this country were in terror of their lives on account of this big, three-toed bear. He ran the cattle ranges without a man's hand raised against him—they were all afraid of the monster. Even this big reward didn't bring out any hunters that were anxious to run foul of him. There were two or three men that had gone to the hills to look for him—and they never returned, and their bodies were never recovered—this was the reason that the scattered residents of the Antelope country were

afraid to go into the hills for him. He pulled down cattle wantonly, destroyed calves and colts, tore down fences, chased the people who lived in the country and conducted himself as an outlaw and degenerate. He carried on this reign of terror for several months, and then disappeared from his usual haunts—and I tell you that there was a feeling of relief in this section when he left. The following spring I was on a trip over here on Beaver Creek—just about twenty miles from Canon City—and as I was going up the stream I was astounded to come upon the track of Old Mose. Now, I have an idea that he would travel at least 200 or 300 miles to get across this country. He would have to follow up the Continental Divide, cross the Sangre de Cristo across the Arkansas River at his old crossing near Spike Buck, up on Tallahassee Mountain, then through the broken hills down there on Beaver. While I was down in Antelope Park the natives say that they heard of his depradations all along the Utah line. Oh, I tell you that he was well known all over the cattle country, and he has cost them thousands and thousands of dollars. I have hunted him for a good many years, but was unsuccessful in even getting a glimpse of him. That old bear was a heap more cunning than a fox—and I have never heard of but a very few hunters that got a shot at him, and then it was at long range. He seemed to know when a man was armed and acted accordingly; unarmed he would make his appearance and frighten a man out of a year's growth—armed, he would discreetly withdraw and disappear, although his tracks were still warm. I had a wholesome respect for him, and after looking his carcass over I am free to say that I am thankful that I never came face to face with him."

Jack Bell

RED LETTER DAYS
IN BRITISH COLUMBIA

by Townsend Whelen

In the month of July, 1901, my partner, Bill Andrews, and I were at a small Hudson Bay post in the northern part of British Columbia, outfitting for a long hunting and exploring trip in the wild country to the North. The official map showed this country as "unexplored," with one or two rivers shown by dotted lines. This map was the drawing card which had brought us thousands of miles by rail, stage and pack train to this out-of-the-way spot. By the big stove in the living room of the factor's house we listened to weird tales of this north country, of its enormous mountains and glaciers, its rivers and lakes and of the quantities of game and fish. The factor told us of three men who had tried to get through there in the Klondike rush several years before and had not been heard from yet. The trappers and Siwashes could tell us of trails which ran up either side of the Scumscum, the river on which the post stood, but no one knew what lay between that and the Yukon to the north.

We spent two days here outfitting and on the morning of the third said good-bye to the assembled population and started with our pack train up the east bank of the Scumscum. We were starting out to live and travel in an unknown wilderness for over six months, and our outfit may perhaps interest my readers: We had two saddle horses, four pack horses and a dog. A small tent formed one pack cover. We had ten heavy army blankets, which we used for saddle blankets while traveling, they being kept clean by using canvas sweat pads under them. We were able to pack 150 pounds of grub on each horse, divided up as nearly as I can remember as follows: One hundred and fifty pounds flour, 50 pounds sugar, 30 pounds beans, 10 pounds rice, 10 pounds dried apples, 20 pounds prunes, 30 pounds corn meal, 20 pounds oatmeal, 30 pounds potatoes, 10 pounds onions, 50 pounds bacon, 25 pounds salt, 1 pound pepper, 6 cans baking powder, 10 pounds soap, 10 pounds tobacco, 10 pounds tea, and a few little incidentals weighing probably 10 pounds. We took two extra sets of shoes for each horse, with tools for shoeing, 2 axes, 25 boxes of wax matches, a large can of gun oil, canton flannel for gun rags, 2 cleaning rods, a change of underclothes, 6 pairs of socks and 6 moccasins each, with buckskin for resoling, toilet articles, 100 yards of fishing line, 2 dozen fish hooks, an oil stove, awl, file, screw-driver, needles and thread, etc.

For cooking utensils we had 2 frying pans, 3 kettles to nest, 2 tin cups, 3 tin plates and a gold pan. We took 300 cartridges for each of our rifles. Bill carried a .38-55 Winchester, model '94, and I had my old .40-72 Winchester, model '95, which had proved too reliable to relinquish for a high-power small bore. Both rifles were equipped with Lyman sights and carefully sighted. As a precaution we each took along extra front sights, firing pins and main-springs, but did not have a chance to use them. I loaded the ammunition for both rifles myself, with black powder, smokeless priming, and lead bullets. Both rifles proved equal to every emergency.

Where the post stood the mountains were low and covered for the most part with sage brush, with here and there a grove of pines or quaking aspen. As our pack train wound its way up the narrow trail above the river bank we saw many Siwashes spearing salmon, a very familiar sight in that country. These gradually became fewer and fewer, then we passed a miner's cabin and a Siwash village with its little log huts and its hay fields, from which grass is cut for the winter consumption of the horses. Gradually all signs of civilization disappeared, the mountains rose higher and higher, the valley became a canon, and the roar of the river increased, until finally the narrowing trail wound around an outrageous corner with the river a thousand feet below, and looming up in front of us appeared a range of snow-capped mountains, and thus at last we were in the haven where we would be.

That night we camped on one of the little pine-covered benches above the canon. My! but it was good to get the smell of that everlasting sage out of our nostrils, and to take long whiffs of the balsam-ladened air. Sunset comes very late at this latitude in July, and it was an easy matter to wander up a little draw at nine in the evening and shoot the heads off three grouse. After supper it was mighty good to lie and smoke and listen to the tinkle of the horse bells as they fed on the luscious mountain grass. We were old camp-mates, Bill and I, and it took us back to many trips we had had before, which were, how-ever, to be surpassed many times by this one. I can well remember how as a boy, when I first took to woods loafing, I used to brood over a little work which we all know so well, entitled, "Woodcraft," by that grand old man, "Nessmuk," and particularly that part where he relates about his eight-day tramp through the then virgin wilderness of Michigan. But here we were, starting out on a trip which was to take over half a year, during which time we were des-tined to cover over 1,500 miles of unexplored moun-tains, without the sight of a human face or an axe mark other than our own.

The next day after about an hour's travel, we passed the winter cabin of an old trapper, now deserted, but with the frames for stretching bear skins and boards for marten pelts lying around—betokening the owner's occupation. The dirt roof was entirely covered with the horns of deer and mountain sheep, and we longed to close our jaws on some good red venison. Here the man-made trails came to an end, and henceforth we used the game trails entirely. These intersect the country in every direction, being made by the deer, sheep and caribou in their migrations between the high and low altitudes. In some places they were hardly discernible, while in others we fol-lowed them for days, when they were as plainly marked as the bridle paths in a city park. A little further on we saw a whole family of goats sunning themselves on a high bluff across the river, and that night we dined on the ribs of a fat little spike buck which I shot in the park where we pitched our tent.

To chronicle all the events which occurred on that glorious trip would, I fear, tire my readers, so I will choose from the rich store certain ones which have made red-letter days in our lives. I can recol-lect but four days when we were unable to kill enough game or catch enough fish to keep the table well supplied, and as luck would have it, those four days came together, and we nearly starved. We had been camped for about a week in a broad wooded valley,

having a glorious loaf after a hard struggle across a mountain pass, and were living on trout from a little stream alongside camp, and grouse which were in the pine woods by the thousands. Tiring of this diet we decided to take a little side trip and get a deer or two, taking only our three fattest horses and leaving the others behind to fatten up on the long grass in the valley, for they had become very poor owing to a week's work high up above timber line. The big game here was all high up in the mountains to escape the heat of the valley. So we started one morning, taking only a little tea, rice, three bannocks, our bedding and rifles, thinking that we would enjoy living on meat straight for a couple of days. We had along with us a black mongrel hound named Lion, belonging to Bill. He was a fine dog on grouse but prone to chase a deer once in a while.

About eight miles up the valley could be seen a high mountain of green serpentine rock and for many days we had been speculating on the many fine bucks which certainly lay in the little ravines around the base, so we chose this for our goal. We made the top of the mountain about three in the afternoon, and gazing down on the opposite side we saw a little lake with good horse feed around it and determined to camp there. About half way down we jumped a doe and as it stood on a little hummock Bill blazed away at it and undershot. This was too much for Lion, the hound, and he broke after the deer, making the mountainside ring with his baying for half an hour. Well, we hunted all the next day, and the next, and never saw a hair. That dog had chased the deer all out of the country with his barking.

By this time our little grub-stake of rice, ban-nocks and tea was exhausted, and, to make things worse, on the third night we had a terrific hail storm, the stones covering the ground three inches deep. Breakfast the next morning consisted of tea alone and we felt pretty glum as we started out, determin-ing that if we did not find game that day we would pull up stakes for our big camp in the valley. About one o'clock I struck a fresh deer trail and had not followed it long before three or four others joined it, all traveling on a game trail which led up a val-ley. This valley headed up about six miles from our camp in three little ravines, each about four miles long. When I got to the junction of these ravines it was getting dark and I had to make for camp. Bill was there before me and had the fire going and some tea brewing, but nothing else. He had traveled about twenty miles that day and had not seen a thing. I can still see the disgusted look on his face when he found I had killed nothing. We drank our tea in silence, drew our belts tighter and went to bed.

The next morning we saddled up our horses and pulled out. We had not tasted food for about sixty hours and were feeling very faint and weak. I can remember what an effort it was to get into the saddle and how sick and weak I felt when old Baldy, my saddle horse, broke into a trot. Our way back led near the spot where I had left the deer trail the night before, and we determined to ride that way hoping that perhaps we might get a shot at them. Bill came first, then Loco, the pack horse, and I brought up the rear. As we were crossing one of the little ravines at the head of the main valley Loco bolted and Bill took after him to drive him back into the trail. I sat on my horse idly watching the race, when suddenly I saw a mouse-colored flash and then another and heard the thump, thump of cloven feet. Almost instantly the whole ravine seemed to be alive with deer. They were running in every direction. I leaped from my horse and cut loose at the nearest, which happened to be a doe. She fell over a log and I could see her tail waving in little circles and knew I had her. Then I turned on a big buck on the other side of the ravine and at the second shot he stumbled and rolled into the little stream. I heard Bill shooting off to the left and yelled to him that we had enough, and he soon joined me, saying he had a spike buck down. It was the work of but a few minutes to dress the deer and soon we had a little fire going and the three livers hanging in little strips around it. Right here we three, that is, Bill, the dog and myself, disposed of a liver apiece, and my! how easily and quickly it went— the first meat in over a week. Late that night we made our horse camp in the lower valley, having to walk all the way as our horses packed the meat. The next day was consumed entirely with jerking meat, cooking and eating. We consumed half the spike buck that day. When men do work such as we were doing their appetites are enormous, even without a fast of four days to sharpen them up.

One night I well remember after a particularly hard day with the pack train through a succession of wind-falls. We killed a porcupine just before camping and made it into a stew with rice, dough balls, onions and thick gravy, seasoned with curry. It filled the kettle to within an inch of the top and we ate the whole without stopping, whereat Bill remarked that it was enough for a whole boarding-house. According to the catalogue of Abercrombie and Fitch that kettle held eight quarts.

We made it the rule while our horses were in condition, to travel four days in the week, hunt two and rest one. Let me chronicle a day of traveling; it may interest some of you who have never traveled with a pack train. Arising at the first streak of dawn, one man cooked the breakfast while the other drove in the horses. These were allowed to graze free at every camping place, each horse having a cow bell around its neck, only Loco being hobbled, for he had a fashion of wandering off on an exploring expedition of his own and leading all the other horses with him. The horses were liable to be anywhere within two miles of camp, and it was necessary to get behind them to drive them in. Four miles over these mountains would be considered a pretty good day's work in the East. Out here it merely gave one an appetite for his breakfast. If you get behind a pack of well-trained horses they will usually walk right straight to camp, but on occasions I have walked, thrown stones and cussed from seven until twelve before I managed to get them in. Sometimes a bear will run off a pack of horses. This happened to us once and it took two days to track them to the head of a canon, fifteen miles off, and then we had to break Loco all over again.

Breakfast and packing together would take an hour, so we seldom got started before seven o'clock. One of us rode first to pick out the trail, then followed the four pack horses and the man in the rear, whose duty it was to keep them in the trail and going along. Some days the trail was fine, running along the grassy south hillsides with fine views of the snowcapped ranges, rivers, lakes and glaciers; and on others it was one continual struggle over fallen logs, boulders, through ice-cold rivers, swifter than the Niagara rapids, and around bluffs so high that we could scarcely distinguish the outlines of the trees below. Suppose for a minute that you have the job of keeping the horses in the trail. You ride behind the last horse, lazily watching the train. You do not hurry them as they stop for an instant to catch at a whiff of bunch grass beside the trail. Two miles an hour is all the speed you can hope to make. Suddenly one horse will leave the trail enticed by some particularly green grass a little to one side, and leaning over in your saddle you pick up a stone and hurl it at the delinquent, and he falls into line again. Then everything goes well until suddenly one of the pack horses breaks off on a faint side trail going for all he is worth. You dig in your spurs and follow him down the mountain side over rocks and down timber until he comes to a stop half a mile below in a thicket of quaking aspen. You extricate him and drive him back. The next thing you know one of the horses starts to buck and you notice that his pack is turning; then everything starts at once. The pack slides between the horse's legs, he bucks all the harder, the frying pan comes loose, a side pack comes off and the other horses fly in every direction. Perhaps in an hour you have corralled the horses, repacked the cause of your troubles and are hitting the trail again. In another day's travel the trail may lead over down timber and big boulders and for eight solid hours you are whipping the horses to make them jump the obstructions, while your companion is pulling at the halters.

Rustling with a pack train is a soul-trying occupation. Where possible we always aimed to go into camp about three in the afternoon. Then the horses got a good feed before dark—they will not feed well at night—and we had plenty of time to make a comfortable camp and get a good supper. We seldom pitched our tent on these one-night camps unless the weather looked doubtful, preferring to make a bed of pine boughs near the fire. The blankets were laid on top of a couple of pack sheets and the tent over all.

For several days we had been traveling thus, looking for a pass across a long snow-capped mountain range which barred our way to the north. Finally we found a pass between two large peaks where we thought we could get through, so we started up. When we got up to timber-line the wind was blowing so hard that we could not sit on our horses. It would take up large stones the size of one's fist and hurl them down the mountain side. It swept by us cracking and roaring like a battery of rapid-fire guns. To cross was impossible, so we back-tracked a mile to a spot where a little creek crossed the trail, made camp and waited. It was three days before the wind went down enough to allow us to cross.

The mountain sheep had made a broad trail through the pass and it was easy to follow, being mostly over shale rock. That afternoon, descending the other side of the range, we camped just below timber line by a little lake of the most perfect emerald hue I have ever seen. The lake was about a mile long. At its head a large glacier extended way up towards the peaks. On the east was a wall of bright red rock, a thousand feet high, while to the west the hillside was covered with dwarf pine trees, some of them being not over a foot high and full-grown at that. Below our camp the little stream, the outlet of the lake, bounded down the hillside in a succession of waterfalls. A more beautiful picture I have yet to see. We stayed up late that night watching it in the light of the full moon and thanked our lucky stars that we were alive. It was very cold; we put on all the clothes we owned and turned in under seven blankets. The heavens seemed mighty near, indeed, and the stars crackled and almost exploded with the still silver mountains sparkling all around. We could hear the roar of the waterfalls below us and the bells of the horses on the hillside above. Our noses were

very cold. Far off a coyote howled and so we went to sleep—and instantly it was morning.

I arose and washed in the lake. It was my turn to cook, but first of all I got my telescope and looked around for signs of game. Turning the glass to the top of the wooded hillside, I saw something white moving, and getting a steady position, I made it out to be the rump of a mountain sheep. Looking carefully I picked out four others. Then I called Bill. The sheep were mine by right of discovery, so we traded the cook detail and I took my rifle and belt, stripped to trousers, moccasins and shirt, and started out, going swiftly at first to warm up in the keen mountain air. I kept straight up the hillside until I got to the top and then started along the ridge toward the sheep. As I crossed a little rise I caught sight of them five hundred yards ahead, the band numbering about fifty. Some were feeding, others were bedded down in some shale. From here on it was all stalking, mostly crawling through the small trees and bushes which were hardly knee-high. Finally, getting within one hundred and fifty yards, I got a good, steady prone position between the bushes, and picking out the largest ram, I got the white Lyman sight nicely centered behind his shoulder and very carefully and gradually I pressed the trigger. The instant the gun went off I knew he was mine, for I could call the shot exactly. Instantly the sheep were on the move. They seemed to double up, bunch and then vanish. It was done so quickly that I doubt if I could have gotten in another shot even if I had wished it. The ram I had fired at was knocked completely off

"The instant the gun went off I knew he was mine, for I could call the shot exactly."

its feet, but picked himself up instantly and started off with the others; but after he had run about a hundred yards I saw his head drop and turning half a dozen somersaults, he rolled down the hill and I knew I had made a heart shot. His horns measured 16½ inches at the base, and the nose contained an enormous bump, probably caused in one of his fights for the supremacy of the herd.

I dressed the ram and then went for the horses. Bill, by this time, had everything packed up, so after going up the hill and loading the sheep on my saddle horse, we started down the range for a region where it was warmer and less strenuous and where the horse feed was better. That night we had mountain sheep ribs—the best meat that ever passed a human's mouth—and I had a head worth bringing home. A 16½-inch head is very rare in these days. I believe the record head measures about 19 inches. I remember distinctly, however, on another hunt in the Lillooet district of British Columbia, finding in the long grass of a valley the half-decayed head of an enormous ram. I measured the pith of the skull where the horn had been and it recorded 18 inches. The horn itself must have been at least 21 inches. The ram probably died of old age or was unable to get out of the high altitude when the snow came.

We journeyed on and on, having a glorious time in the freedom of the mountains. We were traveling in a circle, the diameter of which was about three hundred miles. One day we struck an enormous glacier and had to bend way off to the right to avoid it. For days as we travelled that glacier kept us company. It had its origin way up in a mass of peaks and perpetual snow, being fed from a dozen valleys. At least six moraines could be distinctly seen on its surface, and the air in its vicinity was decidedly cool. Where we first struck it it was probably six miles wide and I believe it was not a bit less than fifty miles long. We named it Chilco glacier, because it undoubtedly drained into a large lake of that name near the coast. At this point we were not over two hundred miles from the Pacific Ocean.

As the leaves on the aspen trees started to turn we gradually edged around and headed toward our starting point, going by another route, however, trusting to luck and the careful map we had been making to bring us out somewhere on the Scumscum river above the post. The days were getting short now and the nights very cold. We had to travel during almost all the daylight and our horses started to get poor. The shoes we had taken for them were used up by this time and we had to avoid as much as possible the rocky country. We travelled fast for a month until we struck the headwaters of the Scumscum; then knowing that we were practically safe from being snowed up in the mountain we made a permanent camp on a hillside where the horsefeed was good and started to hunt and tramp to our hearts' delight, while our horses filled up on the grass. We never killed any more game than we could use, which was about one animal every ten days. In this climate meat will keep for a month if protected from flies in the daytime and exposed to the night air after dark.

We were very proud of our permanent camp. The tent was pitched under a large pine tree in a thicket of willows and quaking aspen. All around it was built a windbreak of logs and pine boughs, leaving in front a yard, in the center of which was our camp fire. The windbreak went up six feet high and when a fire was going in front of the tent we were as warm as though in a cabin, no matter how hard the wind blew. Close beside the tent was a little spring, and a half a mile away was a lake full of trout from fifteen pounds down. We spent three days laying in a supply of firewood. Altogether it was the best camp I ever slept in. The hunting within tramping distance was splendid. We rarely hunted together, each preferring to go his own way. When we did not need meat we hunted varmints, and I brought in quite a number of prime coyote pelts and one wolf. One evening Bill staggered into camp with a big mountain lion over his shoulders. He just happened to run across it in a little pine thicket. That was the only one we saw on the whole trip, although their tracks were everywhere and we frequently heard their mutterings in the still evenings. The porcupines at this camp were unusually numerous. They would frequently get inside our wind break and had a great propensity for eating our soap. Lion, the hound, would not bother them; he had learned his lesson well. When they came around he would get an expression on his face as much as to say, "You give me a pain."

The nights were now very cold. It froze every night and we bedded ourselves down with lots of skins and used enormous logs on the fire so that it would keep going all night. We shot some marmots and made ourselves fur caps and gloves and patched up our outer garments with buckskin. And still the snow did not come.

One day while out hunting I saw a big goat on a bluff off to my right and determined to try to get him for his head, which appeared through my telescope to be an unusually good one. He was about half a mile off when I first spied him and the bluff extended several miles to the southwest like a great wall shutting off the view in that direction. I worked up to the foot of the bluffs and then along; climbing up several hundred feet I struck a shelf which appeared to run along the face at about the height I had seen the goat. It was ticklish work, for the shelf

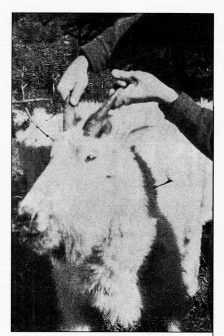

Head of a big goat.

was covered with slide rock which I had to avoid disturbing, and then, too, in places it dwindled to a ledge barely three feet wide with about five hundred feet of nothing underneath. After about four hundred yards of this work I heard a rock fall above me and looking up saw the billy leaning over an outrageous corner looking at me. Aiming as nearly as I could straight up I let drive at the middle of the white mass. There was a grunt, a scramble and a lot of rocks, and then down came the goat, striking in between the cliff and a big boulder and not two feet from me. I fairly shivered for fear he would jump up and butt me off the ledge, but he only gave one quiver and lay still. The 330-grain bullet entering the stomach, had broken the spine and killed instantly. He was an old grandfather and had a splendid head, which I now treasure very highly. I took the head, skin, fat and some of the meat back to camp that night, having to pack it off the bluff in sections. The fat rendered out into three gold-pans full of lard. Goat-fat is excellent for frying and all through the trip it was a great saving on our bacon.

Then one night the snow came. We heard it gently tapping on the tent, and by morning there was three inches in our yard. The time had come only too soon to pull out, which we did about ten o'clock, bidding good-bye to our permanent camp with its comfortable windbreak, its fireplace, table and chairs. Below us the river ran through a canon and we had to cross quite a high mountain range to get through. As we ascended the snow got deeper and deeper. It was almost two feet deep on a level on top of the range. We had to go down a very steep hog-back, and here had trouble in plenty. The horses' feet balled up with snow and they were continually sliding. A pack horse slid down on top of my saddle horse and

started him. I was on foot in front and they knocked me down and the three of us slid until stopped by a fallen tree. Such a mess I never saw. One horse was on top of another. The pack was loose and frozen ropes tangled up with everything. It took us half an hour to straighten up the mess and the frozen lash ropes cut our hands frightfully. My ankle had become slightly strained in the mix-up and for several days I suffered agonies with it. There was no stopping— we had to hit the trail hard or get snowed in. One day we stopped to hunt. Bill went out while I nursed my leg. He brought in a fine seven-point buck.

Speaking of the hunt he said: "I jumped the buck in a flat of down timber. He was going like mad about a hundred yards off when I first spied him. I threw up the old rifle and blazed away five times before he tumbled. Each time I pulled I was conscious that the sights looked just like that trademark of the Lyman sight showing the running deer and the sight. When I went over to look at the buck I had a nice little bunch of five shots right behind the shoulder. Those Lyman sights are surely the sights for a hunting rifle." Bill was one of the best shots on game I ever saw. One day I saw him cut the heads off of three grouse in trees while he sat in the saddle with his horse walking up hill. Both our rifles did mighty good work. The more I use a rifle the more I become convinced of the truth of the saying, "Beware of the man with one gun." Get a good rifle to suit you exactly. Fix the trigger pull and sights exactly as you wish them and then stick to that gun as long as it will shoot accurately and you will make few misses in the field.

Only too soon we drove our pack-train into the post. As we rode up two men were building a shack. One of them dropped a board and we nearly jumped out of our skins at the terrific noise. My! how loud everything sounded to our ears, accustomed only to the stillness of those grand mountains. We stayed at the post three days, disposing of our horses and boxing up our heads and skins, and then pulled out for civilization. Never again will such experiences come to us. The day of the wilderness hunter has gone for good. And so the hunt of our lives came to an end.

Townsend Whelen

HUNTING AFRICAN LIONS
WITH PAUL RAINEY by ER. Shelley

PART 1

Mr. Rainey and party had been granted permission to hunt lions in the southern game reserve of British East Africa. The permit came partially in the form of a request from the government, possibly for two reasons: First, the landowners along the reserve had lost heavily in ostriches and cattle by kills of lions. They claimed that they could kill all the lions that infested their lands, but it did no good as the reserve was their breeding grounds and as fast as they succeeded in killing them, others came in out of the reserve and took their places; secondly, we had broken the record for killing lions in the Southern Guaso Nyero River district. We went into that country with a small pack of dogs, the first that were ever tried in lion-hunting, and to Mr. Rainey is due full credit for originating this new and greatest of sports. Our success with this small pack proved that with a larger one of trained dogs we could almost exterminate the lions anywhere we should choose to hunt them. Mr Rainey was so highly pleased with the sport he had originated that long before the trip was over he had sent in a runner to cable to America

for thirty-three more dogs, and by the time we had returned to Nairobi the dogs were on their way.

Up to this time lions were classed as "vermin," and were on the free list with no restrictions by the government as to the number or method of killing them. However, after our return the government took a different view of the situation and there was talk among the officials of putting a limit on them. They were issuing many £50 licenses to hunters and every safara visited this district, and naturally every hunter that came to Africa for big game hunting wanted to kill a lion. There was talk that if we should return with our large pack of trained dogs and make another record kill there would be circulated the report that we had killed all the lions in the country. The government did not refuse outright that we should return, but requested us not to do so,

The author and the lion dogs.

Grass hut dining room on safari.

and at the same time tendered us permission to have a hunt in their game reserve along the line of settlement. We thought it fair that we should first hunt in the settled district, and so accepted.

We spent a few days hunting from the Athi River to Ulu Station, along the outside of the reserve, and on the Kapiti Plains we killed a good lion and lioness and caught two cubs, also killed four leopards, two cheetas and caught two cheeta cubs.

The morning of Sunday, October 1, 1911, our safara marched into Ulu Station on the Uganda Railroad, the north boundary of the great game reserve.

Our party consisted of Mr. Paul J. Rainey of New York, Dr. Johnson of Lexington, Kentucky, and white hunter Herald Hill of Roosevelt fame, Roy Stewart and myself. We were joined here by Captain Murray and white hunter Percival, with their large safara, also Chief Game Ranger Mr. Ousman, with his safara which included two Masia native guides. Monday morning we crossed the railroad into the reserve and the hunt was on.

The safaris, which consisted of over 100 porters, each carrying a 60-pound load upon his head, 16 pack mules, one ox-wagon drawn by 18 oxen, and dog gary, drawn by six mules, were sent across country to the first water, which was eight miles northwest, while we hunted to the north and cast up a stony dongo with occasional pools of water. There were many giraffe along the line of hunt and every water-hole had fresh rhino spoor about it. Partridges, fowl and wild guineas were flushed at every turn. Much damage had been done by lions in this vicinity, but we saw no signs of them, except one old track that had been made a day or so before. We saw many signs of leopards along the wooded spots, and one track was fresh enough for the hounds to trail a quarter of a mile or more. Had we hit this trail earlier in the morning the dogs would have worked it out, but as it was, the sun was shining on dry, parched grass and only the best hounds living could get even scent from the trail at all. Just at this time there were herds of Marsic cattle feeding along the watercourse, and while lions are very fond of cattle they do not like being disturbed in the day and no doubt had left for a more secluded spot.

We reached camp about 2 p.m. The dog gary had met us shortly after leaving the dongo, which saved the dogs a long tramp through the hot sun. After lunch a couple of hartebeests were killed, one for the dogs and one for lion-bait out on the plains to the west.

Monday, October 2nd, we started before dawn and made straight for a water-hole three miles out on the plains, known as Hills Spring. As we passed the hartebeest there was a string of hyenas and a pair of jicking leaving the spot, and only a few bones remained. There was a lion track at the water-hole but it was too old to run with the dogs. We expected to see lions that had spent the night on the plains and on their way to cover at daybreak, but in this we were disappointed, so we unloaded the dogs and started hunting down the dongo that ran to the east. There we found very scant cover and no water, so we finally turned up a dongo to the north, running almost towards camp. About a half mile up this dongo the dogs began opening at intervals. Some of our best dogs were giving tongue and we knew they had struck a lion-track. Farther up they struck the trail again going away at full speed, only to lose it just as our hopes were rising. Very shortly old Buster opened again farther up and away went the pack. They trailed to a small thicket about 10 feet in diameter and as they circled this the loud growling of a lioness was heard. We saw her break cover a couple of times trying to catch one of the dogs. She was about one-third grown and we mistook her for a small cub, so Mr. Rainey decided to rope her. He took down his rope and made ready to bag her the next time she broke cover. Suddenly he noticed her eyeing him from the cover showing signs of charging, and he immediately saw that she was larger than he had supposed. His gun was in the scabbard of his saddle so he drew his big .45 Colts Automatic and placed a bullet in her brain. We then felt sure there would be others of the same litter, or, perhaps, a grown lioness in the scant cover farther up the dongo, but were again disappointed.

We returned to camp and at lunch one of our boys came in from Ulu with the report that lions had killed a congony almost at the station door and had entered the Masia birma; also that one of their women had been caught and mauled as they were trying to drive the brutes away with firebrands. Mr. Ousman was anxious to kill these lions as they had done much damage among the natives, and a month before had killed two oxen belonging to Lambert and Wilson, who had come to Ulu for freight, camped within a stone's throw of the station and in spite of the fact that the native drivers had fires built all around them.

After lunch more hartebeests were killed to feed the dogs and boys, and a couple more left for bait out near the water-hole. The next morning the safaris returned to Ulu, and we started while it was yet dark. They hyenas and jackals had again feasted upon our bait. We spread out over a lot of territory scanning the horizon with our powerful glasses, but nothing was seen. We unloaded the dogs, hunting them down the main donga to Ulu, and many likely places were hunted out but with no result. The next morning we were awakened long before dawn by the growling of a lion far away, but his bass voice at three miles sounds much like the bellowing of a huge bull a quarter of a mile away. We were up and dressed at once, ate our breakfasts by light of the lanterns, the dogs were loaded into the gary, and we were on our way before dawn. The direction of the sound took us to the railroad track where the gary could not cross. As soon as we should pass over the first hill we expected the dogs to pick up his trail, but we went on and on, and in the third donga there was a lion-kill—only the legs and head of a congony remained. The dogs took up the trail but we saw at once it was not fresh. They ran in a semi-circle to the north where the trail was lost for the moment. Old Lee and Hunter opened and started back up the donga towards where we had started. Buster opened to the left and scented on a good trail, but the remainder of the pack cut in with Lee and Hunter, so we cut Buster off. They took us back to the place of starting on the trail, no doubt the one the lion had come in on, seemed greatly puzzled, and we cut them off and galloped back to where Buster had been running, and he proved right, as the pack took up the trail and carried it beautifully over a mile to the east. When on the highest point the scent got stronger and the dogs began going almost at their top speed.

It was a fine sensation galloping at a good pace with the sound of 30 voices in our ears and watching the pack all strain for the lead. On this high ground was, no doubt, where the lion had been growling a couple of hours before. As we mounted the next rise we all saw at a glance that we were doomed to another disappointment for all of the ground for a two-mile strip had been freshly burned. We knew that as soon as the dogs would strike this their nostrils would fill with the dry ashes of burned grass and the scent would be lost. There was one hope left—that he would turn up or down the donga, which he did not do. He made straight upon the burning, his big spoor at one place being plainly visible. The dogs now got down to a walk, and trailed him a yard at a time. The sun by this time was mounting high. We took the dogs across the burning in hopes of finding where he had come out into the grass again, but this we failed to do, and we returned to camp, somewhat disappointed but not discouraged, all of us entertaining the feeling that this kind of luck would not continue always. Besides, we all fully enjoyed the gallop in the morning air and were pleased with the good work of the dogs, up to the time we struck the burning.

The next morning we heard no lions, possibly because they had heard the dogs and saw us galloping, and had pulled out. At least, we hunted the country closely the next day, with no result, and in the afternoon moved back to the camp we occupied the first night in the reserve.

We had only two weeks allotted to us for this trip in the reserve, and in this time we hoped to break our former record kill of twenty-seven. Five days were already gone and we had only one small lioness.

The next morning we made another early start, moving camp to the Stony Athey River, 20 miles to the east. We had breakfast at 4:30 and by the time we left the table all tents were down and loaded. We took our guns and stepped into the saddle and started, spreading wide apart as day broke so as to command a view of as much country as possible.

ER. Shelley and one of the lions killed.

As we left the camp the dog gary fell in behind us, next came the huge ox-wagon with the long string of cattle leaning into their yokes, closely followed by the porters, each with his 60-pound load balanced upon his head, and the heavily-loaded pack-mules following behind the safara. The Askarias with long rifles were scattered up and down the line, the tent boys and cooks walking leisurely along without loads, the sicis leading the extra horses, the head porters and one Askara in the lead, and the headman bringing up the rear. Within 15 minutes the old camp was deserted and all were on their way.

We spread over a couple miles of country, a trifle to the right of the course followed by the safara. Game seemed rather scarce; a few bucks were occasionally passed and two or three rhinos were sighted in the distance, but no zebra were seen at all—a possible cause of scarcity of lions, as the zebra is their favorite food. We had gone six or eight miles on our way when one of the safara boys came to us on a run. The safara had passed three lions that did not run at sight of them, but laid down in the grass as they passed. We signaled to each other, the dog gary was close at hand, and we followed the boy back, and upon meeting the safara another boy told us they had gone down a donga, that had only an occasional tree for shade. Our hunter, Hill, was first to sight them—two big lionesses lying in the grass near the donga. We turned on the dogs, first giving Captain Murry two shots at them, and at the crack of the gun away went the dogs, the entire pack taking the one to the right. Away they galloped, with

dogs gaining upon them. As we mounted the hill the big brute was at bay, the dogs in a complete circle around her. She was making mad rushes at the dogs, and, as is usually the case where there is no cover, she managed to catch two or three of them. Mr. Rainey's .470 rang out, but he held too high; the second barrel knocked her down. Just then the other lioness rose out of the grass 100 yards to the left and galloped away. Captain Murry, his hunter, Percival, and Ousman galloped after her. It was our intention to let the captain kill her, and he was backed up by three good guns. We did not wish to turn the dogs in unless it should be necessary to do so. As he began firing, the dogs began going to him in spite of us. The captain was handicapped somewhat from the fact that when she laid down she could not be seen and when she got up he had to take a running shot. He hit her twice, knocking her down with the last shot, before the dogs came in. In an instant she was up and surrounded by dogs and was charging madly at them, as we expected, and got two or three before Mr. Rainey put a bullet through her brain.

The crippled dogs were put into the gary and we began to look for the third lion. The boys had run a half mile farther in, and two grown ones were sighted by Dr. Johnson. I tried to hold the dogs back at a respectful distance while the others galloped them down. They were young and gaunt and put up a good chase. The dogs followed leisurely along until I crossed the trail, and away they went in spite of me. The horsemen were now a mile and a half away and were dismounting to shoot just as

The author and lioness killed by him on this hunt.

the dogs came up. Mr. Rainey finished one and the captain the other (his first lion). The dogs were removed to shade, their wounds sewed up and strong disinfectant administered. They were then loaded into the gary and we started anew, the big trees in the distance marking the source of the Stony Athey. The belt of timber looked only a short distance across the open plain, but we marched on and on, and the sun had fallen low into the west by the time camp was reached. Everything was in except the ox-wagon, which was now in sight, the tents were up and luncheon ready for us.

We had had a hard day; horses, dogs and men were thoroughly tired, so the next morning we slept until 7:00 and started late. We left the dogs and horses in camp and rode extra mules, taking some boys to drive out reed-beds below the camp. We went only three or four miles down the dongo of the Stony Athey and began driving up towards camp, and when within less than a mile we came to a reed-bed 10 to 40 yards in width and 200 yards long. There were signs of lions along the dongo and spoor that looked to be fresh along the rushes. The 20 boys were marching through the rushes hitting them with their long sticks and shouting loudly. Mr. Rainey took a stand high upon a rock well ahead to the left, while Captain Murry and his hunter, Percival, stood under a tree well ahead on the right bank of the rushes. Mr. Ousman, our hunter, Hill, Roy Stewart and I walked slowly along, keeping in line with the boys. All of a sudden there was a tremendous rustle in the rushes as some huge brute raced through them. We could plainly see the line of his flight by the moving of the rushes, and he broke 50 yards in front of us. It proved to be a huge lion with full mane, going at top speed. The huge brute in his 20-foot strides was

a sight worth while. I had him covered as he broke cover, but Mr. Ousman said, "Don't shoot yet or he will turn upon us." I held my fire until he was 150 yards away, when three or four rifles rang out at the same time. Someone hit him, for he stopped stock still swinging his tail in big circles, looking to right and left and growling fiercely. All of a sudden he spied Mr. Rainey on the rock and started straight for him. There was another volley poured in upon him from three directions. Mr. Rainey was the closest and his bullet took him full in the chest, when he fell in his second stride. There was a momentary silence when one of the boys shouted "Symba engeane!" meaning "another lion!" Not a word was spoken as we faced them again, and all were silent as death when of a sudden the rushes began swaying again. The lioness broke cover at about the same place as did the lion, but on the opposite side. As she mounted the bank a volley was fired but no one hit her. She passed on into the opening opposite Captain Murry and Percival, and as she ran along the edge of cover they both emptied their big double-barrels at her. The captain grabbed his small gun and had a farewell shot as she disappeared in the heavy cover near the timber. I turned to Stewart, handed him my big .470, taking the small .9 in its place, as I saw at a glance the dogs were the only chance of getting her.

The sun was now high and grass as dry as powder, and scent would not last long, so I must get the dogs to the place as soon as possible. Mr. Rainey joined me and we went to camp at a smart gallop. My mule seemed most willing so I took the lead. We rode to the edge of camp, called the dogs, and started back. Dr. Johnson did not go out that day and though he came out to meet us we were away without a word. We struck the trail about midway up the opening, but the dogs showed no signs of scenting it. Our mules walked slowly along the trail as we encouraged the dogs to cast about. Finally old Dewey struck and opened, and away went the pack after him at full cry. There was a momentary loss when she went to cover, but when the old dog, Doc, picked up the trail in the heavy cover as the pack was going to him he came upon her and we heard her growl fiercely. She stood her ground at first, but as the full pack came in she broke and ran, almost knocking down a bunch of boys that were running to the scene from camp. She broke cover here, but was into the next jungle at a bound. The dogs came through on her trail 100 yards behind. As she left this thicket and crossed an opening the captain was afforded another chance and he fired both barrels of his .450. On she went, still unharmed. She was now in dense cover and circling so as to avoid the dogs. We rode at a gallop down a road until we came to an opening. I was ahead and first to dismount, but no sooner had I balanced myself upon the ground than she broke cover 30 yards from me. I fired, threw a second cartridge into the chamber and fired again before the others were ready. Mr. Rainey, Captain Murry and Percival all fired with their big guns within the fraction of a second after my second shot. I fired the third time with Mr. Rainey's second barrel, just as she came down, and I then gave her another in the chest so she could not hurt the dogs. By this time she was literally covered with dogs.

This was another example of the difference between hunting with and without dogs. Nine times out of ten the lioness is more dangerous than the lion, yet this one ran like a hunted hare from the dogs and showed no signs of charging, while the lion, which was not chased by dogs, was very angry and ready to charge anyone in sight. There is no question but that the dogs divert the attention of the lion from the hunter. They do not always fear the dogs but seem to realize that the noise will call attention to them and so try to throw them off by running and hiding. When one finally comes to bay he must stand and keep turning to keep from being bitten on the tail, so that the hunter can walk up to him apparently unnoticed, take his time and shoot him when he likes, while the infuriated beast uses his energy in trying to catch the dogs. There was a total of seventeen shots fired at the lion, six taking effect, and eighteen at the lioness, four taking effect.

Dr. Johnson, who had remained in camp, came running up with all of his pockets full of shells of the several different calibers, as he thought the reason we had stopped firing was because we had run out of ammunition. The lion weighed probably over 500 pounds. He was 9 feet 6 inches in length. The boys ran sticks through in under him and carried him to camp, then sang and danced around him while the skinners removed his hide.

The Askaria on duty aroused us early the next morning stating that lions had been growling to the north all the late part of the night, and as we were dressing we heard them far down the Stony Athey. We decided to go to the railroad, seven miles below, and hunt back to camp, and when within a couple miles of the railroad we heard one growl a few times near the dogs. Instead of going straight to the sound, we went on according to plans and then started up the dongo. When we were close to where we heard the lion, Mr. Percival found fresh spoor a quarter of a mile to the left of the donga. We took the dogs over and put them on the track up the trail at once, but was running out straight away from the donga and to where there appeared to be no cover. We thought they were going wrong as lions always take

to cover at this time of day, and we made the bad mistake of cutting them off. Most everyone seemed to think the lions were in the donga and that the dogs would soon strike should we continue on up the donga. We hunted on into camp without striking again. Mr. Ousman rode over the ridge in the direction the dogs were running where he sighted timber and a big stony donga. We could then plainly see our mistake, that had we followed the dogs we would have been certain to make a kill. In the afternoon Captain Murry and Percival, Mr. Rainey and myself rode over to the cover, described by Mr. Ousman, to prospect and, if a likely looking place, would lay a bait. As we mounted the rise we saw at a glance that there was splendid cover for lions, a fair sprinkle of large trees with wide-spreading branches, small clumps of brushes, and the ground was nearly covered with rocks and boulders.

We soon came upon a beautiful pool of clear water held in the basin of solid rock. Here were game trails showing much use, leading to the water from every direction. It was a choice bit of lion country and we decided to lay baits at once. A dozen or more hartebeests stood upon the hillside in sight of the water. Mr. Rainey and Percival knocked down two of them almost side by side, but one rallied to his feet and passed over the hill top, Percival going after him, and as he disappeared over the crest of the hill he began shouting at the top of his voice. I was nearly up the hill myself and as I came in sight of him he was running back to meet his sici who was trying to pull his mule into a trot to meet him. Captain Murry and myself passed the sici, at the same time casting an inquiring glance at him as he said, "Symba tarto," meaning "three lions." We galloped on after Percival and soon came upon him standing quietly and looking closely in front of him. He said, "Here is where I saw them last. Don't ride in until we can spot them again. If you get too close they will come in with a rush and take you off your mule." Just as Mr. Rainey came up I saw one in full flight over a quarter of a mile ahead. I pointed him out and away we went in pursuit. We were gaining rapidly and looking for him to turn and face us. I cast my eyes to the left, and there on the edge of the open plain stood a big full-maned lion. I called to the others and as we pulled rein we could hear him growling plainly. He had stopped at 400 yards, determined to fight for it. We sat in the saddle looking at him when he turned and trotted slowly out on the plains. We followed, taking care to keep without the 300-yard limit. He stopped and faced us again, but this time we were dismounted, all sitting down upon the ground resting our rifles across our knees. He was now lying on the ground, with face towards us, swinging his big tail and growling loudly. We opened fire and he made for us, though he was hit and his speed impeded, but on he came as best he could. The bullet from my second barrel struck him behind and turned him around broadside, two or three bullets hitting him at the same time, and he rolled over dead. Mr. Percival jumped upon his mule and tried to catch up with the other two, and though he got in sight of them once they made to cover in the Stony Athey. It was then too late to attempt a further search, so we started for camp, arriving long after dark. The Askaria went with lanterns to meet the shouting boys left far behind us.

PART 2

The next morning we started up the Stony Athey. Mr. Rainey and I kept close to the donga along with the dogs, while the others spread out on both sides and well ahead. Finally when about six miles from the starting-point, I saw some of the hunters galloping to and fro about a mile or two ahead. They were motioning to us with hats and rifle shot, and we rode across the donga and down a game path as fast as the dogs could follow. Mr. Hill had seen two large lions fighting, and at his shot they disappeared into a reed-bed, and as we came up other lions were spotted filing down from the plains to the rushes, seventeen in all. We decided to gallop them and shoot what we could before they made for cover, and then put the dogs after them. I took the dogs back to the gary while the others of the party galloped after the lions. To the surprise of everyone they did not stop in cover, but crossed the donga and headed straight out upon the plains. One large lioness stopped to fight, but she was shot and severely wounded. The riders made a wild detour around her and went in after the others. I had returned from the gary and started to cut across the semi-circle in which they were now running. There was a lot more firing and the bunch split, two lionesses and five grown cubs running my way. At 300 yards they dropped in the grass so that only their ears were visible. The other bunch was working for the reed-beds along the donga, and there was almost continuous firing behind them. Five of the lot reached cover. Dr. Johnson, who had fallen behind, now came up and we sat in our saddles and watched the galloping and firing in the distance, at the same time keeping an eye on the seven pairs of ears in front of us. At last the firing ceased and the five hunters galloped to us. We rode a few steps nearer; they got up and tried to escape. We galloped about 300 yards when they all turned and faced us. The two lionesses went down with the first volley from seven guns; the cubs started away, but soon faced us again. Just as we were dismounting one of the cubs started in 300 yards away, and was not killed until within forty yards of us. The others were fin-

ished shortly after the dogs were taken from the gary and we went with them from one lion to another, finding all quite dead except the first lioness. She was hid in the grass when the dogs surrounded her, and jumped up, making mad rushes at the dogs, catching two of them, which she mauled rather severely before we could finish her.

We counted up what had been killed that morning, a total of eleven. It was past noon now and we had no lunch, nor water left in our canteens, but we started for the donga. There were at least a half-dozen lions hid along in the rushes. We first jumped a couple of hyenas, which the dogs did not follow. Soon we reached the big reed-beds and a lioness was jumped at once. She held her ground well at first, but finally began shifting as the dogs crowded her from one end of the rushes to the other. It was nearly an hour before she broke cover, and then for only a single bound, but it was enough for Mr. Rainey to plant a .470 behind her shoulder, and she fell dead.

We continued on down along the reed beds. The boys were catching up with the lion skins. The skinners had finished their work only to find another awaiting them at the very minute they reached us.

The dogs soon jumped another lion, but this time it was short work. He galloped through the rushes past us and opposite Dr. Johnson and Percival, both hitting him a death shot. On we went until we killed two more in the same way, and caught a cub. It was now nearly sunset, and the big ones that Hill had seen fighting early in the morning were not far ahead of us, but camp was seven miles away and we were tired and hungry. The skinners could not finish what had already been killed before sunset, so we called it a day and left for camp. It proved another record-breaker for one day—fifteen killed and one caught alive.

We figured that we had only four or five days left and the real lion country was still in front of us. We planned for an early start, but felt more like sleep the next morning. It was a matter of twenty miles to the nearest waterhole, a tributary to the Athey River. Everything went smoothly and we reached the water shortly after noon. No sooner had we finished our lunch than we saw a man approaching on a white mule. He told us there were three large noble lions under the shade of a tree about two miles below us. They had killed a zebra and were lying near the kill. The gentleman proved to be Mr. Woodhouse, a quarantine veterinarian in the employ of the government. He had seen some of our boys that were sent in to the Athey River station with lion hides, and was on his way out to our camp to see a couple of days' sport. We gave him a drink and a sandwich to eat as he rode, and started without delay. I rode a short distance

Boys skinning zebra.

behind with the dogs, Roy Stewart riding behind with his long whip, keeping them at heel. The distance proved to be over four miles instead of two, but it did not matter, as the view we had of the country was rather charming. We rode nearly the entire distance down a large hogback that sloped gently to a donga on either side. We were in a game country now. Besides the countless number of hartebeests and zebra there were great herds of beautiful imperla and wildebeest, the latter looking not unlike our American bison. There were great numbers of gazelle, both Thompson and Grant, and a bunch of water buck and eland were feeding on the hillside across the donga. Diker, sten-buck and dick-dick were continually jumping as we rode along. Mr. Woodhouse had left our askari to keep watch of the lions until we could come up. He had the grass carefully knotted where they had crossed the road, and pointed to a tree 100 yards from cover where he had last seen them. We supposed, of course, they had gone on into cover, so rode openly to the spot, intending to trail them with the dogs. As we neared the tree, up they jumped, three large ones with beautiful dark manes, Mr. Rainey and Dr. Johnson firing at the same time just as they reached cover. Away went the dogs so fast that they were out of hearing in a minute. One of the lions was hit behind, and lay in the edge of cover, growling. The Doctor was first to see him and put a ball through his brain. We mounted and galloped after the dogs as fast as possible and came upon them a half-mile down in dense cover. The lion stood in tall grass and was also protected by a thick bush in which he stood. Some of the dogs were barking over to the right and we supposed both lions were at bay. Mr. Rainey and I both climbed high in

near-by trees in an attempt to get sight of them. Mr. Rainey caught sight of one to the left and took a chance shot. It was a lucky one, breaking his neck and killing him instantly. The dogs continued to bark and it was fifteen minutes before we could make out for sure that he was dead. We then sent the dogs in where we supposed the other to be, but nothing happened. We spent another quarter of an hour casting about, with no result, and finally decided to go back where the lions jumped. It seemed the only hope of getting the other big fellow. We spent a little time here when two or three of the dogs opened to the left; the others flew to them and away they went. It was a severe test upon the dogs, as the sun had shone brightly all day upon the already dried-up grass and it did not seem possible that they could carry the trail. They ran over the trail in 300 yards, which gave us a chance to catch up with them. We sat upon our horses watching the dogs try to figure it out. The black-and-tans, Buck and Jim, struck almost at the same time, and away they went, old Dewey taking the lead away from them. Another 200 yards and they lost again, Buck and Jim again showed their superior nose by picking up the trail, and again old Dewey showed his superior speed by taking the lead away from them. They lost for the third time, but only for a minute, when Buck picked it up and carried the pack straight to a thick reed-bed. It was 200 yards long and nearly as wide. The dogs dashed into it and the fierce growling of the big lion was soon heard. He was at the north end, but when the dogs came up, he broke, running nearly to the south end, which ground he held for some time, and the eight guns took stands nearly around the cover. He broke again, making a circle to the point where the dogs first found him. My stand was on the right side, nearly to the south end. He broke again and all were silent for a minute. A gun-bearer was pointing in front of me. I saw the rushes bending, but it was only for a moment, when he broke cover within twenty yards of me. No sooner had he struck the open than he realized the mistake, and his second lunge was back for cover. He was at top speed when I fired the right barrel of my big gun and he changed ends completely, falling inside the rushes. I fired my left in the opening he had made when falling, but he dashed on, growling at every jump, and thirty yards out in the jungle he stopped; his growls turned to moans for an instant, then he started roaring, the same as he had always done in his rambling on the plains. He seemed to be trying to call his last farewell to his mate in some distant donga, and his roars became lower and lower until at last they died away. We stood looking at the blood-stained trail that he had left in the rushes.

Finally, Mr. Rainey said it was my lion and suggested that I go in and see what had happened. The dogs did not appear to know whether the big brute was dead or not, and they nearly tripped me up dodging back and forth as I walked down the blood-stained path. I walked slowly on, peering cautiously at every step and finally came upon him, and some of the dogs were already tugging at his long dark mane. My first shot had entered his heart and the second one cut off a chunk at the root of his tail. He was a beauty, over nine feet, his skull eighteen and one-half inches long and very dense. These three were the best we had yet killed, all fully developed with splendid manes. I hope to keep this beautiful trophy as long as I am allowed to remain upon this earth. In years to come it will bring back recollections of this great chase and the final kill and the last calls of the huge brute will always remain fresh in my ears.

The sun had fallen low in the west. The skinners were hard at work when we left for camp, arriving just at dark.

We sent the askari with rifle and lantern, and a few boys out to meet the others who were coming in with the skins. We had only two days left and had already equaled our former record of twenty-seven, this time in two weeks, and we hoped to make another kill.

The next morning found us out early again. I saw a large male cheetah that looked like a lioness, the spots not being visible in the early light. We put the dogs on and had a splendid run, treeing him twice in low bushes. He jumped for the second time and we saw him charge for the next cover, where he was bayed among huge boulders. He was fighting hard for his life and Mr. Rainey shot him to save the dogs for another chance. We started up the donga leading to camp and the next find was a big leopard. He ran a quarter of a mile up the donga into a large reed-bed, and here he held his ground stubbornly. I was the only one to get sight of him, and saw only his ears for a second as he thrust his head into a small opening. I fired, but only pierced one of his ears. He was faster than the big lions and continually caught the dogs, mauling some of them severely. After a couple of hours we called off the dogs and set fire to the rushes, which burned slowly, but finally forced him out and he fell to Mr. Hill's gun.

It was past noon now, the dogs were tired and some badly scarred, so we loaded them into the gary and started for camp. It was unlucky that we found the leopard at all, as the best cover for lions was still ahead of us. The Masia guides insisted there were always lions in there. We had only one dog left and decided to hunt down the donga while the safaris moved into the station. We went across and struck the Athey five miles above the station, and no sooner had we begun hunting when we saw large crocodiles in the deep holes, and there were many hippo paths near the water. The dogs insisted upon running to the river for water and we feared a crocodile would catch them, so we left the cover, called the bout off and went straight across to the station.

Mr. Rainey ordered a special train for Nairobi, and the party split here, Mr. Rainey, Dr. Johnson, Capt. Murry, Ousman and Percival, with Ousman's safari, going into Nairobi, and the Captain's safari remained at the Athey until they should return and continue on to the Tana river. Our safari, Stewart, Hill and I, returned to Mr. Hill's ranch on the Kapatia Plains for a few weeks' rest prior to our next trip to the Taney river after Hippo, Rhino and Buffalo.

I cannot remember of ever having been thrown into contact with a better lot of fellows, and expressed regrets that the hunt was so soon over, and that we must part.

E.R. Shelley

KENAI MOOSE

AND BLACK BEAR by Russell Annabel

It came to pass that in the twilight of a September evening we hazed a string of packhorses down the west slope of the Kenai hills and made camp at nightfall in a grove of tall cottonwoods on the bank of the Chickaloon River. There were three of us, Gunn Buckingham, a sportsman from Memphis, Tenn.; Rolland Osborne, seventeen-year-old combination cook and wrangler; and myself, the guide. We had outfitted at Moose Pass Station, Mile 29 on the Alaska Railroad, and had come down the peninsula by way of the old Russian trail leading up Devil's Creek and across the forks of the Resurrection Creek. We were after moose and black bear, and planned to remain in the field at least thirty days.

A short distance below our camp in the cottonwoods the Kenai hills melted down into an immense reach of marshland—the Chickaloon flats—which is unquestionably the finest, or at least one of the finest, summer moose ranges on earth. At this season of the year, when the nights were getting frosty and the flies had disappeared, the moose were coming up into the timberline pastures for the beginning of the rutting period, with the cows and yearlings in the lead and the old bulls following a few days behind.

On the morning after our arrival Buckingham and I saddled up and rode down to a birch covered ridge on the margin of the great flat. About an hour after leaving camp, while riding through the close-packed trees, we saw a large black bear on a hillside ahead of us. He was in an opening, and there was just time for a shot before he would cross it and enter a tangle of alder bushes. Buckingham dismounted and pulled his rifle, a .270 Model 54 Winchester, out of its saddle boot.

"Think you can hit him?" I asked. The bear was about 350 yards distant.

"Reckon I'll try a shot for luck," he said.

I'd have bet money right then that the bear was going to get away without a scratch. Three hundred and fifty yards is a long shot at game in any man's country; and this bear was moving along the hillside at a good pace and was partially concealed by a stand of tall red-top grass. But I kept quiet, as a good guide should, and focused my glasses on the animal in order to call Buckingham's shot.

He lay down prone, spent a moment fussing with his Lyman sight, adjusted his sling strap, and fired just as the bear reached the edge of the bushes. I saw the grass weave under the muzzle blast; saw a spurt of gray rock dust puff up behind the bear; but I could not tell for certain whether he was hit or not. It was mighty close, though, and Buckingham's stock took a rise in my estimation. The bear turned, leaped a shallow gully, and started galloping back the way he had come. Buckingham grumbled something under his breath as he cast the exploded cartridge. Then—

Wham!—the little .270 crashed out again. This time I heard the indescribable slap of the bullet striking flesh. The bear stopped, half turned to face us, sagged slowly against the hillside, and suddenly came rolling end over end. A pretty bit of rifle work. I held out my hand to Buckingham in token of apology and congratulation. "You sure fetched him with that second shot," I said admiringly.

"Shucks," he said. "The first one was too far back—through the flanks. I pulled off, I guess."

And when I rolled the bear, a toothless old male, out of the rock pile he had come to rest in, I found two bullet holes in him—one through the flanks and the other through the lungs. The appropriate observation will occur to the reader without my writing it.

The bear measured six feet seven inches from nose to tail: not a record, but one of the largest I had ever seen. We loaded the pelt, skull and tenderloins on my saddle horse and returned to camp. The game trails we crossed on the way back were cut up with fresh moose tracks, and twice we saw spruce saplings which had been stripped of bark and limbs by some bull rubbing his antlers against them.

In the afternoon, while Rolland fleshed the bear pelt and cleaned the skull, Buckingham and I climbed a hill behind camp and killed a half dozen willow ptarmigan. The birds were just changing into winter plumage and their piebald coloring, brown and speckled white, gave them a curious camouflaged appearance against the green hillside. They were little giants of vitality. Two of them, shot through the breast with .22 longs, flew nearly to the base of

The author.

the hill before they dropped. Another, shot through the head, rocketed straight up, spun for a moment in an erratic circle, then set its wings and sailed a few yards into a clump of alders.

Just before sundown that evening we located seven moose browsing on a little plateau about five miles down the valley. At least three of them were bulls. In the slant rays of the sun their polished antlers gleamed like heliograph mirrors. At this time of year the bulls are the most conspicuous animals in the hills, the flash of their antlers in the sunlight often betraying them to the naked eye at a distance too great to pick out their bodies even with binoculars.

The next morning, September 28, broke, clear and cold, with a steady wind blowing in from the ocean. We rose early, and after an imperial breakfast of broiled ptarmigan breasts and bear steaks, saddled up and rode down to the plateau on which we had seen the seven moose. There was not an animal in sight, but I figured they were sleeping in a jack-spruce grove close by. We circled for the wind and approached the place slowly. I didn't want to jump them unexpectedly if I could help it; there is nothing more awkward than trying to pick the best head out of several stampeding bull moose. We

crossed the head of a grassy swale and rode down to the point of the jack-spruce grove.

Suddenly my horse, a spooky Oregon cayuse, threw up his head and snorted. We reined in and dismounted. Presently, swaggering through the emerald shadows under the trees, came an ancient bull. Ribbons and tatters of velvet dangled from his gnarled and twisted antlers. He was grizzled, sway-backed and lean. As he poked along he uttered deep, chesty grunts—Aghr-r-ugh, aghr-r-ugh.

It is a fact that bull moose aren't particularly bright during the rutting season. This old fellow was no exception. We walked along behind him, leading our horses, for 100 yards without attracting so much as a suspicious glance. Maybe he thought we were just two more moose. When he reached the denser part of the spruce grove, Buckingham and I tied our horses and followed more cautiously. In a moment he turned into a tiny opening, a sort of moss-carpeted arena. Here we witnessed a most curious sight.

Our ancient bull swaggered—he really tottered, I suppose, but there was a comical air of bravado about his progress—into the opening. Then, presto! there were four moose instead of one. A cow and two young bulls had come out from the timber on the opposite side to meet him. At once the trio of bulls began maneuvering about with obvious belligerent intent. As none of the heads was worth taking, I got out my camera and prayed there would be light enough to get pictures of the battle royal that seemed imminent. But no combat occurred. After a good deal of grunting and a number of warlike movements they suddenly jammed their antlers together with a clash and stood as motionless as statues. So closely was the pile of antlers interfretted that it was actually impossible at fifty yards to tell for certain which antler belonged to which bull. The cow walked around them once or twice, apparently quite as curious and interested as we, and then went off to nibble at some alder twigs. I didn't look at my watch, but we must have waited where we were for at least a quarter of an hour. When we left, they were still standing with their heads together. Buckingham suggested that the ancient one was probably imparting some of the facts of life to the other two.

Late in the afternoon we jumped four moose in a hillside burn—a yearling, three cows and a bull. The bull, a young fellow with a set of antlers that was almost in the trophy class, sported a splendid bell. It hung twenty inches or more below his throat. Old bulls with heavy, wide-spreading antlers almost never have bells of any length. I don't know whether they simply disappear with age or whether they freeze off during hard winters or are torn off in fights.

The next day, about four o'clock in the afternoon, we killed another black bear. We had crossed over a high summit to the head of a valley that ran down to another watershed, had seen several moose, none of which Buckingham wanted, and had started back to camp when the bear walked into the trail about 200 yards ahead of us. Buckingham tumbled off his horse and opened fire. At the first shot the bear started down the mountain like a streak. The second shot went wide, ricocheting off a slab of shale. Buckingham said something unfit for publication even in expurgated form. Then he knelt, pulled another bead on the bounding animal and managed, just as it crashed into the edge of an alder clump, to get in a finishing shot.

In this bear, as in the first one, the entrails were reduced to an unrecognized pulp by the 130-grain bullets. I had read an article in an issue of *Outdoor Life* praising the .270 Winchester but had never seen it tried on game before this hunt. It is all that was claimed for it. I have since seen it used on sheep, goat, caribou and Kodiak bear, and one properly placed shot always brings down the game with neatness and dispatch.

It was nearly dark when we got back to camp with the pelt. Rolland had a steaming, savory and most welcome rabbit stew waiting for us. He had shot the rabbits—low-bush moose, he called them—with my .22 pistol that morning while rounding up the horses.

The following week we were in the saddle each day from dawn till dusk, riding up first one creek then another. The rut was in full swing now, and there were moose everywhere. Buckingham passed up so many fine bulls that I began to suspect he was out for a record-breaking trophy and would be satisfied with nothing smaller.

The morning of October 5 came in full of sun and sweet mountain breeze. A shift of snow had fallen during the night and there was a keen tingle in the air, as if it were strained through ice. The cottonwoods in the bottoms had turned yellow; aspens were flaming on the ridge crests; Arctic heather smouldered blood red among the rough-strewn boulders on the hillsides. When we woke at daybreak this morning a great flight of sandhill cranes were circling above the hills, their wild, chuckling cries coming as clear as bell notes through the frosty atmosphere.

After breakfast we put up a lunch and rode across the range to the valley in which we had killed the second black bear. About three o'clock in the afternoon, while riding along the edge of an old burn, we saw our Kenai bull. He was standing back in a strip of spruce timber intersecting the burn and was rubbing his antlers against a sapling. It was hard to obtain a good view of him, but even a glimpse sufficed to convince us that he ranked high as a trophy—far and away the finest bull we had seen. He was late out of the velvet and the upper surfaces of his antlers gleamed under the trees like polished ivory. The blades looked broad and massive, and it seemed to me, from the fleeting sight I had of them, that they were fitted out with a wonderful array of spikes.

We tied our horses in an alder thicket and started toward him for a closer inspection. The wind was right and the stalk seemed a comparatively simple matter. The only trouble was the bed of a dry pond

Autumn moose country. This timberline valley runs down to the headwaters of Chickaloon River. From the rocky point shown in the picture I will guarantee to locate from six to a dozen moose on any autumn day after September 25. Figures left to right: Gunn Buckingham, Rolland Osborne.

that intervened between us and the timber. Coarse, dry grass, which made a terrific rustling and crunching under foot, was standing here. There was no way to avoid it, either; from any other angle of approach the wind would be wrong. So we crossed over as best we could, aware that we made enough noise to frighten an alert bull half out of his wits.

After a dozen paces into the timber I knew the stalk had gone wrong. The bull had moved deeper into the gloom of the trees. As the strip of timber was not more than fifty yards wide, I expected he would leave it from the opposite side and run out across the open burn. We ran to head him off, careless of noise now that we believed he knew of our presence—hoping only for a look at him before he was too far away.

The thrill of the stalk with a possible kill as its object had suddenly taken hold on Buckingham, and he sprinted after me through the bushes with surprising energy. We broke into the open, and came to a dismayed halt. No bull. Well, then he was still back in the timber and probably had not heard us at all.

We commenced working upwind through the spruces, with elaborate caution now. The bull having eluded us twice, we were sure he was the veritable Pearl of the Kenai. Buckingham played Uncas to my Hawk-Eye, putting his shoepacs down with a softness and precision that could not have failed to win a nod of approval from the grim old Sagamore himself. He carried the .270 at ready, with his thumb curled under the safety catch.

After five minutes of such progress, with the end of the timber almost in sight, I began to wonder if the bull might not have doubled back and entered the burn on the other side. By this time I would have taken oath that he was a Field Museum specimen. The thought of losing through a blundered stalk the only moose Buckingham had shown any real interest in, was gall and wormwood. My professional vanity, I thought, was going to be reduced in amperage after this affair. (Why the merry Hades hadn't I persuaded Buckingham to shoot when we first saw the bull, taking a chance on his being a good trophy? Then there would at least have been an alibi in the outcome.)

Well, we were nearly to the end of the timber. There was one thing left to do—separate, on the off chance the bull was on one or the other side of the burn and still in sight. If Buck saw him he could judge the head for himself and try his luck if it suited him. If I saw him, I could return and try to find Buckingham in time to get him back for a shot. Dismal prospect. Then—

A brown shade showed through a tracery of low-hanging boughs. Although motionless and formless, it was a color our eyes had learned to distinguish and register automatically. It was the bull. He was standing in a pool of deep shadow, and behind him were a cow and a yearling. The cow was looking straight at us, with her great ears turned forward and her bright little eyes staring hard. Only the superb indifference of the bull kept her from headlong flight.

The bull swung his head slowly from side to side. He grunted: Aghr-r-r-ugh, aghr-r-r-ugh. That was moose talk. He was telling his lady what a great fellow he was, and what he'd do to any presumptious young upstart bull who dared come within half a mile of her. He was modestly requesting her to observe that he was carrying the widest and heaviest spread of antlers that had yet come up Chickaloon River from the marshes—and please notice the number of points and pothooks, my dear, and the really exquisite symmetry of these brow antlers.

I had my 12-power glasses trained on him from a distance somewhat less than fifty yards and could see that he was a fine trophy. But I hesitated. He was facing away from us, and somehow that always makes a game head appear larger than it really is. I waited until he swung broadside: then I was convinced.

"Take him, Buck!" I whispered.

The .270 came up, wavered on line for a heart beat, held steady as a rock. Wham! A spurt of orange licked out against the shadows and the muzzle blast made the leaves dance. The bull slewed sidewise, half fell, then caught himself and staggered after the cow, who was already in full flight. The shot had taken him too far back: it had missed the chest cavity.

Again the shadows flickered as Buckingham's rifle crashed out. This time the bull went to his knees. His great head was in the grass; he groaned abysmally, drew up one long foreleg in a last struggle to rise. Midway of the movement he died, and rolled over.

A noble kill, lying there in the wind-dried grass and the fragrant Hudson Bay tea bushes. We stretched a steel tape across his antlers and gaped at the reading—sixty-nine inches. He would be a lucky hunter who took a larger head out of Alaska this year.... Tomorrow we would bring all the horses to the carcass and pack in the hide, head and meat. Perhaps the meat would keep long enough to permit packing it out to the railroad, where we could give it to the Indian school at Seward. An odd thing to think about—white

Taking off the cape. This picture was snapped just before the grizzly bear arrived on the scene.

men packing meat to husky young natives while they learned about algebra and toothbrushes.

I started taking off the head and cape. When I had worked down to the brisket on both sides, I straightened up to let the kink out of my back and to sharpen my knife. At that moment Buck gave a startled exclamation and dove for his rifle, which stood against a tree several yards distant.

Looking hastily over my shoulder I saw—by all the Red Gods—a three-year-old grizzly. He was not a hundred feet away and was ambling nonchalantly toward us, straight into the wind reeking of smokeless powder, blood and man scent.

I heard Buckingham's rifle bolt rattle, and an instant later the shot, fired directly behind me, nearly exploded my ear drums. The hollow-point bullet struck the bear with a smart whoo-oup, and I knew that this shot also was too far back to kill immediately. The grizzly went down, however, bawling, somersaulting and tearing up the moss. Buck fired again—and missed; he ran forward a few paces as the bear rolled behind a windfall.

Then, whang!—a third shot. The grizzly was still very much alive. Buck cast the empty cartridge just as the wounded animal gained his feet and made off in a crazy, stammering gallop. The next sound that broke the quiet was a metallic click: the .270 was empty of cartridges. Upshot: the bear escaped. Moral: keep the magazine of your rifle filled.

Back to camp in the clear Alaskan dusk. A mere bronze shaving of a new moon rose as we topped the summit and looked down upon the valley in which our camp was pitched. Far below, in the shadowy cottonwoods, we could discern the soft, luminous glow of the candle-lit tent walls. A thin stratum of wood smoke, shot through with starlight, hung like a purple veil above the trees.

As we worked down the slope, letting our horses pick their own way over the loose shale, Buckingham began to sing. The hunt was over, and it had been one to remember. It was marred only by thoughts of the grizzly lying out somewhere in the alders with a couple of bullet holes blasted through him. Perhaps he got well. I hope that he did, and that he will remember never again to walk into the wind when it carries man scent. Perhaps we'll meet him on the Chickaloon burn another autumn day.

Russell Annabel

THE LOST ART
OF STALKING by Howard Hill

PART 1

Through long hours of silent waiting, I used to sit atop a jagged cliff, and, with a pair of binoculars, watch some alert creature of the forest as he grazed, played, or rested, knowing that to stalk him was beyond my ability as a woodsman. A hunter with a rifle might easily have got within gunshot, but a man, attempting a shot with the bow and arrow, never!

Many bitter disappointments were mine when I first began to hunt big game with that ancient and discarded weapon, the long bow. Then I began earnestly to master the art of stalking, for only by proficiency in that art can a hunter ever hope to obtain game with the bow and arrow.

To me, it is sportsmanship to match my skill and stalking ability against the defensive skill of an animal, and win. But I feel that it is wicked to cripple an animal, or have him escape when painfully injured. Many more animals are crippled by long-range shooting than by any other hunting error, and, too often, they get away from the hunter before he can get in a telling shot. It is estimated that one deer out of every five that is shot at long range gets away wounded. In most cases, the hunter thinks he has made a clean miss and does not investigate. If he will observe animal habits a little more closely, and practice stalking more often, there will be no need of shooting at ranges so great that animals are wounded.

After all, most hunting today is not done for the meat, but for the trophy and the joy of the chase. The natural beauty of the forest and the streams is worth a long hike over hill and dale, and I don't have to draw blood every time I go out to appease my hunger for hunting.

The following suggestions on getting near the game are not made entirely from the standpoint of the archer. Any sportsman, photographer or rifleman, will be much better equipped if he has a thorough knowledge of stalking and animal habits. Most of us spend too much time experimenting with sights and grouping our shots. Not that sighting and grouping accurately are not necessary. They are, but a good stalker, with a sound knowledge of animal habits, can take a fair rifle and ordinary leaf sights and get more game and better specimens than another hunter, who has the best rifle obtainable, telescopic sights, and the latest ammunition, but who is short on stalking ability.

Anyone who is willing to give this branch of woodcraft the proper study will have little trouble in getting within 100 yards of most of our American big game, and I am told by widely experienced sportsmen that our own game is much harder to approach than that of Africa, India, Indo-China, and other countries.

A quiet stalker is a close observer. To be able to read animal tracks and other signs will often help a hunter to tell what took place perhaps many hours before. Again, if he is able to read tracks and signs, it helps him to get specimens more readily, and to get better ones. For instance, the hunter might trail a bighorn sheep for days, only to find when he catches up with the animal that it is a ewe. If he had been a little more familiar with the habits and foot costruction of bighorns, he would have known at a glance just what he was trailing.

A little study will enable a hunter to tell a cow elk track from that of a bull, a cow moose's track from a male's, and so on, with but few exceptions, through all animal life. Yet I have hunted with many moderately successful sportsmen who could not tell an elk track from that of a moose, let alone being able to distinguish between the male and the female of a species.

Most sportsmen are not to blame for this lack of observation, because they hunt with guides, and, although the guide probably knows these things, he never thinks of teaching them to the hunter. The hunter himself probably does not realize that anyone knows these distinctions, and that he could learn them in a short time. The veriest tyro can soon learn to tell whether an animal was trotting, walking, running, or casually feeding, simply by the tracks.

Every hunter since the days of Nimrod has had a desire to be able to stalk game successfully, but I seriously doubt that many white men have ever deserved to be called expert stalkers.

Just what does the word "stalk" mean to you? When I see the word, I instantly recall a bobcat I once saw creeping stealthily toward an unsuspecting rabbit in the Florida Everglades. There was no blundering or awkward movement in the entire procedure. To me, that feline advance on the prey was the epitome of stalking.

No hunter can ever hope to obtain the balance and coordination, the noiseless grace and ease of the bobcat. But, by careful study and long practice, he will be surprised to find how quietly and smoothly he can traverse the forest on the trail of game. There are several lessons in stalking that can be learned from the bobcat.

If a hunter is to stalk quietly, correct movement of the feet is by far the most important point to master. Because of the high center of gravity of the human body, and the fact that man walks on two legs instead of four, it is extremely hard for the hunter to move a foot forward, while he keeps his weight entirely on the leg and foot that are in contact with the ground, in the way that is necessary in good stalking. Such an advance is easy for an animal, as he has three feet on the ground to maintain his balance while advancing the remaining foot.

For another thing, the construction of the human leg and foot does not lend itself to quiet walking. The knee and ankle joints are directly in line with the leg bones, and the only possible way you can absorb vibration when putting your foot is by touching the ground first with the ball of the foot, then lowering the heel. If this is done without placing any body weight on the advanced foot, and with the knee slightly bent, a great amount of vibration is absorbed, and noise eliminated. For this reason, the stalker should never allow any of the weight of the body to be forward when placing the foot for the next step.

At first, few white men can walk in this manner without losing their balance, but it is the natural gait for the Indian. It was after very careful study of the gait of Charlie Snow, a Florida Seminole, that I found he never carried any weight forward until a foot had been advanced and securely placed.

When I discovered this essential difference between his gait and mine, I could understand how he could stop sharply with an advancing foot only a few inches from the ground, yet not touching it, and, at the same time, never lose his balance. Once

While one foot is being advanced for a step, the weight of the body should be kept on the other foot.

As the heel of the forward foot touches the ground, the weight is shifted, and the other foot advanced.

when he and I were quite close to a wild turkey we were stalking, he stepped over a small log, and, with his foot three inches above the ground, stopped abruptly, and stood for at least a half minute before lowering the foot. Had I tried to do likewise I would have been compelled to finish the step, or would have fallen on my head. Later I observed that not only the Seminoles of Florida, but the Blackfeet of Wyoming, the Mojaves of California and other Indians, all walk in this way.

Many times while hunting with Charlie Snow in the Everglades, I have left him, agreeing to meet a few hours later at some spot known to us both. No matter how much time I killed looking for arrows or stalking game, I always reached the meeting place first. On arriving, I would listen and look for Charlie, but invariably he would be within thirty feet of me before I saw or heard him. Imagine the lonesomeness of the 'Glades, with the shadows closing quietly down, then to discover suddenly an Indian standing only a couple of feet away. It gave me a creepy feeling.

After about ten years of practice, I have become fairly proficient in the Indian method of walking, but find that, if I don't execute the movement very slowly, I lose my balance, and my gait becomes jerky. To me, this style of walking is extremely tiring, and I have to think constantly to execute it correctly. Before mastering it, I killed only one deer with a bow and arrow, but since then I have killed eight or ten deer, two bears, a wild boar, a buffalo, a mountain sheep, two elk, an antelope, alligators, two wild turkeys, coyotes, and other game. Most of these animals were killed at a distance of less than fifty yards.

If you wish to get extremely close to a quarry, it is good policy to get on the hands and knees at times. By so doing, the hunter can take advantage of much shorter, and usually more dense, cover. Cover is always a great help in stalking, and the hunter should use every particle that is available, no matter how scant, for it helps obscure the bulky outline of a man. The mountain sheep, the antelope, and the wild turkey are three creatures that even the best Indian stalkers cannot approach without the aid of cover. Bear, moose, and, in some instances, the deer and elk, can be approached within bow range without any appreciable cover.

Patience and perseverance should be cultivated by the hunter. Anyone who already has these two traits highly developed has a wonderful foundation to build on. A high-strung person, though he may be persevering, is handicapped because of his impatience, while a man who is slow and easy-going is almost invariably lazy. No matter what type he may be, though, the hunter must have bulldog determination to accomplish the desired results.

I have seen a few white men and many Indians who were lazy so far as performing everyday tasks was concerned. Put them in the woods, however, and they never knew when they had enough. To give up any quarry without exhausting every possible means of getting it would be to these men a disgrace. Particularly is this true of the red man, and no better stalker ever drank from a mountain stream.

The psychology of the Indian is worth consideration. Dave Coleman, an Algonquin, has told me that he hunts each individual animal as though it were the last game he would ever see. He also told me to remember that most animals can see, hear, and smell at least three times as keenly as man, and that they know they live only because these senses are acute. This I have found to be very sound reasoning, and, when applied, almost always brings results.

Some of the Indian hunter's customs are, I feel, not only practical, but must be adopted by anyone who hopes to be a finished hunter. Most of the Indians I have hunted with have been men who live by their wits and are their own bosses, so far as government will let them be. More important still, they retain their self-respect and native pride. The usual tourist Indian, I have long since learned, is abnormal, and usually knows nothing of wood-craft. However, the unspoiled red man still knows how to hunt and stalk, and his knowledge of game and its habits is often uncanny. He can outguess any animal, and his ability to call game far surpasses the best efforts of white men.

In luring game, the Indian does not always use the call of the animal he is hunting. For instance, Charlie Snow's method of getting a wildcat out of the scrub palmetto so it could be seen is to conceal himself in a convenient patch of switch grass, then imitate perfectly the call of a hen bobwhite. If this fails, he waits a few minutes, then sends out the call of the turkey hen. Or he may try the shrill cry a rabbit makes when caught by some enemy. Invariably the cat comes slinking out of the palmetto patch to investigate.

Charlie will never use the call of the turkey hen unless there are wild turkeys in the vicinity, saying he has learned that, if he uses the turkey call when there are no turkeys around, the cat becomes suspicious. I cannot vouch for the accuracy of his statement, but it seems reasonable.

Indian dress is better adapted to the woods than that of most white hunters. Soft-soled moccasins are quieter than ordinary shoes, although in some cases not so safe. For instance, in rattlesnake country in Florida, or on snow-covered ridges, it is, of course, much better to wear boots. The Indian's loin cloth and moccasins are perfectly quiet, but the white man is far too soft, and has skin too tender for this dress. His pale skin would be too easily seen, and the cold rain and wind in most parts of the country would soon kill him. Even the Indian of today has added to this scanty costume.

However, the hunter can wear moccasin-type boots and clothes that fit snugly enough to let him feel any twig that touches him. Clothing should not be too tight for comfort and easy motion, but no hunting attire should be loose and floppy. A balloon sleeve can hang on a twig and break it easily before the wearer knows it. At close range, a snapping twig would, to most animals, be like shouting out, "Here I am!"

I have hunted with some men whose clothes, flapping in the breeze, would have frightened every animal within a mile—long four-in-hand neckties, loose coat tails, and balloon sleeves. To make it worse, they wore heavy-soled, hobnailed boots.

In selecting clothing, we should be careful to get colors that will blend with woodland tints in the country where we intend to hunt. I would not wear the same color in Mojave Desert as I would in the Florida Everglades or in the Wyoming Rockies. In every case, however, I would select different shades of mixed colors, leaning toward the darker ones. Any solid color presents a definite outline, and is, therefore, more easily detected than mixed colors.

This is seen in the protective coloring of animals. A bobcat is one of the hardest animals to see in any cover. He is not black, brown, gray, or yellow, but a combination of these and other colors, and he matches almost any background except green. Therefore, green, brown, gray, and a touch of black in a tweed mixture makes about the best combination of colors for a hunting costume in most locations.

When I get to the Happy Hunting Ground, I will be perfectly blissful if I can be clothed as unobtru-

sively as the bobcat, and can stalk, if not so perfectly as he, at least as well as Charlie Snow.

The same method of approach will not do for all animals. To get close enough for the most effective shooting, it is necessary to take advantage of the weak points of the game being hunted, and to circumvent its strong points. What North American game animals are hardest to stalk, what are their weaknesses, and how can the hunter get close to them? These are important questions, but the answers must wait for the concluding part of this article.

PART 2

To become a finished stalker, you must, in addition to knowing the secrets of silent walking, inconspicuous dress, and using cover to best advantage, know the weak points of each animal species, and how to take advantage of those weaknesses.

Although all animals and birds have habits peculiar to themselves, it is never safe to say that an animal will always do this or that, for there are exceptions to all rules. Anyone who becomes dogmatic about what a species will or will not do, is going to have an individual of that species make a prevaricator out of him. I shall never forget how a cub bear in the Yellowstone Park once made a plain liar out of a ranger.

At the bear-feeding grounds near Old Faithful Geyser, this ranger was lecturing the tourists on bears, while they watched the hungry bruins devour garbage on the "Salad Plate," as the feeding ground is called. The young ranger was closing his address by mentioning a few of their habits.

"Folks," he said, "bears have their own minds, but there's one thing I can say without fear of contradiction. A bear never descends a tree head first."

On the feeding ground, one little, black cub had chased his brown, furry brother up a spruce. Just as the ranger finished speaking, every one started laugh-

Chatting with Charlie Snow, a Seminole, who taught the author many stalking secrets.

ing, for, at that instant, the two cubs came down, the brown one tail first, in the customary manner, with the little, black rascal following head first. In spite of such apparent contradictions, however, we can be fairly certain that, in most cases, an animal will do certain things and not do certain others.

Of the great many North American game animals and birds, I consider the following the hardest game to stalk, rating in the order named: 1. Wild turkey; 2. Rocky Mountain bighorn sheep; 3. Pronghorn antelope of Wyoming and Montana; 4. Canada goose; 5. Wild burro in the Mohave Desert; 6. Eastern white-tail deer; 7. Elk of Wyoming; 8. Mountain goats of Montana; 9. Rocky Mountain bear; 10. Alligators in Florida.

The bobcat, coyote, wolf, mountain lion, wild boar, crow, crocodile, and British Columbia moose deserve honorable mention, but the animals listed are superior. For instance, all the felines feed mostly at night, and offer very little opportunity for stalking. The coyote and wolf also are night feeders. The wolf, too, is becoming very scarce. I did not include the moose in my first selection because I have seen too many of them that were nothing less than plain dumb.

The wild-turkey gobbler truly deserves top rank, if we stalk them in daylight, without using blinds or decoys. In the first place, the turkey has a marvelous eye, and its hearing is almost unsurpassed. It does not have a good sense of smell, but its eyes and ears, coupled with an alert brain, make it a worthy match for any hunter. Its lack of any curiosity and its decided fear of man, can be considered its greatest assets in eluding the would-be stalker. As Charley Snow, the Seminole, once said to me while hunting turkeys in the Everglades of Florida, "Turkey see—he go. Turkey hear—he go. If turkey no see, no hear—he go anyhow." To me, the turkey has never revealed even one weakness that would simplify stalking. Yet decoys, calls, dogs, and blinds can be used very effectively in getting it within shooting range.

The wary, Rocky Mountain bighorn comes a good second. Its eyes surpass those of any other creature on the American continents. It is wise and, in most cases, shows good common sense. While I was in Wyoming, making a motion picture of wildlife with Ned Frost, the guide, I watched a couple of big rams on a high divide, through a pair of 10X binoculars. The sheep were at least seven miles away.

They were feeding quietly, and looked about the size of young lambs, yet, when we passed an opening only a few yards wide while descending, one of the old ones raised its head, looked in our direction, and immediately trotted up the mountain. There was no doubt in my mind that the ram had seen us and knew that we were human beings.

On the other hand, we spotted a sheep, a few days later, on the side of a mountain. It was lying quietly under a ledge some twenty feet high, and, when we came up over the ridge behind it, we moved up within a few feet without disturbing it. We could not see the ram, but I got my bow into shooting position, while Ned rolled a small stone down the mountain side to rout the bighorn out. When several rocks failed to get results, Ned bleated like a sheep. Still nothing happened. Thinking the ram had gone, we began talking in normal tones, and sauntered up to the brink of the cliff. As I peeped over, I got a glimpse of horns. The old ram was as peaceful as if there was not a man within a thousand miles.

I nocked an arrow, and shot the ram through the neck, and it was dead in a few seconds. By actual measurement, the distance at which it was shot was less than fifty feet. After this, I many times got within close bow-range of sheep. In no case did I take any particular pains to be quiet, nor did I bother much about the wind. Ned told me that, in more than forty years of hunting bighorn, he never worried about their nose and ears. Their eyes are their chief protection.

In most cases, the feeding ground of the sheep today is about 9,000 feet high, and this elevation gives the sheep a great advantage. With its powerful eyes it can comb the trails and streams miles below. When a sheep has once seen you, you might as well kiss it good-by, because it will leave the country, for a few days at least. The sheep's extraordinary eyes and good judgment, coupled with the natural advantage given it by its haunts, make it worthy of second place. If it had good ears, and if its sense of smell were acutely developed, it would be in first place.

The antelope has long-range eyes and its sense of smell is acute. Its hearing is also keen, but its natural curiosity drops it to third place. This animal seems to be getting wiser as the species grows older. I am told by many old-timers in Wyoming and Montana that, in the early days, you could put a red rag on a pole, and lure all the antelope in the vicinity to within shooting range.

The open country, which the antelope refuse to leave, is a great advantage to them. Many of the Western animals once roamed foothills of the Rockies, but encroaching civilization has forced them to take to the high mountains and timber. Before the white man invaded the West, mule deer, elk, mountain sheep, and even grizzly bear and cougar were often found in the foothills and in the open plains country. Today, not one of these animals, with the exception of the cougar, ever visits its old haunts.

A valuable asset of the antelope is its terrific speed. On several occasions, a herd has been followed over dry lake beds at the amazing speed of sixty-eight to seventy miles an hour. They do not have the bouncing motion common to most deer and other fast game animals, but run like a horse. Their hind legs are carried wide apart, and they overlap the front feet by great distances. The antelope, however, is not so alert as the sheep, and, when excited, shows little judgment.

One interesting peculiarity of both the sheep and the antelope is the odd arrangement of their eyes. Their eye sockets are somewhat more on the side of the head than is usual in animals, and their eyes bulge considerably. These boldly protruding eyes enable them to see almost as well behind and to the side as they do in front. There is no such thing as sneaking up on the blind side of an antelope or mountain sheep. They haven't any.

The Canada goose is a wise and wary bird, feeding mostly in open country, and passing the night on large lakes and rivers. Nevertheless, any smart hunter who has studied their feeding grounds, can usually bag one by concealing himself near one of these places, because the birds ordinarily come into their feeding grounds at a low altitude, within easy gunshot or bow range. If you ever allow these birds to settle on the feeding grounds, however, you have a real job to make a successful stalk, for they usually have two or three sentries out. Once, in a central Alabama wheatfield, I lay in a hedgerow for four hours, watching a flock of Canadian honkers feed over about twenty acres. Not once were there fewer than two birds on guard. I thought they would probably feed close enough to my hiding place for a chance shot, but they were too wise. About ninety yards was as close as they ever got. This was near enough for a rifle, but very uncertain for a long bow. I am convinced that the geese depend mostly upon their eyes for protection, although they also are known to hear exceptionally well.

The wild burro of the Mohave Desert is not widely recognized as a game animal, but he should be. In the sixteenth century, Spanish gold seekers invaded the desert with pack burros, and often became lost or perished from lack of water. The animals, left free to roam the desert, would by smell find some hidden spring or seepage in the canyons. These burros began to breed on the desert. The California gold rush of '49 brought more men to the same region, and they, too, had pack burros.

Ready to loose one of the arrows with which he has killed almost every species of large game in this country. The author is shooting from the position most favored by the Indians.

Some of these mixed with the Spanish jacks. It is the strain of Spanish burro blood that makes the present Mohave jack so wild, and sometimes so fierce.

I have hunted these creatures for four years, and I consider no other game makes better sport for the bow and arrow. As a food, they are as delicious as corn-fed beef. Unlike the lazy, ungainly tame burro, they are as alert as deer, and often use sentries when roving in droves. Their eyes are good, their ears are better, but their sense of smell is unequaled. Often I have been scented by them a quarter of a mile downwind. Once a burro sees you, there is no way to get within shooting range except to run it down, and you have to have a couple of good horses when you attempt that.

As soon as it is chased, a burro makes for rough country, and, among the ditches and bowlders, a horse does not have a chance with him. Once he gets into the mountains, he is almost as active as a mountain sheep. A man can hardly follow on foot, let alone on horseback. The jack is as tough as a grizzly bear. Cliff

Barnes, a friend of mine who owns a ranch some fifty miles south of Death Valley, tells me he has often hit old jacks with three or four .30/06 bullets without stopping them. They are game to the end, and a man that gets one cornered is in grave danger. The open country where these wild burros range gives them an advantage in spotting a hunter, but the innumerable ditches lining the foothills offer ideal stalking conditions for the sportsman.

The white-tail deer, though one of the most sought-after big game animals on the North American Continent, has a curiosity, and an apparent cunning that often proves in the end to be stupidity, that keep him from ranking higher than sixth on my list. That one look he gives the hunter before he attempts to get away, seems to me to be crass stupidity in a species hunted as frequently as the white-tail.

Very few stalking hunters have ever killed a white-tail without having first been seen, heard, or smelled. But the deer's curiosity overcomes his fear until it is too late. I have, many times, seen a deer stand for half a minute, shaking like an aspen leaf, yet staring straight at me in plain sight, less than fifty yards away. A turkey or a mountain sheep would cover half a mile while the deer was making up his mind to start.

A grave weakness of the white-tail is trying to hide to let a hunter pass him by. If a hunter knows this trick, he can often get a good, close shot. Whenever I see a white-tail in country where the dry leaves make stalking impossible, I never try to stalk him in the regular way. I avoid looking directly at him, and make no pretense of hiding, but take a course to the right or the left, and walk normally. I stop every few paces to examine some tree trunk or bush as though I, myself, were browsing. I never move quickly or abruptly, and never walk in a straight line.

It is fatal to look directly at a deer when using this method of approach. A safer way is to steal a side glance every few seconds. The instant you get in a hurry the deer becomes suspicious, but, if you move along slowly and uninterestedly, it is surprising how close you can get. I have often got within forty yards of a deer before he moved away, and in some instances, when he did decide to go, there was a broadhead in his chest.

Of course, by standing perfectly motionless, deer often do escape being seen, for inexperienced hunters usually expect to flush game before seeing it, hoping to kill the quarry on the run, or to get a long-range, standing shot. To me this is the poorest way to hunt most big game. It is better to look for the game before it is flushed.

Sometimes I believe that the deer can think, because he deliberates so long, and usually does the most sensible thing possible when he has decided what action to take. He doesn't lose his head in a crisis, like the antelope. A turkey does not stop to think, getting out of the danger zone before he has time.

The elk has eyes, ears, and nose that are acutely developed, but he is a sucker for lures. Anyone who is able to imitate his five-noted bugle can easily attract the bull elk during the mating season. It is also possible to lure him by hiding in the brush and beating a dead stick between a couple of saplings. He thinks this is a rival, and often will come near enough for a shot.

The mountain goat of Montana is another animal that has the senses of seeing, hearing, and smelling all pretty well developed. In several ways, he ranks close to the bighorn sheep, but the nature of his haunts makes it possible to stalk him easily. The cliffs he lives among are usually so abrupt, and the canyons so narrow, that you can often get within range before he sees you.

The bear has the keenest nose and ears of almost any animal in America. Were it not for his extremely poor eyesight, he would easily be very near the top of the list. When stalking him, it is necessary to do so upwind, but almost any hunter can take advantage of his fatally weak eyesight.

In some cases, the alligator is very hard to approach, but, if you find one on a sand bar, where the surrounding ground is not covered with water and dense grass, it is a comparatively simple matter to get within forty or fifty yards. If you are lucky enough to catch him asleep, as you often can, on hot, summer days, it is possible to get within even twenty-five to thirty feet. But, in the Everglades, where these creatures are still fairly numerous, the surface water and dense saw grass which usually surround their haunts, make quiet stalking impossible.

To me, mastering the science of stalking has been thoroughly enjoyable. And it's well-worth-while, for good stalking makes a good hunter. The latter invariably is a good conservationist. So let's learn stalking, and give our game a break. If not that, then let's learn it for the unsurpassed thrill that comes of matching our skill against the game's—and winning.

Howard Hill

A BOW AND ARROW ADVENTURE
WITH A POLAR BEAR by Lester C. Essig, Jr.

Feat enough it is for anyone to kill an 1,800-pound polar bear. It's more of a feat when the hunter is a 14-year-old boy. And more still when he uses only a bow and arrow!

But that wasn't enough to suit Lester C. Essig, Jr. He sat down and wrote, unaided, a crisp, exciting account of his adventure—one that any veteran writer of outdoor articles would be glad to claim. So, to give young Essig his full due, we publish the story exactly as he sent it to us not a word or a comma changed. Read it, and be just as amazed as we were.—The Editor (1940)

The ice waters of Moose River were slapping against the hull of our boat. The rattle of anchor chains, the ringing of bells and the chug of the engine were ringing in my head. All the noise and confusion were music to my ears for dad and I were at last pulling out of Moose Factory, Canada, for James Bay—headed for a polar bear hunt which we had been planning for months.

The "Joy H" was certainly going to be a joy to us for the next few weeks for she was a dandy boat. Mr. Cargill, manager of Hudson's Bay Company Moose Factory Post, had outfitted us and had done a swell job of it. The boat was fifty feet long and had a twelve foot beam. She had two masts, a jib sail and an Arcadia engine. Cabins, engine room, and galley were below deck. The galley was in the bow and was large enough for the crew's quarters. Dad and I had two bunks amidship and a table on which we ate our meals. The cook served us through a small sliding window between our cabin and the kitchen. Many bags of sand lay in the centre for ballast. The engine room and a storage place were in the stern. A huge drum of gasoline was roped to the railing on each side of the deck. A canoe was tied to the port side. Anchors were fast to bow and stern. Thanks to Mr. Cargill—the "Joy H" had everything including plenty of food and a fine crew. Three Cree Indians, a Skipper, engineer and cook, made up our crew as we pulled out, and we picked up an Eskimo pilot later on.

We sailed down the Moose River and arrived at the mouth about six-thirty. We dropped anchor

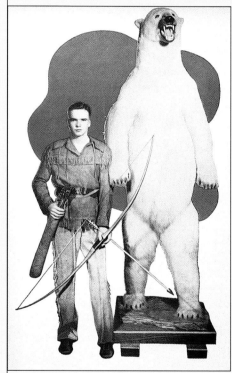

I am very proud of my polar-bear trophy. It stands almost nine feet high.

for the night. To benefit by the flow of the tide, we sailed into James Bay at four o'clock the following morning. I ate a slice of bread and jam and gulped some cocoa. I was all pepped up to hurry on deck and help the crew. But the boat began rolling and my stomach rolled with it. The deck tried to hit me in the face with every step I took. There was no use—I dug back into the bunk. About eight o'clock I tried it again. The foresail was up and the fog hung milky over the water. The sea was heavy and we were rolling and tossing about like a peanut shell. I thought a heavier breakfast might do some good so I stowed away some bacon and eggs. That didn't help matters and I took to the bunk again.

At ten o'clock I was up and on deck. The wind had quieted down, the sun was out, and I felt fine. We let out all the sails. I took my turn at the helm and learned to read the compass. At Woods Bay we picked up a temporary pilot. Tootoo, the engineer, had been seasick, and when I heard that I didn't feel like such a rooky.

While we were anchored the second night, Thomshee (the cook) went ashore in the canoe and brought out regular Eskimo pilot, Wetaltak, aboard. Wetaltak piloted the "Joy H" for the remainder of the trip and he knew the waters well. He took us safely through uncharted reefs that I could not see until we were upon them.

The third day we headed for Comb Hills. We anchored at sundown in a small bay. Dad and I took our guns and paddled ashore in the canoe. We brought down geese, snipes and yellow-legs and Thomshee cooked them for dinner. What a feast we had. Dad and I decided that we would get more of them at the first opportunity.

The following morning we were kept in the harbor by a squall. When it blew over we hunted for more snipes and yellowlegs. Dad and I filled up on Indian water berries. Dad tested our gun sights and I practiced with my bow and arrows. I had brought them along in hopes of getting a duck, goose or maybe a seal with them. Wetaltak and I made trips back and forth in the canoe for fresh drinking water which had collected in the formations and crevices of the rocks.

On the fifth day the weather was clear and bright. A fine breeze filled our sails. Tootoo started the engine and we headed for Twin Islands. The day was perfect for loafing on deck. We took pictures, gazed through the marine glasses, and tinkered with our equipment.

Dad and I took turns scanning the water for seals and white whales. I was sharpening my hunt-

Ready for a short hunt, I test my bear-killing bow. That's Wetaltak in the middle, and Tootoo at right.

ing arrows, and dad was on the bow looking over the water through the glasses, when suddenly—he shouted "NANOOK." If a bomb had exploded it wouldn't have caused any more commotion. That one word told Crees and Eskimo that a polar bear had been sighted. Dad's one thought was for the movie camera. Without stopping to point out the bear, he dashed for the cabin. We had a trick ladder that was practically vertical, and I think dad succeeded in missing all of it. He landed on the floor talking a language all his own. He was back on deck in a few seconds and ready for action. I was afraid to risk dashing below deck for a rifle so I grabbed my bow and arrows and yelled—"Dad, let me get him."

When dad pointed him out we discovered we were headed the wrong way. Dad yelled orders to the Eskimo, but it didn't help for the Skipper had to interpret everything for him. The Skipper got excited and rang the bell to "slow down" but shouted "full speed ahead." Tootoo put the engine in reverse and Wetaltak steered the wrong direction. Thomshee was starting to the galley with our last half dozen eggs and dropped them on the deck in all of the excitement. Confusion reigned for a few seconds until dad calmed us down.

As we neared the white object bobbing around, I realized that it really was a huge polar bear. When we got within seventy-five feet of the bear dad shouted, "Take a shot at him, Pal." I could feel my nerves tightening as I drew the bow I was so very anxious to aim well. The arrow landed in his left flank. With a roar and a splash he dived under, came up snarling, and snapped off the arrow with one swipe of his mighty paw.

A little thing like an arrow head buried in this old boy didn't seem to bother him. He kept right on swimming away from us. The speed he made was surprising for blood was pouring from the wound. I tried aiming a couple of times without releasing the arrow. I wanted to get the timing of the waves for our seaworthy little boat was bobbing up and down on James Bay like a fisherman's cork. As we swung into a better position I let another arrow fly.

The steel point struck his shoulder bone with terrific force, and the shaft shattered into splinters. The bear let out a roar, dived under, came up turning and plunging frantically—then dived under again. He was plenty mad now. He growled and roared and thrashed the water into a bloody foam. He was wounded but far from fatally injured. He turned on our boat and came at us roaring and gnashing his teeth as though he would tear us to pieces.

By this time I realized that mister bear was enormous. I would have to pierce his heart soon or lose all my arrows and get no polar bear. I climbed farther out on the bow and relaxed for a second. Timing my aim with the rolling of the boat, I shot one into him just behind the shoulders. The moment the arrow hit, the bear let out a blood-curdling roar, and with one big splash folded up in the water. The water about him became bloody and he lay still.

Dad said, "There's your trophy, boy, bring him in." But bringing him in wasn't so easy. Tootoo and I climbed the masts and put up double block and tackle, but it took all hands on deck before his heavy body landed on board with a thud. The crew judged the bear's weight at 1800 pounds, and the Eskimo said it was one of the largest he had ever seen. The bear was too massive to skin on board so we tied him to the canoe and towed him ashore.

We spent hours skinning him, quartering the meat and fleshing the hide. I helped with all the work for although I had skinned my moose, caribou, mountain sheep, black bear and brown bear—this was my first polar bear and I wanted the experience. We gave the meat to the Eskimo and Tootoo. They appreciated it for food is scarce in that barren country.

Dad and I went hiking and left the boys to finish scraping the bones and to pack the meat in metal casks. We thought we would do a little exploring. We were trudging over a hill when a white object came up slowly out of the bushes hardly fifteen feet below us. It was the head of a huge polar bear and we stopped in our tracks. He was in a hole in the side of the hill and had raised up to see what was coming near his den. The wind was in our favor but the noise of our boots had warned him of our approach. We could only shoot movies as our polar bear quota was filled. We hurriedly got the cameras into action.

The enormous white head kept swinging from side to side. He sniffed, snorted and champed his huge jaws together; he wrinkled his great nose, sniffed again and bared his long teeth. He kept doing this over and over. He sensed danger but the sun was in his eyes and he couldn't make us out clearly. I kept taking pictures as fast as I could, but the blood was pounding in my ears and I could hardly think. All I could see was the slushy inside of a mouth so big that at the moment it looked like the opening of a cave. It was a vivid, purplish shade of blue which made the long, white, fanglike teeth stand out and sparkle in contrast. All the time I was grinding away on the camera I kept wondering why his mouth wasn't red.

Dad shouted, "Pal, we have the finest close-ups in the world of a live polar bear. Go down around the side of the hill and try to get some full length shots." I dashed down the side of the hill very willingly and glad to get clear of this big fellow. I looked back just in time to see the bear go

It was hard to realize I was the first to bring down a polar bear with a bow and arrow.

after dad. I screamed to dad to look out and attracted the attention of the crew down on the beach. They began shouting for dad to run. With all that noise the old bear decided it was time to retreat. He went loping down the other side of the hill and off down the shoreline into the distance. What a thrill he had given us!

We helped the boys load the meat into the canoe. They had to make two trips to get the hide, meat and us back to the boat. We started to salt down the hide and Thomshee discovered there wasn't enough salt on board to do the job. The Skipper said our only chance to save the skin was to make a run for salt to Old Factory River. Jack Palmquist has a trading post there and plenty of salt. We decided to go for the salt the first thing in the morning.

We started for the trading post early the following morning and ran into the heaviest storm that we met while on James Bay. It was a honey. If we went down into the cabin, we had to hang on to the bunks for dear life to keep from being tossed about like straws. If we went on deck, we had to hang on to the masts to keep from being blown overboard. We took movies of the storm for we wanted a record of all our experiences. We made Old Factory River and picked up the supply of salt, but it sure was tough going.

Wetaltak said the women of his family would flesh the hide much better than we had done and would be glad to do it for us. We appreciated the offer, and told the Skipper to sail on over to Wetaltak's home on Cape Hope. The Eskimo women sat for hours going over every inch of the hide with large circular knives. When they finished, it was a job that only natives can do. We paid them with fresh vegetables, tea, tobacco and matches. They were very grateful. These items are a rare treat and money cannot be spent on Cape Hope.

I enjoyed looking around the Eskimo village for I saw some unusual customs and strange sights. Huge drums of seal oil stood at the door and everything reeked with the odor. I could hardly imagine having to depend on seal oil for light and warmth the year round. Wetaltak's home was neat and clean, but rather bare. The only furniture was beds, chairs and tables. Hides were thrown across the beds for fancy bedding and sheets were unknown.

All of the little colony seemed to be children, nieces, nephews or grandchildren of Wetaltak's. They were quick to discover a few of our belongings that they wanted. Dad and I gave them out sun glasses. They prize sun glasses highly as they help to ward off snow blindness. Wetaltak liked a small whetstone of dad's, so dad gave it to him. We discovered that the women smoke so we unloaded all the tobacco that the crew could spare. Wetaltak does beautiful ivory carving and he traded some of it to us. He also gave me a harpoon and seal floater used in catching seals, and taught me how to use them. Our little visit to Cape Horn was an experience.

When we returned to Moose Factory we luckily arrived on the native feast day of the Cree Indians. The Indians are classed "Coasters" and "Inlanders" and they get together once a year with their chiefs for a feast. Mr. Cargill introduced us to the chiefs, and they invited us as guests of honor. Over two hundred ducks were served and we ate until we were ready to burst. After dinner there was a dance that was loads of fun. The "oldtimers" did a rabbit dance and the others did a square dance. The square dance was brought over by the English and is called "the dance of 1760." The "calling" is done in English which the Indians cannot understand. However, originally they learned the calls in English and learned the steps which go with them. They still hand down the steps and the directions for dancing them although they do not know the meaning of the words.

When the news got around that I had killed a polar bear with bow and arrows, the Indian boys stood and stared at me. They had never heard of such a thing.

The following day dad and I started on our way home. We changed trains at Cochrane. A newsboy was yelling, "Modern Robin Hood kills giant polar bear with bow and arrow." We passed the boy and heard him call the same thing two or three times. I asked dad what the boy was talking about. We both stopped to listen and had a good laugh. I got a big kick out of it when I discovered that I was the cause of all the shouting.

Lester C. Essig, Jr.

A DOE WILL DO by Allen Parsons

The car rolled down the steeps on the New Jersey side of the Delaware River, rumbled across the bridge, and paused at the tollhouse on the Pennsylvania shore. I looked at my watch. It was 10:30 of a December night and misgivings seized me.

"How are Tom and I to get our hunting licenses at this hour?" I queried.

"The squire's the most obliging man in the world," Frank assured me. "If he's asleep, we'll wake him up. He won't mind."

We went through Dingmans Ferry and came to small building by the roadside which seemed to share in three major industries, gas-filling, stomach-filling, and liquid refreshment for those in search of cheer. We banged upon the door. Eventually a clunky, middle-aged man opened it and looked on Frank with a sleepy eye.

"I thought it vas you," he said. "No puddy else puys licenses ven people are in ped."

The squire is of that race, peculiar to his state, known as "Pennsylvania Dutch." About two centuries in America, they still talk a strange dialect of their own and diligently cultivate some of the best farms in the country.

As he handed me my license, the squire looked at me appraisingly.

"My, you vas yoong fer your aitch," he said. The "age" remark was a mystery until a day later when examination of my license disclosed that the squire had made me ten years older with a stroke of the pen.

"Hope you get luck," he went on, "and get a goot puck. Not many pucks killed t'is season. Many toes."

"I'm not particular, squire. A doe, any doe, will do."

Does "did" for many hunters last year in Pennsylvania, when the state—in an effort to balance its big herds—opened the season for female deer. Great state, Pennsylvania—she stands at the top in deer hunting. In the 1940 season for instance, some 187,000 deer were taken by hunters. Such a kill is beneficial, because depleting the herds somewhat results in adequate browse for the remaining deer, and eliminates runts.

Our car left the concrete and took a narrow country road leading upward into the hills of the back country. Woods, woods, woods, with now and then a bleak and snowy field. There's a lot of wilderness in Pennsylvania's Pike County. The window beside Tommy was open, and a nipping chill came through it, so the three of us sat squeezed together on the front seat. The car skidded dangerously on every turn and there were many!—for the road wriggled and squirmed like one of the famous Pike County rattlesnakes.

Finally we came to a steep hill on the ancient farm road. Tom shifted gears and gave the car the gun. It was touch-and-go, but she made it. Then we rounded a turn and came to a dead end with a cabin as an exclamation point. Its windows were lighted and there was the pungent smell of wood smoke from the wide chimney. The door opened, and against the rectangle of light appeared the wide, square figure of Jack Stewart, who had come the day before to open the cabin.

Inside was comfort. An enormous field-stone fireplace, taking full lengths of cordwood, occupied nearly all of one end of the main room, and in it big logs were giving out welcome heat. A wide plate-glass window permitted a view over miles of moonlit hills. Four bunks in tiers of two, a folding cot, and long couch provided sleeping accommodations for six. In the tiny kitchen were cooking range, kitchen cabinet, table, chairs, and shelves for provisions.

Early the next morning the guides came streaming in before we had finished our flapjacks and scrapple. There was much clicking as rifles were examined and cartridges fed into magazines. The snow crunched under foot as we slipped and slid down the camp road. At the Four Corners, where two wood roads and two fire lines met, we stopped, and Frank gave instructions.

"We'll take the Point Peter drive first," he told Henry Snyder, the head guide. "Afterwards we'll move over to the Huckleberry."

Henry nodded, and the three drivers went over the ridge. Frank led the rest of us down the wood road to the left, leaving Jack Stewart at the first stand to cover the Four Corners with its view of fire lines and wood roads. I was stationed against an oak tree right where a fine deer runway crossed the road. Here a rise protected me from Jack's crossfire, and another, 150 yards to my right, guarded me from

Tommy who had the next spot. And beyond Tommy, at a fork in the road, Frank was to stand. All the stands, on each of the drives, had been so picked as to permit a wide arc of shooting with a minimum of danger. I broke the crust at the base of my tree, crushing it to powder with my feet. Thus, if it became necessary for me to move my feet, I could do so without making a noise. I took another look at my Winchester Model 64 .30/30, and then assumed as comfortable a position as I could.

This business of waiting motionless on a stand is a trial of the nerves. You are afraid to move lest you alarm a hidden and watchful deer. Your nose begins to itch and you dare not scratch it. Standing in the snow, there comes a time when even your heavy woolen socks cannot keep out the cold and your toes become numb. The woods are lifeless, with not a sound to break the deep silence. Your companions might be in Canada for all that you can see or hear of them. The drivers beyond the ridge, drive silently, only breaking a stick now and then to keep contact and to warn where they are. The chill of the steel in the rifle barrel penetrates your woolen gloves. You are tense with excitement.

It was an hour by my wrist watch before I heard a cracking stick at the crest of the ridge. Was it a deer? No, it was not. Henry Snyder came striding through the scrub, the red of his sweater like the red of the swamp maples in early fall. Then, to right and left, appeared other drivers. There had been no sound of shot. That drive had brought nothing. Henry's shrill whistle summoned the other hunters, and they came in singly along the wood road.

"I see three deer scootin' ahead of me," Henry told us, "but they turned right back through the drive. Wild as hawks. Been shot at so much the last ten days. We'd ought to have twice as many drivers. Where next, Frank?"

"The Ring Tree, Henry," said Frank. "There are deer in the swamp over there most always. It's worth trying anyhow."

The aim in these drives is to push upwind wherever possible. It startled, the white-tail deer may run downwind a little way, but he doesn't like to, and turns at the first opportunity. The wind was in the south, which meant that the Ring Tree drive would be upwind.

We went back to the Four Corners and walked south along the fire line. Jack was stationed on a rock at the edge of the swamp, about fifty feet from the road. I was given a stand facing the swamp and at right angles to the wind.

There was a fallen tree there, and I slumped on it with a grunt of relief. Frank and Tommy disappeared in the woods, walking south. The swamp was open woods, with scattered patches of thick brush, and

an occasional clump of pines. Before me was a black alder—the winterberry—covered with red berries and looking very gay and Christmasy. Near me a little brook babbled in a chatty, intimate way. From behind, and not far away, came shots, single and in groups. Someone was finding game. Time dragged endlessly. Eventually the drivers appeared, working from the north, and a whistle summoned all hands. No one had seen a deer, though Henry had spotted the fresh tracks of a buck that broke out ahead of him and then cut across the ridge to the east before he had come abreast of my stand.

"I was up here on the second of December, the opening day of the season," said Frank. "I saw at least twenty does within easy rifle shot. I could have had my pick but wanted to wait for a big buck. Now we can't even see one doe. Looks as though I'd waited too long. I haven't seen one buck track today."

"Bucks is awful scarce," said Henry. "Twenty does to one buck, and not a good head to be found. Woods are too noisy. Deers are lyin' close an' you have to kick 'em out."

After lunch the Huckleberry and Birch drives were worked without sight of a deer. When we went back to the camp in the gloaming a fine rain was falling, and road guts were filled with water. A big dinner of thick steaks, smothered with onions, and a gallon or two of hot coffee, prepared by the skilled hands of Jack, restored our spirits. A wind was roaring around the cabin.

"This means a drop in temperature," gloomed Frank as we gathered before the fireplace and felt the cabin shake. "Tomorrow there'll be a worse crust than we had today, and the woods will be twice as noisy."

Before we turned in we looked at the thermometer outside the cabin door. It was then down to 20 degrees, a drop of fifteen within a few hours. This wind was out of the north. Knowing how cold the cabin would get after the fire died down, I took off only my boots, and slept in my clothes.

The next morning was snapping cold, and gray clouds raced by, urged on by the gale. The snow, in the open places, was almost gone. Before breakfast was out of the way Preston Lum drove up, ready to join the hunt. Braw lad, Preston. His father, mother, two sisters, three brothers, and he total the impressive height of forty-eight feet—and Preston is above the altitudinous average.

The sky had cleared a bit in the west, but the wind made the brown leaves on the oak trees whip and rustle and sent down dead limbs and twigs; every step in the snow sounded like a brick going through a windowpane. Henry looked unhappy.

"Bad day fer huntin'," he told us.

It was. We drove and hunted all day. Each time we stood on stand the cold wind pierced our red mackinaws and numbed feet and fingers. When we met after each drive, breath floated like smoke in the air and red faces looked hot—but weren't.

That night a multitude of stars burned in a cloudless sky, but the moon came up encircled with an enormous ring. Five deerless hunters bewailed their luck before the fireplace.

"Well, tomorrow I'm going to take my camera and get some pictures," I told the boys. "The light probably will be good for the first time in days and I've sort of given up on the deer."

"The camera will be in your way if you should get a shot," suggested Frank.

"I don't expect to get one," was my reply. "In two days' hard hunting we haven't seen a deer. At least I'll be sure of some pictures and that will be something. You fellows won't like it much, but I'm going to fasten myself on you tomorrow morning. First I'll stick with Tommy on his stands. Then, Frank, you'll have to put up with me. But I'll keep out of your way; you know—just like the deer!"

The next morning in rolled Carleton Lum, another of the lofty Lums, and Bob Lester. Lester had got his deer the first day of the season, but Carleton was still on the prowl for a shot.

"Swell!" said Frank when he saw them. "Now we can have a real drive!"

The first drive was the Ring Tree again. Tommy's stand was on a big rock at the southwest corner of the property. I got to one side of him, took a light-reading with my meter, and readied my camera to shoot. A full half hour passed. Then, suddenly, I stiffened and my heart began to pound. About seventy-five yards away there appeared miraculously a gray shape, sneaking along with white flag saucily erect. There were no antlers and it looked like a small doe. Tommy, hitherto as still as the rock, aimed his rifle. The shot and the clicking fall of the camera

shutter came as one sound. The deer, who'd seen the movement of the arms as the rifle was leveled, made a great leap, slammed head-on into a tree, then fell in a heap. The blood gushed from its shoulder, staining the snow. Hardly knowing what I was doing I wound the tension spring, focused the camera, and took picture after picture. At last we had a deer!

It was a young buck that had lost its antlers. The zero weather of the previous week, we later found, had caused many of the bucks to shed their antlers earlier than usual. Frank came up on the run, and while he and Tommy dressed out the deer, I hopped around and was lavish with film. The buck was a small one, and Tommy was able easily to shoulder it and carry it out to the road over his shoulders.

"I *would* kill my deer as far away from camp as it's possible to get," he told us, after a half mile of back packing—with a lot more to go.

"What of it? You've saved the day for us. What's a deer hunt without a deer?" I asked him.

The next drive was the Birch Tree and, with Frank, I took my stand on a bold ledge overlooking a flat where birches were as thick as hay in a meadow. A ruffed grouse sprang into flight as we approached, so near to us that the dark band at the outer edge of the fanlike tail was plainly visible. Frank stood upon a hump carpeted with pine needles, while I took a seat on a log to the rear, again with camera ready. The Birch Tree is a short drive and if deer are there, gives quick action. Soon I heard Frank signal softly.

At first I could see nothing. Then, to the left, and more than 100 yards away, I saw the gray shape of a deer drifting along. Once it stopped and looked back over its shoulder toward the distant drivers. Then it came on, amazingly silent over the crusted snow. Again it stopped, held its head in the air, and sniffed. Now it crouched with belly to ground like a cat, and crept swiftly toward a low ridge that would give it refuge. It had caught our scent.

"Buck," whispered Frank. "Does don't act like that."

He waited for the deer to pass an opening in the birches where a better shot was possible, and shifted his position a little to get a clearer view. In so doing a piece of ice became dislodged and slid noisily down the slope. The buck leaped for shelter and Frank fired. I heard the smack of the bullet, and saw the buck collapse into a heap, kick a little, and lie still. He was about seventy-five yards away, and the bullet had hit just behind the point of the shoulder—a lethal shot. Just as Frank had said, though antlerless, it was a buck that had shed its horns. Our luck was now all good and coming in a bunch.

"Two down and one to go," said Frank, as he dressed his buck. It's up to you now, Allen, and

Heaving Parson's big doe into the car, Conlon grunts under its weight.

you've only about three hours to get yourself a deer before it gets dark. Better leave that camera of yours at the camp and hunt in earnest this afternoon."

But I didn't leave my camera behind. I wanted pictures almost as much as I wanted a deer, and that afternoon saw me at my stand on the Point Peter drive with the camera still strung around my neck. There were plenty of drivers on the job. The boys were anxious that the Lums and I should get a shot, so Frank, Tom, Jack and Bob Lester joined the drivers in a real sweep. I could hear the long line crunching through the crust, and again my heart began to pound just as it had on the first day. Then my waiting ended. Tom was shouting below me.

"Watch out, Allen!"

The side of the ridge on which I stood was covered with shrubby oaks, their brown leaves still on. Way down the slope I saw four white flags stiffly erect, and heard the swish of leaves and brush and the pounding of hoofs. The deer were coming like the wind and headed for the wooded ridge behind the camp. With my big camera bumping and bobbling against me, I started on a run for the ridgeside road I knew the deer would have to cross. My feet felt leaden, and it seemed as though I were packing a ton. I arrived at the road panting and out of breath. Swish! A big doe cleared the road with one tremen-

dous leap, while my rifle barrel wobbled all over the horizon. I was so winded that I just couldn't hold it still. Swish! Another doe streaked across a second later. Another swish and another doe. Why wouldn't that cussed rifle stay still? Now came the last big white flag, riding above the scrub like a speed boat over the waves, as the fourth doe leaped into the open. For a millionth of a second the sights were in line on her shoulder. Wham! Down went the doe and up into my throat came my heart. The doe scrambled to her feet, and as she did so I fired again. She went down for the last time very dead with one shot through her neck.

Somehow, most miraculously, at the last possible moment my tortured nerves and lungs had behaved. I, who am not a good shot, had put two shots right on the button, while a big camera was hanging in front of me. Yes sir, I now believe in luck. Only luck could have given me that doe. I ditched my camera and ran to my deer, Frank and Tom close behind, shooting pictures as they came.

That was the biggest doe I ever hefted. We estimated she would weigh 150 pounds, live weight. I looked at my watch. I had killed my deer in the last hour and on the last day possible in the 1910 hunting season.

Allen Parsons

A DAY IN
RAM HEAVEN by Jack O'Connor

Every hunter of mountain sheep has, I suppose, dreamed of a time when great rams were on every side—so many rams that he was embarrassed and confused by their numbers. Every sheep hunter has also dreamed that in this ram heaven he'd find his fabulous forty-inch head, the very top trophy in American big-game hunting. In many years of sheep hunting I had dreamed such dreams, but they had never come true. I had hunted sheep from Sonora, Mexico, to the Yukon, and I had never seen a forty-inch head among the many hundreds of big rams I had put the glasses on.

I hoped that when I got to hunt Stone sheep I'd find a forty-incher; but hundreds of expeditions into the northern Rockies, where the Stone sheep dwell, have brought out only about forty rams with curling horns that long. All "outside" sheep hunters are trophy hunters, and the Cassiar district of British Columbia's Stone-sheep country has been hunted for half a century. That a couple of hunters could glass several rams in one day with curls of more than forty inches is so fantastic that it seems incredible.

Nevertheless, that is what happened to Doc DuComb and me one September day on a big mountain off the Prophet River up in the northern part of the province. From a slope on the other side of the river we had seen rams the previous evening, so the next morning we were up early to make the long, tough climb and look them over. I was going to hunt with Frank Golata, the outfitter, and Doc with Mac, the other guide. The frost was still on the grass when we set out and I was chilly even in wool underwear, wool pants, and two wool shirts. I carried a camera, a pair of binoculars, and a rifle. My 20X spotting 'scope was in Frank's rucksack. Doc and Mac each had powerful binoculars and of course Doc carried his 'scope-sighted .30/06.

We first hiked about two miles to the foot of the mountain. There, before beginning the first stage of our climb, we parted. Frank and I were going to hunt the far side of the mountain, Doc and Mac the near side. Since Frank and I had to go farther, we had to travel faster. Speed in climbing a sheep mountain is only relative, however, and as we toiled

up 2,500 feet to timberline we would have looked like a couple of snails to an eagle or a man in a plane.

The mountainside was very steep. First we fought our way through thick black spruce, then through equally thick aspens. Next we struck a belt of high, thick willows, followed by a shale slide so steep that every bit of rock was looking for an excuse to roll a couple of thousand feet. Just before we got over the hump we had to climb a slope carpeted with high slippery grass.

At last, though, we came out on top of the world, in a land of rolling arctic sheep pastures—soft and spongy underfoot, clad in a thick, damp carpet of mosses, lichens, grasses. These pastures were really a series of hilltops that formed a shoulder of a great mountain. They were cut by deep canyons, black with shale, formidable with cliffs; and behind them rose a mighty series of crags black as ink, criss-crossed with the glittering white of everlasting ice that clung to their crevices.

All around us were other upland pastures, tinted in yellow, rose, and umber by the frosts. We looked down on great black canyons, purple timber, and the blue Prophet River meandering through yellow muskeg meadows and dark forest. The great mountain peaks across the river were powdered white with snow, and on their lower slopes patches of golden aspens glowed bright like candles in the night.

We saw sheep almost the instant we put the glasses on the grassy slopes that were still above us—many sheep. Here half a dozen were grazing. There another bunch was lying down. They were more than a mile away, but even at that distance our binoculars showed us that some of them were rams—

probably all of them, since in September rams are seldom found with the ewes.

So we set up the spotting 'scope in a little saddle six sheep were feeding. At least three of them were good rams, all of the dark Stone type. Two looked so-so, and one was evidently very young. Above them, lying down on some shale, were three rams—a dark Stone with medium-gray face and neck, and two big rams with faces and necks that were so light they looked almost white, like those of the Fannin variety found in the Yukon. In color pattern the true Fannin is an intergrade between the all-dark Stone and the typical pure-white Dall of Alaska and the Yukon. We were to see other dark-saddled, white-headed Stone sheep that day, but we called them, simply, "Fannins"—and that is how I shall refer to them hereafter.

As we took turns using the spotting 'scope, we picked up other sheep until we had counted twenty-seven in all. That's a lot of sheep, and as far as we could tell all were rams.

The logical way to approach them was to go around and above them, but the wind was wrong, and we were afraid that if we got in line with them, they'd smell us and be off. Frank decided that our best plan was to cross a couple of canyons, then work up another on the far side of the rams, get above them, and come down. To do so we'd first have to lose almost 1,000 feet of our hard-won altitude, but those two Fannin rams looked as if they were worth it. Frank guessed their horns would go close to forty inches, though at that distance it was hard to tell.

Walking rapidly, we started off. We were out of sight of the sheep and had the wind right, when I

Frank Golata using a spotting 'scope to size up two likely-looking rams we had already glassed.

happened to glance to the left and saw a ewe standing on a ridge about eighty yards away starring at me.

What that lone ewe was doing up there on the mountain with all those rams I do not know. Probably she wasn't all she should be, and anyway her presence was embarrassing to us. If we frightened her and she ran, she might spook all the rams and we'd be out of luck. There was but one chance.

Looking as innocent as possible—as if sheep hunting were the last thing we'd think of—we turned away from the ewe and headed downhill, but she followed along the ridge staring and snorting at us. A little later we could see that she was with four rams that had been hidden from us by a fold in the ground. They were alert, but not very frightened, and they trotted off.

We dropped down into a deep canyon, climbed out, went over another shoulder low enough so the rams could not see us. Now and then we'd stop to get our wind and to put the spotting 'scope on the big fellows. Our two big Fannins were still at their stand, but most of the sheep had worked somewhat higher. Everything was still under control.

By noon we were at the edge of a tremendous canyon and well on the other side of the rams. If our luck held we could work along for another mile, then climb above the rams, size up their heads once more, and work near enough for a shot. Then two things happened which sent my heart right to the bottom of my hobnail boots. First I heard Doc shoot four times on the other side of the mountain, and I was afraid that those two big Fannins would pull out for the cliffs. Next we rounded the bend of the canyon and ran into four rams. We were afraid that they would run over the crest and scare the others.

Actually, one of the rams wasn't a bad one. His horns would probably have gone thirty-eight inches—maybe thirty-nine. He and three smaller rams lay in beds that they had pawed out of the shale across the canyon. They were about 250 yards away and they saw us instantly as we came around the bend, picking our way precariously along our side of that cliffy canyon.

They watched us. We watched them. They grew more and more nervous, and finally they got up and ran in single file along the side of the canyon, down into the bottom, and then finally up the head of one fork and out of sight. We had a break there. If they had crossed the canyon to our side but higher up and run over the ridge, the rams we were stalking would have seen them and would have known that something was amiss.

At last we negotiated our mile along the wall of that canyon. We were about six miles from camp and something like 3,500 feet above it. We had only to climb to the crest of the ridge to our left and, staying under it, work up higher than the rams. Then, after crossing the head of the canyon that separated us, we would be above them.

We had got almost to the top of the ridge when we paused for a moment to get our wind. I happened to put the glasses on the head of the right fork of the canyon we had just left—and there in the saddle, about a mile away, I could see twelve rams. About half of them were lying down. The other half were feeding. Through the binoculars they looked good; and through the spotting 'scope one of them looked colossal. Even at a mile it was easy to see that here was one ram in many hundreds, a fellow with long and massive horns.

"Get a load of that fellow lying down in the middle of the bunch," I told Frank. "If that isn't a forty-inch head I'll never in my life see one!"

Frank took a long, long look through the 'scope. Finally he passed judgment: "I think that will go forty inches myself!"

"O.K.," I said, my aching joints forgotten, "let's take out after him."

To get a shot at the big boy, we would have to climb up a very steep, boulder-strewn canyon, then go over a ridge, up to the head of a second canyon which headed close to the saddle where that big bunch of rams were resting and feeding. In doing this we'd have to turn our backs on the two big Fannins we had been stalking since morning, but the chance was worth taking.

So, instead of getting above the first rams we had put the finger on, we began the long and painful climb over the boulders of that big canyon. The sun was bright and warm. We hadn't had a drink since early morning and we were very thirsty. As we clambered from boulder to boulder we could hear water running through the rocks below us. Our mouths were cotton-dry and the icy tinkle was tantalizing. It was tough going, as some of those boulders were too smooth to hold hobnails.

Gradually, though, we pulled up higher and higher. We found a little old snow, ate it, and thus relieved our thirst. Finally we had only about 100 feet to climb until we could get over the ridge into the next canyon and begin the final stage of the stalk on this fabulous forty-incher.

Then, right over where the two big Fannins were, we heard a fusillade of shots: One-two-three-four-five-six-seven-eight. . . . From the fact that sometimes we could hear the crack of the bullets before we heard the boom of the report we knew that Doc was shooting across the next canyon in our direction. He had got into the big bunch of rams we had planned to stalk before we saw that forty-incher.

My heart sank. It looked as though our day was wasted; all that heartbreaking, leg-straining climbing in vain. Big rams are wary creatures, or they don't live to be big rams, and I was sure that our forty-incher had pulled out by the time the second shot went off, even though he was more than a mile away.

"Oh, nuts! What a break!" I moaned. "We might as well forget that big baby!"

"Don't feel too bad," Frank tried to comfort me. "We're in a good spot, with only a ridge between us and all those rams. Maybe something nice will run over us."

There was nothing for us to do except to sit and see what breaks we got. If some of the rams ran directly away from Doc and tried to put a ridge between them and the muzzle of his rifle, they would come around the point and along the other side of the canyon where we sat. That looked like the best bet at the moment, so we waited. . . .

To back-track for a moment: Earlier in the morning Doc and Mac had seen a good lone ram on the other side of the mountain. Doc didn't get a good shot at it and his four bullets failed to connect. They then decided to hunt up some more rams, so they had climbed high and had innocently drifted over in our direction.

As luck would have it they ended up on the ridge toward which we had originally headed, but they saw nothing there. Since we had last glassed them, all the bunches of rams we had seen early that morning had come together for a slumber party during the middle of the day, when all respectable rams lie down. They had pawed out beds right at the foot of a cliff. Such being the inscrutable ways of fate, Doc and Mac had decided to go right to the top of this very cliff to look out and see what they could see.

Imagine their surprise to hear rocks rolling, and look down upon something like thirty-five rams, all getting out of there in every direction right under their feet! Some went up the canyon, some down the canyon, some crossed to the other side. Forced to make a hasty choice, Doc decided on a big Fannin with a very wide spread and rolled him over in two or three shots. Then he opened up on a dark Stone-type ram with a massive broomed head. The ram was across the canyon, but finally he got him down.

In the meantime I sat across the ridge in the next canyon with a cartridge in the chamber of my lightweight, fancy .270, muttering to myself and full of gloom. In a short time I saw a ram poke his head over the ridge.

"There's a ram," Frank said.

"He's not worth shooting," I growled.

"Maybe some more will come around."

The ram, about five or six years old, stopped just on our side of the ridge and glanced in our direction, but did not notice us because we remained absolutely frozen. Then another ram showed up, a good big Stone with a fine massive head and what I judged to be 38 or 39-inch curls.

"That's a nice ram," Frank whispered.

"He won't go forty inches, though," I said.

"No," Frank agreed. "I don't think he will."

Then a third ram came around. He was a husky Fannin, probably one of the two we had seen that morning. Right at his heels came a fair-to-middling Stone. All looked back over their shoulders at the place where the shots had come from, but they didn't appear very frightened and they had not detected Frank and me.

I laid my rifle over my knees and picked up my binoculars. The Fannin was an excellent ram. He had a good long curl with one perfect point and the other slightly broomed, but I wasn't sure they were long enough to suit me, and I couldn't afford to blow my last chance at a forty-incher.

"Think the big Fannin will go forty?" I whispered.

"Close but not over," was Frank's verdict.

The four rams moved slowly along the other side of the canyon less than 200 yards away. The glasses told me that the big boy had a complete curl and

then some; but that doesn't necessarily mean much, for I have seen thin-horn rams, both Stone and Dall, that had more-than-complete curls yet didn't go thirty-eight inches.

Then, as the big Stone and the Fannin happened to be side by side, I noticed that the Fannin was a much larger sheep; and on a sheep with a big head and body, the horns do not look so large as they really are.

Right then and there I decided to take him. He was above me and quartering away. I slipped my left arm into the loop of my sling, shifted my heels a little so I was in as solid a sitting position as I could manage on those rocks, and put the intersection of the cross hairs low behind his right foreleg. As I squeezed the trigger I heard the bullet strike and saw the ram spin around.

"His front leg on the off side is broken high!" reported Frank, who was watching with the glasses.

I worked the bolt and shot again. The ram stayed on his feet, so I fired a third shot. At this the sheep went down—and for keeps.

Slowly, wearily, painfully we crossed the canyon and climbed up to where the ram lay. He was a big fellow, as large as most bighorns, and by far the heaviest thin-horn sheep I have ever seen. As we worked closer and I saw those great horns, I could tell they were larger than they'd seemed from across the canyon.

"Will they go forty?" I asked Frank.

"Golly!" he said. "They'll go more'n that! This is the third forty-incher I have ever seen!" (The two others, by the way, were No. 1 and No. 2 in the record book of North American big game.)

Neither of us had a tape, so definite measurements would have to wait until we got to camp. Those three shots of mine, we found, had all struck low behind the shoulder. They had just missed the heart, without opening up much, but together they had almost torn the left front leg off just where it joined the body. It was one of those things. The Stone I had shot previously had been killed instantly with one shot in the same place. This ram had taken *three*!

I used the barrel of my rifle to get a rough measurement and I couldn't see how those horns would go less than forty inches, but to keep myself from being disappointed I tried to tell myself I wouldn't be *too* bitter if they went only thirty-nine and a half.

Frank and I ate a sandwich apiece and washed them down with snow. Then, while I started to skin out the head, he went over the ridge to see what had happened to Doc. He came back in time to help me take the head off, cut out the backstraps and hindquarters. Doc and Mac, he told me, were well to the east and toward the bottom of the canyon skinning

Those horns, I was convinced, would measure at least forty inches along the curl, though I tried to tell myself I wouldn't be too bitter if they didn't.

out a couple of heads, one of which looked fine through glasses.

Camp was about six miles away—and six tough miles. It was then around 3:30 p.m., so Frank and I didn't even go down to see Doc and Mac. Instead we cut straight across for camp. I had the massive 45-pound head and scalp; Frank toted a load of meat. We had hardly started down the steep side of the canyon when I stepped on a loose stone and fell so hard I bounced.

Loaded down as we were, it was a long, tough pull. When we hit the grassy slope I put the big head on my lap and slid a quarter mile down the mountain, using my heels as brakes.

It was 7 o'clock and just getting dark when I staggered up to the cook tent and cried: "Quick, Johnny—the steel tape!"

We laid the big head on the table there in the candlelight of the cooktent. The tape said forty-two inches. I measured it again and got forty-two and a half! Here was my forty-inch head and then some! The circumference at base measured sixteen inches, which is good even for a bighorn, and simply terrific for a Stone sheep.

It was an hour later and pitch black when I thought I heard footsteps. I went out of the tent and yelled. Doc answered me. He and Mac had missed the tent in the darkness. He had two fine heads. One had a curl of forty-one inches—almost as long as mine—and a greater spread. His other ram had a massive, broomed head, with about a 37-inch curl that was very close, for all the world like that of a bighorn.

Our luck had been incredible. Here were two fine heads—both rating places far up in the list of record

Stone sheep—that were taken out of one bunch on one mountain in a single day.

At that, I couldn't forget the one that got away—that fine old ram I was stalking when Doc started to shoot. He was noticeably larger than my 42-incher, and to be that much larger his curls would have had to measure at least forty-six! Doc and I are happy with those two great heads, but we both wonder now and then what our luck would have been if that greatest sheep had been on our side of the mountain!

Jack O'Connor

STAG LINE by Bill Rae

Like hundreds of hunters before us, Chuck Cooley and I had sworn not to shave until I got the elk for which I had traveled from 42nd Street in New York City to the Thorofare in northwestern Wyoming. Twelve days of our hunt had already gone. As I worked my fingers glumly through the matting on my face, Charlie Elliott spoke up.

"Boss, you shore are goin' to be a sensation walkin' down Fourth Avenue next week with that set of muttonchops if we don't fix it for you to kill an elk mighty soon," he said. "You look like you just stepped off a whaling ship."

"Don't worry," I answered. "I'm going back to New York with an elk if I have to stay here all winter."

Chuck, my salty-tongued guide, grinned until the wrinkles around his eyes ran down into his beard like rivulets into a forest. "You know," he said, "if we don't get out of this everlovin' country pretty soon you might do just that anyway."

We knew that was no joke, even though Charlie drooled like a cow moose in a wallow as Chuck said it. We were hunting in the headwaters of the Yellowstone River in one of the last remaining wilderness areas in the United States. Here in the Thorofare, locked in by the ramparts of the Continental Divide and the Absaroka range, great herds of elk work out of the high country down toward the winter refuge in Jackson Hole at this time of year. At the same time, mule deer travel in great numbers the other way through the timber to the high passes in the Absarokas and thence to the South Fork of the Shoshone, where the snows aren't so deep.

Hence the name Thorofare.

But now we had a mystery on our hands. Something had happened to this two-way traffic.

There were no elk, or none to speak of. Our beards testified to that. And since it was just a couple of days short of November 1, it behooved us to find them, collect our trophies, and head for Deer Creek Pass and civilization before the snows blocked our exit through the two-mile high passageway. Once the snows came in earnest, we might just as well resign ourselves to spending the winter in Hammett Cabin.

Hammett Cabin was built, not for dudes like us who practically asked to get snowed in, but for trappers or wayfarers unfortunate enough to get themselves waylaid by winter in the 9,000-foot high valley of Thorofare Creek, whose walls of mountains and ridges soar upward another 2,000 or 3,000 feet. There is never a lock on the door of Hammett Cabin, and the cabin is always well stocked. The only obligation is to leave something in place of what you take for the next fellow—whether food or lantern fuel, soap or fresh-cut firewood.

It was comfortable enough now in the cabin, two-hours' ride by horseback from Bridger Lake. Kenny Hill, a short-order cook in Cody during the winter, was serving up hot biscuits and elk meat with white sauce (the meat from a previous hunt) to a whiskered group of dudes and guides. (I remember once he whipped up a raspberry cake with chocolate frosting.) The amateurs were Elliott, Southern field editor for *Outdoor Life*, Bob Hogg, Atlanta businessman, and myself. The professionals, besides Hill, were Cooley, Frank Lasater, and Don Wildon, guides, and Freddie Zinn, tough young horse wrangler.

All of the latter hail from Cody, Wyoming, which owes its name to the famous scout, hunter, and showman, Buffalo Bill Cody. In fact, our outfitter, Max Wilde of the Lazy Bar F Ranch in Valley, Wyoming, was himself one of Buffalo Bill's scouts. A few days before our arrival, Max had got himself into a rope tangle with a horse while putting out bear baits for our hunt in the Thorofare and all but had his arm torn out of its socket. Unable to come with us, he'd hand-picked these men to herd us through the same wilderness Colonel Cody had hunted in his heyday.

Outside in the night were the 30-odd horses that had carried us and the camp into the Thorofare.

Now and again one of those browsing near the cabin snorted or shook his bell. Beyond, coyotes howled, one answering another, far into the distance. Above the cabin the wind soughed in the spruce and fir. But all these sounds only heightened the cheerfulness of the cabin, until the conversation turned to winter. Then Frank Lasater told of the winter he had trapped into the Thorofare and found two horses, little more than skin and bones, standing deep in the snow chewing the bark off the logs of Hammett Cabin. They were too far gone to save.

Just the presence of Lasater on this hunt underscored our gamble. Frank, an old-time mountain man with eyes the distant blue of the sky, was an outfitter himself, but his hunting parties, like those of all the other outfitters, had departed and he was helping out the injured Max Wilde by serving as a guide for us. In other words, their regular season was over. And now in our straits, he took charge. "We've got two more days to get elk for Bill and Charlie," he said, "and we'll be lucky if the snows don't hit us while we're doing it. We've been up and down every creek within hunting radius of this cabin and haven't had any luck. Now suddenly today I got me an idea."

The idea of hunting in the Thorofare in late October was that of the aforementioned Charles Elliott, the working stiff's Clark Gable, who was squiring me on my first big-game hunt. Charlie has hunted in the Thorofare for 20 years, and is an aged-in-the woods friend of both Max and Frank. For the past 10 years, his ambition has been to get snowed into the Thorofare for the entire winter.

But right now he had something more important on his mind—to see that I got an elk. He had written me lyrics on what magnificent game country this was— elk, deer, bear, moose and, yes, even sheep, but most of all elk. The Thorofare, he assured me, fairly swarmed with elk, that noble American stag which only the encyclopedias seem to call the wapiti. But now the noble stag was letting him down. He chewed his cigar in a circle of gloom.

We'd seen everything else. Antelope stared at us from the plains as we approached Cody, and lit out for the horizon only when we stopped the car. (They've learned the shooting doesn't start until the car stops.) We saw more of them when we made the 45-mile trip from Cody to the Wilde ranch in Valley. After we'd crossed the South Fork of the Shoshone and scaled the heights into Deer Creek Canyon, the first thing I saw, when I dared look down, was a brace of Rocky Mountain sheep.

Weary hours later, when we finally reached Hammett Cabin, a bull and a cow moose watched us placidly from one of the network of beaver ponds laced together by Thorofare Creek. Some days later, when we sought to change our luck by riding down to Bridger Lake for some fishing, we cut a fresh beartrail and my horse nearly climbed out from under me when he got the scent. That same trip I looked down the lake and in a space of half a mile saw six separate moose feeding in the water.

On another occasion, two bulls knocked their horns sportively and hollowly in a little park in the timber not 20 yards from us. A special permit is required to hunt moose in the Thorofare, and not many are drawn. Thus, for the most part unmolested, the moose are bold and brash. On our return trip this day, two more bulls, a young one and an old one, eyed us arrogantly as we rode within feet of them. Chuck kept grunting tauntingly at them, and you could almost read the evil in their minds as they pivoted to watch us.

"What do you do," I asked Chuck, "if they rush you?"

"You ride like hell," said Chuck. "They got good early speed, but a horse will beat 'em out in the long run."

"I hope I'm still with the horse," I said, "but just suppose one of them's good for the distance. What do you do then?"

"You shoot him," said Chuck, "in self-defense. But be sure you hit him—and be sure you can convince the game warden it *was* self-defense. If you can't, you might as well miss."

It was on this day, too, that Charlie rolled a coyote, the only one I actually saw, though I listened to whole choirs of them every night. Deer were a common sight, and a story in themselves. As for fish, we quickly caught our limits of two and three-pound Yellowstone cutthroats both in Bridger Lake and a nearby bend of the Yellowstone River (See "Elk on the Side," November, 1955, *Outdoor Life*.) And as our horses splashed toward the river, we startled a flock of feeding mallards.

As a matter of fact, we even saw an elk the morning of our first hunt, a pretty good-size one, too. But it had a narrow beam, like a V, and we didn't give it a second thought as a trophy as it watched us from the edge of the timber across the meadow. (As the days passed, that beam grew broader in imagination.) The only thing we didn't see, in fact, was a buffalo, and I wasn't sure we wouldn't meet one of those in Deer Creek Canyon that first day out of Valley.

To understand, you have to picture Deer Creek Canyon. From Max Wilde's ranch, a mile above sea level, it's a ride of 11 miles to Deer Creek Pass and, in that stretch, the trail climbs upward another mile. So when you reach that wind-blasted pass across the Divide your altitude is 11,000 feet. Since it's another 17 miles to Hammett Cabin, that first day's ride is something that stays with you a long time, especially if the last time you rode a horse was in the C.M.T.C. at Fort Ethan Allen, Vermont, in 1925.

Yet that last 17 miles is like a canter in the park after you traverse the canyon. In places the trail is little more than an edging on vertical walls, and if you dare look down you can just make out the ribbon of the creek, 1,000 feet below. To add spice, the horses like to walk on the edge of the trail with a sort of casting-off movement of their outside hoofs.

Toward noon, we rode down a series of switchbacks to the bed of the creek where it rushes through the cool timber, and ate our lunch in a nest of huge boulders. It was a great relief. Casually, and hopefully, I asked if we were going to continue to travel at this lower level.

"Why, boy," said Charlie, "that was just a little old rise of ground. Now we climb."

At this point, Chuck Cooley got to reminiscing about the time a stray bison from Yellowstone Park ran head-on into a party of hunters he was guiding. The packhorses in the lead turned tail and tore back through their own string, scattering guides and dudes alike and smashing their packs against rock and tree. It came the turn of a stubby little mule to face this strange, humpbacked, hang-headed monster with horns of the devil. For a moment, she planted all four feet in the trail and dared the creature to come on.

The bison came on.

The mule swapped ends and shot back over the trail like the hot blast from a jet engine, flattening everything in her way.

"We had a husband and wife among the dudes," said Chuck, "and after that damn mule near bowled me over, she shoot through on the inside of them like oversquoze toothpaste, and the horses pawed the air and showed the whites of their eyes like the devil had blowed his breath on 'em. I'm tellin' you I thought the whole shebang was going to wind up in the bottom of the canyon. That mule came to a stop up a draw, trembling like the ague and lookin' back to see if what she saw was true. I wasn't no better.

"Lucky for us the buffalo was as scared as the mule by all the commotion, and it took off the other way. But it took two hours to calm down that string, repack all the gear, and head back in the right direction. That's what makes this old horse here, Croppy, so jittery. He's never got over it. You have to watch him close. Let him see a tree stump, or you pull out

a handkerchief, and he'll get so jumpy he'll spook the whole outfit before you know it."

We soon had an illustration. We began climbing after lunch, as Charlie said we would, and as we neared Deer Creek Pass we began to see the snow that had fallen lightly, the night we hit Cody. Here the storm had been heavier, and the snow had stuck. Where the trail turned away from the sun, stretches of ice appeared and soon only patches of slide rock showed through the blanket of white.

When we surmounted a series of dizzy switchbacks and the trail leveled off again, the horses were up to their hocks in snow.

We were really riding high now. The long train of packhorses stretched out ahead of us with Chuck Cooley in the lead. They rounded the butte guarding the pass and, except for a couple of stragglers, were shut off from view. Kenny Hill and the other guides followed, and the dudes brought up the rear. With that 1,000-foot fall-off below, I leaned my weight toward the canyon wall.

Suddenly there was a lot of yelling, and the horses came around that butte running right for us! I felt my hair rise. Charlie and I had just reached a 90° angle in the trail, like the corner of a room only not quite so straight up and down. It was a steep draw and we headed our horses far enough up it to get out of the trail.

I expected a buffalo to come charging around the butte. Instead, Chuck appeared bellowing curses punctuated by whoa after whoa. Kenny Hill went into action waving his arms and matching Chuck curse for curse. His flailing arms, and probably his red hair, turned the lead horses. Then Kenny whipped out a slingshot he carried to keep the packstring on the prod and stung the end horse on the rump a couple of times to keep him moving back toward Chuck.

The other horses began to retreat, and soon were following Chuck docilely again toward the Thorofare, only this time he led them up over the steep butte instead of by the trail.

I turned my horse, Major, back onto the trail but he was now heading back toward the Valley. I took a deep breath and reined him the other way. Half-way around I said to Charlie, "How much room have I got?"

Charlie looked down at the horse's hoofs on the brink of the canyon.

"You got plenty of room—"

I brought the horse the rest of the way around.

"—a good six inches," he finished.

I did it once more in the middle of the night. When I woke myself up, I was halfway to the bottom of the canyon.

When we topped the butte and began to descend the gentler slopes of the Thorofare, we discovered

horses had spooked. The Pass was belly-
w drifted snow. Chuck had wrestled his horse
gh all right, but the lead packhorse bogged
n halfway across and then began to flounder. It
ned back and panicked the horses behind it. It was
ke a chain reaction, and Croppy's buffalo couldn't
have done a more effective job. Like Croppy, I'd
always remember it.

But Deer Creek was forgotten during the next
12 days, and we became more familiar with the clear,
icy streams which feed into Thorofare Creek as it
gathers its forces to join the Yellowstone River—
Butte Creek, Pass Creek, Scatter Creek, Hidden
Creek, Open Creek, and others without name. All
these creeks—a deceptive term considering the
swathes they cut—have their own canyons, ridges,
and mountain spurs. On a map, and probably, too,
from a point high in the sky, this watershed resembles
a gigantic well-tree platter, only much more ramified.

Consider just one—Hidden Creek. It lies in
Blind Basin, so-called because, except for a spiral-
ing corridorlike trail between two mountains, it is
walled in on all sides by rimrock soaring 1,000 feet.
The day we assaulted Blind Basin the sunless trail
was icy and my horse, Colonel (not a promotion, a
different horse) twice slipped to his knees. With no
place to go, except over the edge, I stuck with the
horse—and it proved to be well worth it.

Blind Basin is 12 or 14 miles long, and is thread-
ed by the coolest and clearest stream I've ever known.
That's Hidden Creek, which bores through the
mountain wall and pours into the Thorofare in a
great waterfall. The valley is like a Shangri-La. I've
seen its like in moving pictures, but never believed
anything like it actually existed. It was almost a
profanation that the only reminder of civilization
we had in the Thorofare, a high-flying airplane,
passed over us the day we hunted Blind Basin.

The rimrock looked like the ruined walls of
great lost cities, like many Angkor Vats perched 1,000
feet above us. Below were the forests of spruce and
the lovely sloping parks in which we hoped to find
elk. From this magnificent retreat a world-record
trophy came years ago. We had pinned our hopes on
it, too—but no elk bugle was to shatter the cathedral
atmosphere of beauty and stillness.

So now with November upon us, we were
worried about Deer Creek Pass again, worried we
wouldn't get our trophies in time to cross it before
the snows buried it completely. There had been
one other storm, a few days after we reached the
Thorofare. Its snow was gone from the sunny
ridges, but still lay on the cold slopes and in scattered patches in the timber.

It helped Walter Griffin, one of our original
party who had had to return to his business in
Jacksonville, Fla., to get a magnificent mule deer.
(See "Blood and Snow," December, 1955, *Outdoor
Life*.) And it helped Chuck and me to dog another
big buck for two days—only to have me miss him
completely, unbelievably and noisily.

Those were the events leading up to the bull-
session at Hammett Cabin which opened this story.
So when Frank Lasater said he had an idea about
the elk, we listened. That morning Bob Hogg and
his guide, Don Wildon, had journeyed beyond the
Yellowstone River to hunt the high country there,
unsuccessfully—and then on the way back to the
cabin, incredibly, had walked right into a couple
of elk jousting in an open valley. It was a good six-
pointer Bob shot. But Don talked us out of going
there. They had seen no concentration of elk.

"Don's right," said Frank. "We ought to go the
other way. We've only had a couple of storms and
there's not more than a foot of snow on those peaks.
It's been a lot milder than we expected. The way I
see it, the elk started down from the high country
with the snow, but when the weather softened up
they went back above timberline. I think we'll find
them up at the head of the Thorofare. I don't think
the big herds ever came down."

Nothing else seemed to make sense, so Frank,
Charlie, Chuck, and I agreed to take out next morning with a couple of tents, a packhorse apiece, set up
a jackcamp at Butte Creek, and then hunt the high
ridges around Woody and Bruin Creeks. It would
be a long haul, so we'd leave early. The rest would
stay at Hammett Cabin, pick up Bob's elk, do some
fishing, and meet us with the rest of the outfit at
Butte Creek in a couple of days.

Next day, we stopped at Butte Creek only long
enough to put up one of the tents and throw our gear
inside. In midafternoon, Charlie and Frank turned
up Woody Creek while Chuck and I rode on to Bruin
Creek, where eventually we wrestled the horses up
the flank of a steep ridge until the timber ran out at
11,000 feet. We tied the horses in some gnarled white-
bark pine, last vestiges of timber, and sprawled out
to look the country over.

Our mystery was quickly solved. First I spotted
a herd of at least 50 elk, and then Chuck picked up
two more herds of about the same size before I
glassed my second bunch and nearly rolled off the
ridge in excitement. In short order, we figured we'd
seen about 250 elk. Frank Lasater had called it. The
elk were only now on the move.

"Hell," said Chuck, as he glassed the peaks
and ridges around us, "this is like hunting sheep.
I've never seen elk so high this late in the season."

There was only one thing wrong in this picture
and, after our first enthusiasm, it sank in. The nearest herd was the first one I'd seen, and that was

Chuck Cooley, my salty-tongued guide, left, and I, had agreed not to shave until we got an elk. The muttonchop matting we're sporting here indicates the extent of our poor luck, which dogged us for 12 days.

high on the slope of a ridge separated from us by a deep canyon. We'd have to drop down half a mile, cross a nameless tributary creek, and climb another half a mile even if we were to take the shortest route without trying to conceal ourselves. And it was already late in the afternoon.

Chuck started grimly for the horses. "Let's go," he said.

"We'll never make it," I said emptily.

"You want an elk, don't you?" said Chuck. "At least we can try."

Suddenly a whistle cut the air. It sounded something like a bo'sun's pipe. It was so near it startled me, and I expected to see Charlie or Frank walk over the crest of the ridge. Chuck flattened me with a downward sweep of his hands. Slowly he crawled to the ridge crest and looked over; then he motioned me up the steep pitch. Keeping me low, he pointed toward some alpine conifers on the reverse slope of the ridge.

"See 'em!" he breathed jubilantly.

There in a shallow basin below us were elk—20, 30, 40? I couldn't tell in the quick look he allowed me. We were at the top of the ridge, and it was as if we were on one slope of a roof and the elk on the other. They were some distance from us, heading for the top, and the way they were quartering they'd be a lot farther from us by the time they reached it.

Chuck backed down till he could run bent over without being seen by the elk and motioned peremptorily for me to follow. Running at a stoop is hard work anyway; doing it all at 11,000 feet is murder. Any exertion sucks the breath out of your lungs until you're left gasping. A couple of times I fell because of the steep pitch. Chuck did once, too, but my heaving pleas to wait a minute fell on deaf ears.

When we'd run like a couple of lopsided [va]guses for a quarter of a mile, and crawled like [turt]es another 200 yards, he stopped suddenly and [coll]apsed behind him, sucking in great gobs of air [tre]mbling from exertion. The slope had eased off [we] were coming to a level topping. Just at that

moment the first of the elk topped the rise and angling slightly away from us. Then they came—spikes, calves, cows, and bulls, in single file.

Chuck was wedged up against me. "Don't move a finger," he whispered in my ear, "and they won't scare. Think you're part of the scenery, and don't shoot until I tell you."

There was nothing between us and the elk, not even a blade of grass. We lay right out in the open, flat on the shale. Maybe 100 yards from us the elk moved slowly, serenely, one behind the other like the clay figures in a shooting gallery. Fortunately, the wind was blowing toward us. In our tearing run, I'd sunk to my knees once long enough to jack a cartridge into the chamber of my Winchester 70. I tightened as a good-size bull came over the rise. Chuck restrained me.

"I saw a bigger one down in there," he whispered.

I was glad to wait. My breath was coming more normally now and my shakes subsiding. I swept my eye along the line of elk parading before us and counted 19 of them. Many of them stared right at us and went on unperturbed.

Only one calf was disturbed by the sight of us. It broke into an alarmed trot and caught up with a cow. It looked back as if to say, "Look, Ma, there's something there." But Ma must have said, "Don't look and it won't be there."

Now on the rise appeared a big rack. Slowly the elk materialized, and Chuck gripped my shoulder. "Get ready," he said. "This is the one."

I waited. It seemed an eternity before the bull carried those big antlers to the point nearest us, a little more than 100 yards away. I held the sights on its shoulder, took a deep breath, slowly let out half of it, clamped down on the rest of it, and squeezed the trigger.

The elk went down with incredible suddenness, crashing heavily to the ground, just exactly as if someone *had* pulled a rug out from under it. Chuck pounded me and I babbled some inanity.

"A beautiful six-pointer," Chuck crowed, "—and now we gotta get out of here. It'll be dark soon."

All we could do was rough-dress it. We'd have to come back for it the next day. It was getting dark as we took the long walk back to the clump of pines where we'd left the horses, and by the time we'd traveled the long ridge to the point where we could begin the half a mile descent to the valley it was pitch dark.

Slanting down a steep ridge through timber in utter blackness is like running full tilt through a back yard strung with clotheslines at night. The horses get through the trees all right but more often than not there's a barrier of invisible branches just about head high—to the horseman. Spice is added when you're not sure whether there's any edge to the trail or anything between you and the bottom 2,500 feet below.

After being jammed against tree trunks a couple of times, and almost decapitated a couple more, I got off to walk. This was worse. I nearly stepped off into space.

"Grab the horse's tail," Chuck suggested. "About 15 years ago I was guiding a bunch of big-league ballplayers, Boston Red Sox they were, and we got into a fix like this. One of those guys grabbed the horse's tail, sat right down in the snow, and let that horse drag him all the way to the bottom on the seat of his pants."

"Don't tell me his name," I said. "He might be one of my heroes."

"Of course," said Chuck, "I think you're better off ridin'. The horse can see better than you can. You learn to trust your horse."

So I trusted him, but, even so, when we reached Butte Creek, where Charlie and Frank had put up the other tent and had a hot supper waiting for us, I had lost every button on my jacket, both pockets were torn, and I had a big right-angle gap in the knee of my pants.

"Where's the wildcat you tangled with?" Frank asked.

There was jubilation that night. Charlie and Frank had come upon elk on one of the lower slopes and Charlie had quickly got the meat bull he'd wanted. So we set out next morning with the four pack-horses to fetch the meat. (It takes two horses to carry one elk.) After we'd quartered Charlie's bull, Frank returned to Butte Creek, but Charlie decided to come along with us and take pictures to record the event.

When we finally reached my elk, Charlie said, "Hey, you guys weren't kidding when you said you were hunting sheep." He'd taken two pictures when it began to snow, and in short order a blizzard plastered us with white. The camera, useless anyway, was forgotten and we worked furiously to cut the [el]k up for the haul to Butte Creek.

"Mr. Elliott," said Chuck, between cussing out [a b]ull blade and sweeping snowflakes from his eyes, ["l]ooks like you got your wish. Lucky we got plenty [m]eat."

[A] couple of hours later as we struggled along [a sk]y-high ridge leading back to the valley, the [snow] suddenly let up, but it was plain there was [more] more where that came from. Still later, as [we move] through the valley, Charlie suddenly stopped [and poi]nted to an opening in the timber above us. A [bunch o]f elk walked into the little park. Then more [came] and in short order we counted 72 of them [wind t]heir way through the spruce. They were still [there w]hen we finally moved on toward the cabin.

Charlie posed me with my six-point bull to record the kill.

"They're on their way to Jackson Hole now, sure enough," said Charlie. When we told Frank later, he said shortly, "If they're in such a helluva hurry to get out of the country, we ought to be, too."

Saturday morning, while the rest of the hands rounded up the horses scattered between Hammett Cabin and Butte Creek, Frank packed them as fast as they brought them in, and sent part of the string on its way with Chuck and Bob Hogg. And when they finally came up with a couple of saddle horses, Frank packed Charlie and me on our way. We eventually caught up with Chuck and Bob at Deer Creek Pass, and as we started down the zigzag trail into the canyon, the wind chilled our bones and whipped the horses' tails between their legs.

But the snow held off. With only 11 more miles to go, it was plain Charlie wasn't going to spend this winter in the Thorofare, either. In fact, he didn't get his wish to be snowed in until nearly four years later—and, of all places, it was at my home just 35 miles outside of New York City.

Bill Rae

MY MOST
MEMORABLE DEER HUNT
by Archibald Rutledge

In my long and happy life, I have killed many bucks. My most thrilling deer hunt occurred in December of 1942. At the time, my son Middleton, his wife Flora, and their nine-year-old daughter Elise were spending a month on the plantation with me.

One morning I took them on a deer hunt, and I decided to drive out to Wambaw Corner, a famous buck place. I put my son on a good stand on the old road facing the drive. I then took Flora and Elise to an inside stand on what we called the Dogwood Hill. There I sat Flora on a pine stump and gave her some instructions.

"Don't try to read; don't smoke; just look straight ahead," I warned her. "There may be a great buck in there, and he may come out ahead of the driver and the hounds."

I then walked down an old road and turned toward a dry pond, in which I took my stand. I had not been there 10 minutes when I heard Flora shoot twice. Then she began to scream.

"Oh my God!" I thought. "Her gun went off, and she shot Elise."

I got to them as fast as I could. When I reached them, Flora was weeping like a baby. She threw her arms about my neck.

"Oh, Dad!" she cried. "The biggest buck in all the world, and I missed him!"

I turned to little Elise.

"Did Mother miss him?" I asked her (an onlooker usually can tell better than the hunter whether a deer has been hit).

"Oh, yes," Elise said casually. "She didn't touch him."

Well, that hunt was over.

Before my children left the next day, Flora came to me and said: "Dad, I want to ask just one thing of you. Someday soon go back to that same stump where I was, sit there, and kill that great buck I missed."

It was a large order.

I admired Flora for knowing that an old buck actually has a home he loves in the woods; that although he may be run out, shot at, and even wounded, in a week or 10 days he will return home; and that

if run out again he may take the very sam[e] took before, especially if he has not bee[n]

I waited two weeks before going stump from which Flora had missed driver, Prince, took the hounds dow[n] to the end of the drive, where he

My gun was loaded, and I silent. I had a premonition that happen. It did.

Between me and the hea[d] a growth of leafless bushes Somewhere in there, as yet a jump. I heard twigs bre[aking] thud of hoofs. The first t[hing] tall antlers rising and fal[ling] straight for me. By tha[t] came nearer, affordin[g] this must be Flora's sands of whitetails to this one.

I once kille[d] run to me by a in my hunt tha[t]

shot a buck while he was running through a thicket of scrub oaks that were still carrying their leaves. When I went to him, I noticed at once the extraordinary width of his 10-point rack.

"He is a stranger here," my driver said when he came up. "Heaben is his home."

But Flora's buck was very special, and I thought I had him. But, Brothers, beware the strategy of an old buck if he discovers that a hunter is near. Something unexpected is likely to happen. It did this time.

The regal stag with the spectacular antlers kept coming straight for me. I had my gun on him, but suddenly he stopped. And he could not have planned better for his security. He almost wedged himself between two big yellow pines. He left nothing exposed but his breast, behind which is the brisket, acting as a shield for the heart. When a buck is dressed, a hatchet is needed to cut down through the brisket.

The huge deer was standing about 55 yards in front of me. I knew that if he suddenly drew back and broke away through the thicket, I would have little chance at him. I had great faith in my old 12 gauge Parker double with 32-inch barrels and in the 16 pellets of No. 1 buckshot in the shell in the left-hand barrel. If the buck would come forward on the outside of either pine, exposing one shoulder and flank, I was pretty sure I could put him down. But there remained the possibility of his suddenly drawing back.

The question was simple, but the answer was hard. Should I shoot or not? At 40 yards a shotgun is deadly. The professional hunters of Africa prefer a shotgun loaded with buckshot to a rifle for stopping a charging lion. But at 50 or 55 yards uncertainty begins, partly because of the scattering of the buckshot. A hunter all alone in the woods must sometimes face problems like these, and they are crucial.

I knew that the buck had not seen me, for I had not moved. If a man sits motionless on a stump or a log in the woods, a deer is liable to run over him. A deer's eyesight, except for detecting movement, is not nearly so keen as his nose. But perhaps the buck had located my scent and would draw back, killing my chances. I decided to shoot.

This was to be a standing shot at by far the biggest buck I had ever seen. I confess that for a moment I had a misgiving about shooting so regal an animal. But that foolish idea soon passed, for I have always been a hunter and here was the chance of a lifetime.

My sight was on the buck's breast and my gun was cocked, so I had nothing to do but steady myself and pull the trigger. At the blast of the gun, the mighty buck stood straight up, looking as big as an elk and as tall as a pine. Then he fell heavily backward. But he got up shamblingly and made his way, listing heavily, into a pine thicket so dense that I could not accurately give him the second barrel. I did not think he could go far. How wrong I was!

So many times we do not think, or else think wrongly. For example, I was once on a crossing in the line of an old fence. A few posts were still standing, and one strand of wire was stretched between them. The wire was not two feet above the ground. After a half-hour wait I saw a buck coming my way far off through the pines. He had a noble rack. He was really shoving off, for my driver was whooping it up behind him. If the buck continued on his course, he would cross the fence about 30 yards to my left— a perfect shot.

But when dealing with a wise old buck, a hunter should expect the unexpected. So certain was I that the deer would jump the wire, that I leveled my gun about three feet above it, planning to take him in the

The regal stag almost wedged himself between two pine trees, leaving only his breast exposed.

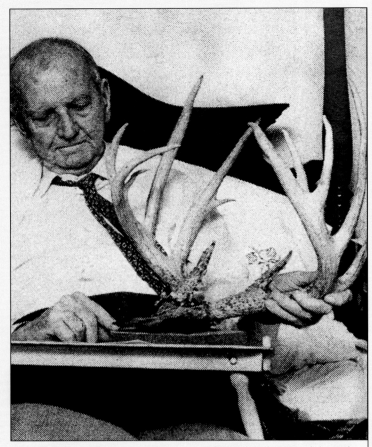

"Actually I have killed 299 bucks in my lifetime," writes author Rutledge, who is pictured above with the antlers of the buck he describes in this story. "If 299 bucks seem just too many for one man, I will remind the reader that South Carolina is a good deer state and that some of its zones have the longest season in the U.S. (4½ months). A hunter is allowed five bucks a season, and I have hunted for 78 years.

"As for the use of a shotgun and hounds, they are imperative in many parts of the South, where the swamps are dense and stalking is impossible. I have hunted deer in the mountains of Maryland and Pennsylvania and can readily understand why the rifle is the weapon to use there and why hounds would be out of place. Everything depends on the nature of the terrain. In the lowland South, because of the level nature of the woods, using a rifle would be dangerous."

air when he made his leap. I had seen him in that part of my plantation several times, so I believed he knew the fence.

As it turned out, that buck knew more about getting past a fence than I did. I had thought he could do it only one way, but there were two.

Just before the buck reached the wire, he dropped to his knees and crawled under the obstruction (tall horns and all!).

Had he sensed that he was in dangerous country and could not afford to display himself by jumping over the wire? I think he never saw me. Because I was so astonished by his maneuver—and perhaps because I momentarily admired him so much for his strategy—I did not shoot at him. Away he went through the forest, still wild and free.

I think it is a great mistake to suppose that all hunters gluttonously shoot everything they see. A good many hunters prefer to give a wild creature a chance, especially if they have an uncertain shot that may result only in a wounded animal. Personally, I will never shoot at a buck unless I am fairly certain I can kill him.

Here I might remark from my experience that too few deer hunters learn carefully how to judge distance. Is the deer 50 yards away, or 150? At 50 yards a buck can be killed with a good shotgun; at 150 a good rifle in the hands of a skilled hunter will take him.

An amateur hunter once told me he had killed a big buck that had been running through the woods 300 yards away. I judged that he really did not know the meaning of 300 yards.

Every weapon has its own capacity to kill game at a certain distance. A hunter should know this capacity and not expect any unreasonable performance. Also, a hunter should remember that there is a limit to the accuracy of his eyesight.

Now to return to the great buck I had shot and thought I would find. Certainly he had left a heavy blood trail. I saw where several times he had lain down and bled heavily. But a natural misgiving chilled me. Had I, like Flora, let this majestic stag get away?

I decided to return to the two pines to see how many buckshot had saluted them. Then I would know how many my buck had received. As I have said, the shell chambered 16 pellets. When I searched the two pines at the right height I found, rather to my dismay, 12 buckshot holes. Only four could have struck the deer. But from his ponderous fall and from the blood he had left, I felt that one of those four had passed the side of the brisket and had gone through his heart.

Baffled, I thought I had better get my driver Prince and the hounds. Prince is a fine hunter and when you're not sure whether there's any edge to the trail or anything between you and the bottom 2,500 feet below.

After being jammed against tree trunks a couple of times, and almost decapitated a couple more, I got off to walk. This was worse. I nearly stepped off into space.

"Grab the horse's tail," Chuck suggested. "About 15 years ago I was guiding a bunch of big-league ballplayers, Boston Red Sox they were, and we got into a fix like this. One of those guys grabbed the horse's tail, sat right down in the snow, and let that horse drag him all the way to the bottom on the seat of his pants."

"Don't tell me his name," I said. "He might be one of my heroes."

"Of course," said Chuck, "I think you're better off ridin'. The horse can see better than you can. You learn to trust your horse."

So I trusted him, but, even so, when we reached Butte Creek, where Charlie and Frank had put up the other tent and had a hot supper waiting for us, I had lost every button on my jacket, both pockets were torn, and I had a big right-angle gap in the knee of my pants.

"Where's the wildcat you tangled with?" Frank asked.

There was jubilation that night. Charlie and Frank had come upon elk on one of the lower slopes and Charlie had quickly got the meat bull he'd wanted. So we set out next morning with the four pack-horses to fetch the meat. (It takes two horses to carry one elk.) After we'd quartered Charlie's bull, Frank returned to Butte Creek, but Charlie decided to come along with us and take pictures to record the event.

When we finally reached my elk, Charlie said, "Hey, you guys weren't kidding when you said you were hunting sheep." He'd taken two pictures when it began to snow, and in short order a blizzard plastered us with white. The camera, useless anyway, was forgotten and we worked furiously to cut the elk up for the haul to Butte Creek.

"Mr. Elliott," said Chuck, between cussing out a dull blade and sweeping snowflakes from his eyes, "it looks like you got your wish. Lucky we got plenty of meat."

A couple of hours later as we struggled along the sky-high ridge leading back to the valley, the snow suddenly let up, but it was plain there was plenty more where that came from. Still later, as we rode through the valley, Charlie suddenly stopped and pointed to an opening in the timber above us. A couple of elk walked into the little park. Then more followed and in short order we counted 72 of them working their way through the spruce. They were still coming when we finally moved on toward the cabin.

Charlie posed me with my six-point bull to record the kill.

"They're on their way to Jackson Hole now, sure enough," said Charlie. When we told Frank later, he said shortly, "If they're in such a helluva hurry to get out of the country, we ought to be, too."

Saturday morning, while the rest of the hands rounded up the horses scattered between Hammett Cabin and Butte Creek, Frank packed them as fast as they brought them in, and sent part of the string on its way with Chuck and Bob Hogg. And when they finally came up with a couple of saddle horses, Frank packed Charlie and me on our way. We eventually caught up with Chuck and Bob at Deer Creek Pass, and as we started down the zigzag trail into the canyon, the wind chilled our bones and whipped the horses' tails between their legs.

But the snow held off. With only 11 more miles to go, it was plain Charlie wasn't going to spend this winter in the Thorofare, either. In fact, he didn't get his wish to be snowed in until nearly four years later—and, of all places, it was at my home just 35 miles outside of New York City.

Bill Rae

MY MOST
MEMORABLE DEER HUNT
by Archibald Rutledge

In my long and happy life, I have killed many bucks. My most thrilling deer hunt occurred in December of 1942. At the time, my son Middleton, his wife Flora, and their nine-year-old daughter Elise were spending a month on the plantation with me.

One morning I took them on a deer hunt, and I decided to drive out to Wambaw Corner, a famous buck place. I put my son on a good stand on the old road facing the drive. I then took Flora and Elise to an inside stand on what we called the Dogwood Hill. There I sat Flora on a pine stump and gave her some instructions.

"Don't try to read; don't smoke; just look straight ahead," I warned her. "There may be a great buck in there, and he may come out ahead of the driver and the hounds."

I then walked down an old road and turned toward a dry pond, in which I took my stand. I had not been there 10 minutes when I heard Flora shoot twice. Then she began to scream.

"Oh my God!" I thought. "Her gun went off, and she shot Elise."

I got to them as fast as I could. When I reached them, Flora was weeping like a baby. She threw her arms about my neck.

"Oh, Dad!" she cried. "The biggest buck in all the world, and I missed him!"

I turned to little Elise.

"Did Mother miss him?" I asked her (an onlooker usually can tell better than the hunter whether a deer has been hit).

"Oh, yes," Elise said casually. "She didn't touch him."

Well, that hunt was over.

Before my children left the next day, Flora came to me and said: "Dad, I want to ask just one thing of you. Someday soon go back to that same stump where I was, sit there, and kill that great buck I missed."

It was a large order.

I admired Flora for knowing that an old buck actually has a home he loves in the woods; that although he may be run out, shot at, and even wounded, in a week or 10 days he will return home; and that

if run out again he may take the very same course he took before, especially if he has not been wounded.

I waited two weeks before going back to the stump from which Flora had missed the buck. My driver, Prince, took the hounds down the old road to the end of the drive, where he would put them in.

My gun was loaded, and I was cautiously silent. I had a premonition that something would happen. It did.

Between me and the head of the drive was a growth of leafless bushes about 10 feet high. Somewhere in there, as yet unseen, something made a jump. I heard twigs break and the telltale heavy thud of hoofs. The first thing I saw were remarkably tall antlers rising and falling. A huge buck was coming straight for me. By that time I had my gun up. As he came nearer, affording me an exact view, I knew that this must be Flora's buck. I had seen literally thousands of whitetails in the woods, but no buck equal to this one.

I once killed a beautiful 12-pointer that was run to me by a strange hound, which had no business in my hunt that day. Another time, on a rainy day, I woodsman, but he is a little deaf. I had a time finding him. When we met an hour later I learned that most of my pack had chased another deer across the river. Prince had with him only Music, a runty, rather bashful little hound, but she had a fine nose.

As we walked up the road together, I told Prince what had happened.

"Music will find him," he said.

The little hound took the blood trail. But before long, somewhat to my chagrin, she began to open and then lit out. From the way she was running, I knew the buck had run a good deal farther than I had thought he would. And following a wounded buck, especially a record one, is always hard on a hunter.

Prince suddenly paused and put his hand on my arm.

"Music," he said, "she quit runnin'."

That should have meant just one thing: she had come on my buck. But it didn't mean that at all, for presently here came Music back, and she was covered with blood. What could that mean? I examined her carefully. The blood was the buck's, not hers. But she was trembling and seemed afraid.

Then, to my relief, we were rejoined by Red Liquor, a big rough rawbone hound, one of the dogs that had taken a buck across the river. As soon as we put Red Liquor on the blood trail, he went howling away. Music followed, but silently and without enthusiasm. Prince and I followed fast after the dogs. Suddenly we came to an old deep ditch.

As we got to the edge of the ditch, Prince and I saw a great pool of blood, where my buck evidently had collapsed. Music apparently had come on him there and, taking wary note of his huge body and tall horns, prudently decided not to take him on. It has been my experience that most hounds are wisely afraid of a buck with big horns. Music, however, had run down into the ditch, probably inadvertently; hence, all the blood she got on herself.

Meanwhile Red Liquor was clambering westward down the old ditch, which, I knew, ran into an incredibly wild old swamp known as the Elmwood Ricefield. Music decided to join Red Liquor, though

delicately. When Prince and I got down in the ditch we picked up the big buck's sprawling tracks. He was running wounded, but I did not think he would go far.

As we hurried down the ditch, Prince paused and again laid his hand on my arm.

"Red Liquor," he said, "he is bayin' now."

As I listened eagerly, I heard Music join in faintly. She, too, was baying, but rather halfheartedly. Either the buck was down or the hounds had brought him to a stand.

The ditch rose to the end of a bank that spanned the desolate ricefield. I walked ahead, my gun ready in case a second shot was needed. It was not. Soon we saw the hounds pulling at something at the foot of a huge cypress. When we came up, there lay my record buck. He was dead.

We were almost in awe. The buck's antlers were beautiful and symmetrical. There were seven points on one side, six on the other. Several of the tines were 14 inches long. His bulk was huge. Later we weighed him on some old scales used for weighing bales of cotton; his weight, before dressing, was 287 pounds. I think it rather rare for a whitetail buck to weigh over 200 pounds. But, as Raymond Ditmars once wrote me after I had reported a nine-foot diamondback to him, "I am not at all surprised. There are giants in nature as in human nature."

Some of the backwoods hunters who had heard of my luck came in to see the big buck. Nearly all of them declared that they had seen him before. Three professed to have shot at him. They were generous in their admiration.

I have killed many other bucks in my lifetime, but none of them ever rivaled that old master. Such was my most memorable deer hunt.

Archibald Rutledge

FISHING

SUPREME MOMENTS
AT ANGLING by Lewis B. France

My friend Lovell has furnished me with the following description of his first experience with the trout.

"Aunt Becky" Tallern, as Lovell was wont to call her, and her son Eli, together with my friend and his young wife, were camped some thirty-five years since in one of the pretty valleys of the Platte. It was Lovell's first experience also at camping. But let him tell his story in his own way:

For the first time in my life I slept out under the stars, courting the novelty. I realized the ambition of the days that were gone when I played at camping out and imagined how grand it must be to indulge in the genuine enjoyment. It was very pleasant lying there and looking up at the bright lights, dreaming of the past and of what the future might have in store for me, listening to the murmur of the river's voices rising and falling on the still air. A small stick, tumbling from its position against the back log of the dying camp fire, made a great noise, I thought, and I looked over to see the little shower of sparks rise in miniature rivalry to the lamps overhead.

As the light of our own kindling fell low again and I courted the sweet influence of the brightly studded vault, I asked myself if its gems were as brilliant as of yore, was the incense wafted to me on the soft air from the pine-clad hills as genial as the fragrance that had greeted me in the old home

of the summer's night? Was there as gentle music in the crystal river sweeping by me as in the whispers of the little brook in the olden time? And the answer came to me soothingly:

"Canst thou bind the sweet influences of Pleiades?" was the question put afore-time and to me, and I answered yes, for I knew of no change, no loss, save of my own working; and why might I not continue to draw sweetness and not bitterness from within?

The night was young yet when I heard away in the distance what I conceived to be the barking of a dog and thought it might belong to the ranchman up the creek. Perhaps had I known what it was on this my first attempt at making my bed in the wilderness I might have grown nervous. Wild animals had not been mentioned, and thoughts of them did not trouble me. The sound was pleasant and homelike and I went to sleep to dream of my old friend Duke. When he vanished I became lost until the sun, shining in my face, advised me of another day and I became aware that my beard was moist from the dew.

Eli, who lay a little way from me snugly wrapped in his blankets, slept soundly. I heard no stir in the tent and considered it a good time to slip out and try to surprise them with a trout for breakfast.

My rod was heavier than Eli's (who was an expert) and better adapted to a different style of angling—the style to which I had been accustomed. I splashed the fly into the water and essayed to draw it along the surface as Eli had instructed me the day before; but I did not succeed until I had made several attempts in decoying one of the denizens of the swirl to possess himself of the deception tendered him. I could not but confess to myself that a trout of ordinary intelligence, even though uncultured, would not be so lacking in discernment as to favor my efforts. At length, however, I prevailed upon one; he was moved, I presume, by the same weakness that prompts the unwary as well as the shrewd man of the world to fall into the shallowest snare that may be laid for him. I felt that self-confidence and innocence are by no means such virtues as should

be cultivated to extremes in the affairs of life; the difference in the dangers attending upon each is so slight that the knowledge of a little wickedness and a doubt of one's self are only to be relied upon. I do not know whether my first trout was a neophyte or well versed in the wiles of our kind. He was very beautiful, however, and I landed him with something of that exultation that no doubt pervades the mind of every man who plumes himself upon his powers of deception. I have heard it said that the expert who cleverly abstracts the contents of a grocer's till or the burglar who defies the skill of the lockmaker prides himself upon his dexterity; that a failure is mortifying to him, not because of the consequences, which are counted in the chances, but because he has demonstrated to himself his own incapacity. No man, whether he be a sneak thief or a minister of the gospel, a poundkeeper or a statesman, can take pleasure in confessing to himself that he is a bungler. While my triumph affected me only and was disastrous to none of my fellows, still it had in it a taint of that voice which attends upon the mind of the successful general or the fortunate pickpocket, and it is well for us that pride goeth before a fall, otherwise this planet of ours would be altogether too limited for our aspirations. Defeat apprises one of his strength and several discomfitures are necessary to some to establish that happy medium between weakness and the strength which leads to healthy success in all wholesome undertakings.

I disposed of my first trophy by laying him gently upon the gravel, a useless precaution now that he was beyond the appreciation of either clemency or indignity. But his beauty appealed to my taste, while his helplessness invoked my magnanimity. Having satisfied my pleasure in the one and quieted my conscience concerning the other by resolving that death is in the Divine order and that the weakest must go to the wall (a doctrine I sometimes hold to be questionable), I again threw the fly upon the current. It came my turn at once to go to the wall, hence my doubts touching the integrity of the prevailing creed. A very large trout seized the fly and without ceremony broke the leader, being materially assisted therein by my unskillfulness. If the tackle maker had only—but I would better not pursue the dominant custom; upon consideration the admission shall stand without qualification. The trout broke the leader, and I looped another fly to the end of the line and sent it on a tour of inquiry. Then I had demonstrated to me the theory that more than one defeat is necessary to a proper appreciation of one's strength or, the other way, that success sometimes begets a confidence liable to lead to disaster. The same trout—filled with conceit or hungry, curious or defiant (he did not communicate his inducement, nor did I consider it delicate to inquire into his motive)—was impelled to fasten upon the fraud; it quickly came his turn to go to the wall and my scepticism experienced a sudden relief. To me he was a marvel of beauty as he lay gasping out his life on the gravel, and I thought only of this: the recovery of my leader and my conquest. The laudations that should be expressed to me in due course added to my gratification. At such supreme moments one cannot easily question the integrity of the "Divine order."

Eli was astir by this time and I heard the voice of Aunt Becky cheerfully issuing her morning instructions to him, wherein the coffee was held in prominent regard.

"And those trout were so nice last night, Eli. I think we might have one for breakfast; can't you take a minute after you get the fire built and catch some?"

The desire of the dear soul jumped pat to my heart; she would have a pleasant surprise of my working, and I—well, it is not the exclusive province of the great successes in life to bring the most pleasure; the little achievements present their full measure, just as the trifling disappointments ofttimes produce the greatest annoyance. Among the other compliments paid me by her was in the avowal, as she had heard; that it required a good man to make a good angler, and that I gave promise of becoming a good angler. She thought, also, that I deserved a cup of good coffee and carried out her conviction.

The golden hue of it, because of the cream which refused to be poured in the exact quantity from the little jug and had to be dipped out with a spoon, and its sublime fragrance, linger in my memory to this day as a delightful dream. It has never been approached and I know will never be equalled. It was never intended in the "Divine order" that more than one such pleasurable experience should visit us in this life. There is always one wife, one trout and one cup of coffee to the man, that stand out paramount to all other exquisite emotions. To possess either more than once would make both insipid.

There is a sublime philanthropy in this restriction that can emanate only from the Divine love and charity for human frailty.

Lewis B. France

A BASS STORY by H.C. Rubincam

I stood on the boat-landing at Seeley's Lake (near Greeley, fifty miles north of Denver) and alternately kicked everything I could reach and "cussed" everything in sight. I had turned out at four that morning to find there was no live bait, and when a Colorado bass takes a notion to live bait the most seductive of artificial bait is of no avail. The Cache la Poudre River was high and minnows consequently scarce so the "boys" came in the night before without a supply, which fact I was unaware of, having retired early in order to do the 4 a.m. stunt. They started for the river shortly after I turned out, but the sun would be high before they returned so I stood there and went through the aforesaid song and dance act with considerable vim and enthusiasm. Rhoads sat in a boat over near the ice house demonstrating the futility of trying "stickle backs" with a placidity that was maddening and I was meditating whether to kick the slats out of the side of the "live-box" or go up to the house and "cuss" a distant relative of the man whose business it was to keep the supply of bait replenished when something in the bait-box attracted my attention. With great caution and a bait net, I approached the box and in a few seconds was possessed of as fine a minnow as I ever beheld. He was nearly four inches long, with yellow and black

stripes running across him—one of the kind we called a "Zebra" and regarded by select Seeley Lake bass circles, as very proper. It was only the day before that I had seen several good sized bass sunning themselves in the shallow water near the ice house, so I immediately rowed over towards Rhoads with my precious minnow carefully housed in the bait can. When I got there I concluded to get in the boat with Rhoads, so he would have no difficulty in seeing what could be done with the proper bait.

After carefully hooking my minnow, I cast him far over to the shallow water near the ice house.

Z-z-z-z-z-z-z-z went my reel before that minnow had time to flap his gills twice. My first impression was that the hook was fast in a log and

Seeley's Lake.

a tidal wave was carrying the boat toward the opposite shore. Then I got busy with the reel and found something hooked good and hard.

"It's a cinch," I said to Rhoads, "that this is either a submarine boat or a twenty-foot shark and if you have your bicycle oil with you please haul it over, so I can oil up this reel before it gets a hot box."

"Look out for your line," growled Rhoads. "If he gets an inch of slack in that shallow water he will get in the moss and then, good-bye fish!"

I started to tighten up on him again and he "broke." Of course, you know what a hasty glimpse one gets of a fish when he breaks water, but I would have taken oath that three feet would not touch the size of that fish and I began to get excited. Then Mr. Fish started in to show me the way they did things when he was a boy and he made straight for the boat. It grieves me to confess that I was then guilty of a very unsportsmanlike proceeding, but remember the circumstances—I had about forty feet of line out, the water over there was only two feet deep, and that fish swam like he was trying to make a track record, so I quickly pushed my rod overboard behind me and hauled in hand over hand. When the fish reached the side of the boat, he was so nearly drowned I picked him up by the gills. As I raised him from the water the magnificence of this specimen of the big-mouth bass tickled an appreciative and responsive chord in my make up. All the people ran out of the house and were much disappointed to find that I was making all the noise. They thought a German picnic had fallen in the lake. Then we went in to weigh the bass and incidentally get some breakfast. Now it is customary to do some acrobatic figuring in computing the weight of a fish and I have a keen realization of the fact that not even my failing hair and general air of respectability can be counted upon to strongly support any fish statement I make, so it is only after due deliberation that I mention, merely to complete the data, that the fish weighed five and one-half pounds. As it is, I would not mention the weight had not several very respectable gentlemen weighed it themselves, both in conjunction with myself and later, as I subsequently learned,

A 5½-lb. bass.

when I was not around, besides which the population of Greeley accustomed to promenading its principal business thoroughfare, viewed a large cake of ice in which his fishship was entombed, prior to its shipment to the Union Pacific's Denver office. It would have been strange indeed if this fish had rounded out the course of his existence on a large platter and stuffed, without encountering some of the experiences of caught fish, and I am sure that as a decent bass he blushed with shame when he was set out on the streets of Denver with a placard announcing his weight as nine and one-half pounds. But then, when it comes to scenery, roadbeds and fish, a railroad must not be held too closely to account.

H.C. Rubincam

THE BLUE JAY FEATHER

by O.W. Smith

I do not know who it was gave the world the well-known saying, "Truth is stranger than fiction," but he might easily have been an angler. As I look back over the ever-lengthening vista of lakes and streams stretching away behind me, I call to mind many a strange incident and peculiar happening, the relating of which would forever place me in the Ananias class. I have no desire for that sort of notoriety, therefore those incidents are recorded in my private note books and the hindmost chambers of my mind. When the wild winds riot about the house in midwinter and the fed flames leap up the open maw of the chimney, with photograph album wide open upon my lap, I recount them for my own delectation and amusement. So I tell these stories to the only person that appreciates, or would believe them— myself. However, today I am going to violate a lifelong rule; I am going to tell one of those stories, let him scoff who will. The story is so unusual, yet withal so satisfactory that the telling of it will be a great pleasure.

There is one white-water stream fished by me which works itself into a very agony of bubbles and foam as it tumbles down hill, hastening to commit suicide in cold Gitche Gumee. Ah, but it is a great trout stream, quiet, slumberous pools, sandwiched in between noisy falls and tumultuous rapids, slippery places, where even the wicked can not stand, and the unsophisticated fisherman comes to grief many times in the course of a long summer's day. (Shall I ever forget the barked shins and aching legs, not to mention the more stable, though not less abused portion of my anatomy?) Just the same I love every rapid, fall and pool, know just where to cast without spying out the land, which, by the way, is the

only successful method of circumventing the wise old trout of a much-fished stream. There are three things which the successful trout fisherman must possess—good tackle, backed up by skill, knowledge of the fish's ways and an intimate acquaintance with the water. Which of the three is the more important I will leave the reader to judge. I must confess I do not know, though sometimes I am more than half convinced it is the last mentioned. At any rate, I have wandered up and down that stream—my stream— in fair weather and foul, until I am acquainted with its every whim and vagary, and have discovered that some mighty leviathans are to be taken from its forest-environed pools and deep rapids.

It was raining proverbial "hammer-handles and pitch-forks" when I caught first sight of the "whale"— only a fleeting glimpse—but enough to send my heart into my throat and cause me to hang my flies high, if not dry, in the tree top behind me. Thereafter, for more than an hour, I cast assiduously, seductively, with all the skill that years of training gives, multiplied by a great desire; but to no purpose; not a fin stirred, not a break in the rain-pelted surface. High on the steep bank above me an upturned stump offered protection from the downpour, and I sought it. Then as the rain did not cease, I built a fire, fried three trout, brewed a cup of tea and sat me down under the stump to think it over. The longer I sat the larger grew the trout and the more remote withal. But you know the feeling. The rain continued. Night shut in early, and I made my way through the reeking woods to camp, discouraged, despondent, disgruntled.

During the night the storm passed, and the next day the sun was not as early as I in getting out of bed. Over night all had changed; I knew, just knew, that I was going to try conclusions with that whale before the sun set. No, it was not the weather, rather the angler temperament. Don't laugh; if an artistic temperament, then in Heaven's name, why not an angler temperament? Every angler has those intuitions, call it seventh sense if you will; we can not give a valid reason for the faith that is in us; we just know.

The tyro would have rushed right up stream to that pool, would not have wet a fly until standing upon its environs; not so the old hand; he waits to warm up, to get his hand in. I began just above camp and fished up, just as though there was no monster trout three hours above me. The day was perfect, the stream in fine condition; that is the beauty of those down-hill streams, the flood runs off quickly. Something had happened to the fish, I found. Where the day before the speckled trout and rainbow were rushing madly to any feathered offering, now I could not stir them to attack. Oh, they were rising to something, and after an hour's unsuccessful casting I determined to discover what sort of food they craved, and supply it if possible.

Imagine my surprise and chagrin when I found that the fish were rising to a pale blue fly, very plentiful upon the surface of the water, and that my book contained nothing at all like it. But I would not give up, and when I neared *the* pool, the home of the whale, I had but six small trout to my credit. I fished the pool from below, from above, but all to no purpose. Then I retired to prepare my mid-day meal and reflect upon the ways of trout, as well as the impotency of mere man.

I let the hours slip unregarded by, for there is little use casting a fly in the middle of a bright day, and what was the pleasure in fishing anyway if the trout steadfastly refused to rise? Sitting there on the shaded bank above the pool I tried to think of some scheme to produce a blue fly out of nothing. I ran the gamut of my fly book through and back again and again, hoping that I might have some fly with a few blue feathers, but no, Fates were against me; anyway, blue flies are not overly common, and I have never found them very successful. I said the Fates were unkind, but underneath it all, back of the disappointment, remained the feeling that I was yet to have the satisfaction of hooking that monster I thought of as calmly reposing somewhere in the depths below me.

The moments had piled themselves up into hours, and it must have been well on towards 3 of the clock, for the long shadows were reaching out from the western bank, when the placid surface of the pool was broken. The fish, such a fish as one sees only in the course of half a dozen seasons, shot into the air, hung for a second, a perfect parabola, then disappeared beneath the water. Once again I experienced that delightful choking sensation and thrilling of the muscles of the right arm.

"My kingdom for a blue feather!" I breathed, and it was more than half a prayer.

Now appears the "impossible" part of the story, the portion that has impelled me to keep it to myself all these long months. A shadow passed over my head. I glanced up to behold a bluejay approaching from the direction of the declining sun. When just

" . . . just where the water shot down in a single volume black and heavy in the center. But with little white foam-circles at the edges."

above me, the bird let fall a single feather, and, darting, ricocheting, eddying, it fell at my feet. I had my blue feather!

Quickly I set to work, for I have some little knowledge of the fly-tier's art, and beneath my trembling fingers there came into existence a blue fly, not the exact counterpart of the particular ephemera the trout had been feeding upon all morning, but near enough to fool old spotted-sides I felt sure.

The fly finished, Fates, or whatever it is that looks out for fishermen, intervened in my favor. Instead of casting directly into the pool, as I had planned to do and had done before, I had a hunch that the proper thing was to cast into the rapids at the foot of the pool; for on my stream, as I have intimated before, rapids and pools alternate; indeed, the pools are all above rapids. You see, away back in geologic ages some mighty Titan dumped several train loads of volcanic rock into the valley through which my trout stream makes its way, and the melting snows and spring freshets of many centuries have worked them—rounded and polished—into the river's bed. The river has rooted and rolled the hard-heads until it has banked them in rapids here and there, through which the water makes its way with much difficulty and noise. And there you have it.

In fly-fishing I have learned wherever possible to fish rapids from below, even though breasting the current is difficult and fatiguing. Casting over fish in swift water is the only way you can be sure of hooking them. So I went below the rapids and slowly made my way up stream, casting to the right and left, touching every wee eddy and back current. My makeshift fly proved an open sesame. I was kept busy taking off medium-sized trout, and I became almost angry with them, for my mind was upon the expected. Just where the water shot down in a single volume, black and heavy in the center, but with little white foam-curls at the edges, I cast, letting the fly fall, an insignificant speck of blue baby ribbon amid the white tresses of some Norseland giantess.

Coincident with the caress of the feathers, there came a flash, a rainbow curve of a radiant body. The fish, my fish, had rose to the feathers, missed by the fraction of an inch and returned to his lurking place amid the eddying bunches of foam. The leap occupied the briefest fraction of a second, yet the curving body of the fish, silhouetted against the white and black water is indelibly photographed on my memory. (I would give a great deal for a camera-made picture.) Quickly I recovered and cast a second time—almost instantly, for all depends at such times upon getting back at once. Again the flash of

". . . some mighty leviathans are to be taken from its forest-environed pools." Some rainbow for a fished-out stream.

a red body, the head of the fish seeming to re-enter the water even before the tail was free from it. But when the trout went back into its lurking place amid the rocks at the bottom, it took my new-made blue-jay fly with it, hooked hard and fast through the lower jaw.

No, I am not going to attempt to describe the battle. Why should I try to square the circle? I have gone back over the descriptions of various ichthyic struggles which I have written and published during the last ten years, and yet they are all inadequate and unsatisfactory. I have been accused of using extravagant language in my attempts to describe angling battles, but I solemnly assert that that is an utter impossibility. You can't make mere words lie when it comes to a fight with a rainbow! Just take everything you have ever read about "ripping lines," "moil of water," "bending rods," "shrieking reel," etc., etc., and roll it all into one gigantic, tremendous description; then you will have the introduction to my battle there in those rapids at the foot of the quiet pool, mirroring the fleecy clouds which floated overhead, all unconscious of the fact that its bright monarch was battling for his life a few rods away.

As I write, the rod which played the monarch lies upon my letter scale at my elbow—I placed it there for inspiration when I began the story—and the little pointer gives the weight as exactly 4¾ ounces. It is a split bamboo from the shop of a man who knows how to make good rods. I want no better. The reel, that quadruple aluminum winch, adapted to the necessities of the fly-fisher, which, filled with G. enameled line, weighs 4¾ ounces—the combined weight of the tackle, if my arithmetic is not at fault, being exactly 9½ ounces. No, it was not overly light, but I desire that you know I took no unfair advantage of the monarch of the pool and foam.

I can not tell you how long the battle lasted; I was not interested in the flight of time; neither can I tell you the number of aerial leaps the rainbow made; I only know that again and again he went into the air, shaking himself until the silvery drops of water rained into the rushing water below. Down stream or up stream, it was all one to him. He would rush up that shoot of dark water, the line bending perilously behind him, as easily as the Maid of the Mist breasts the current below Niagara Falls. Sometimes we were clean down at the foot of the rapids, but never could I coax him into the still water below, neither would he enter the pool above his home. The fish seemed to know that the only chance for escape lay in the rush of the current. But after all, rod, reel, line and hook were too much for him. Long before the battle was won I had the landing net free, ready to receive the doughty fighter. At last, exhausted but not vanquished, he would turn upon his side and

The Editor proves that the stream also shelters good brook trout.

feebly "kick." Then I held the net in the current, and when the bag bellied out down stream, gently led my captive head first to its entrance. Its water-colored meshes enfolded him lovingly, and I splashed over the rounded, slippery rocks to the shore, the proudest, happiest angling editor in all the Badger State.

Did I, after I had mercifully killed him, lay him out there upon the green grass where the rays of the setting sun could play upon his multi-colored body rivaling the sun itself in glory? Did I pass my hand down his velvety sides, gloating exceedingly? Did I "heft" him again and again? Did I sit down by his bigness and just "feel good"? Did I? Did I? You will never know, for I will never tell.

Next season, Red Gods willing, there will be another story, for there are greater fish in that stream of mine which empties into Gitche Gumee known to the Pale Faces as Lake Superior.

ADDENDUM.

In the foregoing story I have failed of my purpose unless I have shown you the value of adaptability, stream-knowledge, fish-knowledge, and stick-to-it-iveness, as well as the prime necessity for good tackle. As to that fly, well, the angler who can not, like Will Wimble, "dress a fly to a miracle," when needs must, is going to fall short of success many a time.

O. W. Smith

LANDING THE
RECORD BROADBILL by Zane Grey

Our big-game fishing editor, William Barber Haynes, in sending us the accompanying photograph and description of Zane Grey's big broadbill swordfish catch at Catalina island, Calif., last July, says: "Zane Grey, noted novelist and sportsman, today holds the world's record for a broadbill catch made with rod and reel. His fish taken recently in Catalina waters weighed 582 pounds, and it took Mr. Grey five hours and thirty minutes to conquer it in what he calls an 'old-fashioned' fight. Mr. Grey holds that there are old-fashioned ways and new methods of doing things, even fishing, and that when it comes to thrill and sportsmanship he favors 'the good old way'."—The Editor (1926)

For ten years I have been trying to catch a record broadbill swordfish—*Xiphias gladius*—the broad-sworded gladiator of the seven seas. During eight of these long, hard summers my brother R.C. has tried it with me.

During this period I have caught twelve broadbill, and my brother has taken six. Although we have had many hard battles with great swordfish, the longest of which endured eleven and one-half hours, we never have brought to gaff a world's record until

Zane Grey and his record broadbill.

this season, when after a tremendous "old-fashioned" battle on the heaviest of tackle I captured a 582-pound fish.

I say "old-fashioned" because the method in vogue here at Catalina during the past few years is a modern one, and like many other modern things in this day and age, is open to question.

Fishermen all over the world hear and read about great swordfish being taken at Catalina, one new record about every year or so. It is very thrilling to read, and no doubt most fishermen wonder how a 400 and 500-pound swordfish can be caught in thirty and forty minutes on rod and reel. But nothing is ever said about the airplane wire leader. This is 15 or 18 feet of wire that holds the hook and is attached to the line. We used to use a piano wire, a very stiff and hard wire, while the airplane wire is thin and pliable, like a cord, and very strong. It loops like a lasso.

Well, the modern method of angling for broadbill is to use this airplane leader, and when the angler gets a strike to slack off a lot of line and let the swordfish get tangled up in it. Sometimes the fish is choked or strangled, and often he is cut to pieces. In any case he is lassoed and hog-tied by this infernal wire. As a result he is quickly pulled in, either dead or unable to fight.

This airplane leader is the deadliest and most unsportsmanlike thing used in this manner that I have ever encountered in fishing. It is also extremely dangerous to the angler. It could very easily loop around his gaff and cut his head off. It would actually do that! And the loss of his fingers is a very great risk.

I did not catch my world's record in this manner. I struck him on a tight line with all the strength I could command and fought him until I killed him. It took five hours and thirty minutes of continuous battling.

If I had not been in splendid physical condition from my hard fishing in New Zealand I never could have whipped the broadbill at all. Nevertheless, I had about all I wanted. My arms and back were badly strained, and my left leg black and blue from constant contact with the arm of the swivel chair. The weight of the fish kept forcing the chair around, and I had to use my legs to get it back straight.

He was not a spectacular fighter. He did not leap or break water. He just fought every way, slow, heavy, with fast runs and deep soundings.

Without the Coxe reel and the Swastika 39 line I never could have conquered this broadbill in any time.

He was the most perfect specimen we ever saw. More than 13 feet in length, 5 feet in girth, with enormous fins and huge, round, curved body, heavy clear to his tail. Without a parasite or a blemish, he was indeed a magnificent specimen of the "King of the Sea."

Zane Grey

TAHITI WATERS by Zane Grey

I am sure that I owe to Charles Nordhoff the discovery of the great game fishing in Tahitian waters.

When we dropped anchor at Papeete my intention was to fish a little around the island, and then make for the Paumotos and the Marquesas, which groups of islands were my objective. We fished quite a little between Moorea and Tahiti, but as we were unable to catch bait and did not see any fish I decided that perhaps there was something in what American yachtsmen had claimed anent the absence of game fish around Tahiti.

It was a happy event for me, and likewise to the angling world, that at the instance of my publishers, Harper & Brothers, I called upon another of their authors, Charles Nordhoff, who lived in Tahiti. When I explained my object and plans to him he said:

"Why go to the Dangerous Archipelago and the far Marquesas when there are great fish right here?"

Then I was to learn how Nordhoff, when out with the natives after bonito, had seen many swordfish and sailfish, the size of some of which seemed incredible. I am bound to admit now that Nordhoff was very conservative. He strongly advised me to stay and give Tahiti an exhaustive fishing. This I did as related in my book, "Tales of Tahitian Waters."

The spring of 1931 was my fourth season at Tahiti, during which time I had fine sport and caught three very notable fish—a black marlin of 810 pounds, a world-record sailfish of 170 pounds, and a mako shark, the only known fish of this species that was ever caught except in New Zealand waters.

It should be recorded that fishing at Tahiti is the hardest of any that I have tried. And any visiting angler must have his own tackle, and make arrangements in advance for boat and engineer. As the sport there is in its infancy these are not easy to procure. But it can be done, and the enthusiastic angler with time and money can be assured of an unforgettable experience.

Travelers go to Tahiti for its unparalleled beauty alone. The angler who visits Tahiti may be assured of many wonderful pleasures besides his favorite sport.

My protegees, the Guilds, who live at Tahiti, started from scratch without any previous experience whatever, and they made a magnificent success of it. They began with a little launch they bought

from me, and some tackle I gave them, and some few days out with Captain Mitchell and me. The story of their blunders and struggles against tremendous odds is not the least interesting of my "Tales of Tahitian Waters." I called them Ham-Fish and Carrie-Finn.

It took Carrie-Finn two years to catch her first marlin. She had strikes from many fish, and had a score hooked before she got one. I mention this here, not only because I want to emphasize their remarkable perseverance against obstacles, and their ultimate graduating into great anglers, but also to prove my contention that for anglers who want only a little sport as well as those who aim at the heights, Tahiti has no peer in the Seven Seas.

My first important catch at Tahiti in 1931 was a 150-pound mako shark. This species has been reported from various waters away from New Zealand, its natural habitat, but no verification of the claim has been substantiated, to my knowledge.

Reports of mako caught at Hermanez, South Africa, off the Japanese coast, around Australia, and other places seem to be unfounded. The photographs presented in two cases absolutely verified another species. But so far as Tahiti is concerned I can prove the mako has been taken off the Queen Island of the sea.

In March, while trolling for swordfish off Paea, I raised a white and blue fish that leaped high out of the water on the strike. It did not resemble a marlin in any particular, yet I took it for one. I hooked the fish and was working hard on him when the hook tore out. My chagrin gave way to amaze when we sighted the fish returning for part of the bait still left on the hook. I had reeled most of the line in. When I saw the fish distinctly I shouted: "It's a mako!" Peter certainly responded to that call. Being from New Zealand himself the word mako was magic. When the darn fool fish took the bait again, right under our noses, we knew it was a mako; entirely aside from classification by sight.

"WHOOPEE! Mako!" bawled Peter.

I jerked with all my might and believed I had made fast to the shark. Nevertheless he pulled free. Still he had not had enough! This is a feature of the mako that is great. You can scarcely hurt, whip or faze him. He came a third time, looking for more. Peter had swiftly hauled in my line to put on another bait. I let it down. The mako swam around it several times, evidently leery of the strange contrivance. Something to eat with a string and a pull in it! Eventually either his hunger or his pugnaciousness got the better of discretion, for he charged the fresh bait and rushed away. I put on a stiff drag and lunged back with all my strength. This time I knew I had hooked him. But mako or not he refused to leap, which was disappointing to us. After a brief tussle I bested him and dragged him in to the gaff. The instant that steel touched him—souse—crash! "Same old mako stuff!" I yelled. We landed him, and could see no difference in the slightest way from a New Zealand mako.

Such classification identified another shark I had hooked at Vairoo two years before. I had let down a live bait, got a tremendous strike, and hooked something heavy. It ran a little way, then came up—a huge blue and white fish, nearly 20 feet long, that evidently saw the boat, for he darted away with inconceivable rapidity. The line simply melted off the reel. At 400 yards it snapped. We had always wondered about the fish. Now we identified him—an enormous mako shark.

March 5 was a day of full moon, always a period of uncertainty at Tahiti. It promised to be a hot clear day with a heavy sea and strong wind. On the way out we met the native who caught flying fish for us. He had a unique method. He put out in his outrigger canoe to leeward of the reef a few hundred yards. His tackle consisted of a dozen or more little floats of light wood, 6 or 8 feet of line to each, mounted with tiny hooks and baited with shrimp. These he scattered around the smooth patch of water and kept his eye upon the floats. When he saw one bob under, reappear and glide away with a ducking motion, then he knew he had a flying fish, so he would paddle over and haul it in. One morning he caught eleven in short order. But that was exceptional. On this particular March morning he had only one. From past experience I knew well

Zane Grey with a Giant Sailfish. This fish, weighing 170 pounds, restored to the distinguished author at the time it was caught, a world's record which he had held and lost.

that a single bait could get an angler into a heap of trouble. This very thing happened that day.

We ran out several miles off Vairoo. The sea was rough and blue, with white caps showing. While I trolled the one flying fish the rest of the outfit searched the sea for signs of birds and bonito. In vain!

As it was pretty rough I decided to run in under the lee of the mountains and try to raise a sailfish. My tackle was a hickory rod, 600 yards of 39-thread line on a 9-inch Coxe reel. My leader was 20 feet long and the hook a Sobey Pflueger 10'. This rig was small enough to be all right for an ordinary sailfish, ideal for a big one, and it would serve pretty well if I had the bad luck to hook a heavy marlin. That is the only way you can fish successfully in these crystal-clear hot waters of the tropics. I had learned to my sorrow that light tackle means only grief. You will hook what you do not expect, and toil in vain.

We were well back in the lee and not a mile from the reef when Jimmy yelled in his deep voice: "Beeg feesh!" I sighted this fish myself just about the same instant. It was a long brown shape on the left side, far back of the teaser, and coming pretty fast. I stood up. The leathery shape resembled a porpoise. But as he shot in toward us I recognized a swordfish shape and I pealed out the old familiar cry: "There he is!"

He rushed that flying fish, his black fin out of the water, and simply absorbed it in a great swirl. He swept away in plain sight, curved and came back. I knew he had my bait by the way the swivel of the leader cut the surface.

"That bloaker wants some more," yelled Peter.

"Sorry we can't oblige him, Pete, but this is the only bait we have," I replied.

Whereupon I put on the drag, reeled in until the line was tight and struck him hard. He lunged out of sight leaving a circling swirl of green water where he had been. When I stuck again I came up on a tremendous weight, and I knew that whatever the fish was I had him hooked.

He got going faster and faster, and at the end of perhaps 100 yards he leaped. We all yelled bloody murder. Peter and I: "Black marlin!" and the natives some name in Tahitian. The second leap was long and low, broadside on, and gave us a chance to estimate his size. He was a dazzling blue-green and silver, a lengthy fish, and very deep in his shoulders. He struck up a huge splash, went under, to heave out in so magnificent a leap that I was stunned with

A giant black marlin, weighing 810 pounds, caught by the author at Tahiti in 1931.

the wonder of it. Then he sounded and headed out to sea.

"Up against it, Peter," I said, grimly, as I faced the ridged sea and the hard job. But there was a degree of exultation in it, too—the fight ahead—the obstacles to overcome.

My angling principles do not approve of following a fish, if he can be stopped and fought. But I doubt that I could have stopped this fellow very quickly, even if I had had him on my big tackle. Peter was evasive as to his size and weight. "He's a big fish," was Peter's only comment. To that I replied: "He's long and 4 feet deep. He'll go 1,000 pounds…. But it's a thousand to one I'll never land him in this sea."

"I'll take that bet," averred Peter.

So we followed him while I hauled and pumped and wound steadily. Mile after mile he led us out, until we cleared the extreme east end of Tahiti and went out in the open sea, where the great green combers rolled. I had to admit that the new boat was a comfort to fish out of. I did not mind the sea at all, except that I worried about the finish of the fight, if it ever came to that. I managed to turn the fish, and he led us back a few miles, for which we were extremely grateful.

Three hours—four hours—five hours—how they fly in a battle like this! At the end of five and a half hours, I stopped the black marlin. He began to act queer, to fool around, to change his tactics. But he was mighty powerful and not yet exhausted. Then to my regret he began what I had feared—to sound. I had to let him go.

When he got down 1,000 feet I knew the pressure of water would kill him. "He's cooked," said Peter. It was my idea that I was the same. Down 12, 13, 14 hundred odd feet. Then he stopped. Probably at that moment he gave up the ghost.

"Well boys, he's whipped. Now let's take stock of the job, and see what can be done," I said.

The rod was bent in a curve and rested in the gunwale. It had the solidity of a rock. I could not raise it off the gunwale, or move it in the slightest. The line stretched like wet gut and sang like a telephone wire in the cold wind. We drifted and we talked. Peter put down 1,500 feet of line, with a heavy lead and grappling hook, but could not tell whether he reached him or not. The sea was not so heavy as it had been, still it made my chance appear hopeless. The fact that the wonderful Swastika line held was the only thing to keep me calculating. By holding the bell of the reel with both gloved hands I was able to keep the line from slipping off when a huge swell lifted up.

Perhaps we had drifted for a quarter of an hour before I noted that the angle of my line had changed.

The Fisherman, anchored off Tahiti and seen in a setting of palms.

First it had been straight down and now it took an angle of 45 degrees. That gave me an idea.

"Rube, throw the clutch in and turn her hard toward my line. I'll see if I can get some back." I said hopefully.

The engine roared, the wheel whirled, the boat turned to short ahead. The tension on the rod eased. I hauled and wound in a frenzy, and I recovered about 10 yards of line before we had to stop.

"It worked," I shouted. "Throw her out. We'll drift and try that again."

In ten minutes the angle of my line slanted off to windward. We tried that plan again. It worked still better. I got in more line. I had to work strenuously, but felt that the short time justified any exertion. I could rest up each time. This method we kept up for three long hours. It took skill, judgment, and endurance. We got back fully 900 feet when Peter conceived a brilliant idea.

"Let's cut that line and thread it on your big rod."

I wondered why I had not thought of that before. They wound the line off my Hardy reel. Then Peter reached down to grasp the line which held my fish and very carefully pulled until he had slack. "Pull some off, Rube," he ordered. "Then cut—and tie a running bow-line knot."

It was accomplished in a few seconds, and there I had the great fish on my big outfit, with only 500 feet of line to recover. The danger, of course, was that with the more powerful rod and reel, and the same line, already stretched and strained to hazard, I might break the fish off. Moreover we could not get

so much of an angle by drifting. But I made headway, and though almost beaten felt that I could last.

Sharks came around the boat—ugly, yellow, uncanny devils. The boys got out the lance and threw it whenever we came close. That is a new sport we have developed, and to anyone who hates sharks it is surely thrilling. The lance is a heavy blade 18 inches long, and screwed into a long pole with a line at the end to recover it. You aim and throw as you would a baseball. The thing goes like a shot and when that blade connected with a shark it was just too bad for him.

At the end of nine and a half hours I dragged the black marlin to the surface. He was huge, almost deformed, black as a black opal, with a short rather light spear. The sharks had mutilated him considerably, but we believed we could patch him up well enough to photograph.

The sun had set, the sea was still rough, and we were 10 miles off land. We had to tow the fish in. Darkness came on, the moon rose, the clouds over the black mountain were grand in the extreme. I sat out on top, in a heavy coat, and rested while I watched. I was pretty severely used up and sagged more as time passed.

At 8 o'clock we got inside the point into calmer water. I flashed my Portolite searchlight which was answered from camp. That was a help and comfort. We got in at 9:30, to meet all my party and half of Vairoo at the dock.

The black marlin weighed 810 pounds as he was. That was a disappointment to me. But despite his length of 12 feet and more and his great depth he was thin. If he had been thick and fat he would have weighed over 1,000. Nevertheless he surely was a superb specimen of that species and lent an added stimulus and thrill to the beginning of our cruise.

Fishing around an island, or among islets, affords unparalleled opportunity of appreciating their dominant features. I made bold to state that probably not one of the many writers who have extolled Tahiti could possibly have had any such impressions as I had. For I have fished all around its shores, and for months off Vairoo, Paea, Teravoi, and those districts on the east side, where the most magnificent scenes are located. You must get out on the sea, at a considerable distance, to be able to appreciate the grandeur of Tahiti, to see the blue and white and gold and green in their successive belts, to get the glory of the pearl clouds on the peaks.

On the third day of our fishing around Vaaru we got outside the reef into the open sea, and we trolled for 30 miles. We did not raise a swordfish. Upon running inside again we began to get strikes. Loren's boat appeared so busy on several occasions that we wanted to satisfy our curiosity; wherefore we called it on the radio. They had caught three good fish, and were on the moment engaged in fighting something heavy. About this time I had a heavy strike—on a feather gig— and saw a sousing splash. But the fish missed the hook. A little later a big wahoo leaped with the gig in his mouth. This one hooked himself and proved to be a hard fighting fish—a wahoo of 60 pounds. That exhausted our luck for the day. We ran inside past the wonderful islands, some of which were inaccessible except for birds, and in every case these were the most beautiful and fascinating ones.

Loren's boat accounted for one 35-pound wahoo, two tuna about 25 or 30 pounds, and a dogtooth tuna of 98 pounds—this last being a splendid specimen of that fish we had discovered at Tahiti. It looked like a bulldog, heavy-jawed and thick through the body, with big eyes and teeth.

Captain Gunderson and our chief engineer, Quady, who had been on many a tuna market-fishing boat, undertook to catch bait with our big net. They reported enormous mullet, but too illusive to be caught in the daytime. Quady also reported 300-pound tuna feeding and leaping in the bays inside of the islands.

It rained the following morning, then cleared off sunny and breezy. We ran to the southwest, out in the open sea, where white breakers and huge black rocks held the gaze. Birds were hard to find. Some bobbies soared about the last castle rock. They were large black and white sea fowl and might have been ganners. Flying fish were conspicuous for

their absence. And the dearth of small bait proved to us that this was an off season. Nevertheless I trolled a split mullet for hours, and at last, about noon, saw a swift flash of bronze coming. I yelled. He hit the bait like an express-train going at full speed. As he turned I struck him hard. He went off, stopped, fiddled around, then stuck up his slender spear. Naturally I was thrilling with the hope that I had gotten fast to one of the rare under-jaw-billed swordfish. He leaped, disclosing the wide flopping sail and enormous tail of a sailfish. That for a fore-runner to a succession of beautiful leaps, after which the fish settled down to a slow fight. He felt pretty heavy for a sailfish, and always eager for a record, I hoped he was not a deceiving fish. Eventually I brought him in, and when the boatman hauled him up on the roller on the stern and to lay flat, I knew I had a magnificent prize. He was bright bronze in hue with violet stripes, very gracefully and power-fully built, and evidently a variation of the regular species of sailfish. His spear was the finest and sharpest I ever saw on a fish. His whole length was close to 11 feet. He weighed 170 pounds, which gave me back the world record for this species, by 7 pounds.* I had lost the previous record at Raiatea in 1928.

Zane Grey

We understand that William Gray has since broken this Zane Grey record by taking a sailfish weighing 180 pounds.—The Editor (1932)

THE DAY ALFANDRE
FOUGHT GERONIMO by Frank T. Moss

In the salty village of Montauk, on the eastern tip of Long Island, New York, they still call Harry Alfandre the unluckiest fisherman who ever lived. Harry was a lean, angular man who had the nose of a beagle for fish, especially tuna. During his days at Montauk, he stirred up storms of excitement and comment by big-city rod and gun columnists.

It was Harry who discovered the famous "Rosie's Ledge" giant-tuna grounds and instigated what amounted to a revolution among East Coast big-game fishermen. Yet Alfandre himself never managed to land one of the great, finned furies that became synonymous with his name. But he tried. Oh, how he tried.

Two weeks before Labor Day in the summer of 1949, Einar Handrup, owner of the commercial fishing dragger Marion H., came into Montauk with a very large bluefin tuna. He had harpooned it some-where east of Fisher's Island. Harry Alfandre saw the fish, talked with Handrup, and lost a night's sleep mulling over what he'd learned.

The next day Harry took Capt. Clancy Pitts, a local charter skipper, and the crew of the Rosie, his own small fishing cruiser, and shoved off across Block Island Sound for Fisher's Island. With Harry's 15-year-old son Ronald and nephews Howard Alfandre and Sandy Hacker, they were five. After several hours of scouting, they'd found no tuna. A lobsterman they met told them where tuna had been sighted the day before.

When they reached the spot, a couple of miles south of Watch Hill, Rhode Island, huge tuna were breaking all over the place. Four draggers were dash-ing about, trying to harpoon the fish. One finally got an iron into a tuna. Harry watched and got an idea.

The next day they returned to the spot off Watch Hill, trolling squid and mackerel baits among the rioting tuna. They hooked two large ones, which they promptly lost to broken lines. That evening, back at the Montauk Yacht Club, Alfandre told some of the local guides what he'd seen. They said he was off his rocker because "Tuna don't grow that big in these waters."

The third day Harry lost another fish. When they got home, tired and disgusted, they found Capt. Don Gross of the charter boat Capt. Don preparing to sail the following morning for the big ones. Don Gross knew how to handle big bluefins, and his client was none other than the then Mrs. Dan Topping, wife of the co-owner of the New York Yankees and no mean fisherwoman.

History records that Mrs. Topping caught more dead weight of tuna in the next four days than the entire fleet of the U.S. Atlantic Tuna Tournament, which happened to be fishing at the same time at the Mud Hole of Hudson Canyon, off New York harbor. The fuss the press kicked up over Harry's discovery of the fabulous new tuna grounds and Mrs. Topping's eye-popping catches resounded from Maine to Florida. In a lyric column in the New York Journal-American, the late Jack Brawley dubbed the spot off Watch Hill "Rosie's Ledge," after Alfandre and his little white boat Rosie. The name stuck.

Local guides quickly quit scoffing and joined the rush to harvest the big fish. Frank Tuma Jr., skipper of the Gannet, brought in seven big ones. Don Gross racked up an even dozen, including the season's largest, a 779-pounder caught by New York sportsman Robert Manger. Captains Ralph Pitts, Bob Tuma, Carl Darenburg, and George Verity, spark plugs of the Montauk charter fleet, helped account for the 25 giant tuna that were weighed in at the Montauk Yacht Club.

Among the tuna at Rosie's Ledge was one monster folks started calling Geronimo. He showed himself occasionally in chum slicks, always far back from the baited hooks. When he joined other tuna in their spectacular surface-feeding, his mighty tail

Harry was whipping the 14-foot sharpie like a jockey as the giant tuna took them through the fleet with spray flying.

swept like the black scythe of Father Time among the sickle-blade tails of lesser fish. Men guessed his weight at between half and three quarters of a ton.

Harry Alfandre saw and coveted Geronimo. He lay awake nights thinking of ways to hook the elusive monster. But luck was not with him. When summer was over, the Rosie's score was high on broken lines and fractured rods but still zero on big tuna in the boat. Nevertheless, Harry was already planning for the next season, nursing the germ of a radical and exciting idea.

As the summer of 1950 began, Russ MacGrotty inflamed tuna-season hopes by his early capture of a 409-pounder at Rosie's Ledge. Tuna guides and anglers flocked to Montauk as the fishing picked up. Chissie Farrington broke her own women's world record with a 674-pounder caught on 24-thread tackle.

Then came the electrifying news that old Geronimo, grown even bigger and more wary, was back. This was all Harry Alfandre needed to hear. He had refurbished the Rosie, bought new tackle, and hired quiet, capable Oscar Rodge as skipper. An old-time Montauker, Oscar had an unshakable Scandinavian faith that anything the crew of the Rosie set out to do, it could accomplish.

Oscar had built Harry a 14-foot rowing sharpie and placed in its bow a cut-down fishing chair. Alfandre's new plan was to try to catch giant tuna from the sharpie in the manner of the old-time whalers' Nantucket sleighride, fighting the fish from the chair in the sharpie with rod and reel. People scoffed, but not to his face. Folk had learned that Harry's vinegary tongue could marinate those who tried to twit him. Even his wife Rose, for whom the Rosie was named, said nothing.

Then came the fateful day, Sunday, August 13. The weather was ideal for tuna fishing and a long file of sport-fishing boats roared from Montauk toward Rosie's Ledge, 12 miles across the Sound. The Rosie, towing her sharpie, wallowed in the wakes of more powerful and dashing cruisers. Most of the fleet was already anchored and chumming when the small, white boat arrived and planted her mud hook.

The art of chumming consists of doling overboard a thin soup of ground menhaden mixed with sea water and laced with chunks of cut whiting or menhaden. It's a messy and often smelly process, but it does attract big tuna. Alfandre placed the heavy fiberglass rod with its 14.0 reel filled with 54-thread line in one of the cockpit rod holders. He hooked on a 15-foot cable leader, baited the 13.0 Sobey hook with a whole, fresh whiting, and drifted the bait deep behind the boat, tending the line by hand. The others, Ronnie, Howard, and Oscar, cut bait or dipped chum.

Suddenly a motor coughed to life down the long line of anchored boats and one of the chumming vessels slipped its buoyed anchor cable, speeding off in circles, fighting a freshly hooked giant tuna.

"Watch for fish in our chum slick," Alfandre warned his crew, knowing that where one big tuna strikes, many more may be feeding.

Then he felt an incredibly heavy weight on his fishing line. He had put the bait down 60 feet under the surface, hoping for a large fish. He stripped a fathom of the fishing line from the rod and reel, dumping the slack into the water so the fish would have loose line to swallow the bait. When the line came tight again he yanked on it as hard as he could with both hands to set the big hook.

"I have one on!" he yelled as he grabbed up the big rod.

They managed to get him aboard the sharpie and into the chair without upsetting the smaller boat. Oscar tumbled in after him, releasing the line that held the sharpie to the Rosie's side. Grabbing up a steering oar, Oscar dug water to swing the small boat's bow after the fish as Harry jammed his calloused thumb down the star-drag wheel to increase the tension.

The rod bucked and cracked. Alfandre shouted. Line whistled out through the guides. Oscar paddled frantically, cursing around his cud of cut plug. The boat started to skim over the water, towed by the hooked fish. Some distance ahead the tuna boiled at the surface. Harry and Oscar caught a glimpse of a great, familiar, scythe tail.

"Suffering catfish, we've hooked Geronimo!" Alfandre shouted.

The sharpie raced through the anchored fleet, spray flying. Harry hung onto the rod with one hand, flailing his fishing cap from side to side in his excitement, like a jockey urging on a reluctant bangtail.

"Outa our way!" he bellowed at the startled occupants of Gene Goble's resplendent Fishangri-La. The tuna took them whizzing under the larger boat's bow.

The sharpie splattered through the gathered boats like an outboard racer that had bucked off its driver. Motors roared into life as skippers suddenly decided to abandon anchor lines rather than risk a ramming from the seemingly jet-propelled skiff and its two wild-eyed occupants.

"Can't you steer this fish outa the fleet?" Alfandre shouted over his shoulder at the drenched, blaspheming Oscar.

Somehow, Oscar managed to shoehorn the sharpie through the mob of boats without scraping paint or chafing the fish line on an anchor warp. Finally, they were clear of the fleet and out in open water. Oscar heaved a sigh of relief, but Harry saw fresh danger.

"Turn the fish back inshore!" he howled at Oscar. "He's taking out to sea at better than ten knots!"

By cramping the boat hard to one side of the tuna's wake, Oscar found he could steer Geronimo back in the general direction of Rosie's Ledge and the chumming fleet.

"Don't let him drag us back into those boats!" Harry screamed.

"Wish you'd make up your mind," Oscar grumbled, wiping tobacco juice and salt spray from his chin.

Meanwhile, the Rosie and another fishing cruiser, the Barracuda, skipped by young Bobby Darenburg of Montauk, were hovering, near, anxious to render aid, but afraid to come too close. The fight between the tuna and the two men in the sharpie settled down to a gut-wrenching slugging match that circled, stopped, started, and zigzagged just outside the fleet.

Once Geronimo sounded and lay doggo, gathering strength. "Gotta get him moving," Harry muttered, yanking strongly at the fish with the heavy rod.

His problem was a special one. A well-handled power boat can chase and hound a hooked giant tuna into making run after run, burning up its supply of body oxygen faster than this vital element can be replaced by water flowing over the gills. Eventually, the fish can be driven to the point of complete collapse. This is the secret of those startlingly swift victories over huge tuna that mystify so many landlubbers. But Harry and Oscar had no motor with which to chase Geronimo.

All Harry could do was to goad the fish into making oxygen-burning runs by banging at him with the rod under heavy line pressure, then quickly releasing the drag pressure to fool the fish into thinking it was free.

It was back-breaking work. Blisters broke on Harry's hands. He and Oscar were soaked with sweat and salt water. They were dying for a drink. The sharpie needed bailing. At odd moments Oscar flung out a scoop or two of water, but most of the time he had to concentrate on steering and shifting his weight to prevent a capsize.

At last the fish showed signs of weakening. Alfandre increased drag pressure and began to muscle in the last 50 yards of line. He had literally to haul the boat up behind and finally on top of the tiring tuna as it cruised slowly along, a few feet under the surface. Oscar tried paddling, but it didn't help much. The outermost 15 feet of the line was spliced double as gamefish rules allow. When Harry got two turns of this double line on the reel spool he clamped down on the drag pressure to the maximum. The Rosie and the Barracuda cautiously came closer.

Then they saw how big the fish was. "His tail's under the stern of the sharpie," Oscar called out.

"His head's two feet beyond the bow," Alfandre marveled. "He's longer than the sharpie!"

Slowly the fish rose to the surface. Harry winched in the last of the double line until the stainless steel snap-swivel connecting the line to the cable leader touched the rod tip. Dropping the rod, he grabbed the leader and hauled the skiff toward the wallowing fish. Oscar shoved the flying gaff at him. Holding the leader with one hand, Harry made a powerful swipe and drove the hook of the flying gaff into Geronimo's jaw.

He separated the stout ash gaff handle from the detachable hook and hauled tight the half-inch manila rope that was spliced to the gaff hook. The Barracuda had backed close to them and Oscar threw the free end of the gaff rope to Bobby Darenburg, who hauled in the slack and took two quick turns around one of the boat's after bitts.

"He's ours!" Harry croaked triumphantly, picking up the rod to get it from underfoot.

Then Geronimo came to life, showering the two boats and the people in them with sheets of spray from his great, slashing tail. Down he plunged,

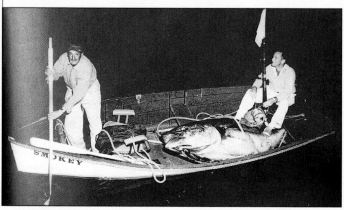

Harry Alfandre paddles sharpie used to fight big bluefins. The angler with foot on conquered fish is A.M. Whisnant.

Ronnie and Harry Alfandre with big tuna Ronnie boated.

snapping the gaff rope like string. Bobby Darenburg stood in the stern of his boat, too stunned even to pick up the broken end of the gaff line that hung over the transom.

"He'll dump us over!" screamed Alfandre, staggering under the weight of the fish on his rod.

Oscar scrambled just in time to prevent a capsize as Harry got the reel drag released so the fish could take out line. When they had themselves and the sharpie under control, they were back where they were before the gaffing, but minus the gaff and with the boat half full of water.

"What'll we do now?" asked Oscar.

"Bail out the water, then tire him out and gaff him again," said Alfandre. "What else is there to do?"

Wounded by the swallowed hook and the gaff in his jaw, Geronimo couldn't last forever. Harry goaded him into a couple of runs, but the old steam was not there. Finally the fish was back cruising slowly under the surface, setting its fins against the pull of the line. Harry could gain no more line. They had reached a stalemate. The splice of the near end of the double line was still two feet under water.

Geronimo's blood stained the water. Harry rested, panting, his arms aching. If he could just get in the last couple of fathoms of single line and put two turns of double line on the reel, he would be able to apply enough pressure to raise the huge fish to the surface. Both the Rosie and the Barracuda were standing by to pass them a fresh gaff. He tried once more to raise the fish a bit and failed. Black spots danced in the backs of his eyeballs with each pounding pulse. He had been fast to the tuna for

more than three hours, and he didn't know how much longer he could keep up the pressure.

The end came with a shocking suddenness. The hot sun, burning down on the drying linen line just beyond the rod's tip, caused the fibers to lose some of their wet-test strength. Harry took a deep breath and tried to lift the fish, applying a few extra pounds of pressure. There was a sharp snap as the line parted. Harry lurched backward out of the fishing chair. Oscar lunged to catch him.

When they regained their feet they could see the broken end of the white fishing line snaking slowly into the depths as Geronimo's mighty, dying bulk sank away from them.

Numbly they let Ronnie and Howard help them back into the Rosie's cockpit. No one spoke.

The Rosie continued to fish for big tuna at Rosie's Ledge and Harry was sometimes in the sharpie, but there was always someone else behind the big rod. Alfandre's zest for rod-handling was slow to return.

Stan Smith of the New York News hooked a 10-foot shark fishing from the sharpie with Harry at the steering oar. Asked if he had fun, Stan replied, "Fun? It was the second closest thing to suicide."

Guessing at Geronimo's size, good tuna men estimated his length at 14 to 16 feet. He certainly was longer than the 14-foot sharpie. For fish caught with rod and reel, the present world-record bluefin is a Nova Scotia 977-pounder. It measured not quite 10 feet long. A 1,200-pounder brought into Block Island in 1956 by a swordfisherman was short of 12 feet. Using these measurements as rough guides, it's safe to say Geronimo probably weighed 1,600 to 2,000 pounds.

It is fitting to note, in closing, that 16-year old Ronnie vindicated his father's faith in sharpie-fishing for big tuna just three weeks after Harry's debacle. Ronnie took a 676-pound bluefin from the tiny boat in the fast time of 30 minutes flat. When the Rosie returned to Montauk that afternoon with Ronnie's big fish, every boat in the harbor blew its whistle or fog horn. Rex, the dockmaster, fired salutes from the little brass cannon at the Yacht Club.

That night, at the Yacht Club Crew's Bar, a beaming Harry was buying drinks for all hands, satisfied to see his son redeem family honor.

Frank T. Moss

HEAVEN IS A
STEELHEAD by Joe Brooks

———◆———

Bill McGuire was into a fish. It streaked across the pool so fast I thought it was going to climb the trees on the far bank. Then it made a dogleg to the right, skittered five feet across the surface, and sank from sight. But it came right out again in an arching leap and headed upstream, still showing plenty of power and speed—a big, going fish if ever there was one.

Bill reeled fast, to keep the line tight. Then the fish came to the top, slowed, swirled, and dropped downstream, still facing into the current but slanting to the right, and with hard sweeps of its tail gained a couple of feet.

These were rough tactics. This steelhead was hard to hold.

Then the fish surged forward a few feet. Bill swept his rod in toward our bank, pulling the fish our way and getting it out of the current, reeled fast, and had the trout coming. Things looked good.

But then that fighting steelhead pulled out all the reserves, shooting toward the tail of the pool and again jumping clear. That effort tired the fish, however, and Bill followed it downstream, easing toward the bank as he went. He got the fish coming good and skidded it up onto the sloping beach.

"About eighteen pounds," Bill said, lifting the steelhead by the gill cover. "What a fish!"

That small bullet-shaped head was made for boring into heavy currents. The body was thick,

deep, and strong-looking. An overall sheen of silver spoke of months in the sea, but the flared gill covers showed a faint blush of crimson, and there was a crimson slash along each side from gill cover to tail.

"He's traveled two hundred miles from the salt," Bill said. "He's beginning to get back his rainbow colors."

Bill took the hook out and put the fish back into the river.

"Go on upstream and spawn," he said. "And thanks for the memory."

That fine fish was the heaviest of eight steelheads Bill landed that day on the Babine River in northern British Columbia. All were taken on flies.

The steelhead, one of the greatest of all gamefish, is almost entirely confined to the coastal waters of western North America. In some places rainbows that run upstream out of lakes to spawn are also called steelheads. But the true owner of that name is the rainbow that goes to the salt and then comes into coastal rivers.

Here is an extremely strong fish that makes amazingly long runs, breasts mighty currents, soars up and over falls, thrashes through rocky shallows— moving relentlessly upstream in answer to the hereditary urge to spawn in the waters of his origin, waters that often are hundreds of miles from the sea. A few spawning steelheads die. But many survive and work their way back to the salt. There they fatten again in the sea's bounteous larder and regain strength so that they can return to the river and spawn once again.

From late August to mid-March (and even later in some rivers) the steelhead hordes enter rivers all along the West Coast from California to Alaska. Like waves beating on the shore, come the steelhead hordes. Then they hurry upstream, heading inexorably for the spawning beds.

There are summer steelheads and winter steelheads. The summer runs occur from late May through October, the winter runs from December or January to about mid-March.

On the Babine River, where I watched Bill McGuire take those eight steelheads, the best period is the last two weeks of September and all of

October. But winter comes early this far north, and icy blasts sometimes send late fishermen out of there on the run.

Part of the thrill of steelhead fishing in the Babine is the wildness and splendor of that country—the dank smell of the forests, the racing rapids, the "feel" of a land that demands the best from every man. It is stern, remote, and wonderful.

In late September and through October—at the peak of the river's steelhead run—the landscape takes on a holiday look. The mountains shove up stands of lodge-pole pine, whose dark green provides a rich backdrop for the flamelike oranges of the aspens and poplars. The mountainsides appear to be dotted with lighted candles.

All of those trees seem to rank up and march down the slopes to the lakeshores, leaving occasional grassy, open spaces in which moose feed.

And along the shorelines you get an eyeful of rising trout.

The same rivers that harbor steelheads are also used by Pacific salmon, which spawn there and die. In the Babine you see sockeye, humpback, chinook, and coho salmon, all bound upstream to perform the last act of their lives. Many of the salmon, already half dead, are blotched with whitish fungus. Gaunt and sunken-eyed, the salmon dig out spawning beds and go about the act of spawning.

The sockeyes are bright red along the body, with greenish head and tail. Their beaklike mouths are studded with sharp teeth. The backs of the males show a decided hump, another manifestation of the spawning phenomenon.

Along the shore, spawned-out and dead fish lie rotting, and from them rises a heavy odor. But the smell is more pungent than unpleasant, so you soon forget it as you fish.

Perched on the fish carcasses are the everhungry gulls, mewing and crying, pecking and pulling at the flesh. Sharing the spoils are dozens of bald eagles, in there getting their share or perched on log jams and trees along the river.

All are part of nature's cycle.

It is sometimes hard to get your offering to a steelhead before a salmon or one of the river's resident rainbow or Dolly Varden trout grabs it. If we did hook a spawning salmon, we tried to shake the hook out. If unsuccessful, we carefully released the salmon, hoping that it would live long enough to make its contribution to the future of its species.

Insurance man Moses Nunnally and I had flown from our homes in Richmond, Virginia, to Seattle, Washington, where we'd met Bill McGuire. Bill is director of research and development for Eddie Bauer Outfitters of Seattle, and he knows the Northwest thoroughly.

In Bill's car we headed for the Canadian border, which we crossed near Sumas, Washington, and picked up the Trans-Canada Highway. At the town of Cache Creek, British Columbia, we turned onto Highway 97 and continued north to Prince George. From there we headed westward on Highway 16.

Five miles south of the town of Smithers we took off on a dirt road. Forty-five miles later we reached Babine Lake. Ejnar Madsen and Jim Clark, owners of Norlakes Lodge, were waiting at a dock with a launch, in which we rode to camp, located 20 miles down the 115-mile-long lake.

The Babine River, which we were going to fish, slips out of the lake some four miles below the lodge, at the Indian village of Babine. The river is wide up there, with long, shallow stretches. Then it narrows and runs faster as it nears a weir three miles downstream. Below the weir it rattles along through breathtaking country for 20 miles and on into an almost impenetrable canyon. It then enters the great Skeena River, main artery for steelheads coming inland from the ocean. The Kispiox and the Babine are two of the Skeena's most famous tributary rivers.

From start to finish the Babine runs for about 60 miles, in a generally westward direction.

The Babine's steelheads average 15 pounds, but many are considerably heavier—the females as big as 15 pounds, some males to 35.

The biggest steelhead reported from the Babine was a 47½-pound fish taken in a net by the Babine Indians. The largest ever taken on rod and reel went 31¼ pounds and was caught on bait by Wendell Henderson of Kelseyville, California. Several other anglers have taken Babine steelheads to 30 pounds, and fish estimated to have been in the 40-pound class have been lost.

The Babine's largest fly-caught steelhead weighed 26 pounds and was taken by Jim Sharp of San Francisco, California, in 1958.

One day Jack Albright of Bellevue, Washington, representative for a ski-clothing manufacturer, and I took the biggest steelheads we'd ever caught on flies. The fish were hooked in the same pool and within a few minutes of one another.

Jack and I had gone downstream several miles below the weir and had stopped to fish a fine-looking pool. It was about 600 feet long and 125 feet wide, with a good current throughout. I fished the head of the pool while Jack waded in a couple of hundred feet downstream from me.

He had just got into position when I saw him wave and point to the opposite bank. On the sandbar at the head of the pool, we had seen within 10 feet of one another the tracks of wolves, moose, and grizzlies. Right away I thought, *grizzly!*

But it was a moose that Jack had spotted, a majestic animal whose antler spread must have been at least 55 inches. Eventually the bull turned and faded into the dense underbrush.

The moose was a good omen. Jack and I were into fish right away.

I made a short cast across-current, heard a splash, and got a strike that made me jump. That steelhead must have been lying just below the surface.

It was a good fish, and he zipped off downstream as if he were going to tear Jack's legs off. But he jumped halfway between Jack and me and fell back with a thump, tossing water far and wide. Then he made a run of about 100 feet, stopped, and hung there.

I edged to shore, keeping a tight line, and walked downstream, reeling as I went. Then the fish raced upstream, fresh and flying, and jumped right opposite me. I got a good look at him, and I knew that this was the biggest steelhead I'd ever had on. Jack saw him, too, and came running.

I finally beached that fish, which weighed 20 pounds.

Back we went to our fishing, and now it was Jack who got the action. He gave a whoop, and I jerked my head around in time to see a tremendous steelhead in the air. It fell back with a splash and tore the surface to shreds as it steamed for the far bank. Then, just as suddenly, it turned, rushed right back at Jack, and came out of the water only 15 feet from him.

I could see that this steelhead was bigger than the one I had just landed.

Jack stayed with that big, strong fish for 15 minutes. Finally he got it into the shallows, where its color blazed up and seemed to tint the water with crimson and pink sparks. The fish was fat and round-looking, its weight riding the length of the body into the tail—a powerful fish from a mighty breed.

Jack skidded the steelhead onto shore. The scales said 25 pounds—a skookum (mighty good) steelhead for sure.

We had released all of our other fish, except a couple that we'd eaten, so Jack and I both felt that we could be excused for keeping these two for mounting. They were the sleekest-looking steelheads I've ever seen—fine products of a great river.

The Babine was loaded with big fish. The next day, I fished the pool below the weir with another

Flamelike foliage forms backdrop as Ejnar Madsen strarts to net big steelhead for Don Ives.

of the camp's guests, Don Ives, a machine salesman from Seattle. I was about 200 feet below Don when he hooked a fish so big that if I hadn't seen the crimson on its sides during a jump, I'd have thought that it was a chinook salmon. The fish streaked downstream with a definite goal in mind, maybe the salt.

Don raced past me in pursuit of the great fish and disappeared around a point. Twenty minutes later he came trudging back.

"He took me down through the next two pools," Don told me. "He got into a pocket behind a rock, and I got most of my line back. Then the hook pulled out. That fish must have been forty pounds."

I could well agree. That was certainly the biggest steelhead I'd ever seen. And Don's reel handle was bent to about a 40° angle from the pressure that had been put on it.

In many steelhead rivers you can occasionally take fish, especially summer-run fish, on dry flies and by skating spiders; or you can take them on flies fished just under the surface. But all of us at the Babine camp tried this kind of fishing at one time or another without luck.

Most of us used a sinking-float line, the first 30 feet of which sinks while the rest floats. With such a line you can make very long casts and put the sinking section out where the fish are. It will go down quickly and allow leader and fly to work in the holding water. The floating section is easily mended, or flipped upstream, letting you keep the fly out there and drifting freely. And the sinker-floater is much easier to retrieve and pick up than is a conventional sinking line.

Moses Nunnally, though he is an old hand at fly casting, had never fished this kind of line before.

"Couldn't I do just as well with a floater?" he asked.

I explained that the fish were holding deep in the riffles and pools and didn't seem to want to come up to take. Now and then they moved up a foot or so, but most of the time they nosed down and picked up a fly as it slid along the rocks on the bottom.

I'd guess 85 percent of all steelheads taken on flies are caught by the users of sinking lines, lines that get the fly right down to the fish. Many anglers use a line that sinks in its entirety, but an old steelheader's trick is to splice a sinking head to a monofilament line or to a level nylon floating line. By using a very heavy head—a 333-grain shooting head, for instance—and splicing a nylon running line to it, you get an outfit with which you can easily make casts of 125 feet. The light nylon will float and so won't be pulled by the current as would a heavier line.

However, the new combination sinking-floating lines, now made by a number of fly-line manufacturers, eliminate the troublesome job of splicing two lines together. The new lines also eliminate another problem—possible weak spots at the splices.

Moses' first cast with the sinker-floater on the Babine was a good one of about 85 feet. But as soon as the fly and line landed, the current grabbed the line and put a big belly in it. I knew that consequently the fly was rushing across the pool far too fast.

"Mend your line," I said hastily. "Flip the floating part upstream so the water won't pull on it and drag the fly away from the fish."

In any steelhead river having a fairly stiff current, the heavy push of water will quickly belly a line and pull leader and fly out of the lies of fish. I told Moses to throw a slack-line cast (a serpentine toss) and then to mend the floating part of the line. That way, the fly floats freely for a longer distance, straight down-current, out where the fish are.

I explained that some fishermen make a cast and feed the shooting line out of their hands or let it run out of the shooting basket (we used shooting baskets on the Babine) so that the fly gets down and works along the bottom.

"After the fly has finished the downstream float and the current starts to pull it across the pool," I told him, "let it go, keeping the rod tip high and imparting no action to the fly. It'll work across the pool and come to a stop directly below you."

"A steelhead may hit at any part of a float—sometimes as soon as the fly lands, sometimes when it's out in the current—or he might follow it across-current and hit on the swing. Most of them do hit on the last part of the swing or just when the fly stops moving and hangs in the current."

"That's what he did!" yelled Moses, who was following my instructions religiously. "I've got one!"

He raised his rod tip, and 30 feet out from us a steelhead took to the air. It was a good, deep-bodied fish, and it fought a great fight. Moses finally beached the trout, which weighed 14 pounds even.

"Not bad," I said. "Two casts and one steelhead."

Some steelheaders bring the line in as soon as the fly's cross-current swing is complete. Others retrieve the fly upstream for several feet, jerking it as they do so, before bringing it in for the next cast. On the Babine I have got hits from steelheads on those slow, foot-long jerks, so I stick with that kind of retrieve wherever I try for steelheads.

Or the Babine, as elsewhere, to get the best float with a sinking line you have to judge the water's depth and force.

Sometimes the current is so great and the water so deep that, even with a sinking line, you must cast well upstream so that the line has time to get down before it reaches the place where you know or suspect the fish are lying. On the other hand, the fish may be holding where the water is shallow and the current relatively slow. In that case you have to toss the line and fly a bit downstream so that the line won't sink too much and catch on rocks.

Moses raised another point that day.

"I've always thought that the longer the leader, the better your chances for fish," he said. "But we're using short leaders."

"When you use a sinking line," I said, "the leader should be no longer than six feet. A ten or twelve-foot leader such as we use in most trout fishing would only defeat the purpose of the sinking line. The heavy line would go down, all right, but the current would force the long, light leader—and the fly—up toward the surface and out of bounds for deep-lying fish. The short leader keeps the fly down where you want it, only inches from the bottom."

(In any big steelhead river, long casts are usually needed. For that reason, as well as for ease in handling the sinking lines, I advise steelheaders to use a 9 or 9½-foot fly rod. With such a stick you can throw either the WF-9-F/S or the slightly heavier WF-10-F/S line. The number in each line designation classifies the weight of the first 30 feet of the line. The designation WF-9-F/S means that the line is a weight-forward floater-sinker in which the first 30 feet weigh 250 grains, thus making the line a No. 9 according to standards set by the American Fishing Tackle Manufacturers Association. The WF-10-F/S is the same type of line but has a 30-foot weight of 300 grains. I like the lighter of those two lines for fairly shallow water and the heavier one for deeper water. The No. 10 line sinks faster and makes long throws a little easier.)

On my first trip to the Babine, Bill McGuire had handed me a shooting basket and insisted that I use it. As I said earlier, most steelhead rivers demand extra-long casts—throws of 80 to 100 feet. To handle that much line while wading, it is almost essential to use a shooting basket.

If you don't, you must loop the shooting line in the fingers of your free hand, and the long coils often drag in the water, twist in the wind, or become entangled and bunch up against the rod's first guide, spoiling what could have been a fine throw.

With the shooting basket strapped around your waist just above your belt, you can strip in line so that it lies in neat coils in the basket. When you make the next cast, the line slips out freely and easily.

"When you're ready to retrieve," Bill had told me, "tuck your rod under your arm, and use both hands to strip the line into the basket in front of you.

You can use a lot more line this way than if you tried to hold it in your hand."

I did as he said, and it was a pleasure on the next throw to see the line's heavy head go out and then to look down into the basket and see coil after coil disappear.

Best fly patterns for steelheads vary according to the river being fished, and they are used both weighted and unweighted. In general, the best patterns, especially for winter steelheads and during late runs in big rivers such as the Babine, show some pink, red, or orange, along with some white. These flies are tied to imitate salmon eggs, on which steelheads feed heavily.

On the Babine we used all the color combinations just mentioned. We started with No. 4 and No. 6 hooks but eventually went to 1/0 because we found that these bigger hooks bit better into the mouths of big steelheads.

Our favorite pattern was the Babine Special, first tied by Bill McGuire. It has an orange body with a pinched-in center, a white hackle, and no tail. Its design is very simple, but that was the fly we all came to depend on.

Rex Palmer of Seattle ties another good one. It has an orange body, white hackle and a green tag. He calls it the Palmer Special.

As far as I have been able to discover, no one has ever taken a steelhead from the Babine on a dry fly. Next time I'm there, I intend to put in some time trying to do just that.

Joe Brooks

ADVENTURE

AN ADVENTURE
IN THE TETON MOUNTAINS

by William O. Owen

There is a widespread notion that numerous of the wild beasts which inhabit our forests and mountains will attack man without any provocation whatever, but there is very little in fact on which to base such an opinion. The truth is that generally even the most ferocious of them will flee upon man's approach, and will attack him only upon receiving a wound, or when the lives of their young may be endangered. An experience of twenty-five years in the Rocky Mountains verifies the above statement; but while this is the rule, there are of course occasional exceptions, and one of the latter I shall attempt to set forth for your readers.

In 1892 I was detailed by the government to project the lines of the public survey into and over that portion of the Snake River Valley lying immediately south of the Yellowstone National Park and at the east foot of the Teton range of mountains—a country of wild and rugged grandeur, and, at the time of my survey, practically unknown to the white man.

Within this area are included "Jackson's Hole," Jackson's Lake and the trio of world-renowned peaks known as the "Three Tetons," the locality in question having recently been brought into prominence through the Indian outbreak of 1895.

Having carried our line over the rugged Gros Ventre Range and the narrow valley of Snake River, we encamped, one evening in September, on the south shore of Jackson's Lake, at the base of the Teton Mountains, whose snow-capped summits rise 13,000 feet above the sea. Jackson's Lake is ten miles long, and its waters lave the very foot of the range. Passage afoot is possible all around the lake, except at one critical point on the west shore, where the

naked granite of the Tetons rises so abruptly from the water that not even a cat could scale it. We did not discover this fact until several days after our arrival, and I have emphasized it as having an important bearing on this narrative. Having finished our work on the east side of the lake we set out one morning to connect our lines on the west shore; and by quitting time we found ourselves five miles from camp and with a stretch of as rugged country between us and supper as one could find anywhere in the state. As usual there was a lively debate as to which was the best way to camp, some urging the shore of the lake, others insisting on a route far up the mountain, through the dense pine timber.

In working on the east side of the lake we had frequently noticed and discussed a long, bare slope of granite which swept down to the water's edge on the west shore, and which was, to all appearances, utterly impassable. Recalling this, it was finally decided to toil westward up the frightfully steep slope immediately to our right and make for camp through the timber, passing entirely around the inaccessible granite slide. Only one member of the party dissented. This was my flagman, and nephew, Neale Roach, an athletic youth of 16 years. He insisted that the lake shore was by far the shorter way, and much easier walking, and expressed perfect confidence in his ability to pass the granite slide—the object which alone determined our party not to pursue the route along the lake. So we parted at the water's edge after a word of caution to the young man, and after three hours' climbing over granite slopes and fallen timber five of the party reached camp just at dusk. But Neale had not yet arrived. We ate our supper, expecting every moment to see the flagman, or hear his shout through the pines, but no such welcome intelligence was in store for us. Nine o'clock came, and still no tidings of the wanderer. We built a large fire that could be seen for miles, and kept it burning throughout the night, filling the mountain fastnesses with deafening yells all the while, but not a sound could we get in return.

The dawn of morning, following, seemingly, the longest night I ever experienced, found Neale still absent, and immediately two parties were made up to go in search of him. One was to go back over the route we had pursued the evening before, while the other was to proceed by boat to the point on the west shore of the lake where the young man had separated from the party. We had been compelled to use a row-boat while working around the lake, and this was fortunately at our camp.

We set out shortly after daylight over the unruffled surface of water and headed straight for the granite slide, which, I had little doubt, had proved too much for Neale, and where I hoped to be able to strike his trail at the point where he had been compelled to turn back. On one point I was quite apprehensive, and that was that Neale might have attempted to pass the slide of smooth granite and fallen into the lake. In such an event it could scarcely be hoped that we should ever see him alive again, for the water is all but ice cold, and no man could live in it long enough to swim to a landing point. I feared nothing else, for he was well provided with matches; and being of iron constitution, fortified by youth, he could stand severest hardship. As we approached the slide the conviction that Neale had never passed became more and more settled.

It is a slope of at least 60 degrees and almost glassy in its smoothness, extending along the lake for about 400 yards, and rising at least a thousand feet above the water in a steep unbroken incline. Along its north and south margins are forests of dense mountain pine. Examining the slide with the glasses, I suddenly became aware of the presence there of a moving object, perhaps eighty or a hundred feet above the water, and clinging like a crab

to the smooth, bare rock. Hope was alive in a moment, for what could that object be but the missing youth?

As we drew nearer I could see that it was a human being, and that he was gesticulating and wildly waving his hat. Imparting this information to my three companions they gave out a lusty shout, and Smith, seizing his Winchester, discharged several shots in rapid succession.

Our nearer approach to the rock developed the fact that there were two live objects there, separated by not more than a score of yards, and in a short time we discovered the second one to be a large mountain lion, or puma. We now discovered that across the face of the slide, for about half its width, there ran a narrow ledge or shelf about four feet wide; and on this shelf, perhaps fifty feet asunder, were our flagman and an enormous cat-like creature eyeing each other savagely—the former erect, the latter crouched down close to the rock, with his head between his paws, in the attitude of a cat about to spring upon its prey.

The trained eye of Sam Smith, our hunter, took in the perilous nature of the situation at a glance. He was a veteran mountaineer and had hunted these animals for years, and knew their habits.

"There's no boy's play here, I can tell you that," he said; "I wouldn't be in that kid's shoes for all the gold in the Teton Range! Don't a man of you open your mouth if you value that boy's life! Be mum as the grave and row a little farther north, where I can get a bead on the cat, and we'll see what this gun's good for." Coming from Smith these words almost stopped my breath, for I knew they never would have been said without abundant grounds for them. Sam's skill with the rifle had won him the nickname of "Old Faithful," and it was a remarkable fact that the tighter the situation in which he was placed the more sure was his aim.

A short pull up the lake brought us to a point whence Smith thought a good shot could be secured, and at his orders we came to a halt. At the same moment the lion, in some way aroused, rose slowly to his feet and deliberately started toward the boy. I closed my eyes, but immediately opened them at a low whistle from Sam, which brought the lion abruptly to a stand. The great cat turned his head eastward and fastened his gaze upon the boat. This was the opportunity Smith had been looking for, and quick as thought the sharp crack of a rifle rang out upon the morning air, followed by a cat-like howl of pain I shall never forget. The huge brute raised himself to full height on his hind legs, and, tottering, fell sideways on the rocky slope and shot down the glassy incline with the velocity of a cannon ball. The carcass struck the water with terrific force and, impelled by awful momentum, disappeared like a flash in the cool, clear depths of the lake. We breathed once more and a shout of triumph went up from every man in the boat. "Old Faithful" had not failed and Neale was saved. I seized Sam's hand and gave him a hug that a bear might be proud of, and was followed in like manner by every man in the crew. The path now being clear we shouted to Neale to retrace his steps and meet us at the west shore of the lake where we had separated the previous evening. Rowing northward we soon had the boy in the boat and provided with a generous breakfast.

Having quieted the pangs of hunger, Neale gave us an account of his adventure. Upon leaving us the night before he had proceeded through the timber close to the lake, and he was making excellent progress, when, emerging suddenly from the forest, he came upon the rocky slide previously described. It looked at first impassable, but turning up hill he found a shelf or rift which, as far as he could see, extended entirely across the slide, and of sufficient width to admit of easy passage. He moved cautiously along the shelf, highly elated with the prospect of an easy trip to camp, but had gone not to exceed 200 yards when he was brought to a standstill by the disappearance of the cleft. He was halfway across the slide and completely balked.

There was nothing to do but to return and overtake the party far up the mountain. He hurried back, but had not gone a hundred feet when he was brought face to face with an enormous mountain lion, standing right on the shelf and absolutely blocking the way. This animal had doubtless been following Neale without the latter's knowledge, awaiting a favorable opportunity to attack him.

For a boy 16 years old and unarmed this was an awful position, and for several minutes he stood completely paralyzed. For perhaps five minutes the two stood eyeing each other, when Neale, having recovered his self-possession, began to move backward, keeping his eye on the lion. The moment he

The Grand Teton.
Under the shadow of which the episode here related occurred.

started the cat advanced, and when Neale stopped the lion did the same. Three times this performance was repeated and ever with the same results. Thinking to frighten the brute, the boy made several quick steps toward him; but the move was an utter failure, for, with a low growl, the lion promptly crouched as if to spring, and Neale promptly retreated. Again the beast rose to his feet, and angrily lashing his tail, advanced a few feet and waited for the enemy to make another move. But no move was made by either party to the contest and absolute quiet reigned again. Night was approaching, and the terrors of the situation came out in stronger colors as the boy began to realize his condition. He stood on a shelf of granite just wide enough to hold him, on a glassy slope of such steepness that a cat could not cling to it. One hundred feet below him, at the foot of the slide, lay Jackson's Lake, 200 feet deep and intensely cold.

The September nights in the mountains are anything but warm, and although provided with matches, there was not a particle of wood within the boy's reach. Darkness now settled down and Neale stood facing the lion, expecting an attack every minute, and fully determined to make the best possible fight for his life, even to dragging the brute off the shelf and rolling into the lake with him, if the worst should come.

With open pocket-knife in hand the boy watched through the long night, confronted by this animal and continually made aware of his presence by an ominous pair of eyes that glistened in the inky darkness like opals in the sun. Far to the south he saw our fire at camp and six miles to the east the light in Sargent's window glinted brightly. Distant and inaccessible as they were they afforded some slight companionship and the assurance that he was not

"I knew Sam would get him the minute that Winchester went up."

forgotten. The dawn came and showed the lion exactly where he stood when last seen by Neale the evening before, the only change in position being that the brute was now lying full length on the shelf, seemingly contented, and patiently awaiting the approach of his intended victim.

Shortly after daybreak the boy turned his eyes for a moment across the lake in the direction of camp and caught sight of our boat. He knew we were seeking him now, and impulsively gave forth a lusty yell, and was rewarded for his trouble in an unexpected manner. With a cat-like spring the lion arose to his feet and started for the boy, who now supposed the critical moment had arrived. Fired with courage born of desperation, Neale raised his knife and rushed at the brute to have it out with him then and there, but the impulsive rush of this boy stopped the lion's advance, and once more, the two adversaries were brought to a standstill, facing each other savagely and not more than thirty feet apart. In a few minutes the lion resumed his crouching posture and Neale retreated to his old position—just as we found them when the boat reached the slide. It was at this juncture that I caught sight of Neale through the glasses, for, fearing to hollow again, he had removed his hat and was waving it violently to attract our attention. His feelings when seeing the boat approach it is unnecessary for me to describe.

"I knew Sam would get him the minute that Winchester went up," said Neale, "and from that instant I felt perfectly safe."

We reached camp shortly before noon and remained there all day to show our thankfulness for the safe return of our boy. The rifle with which Sam killed the lion was my own, and a prime favorite with Smith. He had repeatedly tried to buy it, offering twice its value, but I had persistently declined to sell. But what I would not sell, I now most cheerfully gave; and on a silver plate, subsequently set in the stock of the Winchester, is an inscription which bears honorable testimony to Sam's unerring marksmanship, heroic courage and his never-failing ability to do the right thing at the right time.

William O. Owen

MIDNIGHT ENCOUNTER
WITH A PANTHER by Capt. L.L. Goodrich

In the year 1871 four companions and I left California and came to Texas, finally settling in southwest Texas, where we engaged in sheep raising. We located about sixty miles north of west of San Diego, in Encinal County. Our nearest neighbor was thirty-five miles distant, so it is very easy to see that in that particular locality the country was not very thickly settled. The country was infested by a very hard class of men who amused themselves by stealing horses, killing cattle for their hides, smuggling, murdering, and indulging in other pleasant kindred occupations. Many of these men were outlawed either in the United States or Mexico, and as there were no extradition laws worth mentioning the opposite side of the Rio Grande River meant a haven of rest as far as law was concerned. Still that line was not always recognized by individuals or posses who had a grievance, and it was frequently noticed that some trees bore strange fruit—such trees not being classed as fruit-bearing trees when growing in more civilized and law abiding districts.

However, I am getting away from the road as this article is not intended as a description of the country or its resources. As it is written for a sporting magazine, the matter must be confined to subjects relating to meat, horns, fur, bristles, feathers, snake oil or fish. I have remarked that settlers were scarce; but not so with game. At certain seasons of the year deer could be seen in droves, sometimes as large as fifty in a bunch. There were a few antelope and a good many turkeys, while quail were so plentiful they were hardly noticed, and rabbits and hares were in abundance. Consequently coyotes, foxes, and the different varieties of the cat kind were freely represented. The panther (called the Mexican lion) and the leopard (called the tiger) were the worst animals we had to contend with as they were destructive to sheep and goats. Ofttimes when they got into a flock they were not satisfied to select one for their meal, but would kill seemingly for the pleasure of killing. I have known a pair of leopards to kill thirty-seven goats before they felt satisfied with their labors. In those old times these animals

were quite plentiful, but as the hand of every man and some women were against them, they are now pretty well thinned out.

The panther has a finely developed taste for colt meat and will kill a colt in preference to any other animal. Sheep were herded in flocks containing from one to two thousand head and bedded at night in the open, so it was a simple matter for one of the big cats to slip up and seize a sheep and make off with it before the shepherd would be aroused.

Some flocks had dogs with them that might be called sheep dogs, but not shepherd dogs. They were a wolfish-looking arrangement of no known breed, but seemed just a dog or a cross between two dogs. They would be taken when little puppies and given to a gentle goat to raise, the kid being taken from her. She would soon take the pup and appear much attached to it, which would be evinced by loud bleating when she came to the corral in the evening in apparent anxiety until she found her adopted pup. Young goats are not allowed to run with their mothers on the range until two or three months old, but are tied to a small stake by the foot until they are able to recognize and be recognized by their mothers in a big bunch. They are then let loose, but are kept in the corral until they are old enough to go on the range in the flock; so our pup stays among the little goats until he is big enough to follow his foster mother. She may then be put into the hospital flock where she will not be allowed to travel much until the pup is able to go with her all day on the range. So the pup being raised with the sheep and goats probably thinks that he is a goat—at any rate

he stays with the flock day and night. The flock get accustomed to him being among them and look upon him as a protector. These dogs will come to the fire in the evening to be fed, but will not allow the shepherd to handle them; neither will they sleep around the camp, but among the sheep instead. The courage and fighting qualities that these dogs develop is certainly very commendable, and no matter how good, obedient, intelligent, faithful or fine-haired a dog I may own, when I remember the old wolfish-looking wire-haired beast, I am ready to take off my hat to him. And some of those old Indian shepherds who take the weather the same as their flocks and are as faithful to their charge as if it was their own, are deserving of a pleasant climate in the great hereafter.

I will bear out of the road still farther and relate a short panther story: From January 1, 1878, until August 15, 1879, I was employed as a detective for the Mexican government during the revolution of Lerdo against Diaz. I was in communication with and received orders from the Mexican consul of this city. My range was from Eagle Pass to Browsville, a distance of about 300 miles up and down the Rio Grande River. One time I came into Laredo and found among my mail a letter containing orders to report as soon as possible at Eagle Pass. I struck out, taking the road that ran near the river on the Texas side. I passed the hills called the Hermanos and stopped at the ranch of my good friend, Prudencio Herrera. He told me that the Indians were making things pretty "rapid" between there and Eagle Pass, and advised me to go back. I concluded to strike a route farther from the river and try and keep around them; and, fearing in case I followed my usual custom of lying out in the brush, that I might get lonesome on this particular night, I took my course for a small Mexican ranch that I could reach by nightfall. After supper we lay down early and I undressed as far as taking off my hat, coat and boots. About 2 o'clock I heard some little commotion and slipping into my boots and hat I picked up my carbine and stepped out into the yard. I heard some one hollering in the distance and a dog barking. The old man told me that as a lion had been giving some trouble to the flocks of late, in his opinion, the dog and the shepherds were after him. He further said that his son had just started over there, and requested me, in case I wanted to go, to follow him, as I would have trouble in crossing the arroya unless I went to a certain pass. I thought the old man had made the proper diagnosis, so I lit out, following his son, whose whereabouts I knew from an occasional yell that he uttered, to which I replied in like kind. He did not wait for me to come up, but kept cutting away to the left of where the dog was barking. After the arroya was passed he struck direct for the dog. The timber was nothing but small mesquite trees and bushes, and as the dog seemed coming directly toward me I began to wonder, in case the panther came near, if he might not take me for a stump and hop upon me. But I soon dismissed such thoughts and fears, because I knew that in case I saw him coming my way I would surely convince him that I was a loud and lively being, and ready to do the emigration act with great vehemence.

There was no moon and it was not light enough to hurt. I hurried on, yelling every few moments or oftener, when I finally made out that it had taken to a tree. I rushed on, shouting with more confidence, and was soon there. The panther was lying on a horizontal limb not more than six feet from the ground, and the old dog was barking lustily. We held a short council of fight and lined up within about thirty feet of the panther. We would not have gotten so close, but we could not see him and keep any farther away. The man who had come from the house had a carbine, one of the shepherds had a Colt's pistol, while the other had a machette about thirty inches long. I appointed myself a committee of arrangements and instructed my fighters that I would count and at the word three we would fire at the beast. I also admonished them to be cool, calm and collected. I informed them that after the first volley all orders and commands were inoperative and annulled, and every person was at liberty to use his own judgment and discretion. I tried to explain to them in a hurried manner that discretion was the better part of valor and in case we saw the need or thought best to make use of that virtue, that it would at least look better if I were allowed to lead. I was fearful that the panther would not be pleased with matters as arranged, and that he might offer some resentment. However, we were up to it, and I pointed the gun and in a trembling voice counted three, pulled the trigger hard and dodged down to look under the smoke, at the same time working my gun lever promptly. The little Mexican had either misunderstood me or did not acknowledge me as an authority, for immediately after the report of the guns he rushed in brandishing his old cheese-knife in the air and brought it down on the head of that panther in a manner that showed both skill and determination. It fell to the ground and the old dog proceeded to give him the best he had to spare, but as it offered no resistance he concluded that what had been done to him was a-plenty.

We built a fire so that we could look him over. At the same time he wanted light; we wanted to see and be seen; we felt our importance; we rejoiced for divers and sundry reasons. We had played lucky and had won out without loss; we had rid the range of a menace and had saved mutton, and we had done it in a manner that spoke loudly of valor. If that machette

Mexican had behaved differently and had not shown his utter disregard of fear of the beast, we might have felt that we weighed more. But his conduct clipped our wings a little.

We found that each bullet had found lodgement in his system, and in fairly good locations. He was a very large, old male, fat and sleek. I would liked to have had his weight and measurements, also his hide, but I did not have the time to attend to it and get it where I could have it tanned. I saddled up after breakfast and made for Eagle Pass without meeting the Indians. I afterward learned that they crossed to the Mexican side and disappeared. Several times I called at the little Mexican ranch later, and when I grasped the hands of my midknighted friends, I felt that thrill pass through my frame that can only be felt when men shake hands who have been badly frightened at the same place and moment, and who have ardently prayed that if any one is to be hurt that it will be the other fellow.

Capt. L.L. Goodrich

THE KILLING
OF A BIG BEAR by John L. Pfohl

I have read some very good stories in your magazine about some big-game hunts, and especially about some large bears that have been killed in Alaska, and I thought that perhaps some of your readers would like to hear of a bear hunt which I had last fall.

I have hunted big game in Montana for twenty-five years, and during that time I have killed a great many bears, but the one I killed last fall is the largest I have ever seen. I live in what is known as the Tom Miner Basin, in Park County, Mont., and my ranch is about five miles from the railroad. Last fall we had a very early storm, which came about the 15th of September, and in the hills snow fell to the depth of about a foot. I had seen signs of bear in my locality during the early fall, and this snow afforded a good opportunity to go out for them, as they could be easily tracked, and as a rule just before they hole up for the winter they are quite active in running about. I have an old dog named Swipes. He is a shepherd and 12 years old, and has been a very valuable dog to me in hunting big game, and especially bear, although he is now pretty old and has been badly hurt on several occasions by bear which he has "treed." To make the matter worse, about four years ago, the old fellow, in following a wounded ram, fell over a cliff and broke several ribs, so that he is pretty slow and not much more use in hunting, and perhaps the big bear about which I am going to write will be the last one which old Swipes will ever hunt.

One morning shortly after the heavy snowfall I called up my brother Tom over the telephone and suggested to him that we go out and kill a bear. Tom, being as much a lover of the sport as I am, very quickly responded to the invitation and we arranged to go out that afternoon. I took my .30-40 Winchester, which I usually hunt big game with, and my brother carried a .25-35. We went to the upper end of the basin, and just as we reached the edge of the timber on the side of the mountain we struck a bear track heading into the timber. As I have stated, I have been reasonably successful in making short work of any

bear that I got after, but I am frank to confess that this fellow's track caused me to "sit up and take notice."

I am a man over six feet tall and my shoes do not make a track like Cinderella's by any means, but in comparing my track with those of this bear, mine looked like those of a Chinese lady. The tracks showed that it was a silver-tip, and his long claws made prints in the snow as long as my fingers. If I had been alone I believe I would have either gone back home or started in to hunt smaller game, but as I had my brother with me, and he is something of a bear hunter himself, we concluded that we would see what the old fellow looked like and hoped that our usual good luck would follow us.

I put old Swipes on the trail, which we could see was very fresh, and as rapidly as possible we followed the old dog into the small growth of timber. I have in the last few years learned the habits of bears quite thoroughly and have become acquainted with their methods of living and with their actions generally, but this old fellow that we were following acted differently than any other I had seen. In going through the brush he would occasionally stop at a small sapling three of four inches in diameter and bite pieces out of it, and in some cases would chew the trees clear off, and then after the top would fall he would seize the stump and pull it up by the roots. He acted as though he were mad, and there appeared to be no cause whatever for tearing up the timber as he did. I have often seen a bear stand on his hind legs and claw the trees, but I had never seen one that would bite pieces out of trees and tear them up by the roots as this fellow did, and his actions from what we could see did not help to raise my courage any.

In a few minutes we heard the old dog bark, and we knew that he had come up with the bear, so we hurried in to where the dog was as quickly as possible. The bear had gone into a thicket of small, bushy evergreens, and we could see but a few feet in advance. I was ahead, while Tom was a few feet to my left. I could hear the bear growling at Swipes and knew that he had stopped to fight the dog off. We rushed on, spurred by the noise the dog was making, and I supposed we would find the bear at or near the spot where the dog was, but instead of doing so I ran into the bear about a hundred feet from where I expected to find him, and he was coming in my direction. He appeared to be very mad (I suppose by being worried by the dog), and the sight of me did not help matters any. Men who have hunted bear know that the grizzly never runs away from anything and he fears nothing, and with him it is a fight from the drop of the hat, if you are there for a fight. For this reason the grizzly is becoming scarce, for he will stand up and be shot, while in nearly every case a black or brown bear will get away if he can. When I first saw him he was not more than twenty-five feet from me and coming closer.

I am not considered a man who is scared of his shadow, or one who is afraid of the dark, but if at that particular time I could have been transferred to the top of some good high tree I would have felt a good deal more at home. I don't know how I managed to get my gun to my shoulder; in fact, I don't think I did, but I was so close and the bear so big that I could not very well miss him. When talking the matter over with my hunter friends, as we have been gathered around a good fire after supper, smoking a big pipe of " Union Leader," I received a lot of good advice from them how to kill a bear. One would say, "You should have hit him in the eye." Another one suggested that the proper place to plug him would be in the center of the vertebra, in the small of his back. I agree that this is all good advice and am ready to admit that it reads well in print, but if you will show me a man who, face to face with what I was, will calmly and coolly remove his coat and take off his cuffs and carefully locate the spot on that bear's anatomy where he should hit him as suggested above, I will show you a man whose picture does not look like mine and whose nerve is of a different variety from the writer of this story. I accidently hit him in the heart the first shot, and with a roar that could be heard a mile the grizzly rolled over a couple of times, sawing the air with his big paws and making the brush fly generally. I thought that he was all in, and turned to look for Tom and tell him of the good shot I had made and receive some compliments. In another instant the bear had regained his feet and made a rush for me. I was the most surprised and scared individual you ever saw, as I was not accustomed to see anything get up like that after I had landed on him with that old .30-40,

and for an instant I did not know enough to run and did not think to shoot. I wonder now just what I did do, but I am sure my actions were not strictly professional and not those of a cool and clear-headed bear hunter. I do know, however, that I managed to get three or four more shots into that bear at a mighty close range. I know also that my bullets seemed to have no effect on him. I had been breaking ground all the time, and was just about to follow the advice of the great Napoleon to his soldiers when disaster stared them in the face at the battle of Waterloo, when he said, "Save himself who can." I had about concluded to leave the field and the artillery in the possession of the bear, when Tom came rushing along, sized up the situation at a distance of about thirty feet and broke the old fellow's neck with a first shot of his little .25-35, and it was all over except the shouting and congratulations of our friends.

We went back for a team and another man, for I wanted to take the bear home before skinning him and have a picture taken of him. We had some job loading him into a wagon, I can assure you. Had he been stiff, a load of 750 pounds would not have been a hard matter for three men, but soft and limber as he was, we couldn't load him until we had dragged him with the team to a bank where we could back the wagon up to him and slide him on skids. We

Mr. Pfohl (6 feet 3 inches) pointing to the spot where the bullet struck, breaking the bear's neck.

hauled the bear home and took a picture of him hanging up. He weighed 750 pounds, and I secured 200 pounds of fat from his carcass. The skin measured 9½ feet long and is the largest specimen seen in this locality for years. I had seen his track for two or three years in that locality, but had never been able to see him before, and he had grown old and wise in the game he was playing. His skin has been made into a beautiful rug, and at this writing serves as a great attraction in a local taxidermist shop.

If there is anything to be learned from our little bear fight as we experienced it, it is this: I shot that bear four or five times in vital spots, through the shoulders and lungs and the heart, and he still had enough life in him to kill a dozen men if he could have reached them. Of course there is a great difference in bears, and a shot that would kill one might not kill another. This is noticed by all hunters in all kinds of game, but with this particular bear there is, in my judgment, no rifle made that would have stopped him by a shot in the body, for the .30-40 Winchester is about as effective as any gun made. On the other hand, the shot that put him out of commission was from the little .25-35 when it hit him in the neck.

We hear a great deal about one certain gun being better than another for big game, but my experience teaches me that a little gun is big enough when you hit your game right, and when you don't, none is big enough. In the last few years I have known of several men who have been killed by grizzlies—old and experienced hunters that they were—and I can see how this can easily happen. No man has any business to attack a grizzly alone. He may get him, and he may not; it depends a good deal on the conditions and on his luck. If I am ever so fortunate as to get another shot at a grizzly I will hit him in the head or neck, or I will not hit him at all. These body shots don't work. At least, they did not take effect quick enough on this fellow to suit me. To be charged upon by a wounded silver-tip is a great experience to tell about and reads fairly well in print, but it is mighty trying on the nerves, and if I live one hundred years I will never forget how that old bear looked as, covered with snow and blood, foaming at the mouth and bellowing with rage, he rushed toward me mortally wounded, but game to the very last, to meet his fate.

I expect to keep on hunting bear every year as long as they last, or until one gets me, and I can say now that I will be a little more careful in the future. I know within a mile of where some pretty good-sized fellows are holed up for the winter, and in the spring I'll be after them if I don't lose my nerve entirely. If any of my readers care to take a touch of high life I will be glad to steer them up against a game that will bring out any yellow streaks they may possess.

The time will soon come when the Rocky Mountain grizzly will practically be wiped out. His courage and ferocity, known and admired by every sportsman, will be his undoing. His fight for existence is an unequal one; devoid of fear, he challenges the unseen messenger of death hurled by modern high-power rifles, and he loses in the fight. But though he loses in the contest, unequal and unfair as it is, he has gained, and will retain the admiration and respect and the fear of every man who has carried a rifle in his pursuit. The grizzly is the acknowledged king of American game animals, and when he has run his course and passed out, his memory, like that of the American buffalo, will long remain, and happy is the lot of the sportsman, when old and bent and gray, he can relate to his grandchildren of the future the story of how he in an early day hunted and killed one of these splendid animals, whose strength and fierceness have made him the most dangerous and the most highly prized of all the game animals on the American continent.

John L. Pfohl

While generally the grizzly is more ferocious than any other species of the ursus family, yet we believe our contributor gives him credit for too much pugnacity when he states that he "never runs away from anything, and he fears nothing, and with him it is a fight from the drop of the hat." We have ourselves trailed more than one grizzly bear, and having killed them and being closely associated with men who have killed many of them, we believe we can speak from experience when we say that usually they will run from the hunter if there is a chance to escape (wounded bear close up or mothers with young excepted).—The Editor (1913)

LASSOING THE
GREATEST POLAR BEAR by Walter L. Beasley

"Big Polar, sir, on the ice to the starboard!" This came from the lookout on Paul Rainey's chartered whaler while this wealthy sportsman and big game hunter was recently cruising in Arctic waters for the purpose of capturing for and presenting rare living trophies to the New York Zoological Park. This is one of the small bays of Ellesmere Land, about the 77th parallel. "Full steam ahead; get launch ready for lowering," was the captain's orders in quick response. Sure enough, a mile or so away, was the figure of the fierce Arctic king clearly outlined, standing on the very edge of an enormous pan of ice which extended several miles back to the shore. The great white-coated form stood with his neck thrust well forward trying to get the scent of his pursuers. Here was thrilling sport and excitement, for the monster was destined to be the largest Polar bear ever captured alive and transported unhurt into civilization. Then again the man-eating ice-king was to be taken alive, with the lasso, or "roped," a new experiment in capturing such ferocious monsters at close range. The big animal was evidently on the watch and in search of a batch of young seals, his favorite prey for food. The ship was headed almost straight for him, but when it struck the ice a few hundred yards to his left he made a quick dive from the ice pan. One of the most remarkable things about a Polar bear is his cleverness in diving from an ice pan. The most difficult dive for an expert swimmer to make is from something almost at a level with the water. The bear makes a more beautiful dive than can be made by human swimmer and when he glides into the water he leaves hardly a ripple behind him. Bears cannot stay under the water very long, however; they are not very fast swimmers and are very easily overtaken. When the launch ran close up to him he turned to fight, and then the rope lasso was thrown over his head. In a moment he had thrown the rope off his neck and was free. It was thrown once more and caught again, but as before he fought his way out of the noose to freedom. He rarely stayed in the rope for more than three or four minutes at a time, owing to his frantic efforts. It was then decided that new tactics had to be employed. Instead of getting the rope

A front view of Silver King, the monarch of the ice floes. His favorite pose is on a high boulder.

around the neck it was to be left slack until the animal had gotten his forelegs thru it and then also there would be no danger of choking him. Meanwhile the monster had been swimming among the small broken pans, but the launch soon overtook him. The lasso whizzed, and the big creature was roped just after he had climbed out onto the ice. This time the rope was permitted to lay slack until he had put his forelegs thru it. Soon the launch was got going astern and gradually started to drag the animal into the water. It was a wonderful sight, it is said, to see this enormous brute with a strong rope just behind his foreshoulders. He would rear on his hind legs, bite at the rope and jump up and down as he was surely and steadily dragged toward the edge. Finally, seeing that the inevitable was coming, with a vicious growl he plunged into the water, for he had left the ice pans forever. The ship was signaled to move into open water as plenty of sea room was needed in which to handle the big bear.

On reaching the vessel he was hoisted high in the air and swung over the ship's deck, and in another moment the roaring, raging monster was dropped down in the hold. At once a large cage was constructed, some ten feet long and six feet broad and high.

Arrival of the giant polar bear in New York in a frail cage, the beast being chloroformed before he could be handled with safety.

This proved, however, to be entirely too light and frail. Then the question arose, how to get him into the cage. After starving the bear for four or five days a fine, juicy piece of walrus meat and a tub of fresh water was placed inside the cage, and it was lowered down to the bear. He started directly in for these tempting rations and the trapdoor was dropped, and the mighty beast was in his cage. After this both cage and bear was hoisted on deck. The construction of the cage was much too light, and on a dozen different occasions he very nearly succeeded in escaping.

One night, during a storm, the alarm was sounded and the entire crew turned out. On hurrying to the cage it was found that the bear really had his head and shoulders out. With the aid of a stout boat-hook one of the Eskimo sailors succeeded, however, in driving him back in, and soon the hole was boarded up. It was terrifying to the onlookers to see him grab hold of the smooth side of the cage with his teeth and tear out splinters a foot long. This would cause a wild stampede of Eskimos and sailors, for it looked as if he surely would be out on the deck in an instant. After this a sailor was kept watching the bear day and night, and he is said to have driven several thousand nails into the sides of that cage.

Almost the entire official staff and all of the keepers of the Zoological Park awaited the whaling vessel when she arrived at City Island, New York, with the record Polar bear of the world. On deck, in his rude cage, Silver King, who towered nine feet on his hind legs and weighed 1,200 pounds, growled and charged the frail wooden sides. Several sweeps of his mighty paw tore thru the planking. The boards were reinforced by heavier timber but as his onslaughts continued it was decided to administer chloroform. The anaesthetic was sprayed again and again over his nostrils, and, finally, he succumbed. The cage was quickly placed on a truck and hurried to the Zoological Park. Half-dazed from his big dose of chloroform, Silver King was hustled in his new home—a spacious cage having fine bathing pool, cozy sleeping den, etc. His favorite lounging place is up on a high rock boulder where he growls and watches the close approach of any inquisitive visitors. With his ideal quarters, however, and bountiful rations, he seems to be quite contented, as much so as he was on the ice pans of Greenland.

Walter L. Beasley

CAPTURING A

MOUNTAIN LION by A.R. Stram

Several years ago I read (I have forgotten when or where) an article telling of an old mountaineer's catching of a wild mountain lion by the seemingly simple expedient of climbing the tree and roping the lion in some dexterous manner. That being the first time I had ever heard of such an (as I then thought) extraordinary proceeding, I supposed the man merely did it for the notoriety and adventure; but I was surprised recently to meet a man who has made the capturing alive of wild mountain lions his profession, and is one of the best known and most successful lion hunters in the West.

This man is Bob Bakker, and in the past fourteen years which he has devoted to lion hunting he has captured something like 300 lions. With Mr. Bakker I had the good fortune to attend a lion hunt, and I will attempt to describe this hunt as well as possible, so others who have not been so fortunate as to have had or read of a similar experience may learn the method by which the lions which they have seen pacing their cages in a zoo come to be taken from their wild mountain homes and transferred probably hundreds of miles to an iron cage where they must stand before the gaze of the countless hundreds who pass back and forth with perhaps never a thought of the wild, free life the lion had before being committed to a "life behind the bars."

The lion hunter was stopping with a farmer, not far from where I was staying, and during the week preceding the hunt I am going to narrate he had caught three lions, and had them caged in wooden boxes and locked in an unfinished log building. He figured there was at least one more lion, and perhaps two, in the vicinity; so at 9 o'clock on a Saturday morning the three of us—Mr. Bakker, Mr. Smoot (the farmer) and I—set out on snowshoes up a nearby mountain with high hopes of finding a fresh lion track. The hunter's three dogs were full of life and eager to be off on the first lion track that we should happen to run across.

After about half an hour of traveling we decided to split up, so Mr. Smoot followed along the foot of the mountain and the hunter and I traveled around the side, about half way up.

It was practically my first experience on snowshoes, and it kept me extremely busy to keep up with the hunter, who is an expert on them; and to be honest, I must confess that I believe he set his pace more to mine than I to his.

After about three hours of hard going up and down the steep mountainside, in snow 2 feet deep, the lion hunter shouted to me that he had found the tracks of a lion, and we would get him before the day was over.

We called to Mr. Smoot, who was some distance below us, and were soon joined by him. On going farther we came upon a number of other tracks, all made by the same lion, and while we were trying to decide which was the more fresh, one of the dogs, a 7-months-old pup, started off unnoticed on what later proved to be the freshest track. In two or three minutes after he left we heard him barking, but as he was so young, and was not entirely trained, we didn't think it worth while to follow him, and about half an hour later he came back.

We built a campfire, boiled coffee and ate lunch, and it was about 2 o'clock when we picked out what we thought to be the likeliest track we had found, and turned the old dogs loose on it, holding the pup back so the other dogs would not be hindered in the least.

Not many minutes later we came to the place where we had heard the pup barking before lunch, and to our surprise found that he had treed the lion during the short space of time he had been gone, but as he had not had sufficient training as yet, he didn't know what had become of it after its tracks stopped, and so when he was unable to pick up its trail again he had returned to us. Of course the lion came down immediately, and all the time we had

The author on snowshoes.

been eating lunch it had spent in getting as far from that vicinity as possible.

However, we set out, following the tracks of the dogs, and it was only a matter of a couple of hours until we heard them barking "Treed!"

We made all haste in the direction of the barking, and on arriving at the scene of action, we found that the lion had climbed a large fir tree, over 2 feet thru, and practically without branches. As the lion was a long distance from the ground, it would have been an impossible task to climb the tree, so the only thing to do was to chop it down, which was accomplished at the cost of much sweating and many blisters, as the ax was a small one.

It was interesting to see the antics of the lion when the tree commenced to topple. It seemed to grow frantic and didn't know what to do at first, but as soon as the tree really began to fall it awoke to its peril and leaped about 75 feet to the ground.

We had kept the dogs back out of danger, but as soon as the tree fell we turned them loose. It was probably a minute before they picked up the lion's trail again, and during that time we began to fear that the tree had fallen on the lion—something Mr. Bakker said he had never known to happen—but

just then the dogs gave several joyous barks and were off after the lion once more.

Altho it had not had more than a minute's start, several minutes elapsed before the dogs had it treed again, but once more we were doomed to disappointment, as the lion apparently desired to be high in the world, for this time it had climbed a tall hemlock.

Mr. Bakker made ready his paraphernalia, put his steel climbers on his feet, and then started up the tree after the lion.

Perhaps I had better stop and describe the things used by Mr. Bakker in capturing his lions. To snare the animal he uses a small, but strong, wire cable, which is tied to the end of a long rope; the rope being necessary to pull the lion from the tree, and to hold it when it gets on the ground. His other necessities are several short ropes with which to tie the lion's feet, and a strong leather muzzle to slip over its head; besides a collar and chain for its neck after it is tied up.

To continue my story: Mr. Bakker climbed to within about 15 feet of the lion, then tied himself to the tree, so as to have free use of both hands, fastened the wire cable to the end of a pole which he had drawn up after him, and then reached up and was about to slip the noose—in the end of the cable—over the animal's head, when it took fright and went scrambling up nearly to the top of the tree.

Being unsafe for Mr. Bakker to go higher, he returned to the ground and we immediately chopped that tree down. It only fell about half way and lodged in some other trees. The lion, however, didn't wait to see if it would continue to the ground, but left it in mid-air, but had hardly hit the ground before the dogs were loosed, and they had it treed in a short time. This time it apparently had no opportunity to select as tall a tree as it would have liked, and luckily there was a tree growing within 6 feet of the one containing the lion, and this tree Mr. Bakker climbed, with less danger of frightening the cat higher.

It was so dark now that objects were barely distinguishable, but Mr. Bakker managed to get the noose around the lion's neck and then came down as rapidly as possible and pulled the astonished cat down.

It immediately attempted to get away, and in so doing, wound the rope around a small tree, and was held fast. Mr. Bakker then tied the end of the rope securely, and Mr. Smoot went around behind the lion, and by suddenly taking hold of its tail, stretched it out so that it was held fast at either end so all it could do was snarl and spit. Mr. Bakker then took it by the tail, and with a deft jerk lifted the lion and flung it on its back. Throwing a loop over one hind paw and drawing it back to him, he suddenly reached out and caught the other hind paw with one hand, and by drawing them both back together he was able to tie them securely, and then while Mr. Smoot held the hind paws, he repeated the performance—with considerably more care—with the front ones, after which it was a simple matter to tie front and hind paws together and Mr. Lion was securely trussed up.

Now came the delicate task of putting the muzzle on. It was nearly pitch dark by this time, and the tying had to be done more by sense of touch than by sight, but Mr. Bakker is so used to working with them that he can do it about as easily in the dark, so it was not long before he accomplished the muzzling. First he took a strong stick and let the lion grasp it in his teeth, then with a sudden movement he grasped the lion's throat, removed the stick, and in a short time had the muzzle buckled on its head. A collar and chain was placed on its neck, and as it was too dark to take it home that night, it was tied to the tree with the chain, its feet were loosed and it was left to spend one more night in the woods it was soon to leave forever. The muzzle was left on to prevent the lion from biting the chain and breaking its teeth.

The next day three more men joined us, and five of us (Mr. Smoot remained at home) went back after the lion. Mr. Bakker took a large pack-sack in which to carry the lion home, since it was a female a little over a year old, and therefore only weighed about 75 pounds.

Upon arriving we found that she had spent the night very well, and in a few moments the tying was accomplished and the cat was placed in the pack-sack, with only its head protruding. Each of us then took turns carrying it, "just for the fun of it," but the lion's 75 pounds quickly changed the fun into work, so Mr. Bakker was very willingly allowed to have more than his share of the "fun."

Naturally the lion's head was muzzled, but it was quite a sensation, at that, to have it growling and spitting within a few inches of your ear at every step, and now and then attempting to extract a mouthful of cloth from your coat.

Mr. Bakker stated that many times he has carried small lions in a pack-sack without having a muzzle on the lion, merely putting the collar and chain on its neck and holding its head in a position which made it difficult for it to "chew his ears."

As a general rule when a large lion is caught, it is tied and muzzled, and by tying a rope around its head and front paws it can be dragged to camp with very little trouble.

When releasing one in its cage, Mr. Bakker ties its head to a lower corner of the cage and slips the muzzle off. Its feet are then partially loosened and the cage closed up tight. Then with the aid of wire

Bob Bakker, dogs and captured lion · taking it in alive.

the ropes are slipped from feet and neck, and the lion is loose in its cage.

When one of them is left in a wooden cage for three or four days, it is very apt to gnaw out, and I had the good fortune to be able to witness the recaging of two lions which had escaped from their boxes in this manner.

Lion hunting is an exciting sport, and to attend one is an enjoyable adventure, but if all people were like myself, I don't believe lion hunters would have very much competition in their profession, altho, as Mr. Bakker says, it is, like many other things, simple enough—if you know how.

A.R. Stram

I WENT WHALING ALONE

by Phil A. Moore

Here is adventure—with a capital A! A veteran sportsman, who had tried every other known form of fishing or hunting, decided to go to sea alone in a small boat and harpoon a whale. What happened to him was—plenty! This is the most extraordinary story we have published in a long time and you'll find a thrill in every line.—The Editor (1945)

Having hunted many kinds of big game, I have come to feel that, unpredictable though they are, one who is familiar with their habits when frightened or wounded is pretty well forearmed. Besides, he has a powerful rifle to fall back upon. But harpooning a whale from a small boat—there was something I had never tried!

What would it be like? The very idea of approaching a whale and sticking it with a harpoon seemed a bit presumptuous; about like jabbing a boar spear into a rogue elephant. And why a whale will permit such familiarities was beyond my understanding. Perhaps the dumb beast does not savvy attacks from the surface of the water. Yet whalers tell us that whales that have been chased and stuck and have escaped do learn to be cautious—hard to sneak up on, also dangerous to boats which approach too close.

We have along the southern coast of Nova Scotia many sorts of whales, both large and small. The one most commonly seen in Mahone Bay is a saucy bold monster with a prominent dorsal fin. It's a grampus, according to local fishermen, and it may be a grampus sure enough. Or it may really be a pilot whale, for which "grampus" is a common misnomer. It's certainly not the white-splotched Atlantic killer whale, or orca, which those who've fished off Labrador also call a grampus.

When you see a whale only in the water, and never all of it at once, you can't examine it as you

would a museum specimen; nor are you in any mood to do so! All I can say is that, unlike most Nova Scotia whales, our grampus has a mouthful of teeth, at least in its lower jaw, and, that the bigger specimens run almost as long as a tuna boat. Norwegian whaling skippers hereabouts (war refugees) call them "herring whales." For food they chase large schools of herring, mackerel, and squid, as do the giant tuna and swordfish of this part of the coast. If the fancy takes the brutes, they think nothing of plunging through the herring and mackerel nets, or tearing up miles of trawl. Accidents, of course, but the men who lose the gear say pure malice is to blame.

The fishermen are afraid of the big animals, for they do not scare easily and will smack right up against the keel of an anchored boat, or sideswipe it with a blundering tail. This does not happen very often, but often enough to make everyone aboard nervous when the grampuses get to feeding close by.

However, the urge to stick a whale with an old-fashion whaling iron kept digging at me. I knew it would be impossible, of course, to find one of those delightful little streamline cedar whaleboats, or an expert crew to row it. The best craft available would be an eighteen-foot Grand Banks two-man dory. With a clever boatman in the stern with a steering oar, and the harpooner standing in the bow, such a combination might work. I explained my project to several professional fishermen—and encountered a decided lack of interest.

"Monkey business, we calls it," was the way they expressed it. "And somebody is a-going to get wet."

Many of my fishermen friends cannot swim a stroke. Water to them is mainly a nuisance overlying the marine farm whence they take their crop of codfish. Otherwise it holds few attractions.

I soon gave up the idea of obtaining help from that quarter. But ways and means had to be found.

Among other small craft I have an eighteen-foot boat that is a Grand Banks dory forward and a hydroplane aft. It has a wide stern transom, and may be driven by any outboard motor with an extra-long shaft. Under the forward thwart is a ten-gallon pressure tank for gas. A pipe runs aft with a hose on the end and a valve with strainer. When I wish to fill the tank on the outboard, it is a simple matter to unscrew the filler cap, stick in the hose, open the valve, and fill her up. Three or four pounds of air pressure put in the supply tank with a bike pump will last a long time. A tire-tube nipple is soldered into the tank for this purpose.

The dory has a centerboard and also a sail. She is steered by an oar when under sail. She will plane when driven by a nine-horsepower four-cylinder motor, and can make fifteen miles an hour while carrying two passengers. The outboard consumes an imperial gallon of gas hourly. When turning, the dory will bank like a race horse, and come about in three times her length. In a heavy seaway she is all dory and as safe as a small boat can be. Steering lines extend from the tiller and pass through pulleys clear around the rail. You can steer from any position in the boat.

All this detail has a bearing on my whaling adventure; for I decided to use the craft in my plot against the whales.

For weapons I had a 100-year-old whaling harpoon and 100 fathoms of new nine-thread harpoon line with the inboard end fast to the mast step. Also I had an old whaling lance and 100 fathoms of new six-thread line attached to it—the inner end being made fast to a ring-bolt in the bow. The lance had a double-blade head shaped like a beech-tree leaf, and a four-foot shank fastened to a long pole or shaft. Such lances stab much more deeply into a whale than can a harpoon; and I intended to be fully equipped!

The next step was to try to find some adventurous soul with an active body who would handle the boat while I harpooned the whale. Finally, one guy promised to go, but when the time came to shove off, his wife refused to let him out of her sight. My own wife, long since used to my adventures, took the whole thing with her tongue in her cheek. But

"Don't you dare to land any smelly old whale on my beach," she warned, "or I'll just up and shoulder my pack and pull out for Times Square! Remember, now!"

At least she believed that I could catch a whale and come home to Chester alive. That was something!

I had a vague notion that if I could puncture a whale, it would tow the dory until it tired itself out, when I could pull up on it and stick it again with the lance and maybe kill it, or so wound it that my outfit would do the final towing. I could then take it triumphantly into the home port. Then what? Well, I did not know.

I felt a sneaking sense of relief when my friend's wife refused to let him go along. After all, this expected rendezvous with the whale was a personal affair. My friend had already asked a lot of questions about the enterprise I could not answer. They annoyed me. The only clear picture I seemed to have was of my

boat, with me and my harpoon at one end and the whale at the other.

Practicing ashore with the harpoon, I found it heavy and awkward. The line weighed it down. It was also obvious that the line, when coiled in the boat, must not be behind me as I heaved the harpoon into the whale—if any. If I was between coil and whale I might get tangled in the whizzing line, and be drowned. The short distance I could cast the harpoon made it essential to run the boat practically up against the animal; and perhaps he would not permit such a near approach. Such were the problems that persisted in the back of my mind as I worked over the preparations.

When all was ready I headed out of Mahone Bay. The grampuses had been feeding in the shallow water between Owls Head Island and Southwest Island at the western entrance to St. Margaret Bay— the next bay to the east. The narrow inlet was about eighteen miles from Chester. Herring, squid, and mackerel often passed through it, and apparently the whales found it a convenient place to corner the schools upon which they fed. Making trips after tuna with sportsmen in the previous few days, I had seen several grampuses in water so shallow that their backs showed on the surface much of the time. They had paid little heed to our tuna boats as we trolled through the passage, steering clear of the powerful marine mammals in our anxiety to avoid a possible collision.

Now, as the boat and I skimmed along between the Seal Ledges and the mainland, several whales showed themselves. The water was shallow but there was too much sea room for my plans. Nevertheless, as one of those great masses of muscle slithered to the surface and spouted—quite near to my rapidly moving boat—I could feel goose pimples crawling along my spine. My stomach felt hollow and pinched up. Being a right-handed harpooner, I realized I'd have to approach the quarry on the port side, so that when I cast the instrument the coil of line would be

My dory fairly leaped when I gave her the gun, then poised the harpoon. Along about then, things happened thick and fast.

sure the beast was aware that it was being persistently followed. It did not hurry or act as though frightened. It did not make for either of the outlets to the narrow channel. But it did suddenly disappear. For ten minutes or more I could see no sign of my quarry.

I had about given up hope when I spied its fin right near the high cliff known as Owls Head Island, which marks the northern or inner end of the passage into St. Margaret Bay. There against the cliff the water was some twenty fathoms deep. I steered away from the whale and maneuvered until I could approach from the bay side, and thus drive it back into the shallow water of the passage. Moving at about six knots, my boat and I approached the lolling monster. When about ten fathoms away, I picked up the harpoon and gave the engine the gun. The dory fairly leaped straight at that whale! I twitched the tiller rope to avoid running right up on its back, then poised the harpoon.

Things happened so fast from then on I cannot describe them. I have a memory, a mere impression, of a huge mass of unpredictable muscle suddenly appearing alongside. I slammed the razor-sharp harpoon into the middle of this mass.

The ocean exploded. The boat gave a lurch and was violently thrown sidewise, and all but tipped over. I caught a glimpse of curling flukes hanging over my head as I grabbed for a thwart and hung on for dear life. The line was sizzling out over the bow. I scrambled aft to give the boat a chance to turn if the whale turned, then grabbed the tiller itself and also slowed down the engine. The boat had been running as wild as the whale.

After a few seconds I could determine the course of the whale, by where the pull on the harpoon line was coming from. The animal had headed back into the passage and seemed to have taken a through ticket for the wide Atlantic. The line came at last to its end. The boat was yanked ahead with a powerful jerk. The bow almost went under. I speeded up the engine and this relieved the strain. The water was not deep enough for the whale to sound straight down, and wouldn't be for several miles. Thus it could not sink the boat—not yet!

What sort of whale it was, I couldn't even then be sure. I'd had it in mind to try for a grampus, as I've said; but this fellow—what little I'd seen of him—looked even bigger than I'd bargained for. For all I could tell, I might have tied into one of the smaller finbacks—a pike whale, or least rorqual. And those babies (if you can call them babies) run up to thirty feet or more! Anyway, that animated tugboat was giving me other things to think about right then.

I judged I was being towed along at about fifteen miles an hour—about the speed the boat

on the same side of me as was the harpoon. Anything might happen after that. The whale, when hit, might go under the boat; it might sound and sink me with its flukes. But I had already been over all that. As the dory sped into the passage I had to put what might happen entirely out of my mind.

And there was a whale lolling around directly ahead of the boat! I slowed down and ran up on it. It lazily sounded when I was but ten fathoms away. The water was so shallow I could follow its wake with my eyes. I turned and ran along the wake. The whale broached, veered, and changed its course with a flip of its mighty tail. I yanked on the tiller ropes and veered also. The whale surfaced and turned sharply to its right. This put me on the wrong side in case I should catch up with it. I turned the boat to starboard. Again the whale veered before I could run alongside, this time to port. I overran.

This dodging about kept up for some time. But the whale could not go far, as the proximity of the land and shallow water forced it to turn. I am not could do by itself. So I cut out the engine and let the whale do all the work. As we went out of the southern end of the passage, the whale surfaced and spouted. The sun was shining and I thought I saw blood in the steam. I grabbed my camera and made ready for the next time the whale breached. I hoped to get a picture of the animal as it rode a wave and spouted. But each time I tried to stand up the whale would give a yank, and I would sit down with a bump. All I succeeded in getting were pictures of the sky or ocean, or of the line cutting the water ahead of the bow.

I had stuck my "fish" about 3 p.m. By sunset we were some five miles east of Chester Ironbound Island. The whale had settled down into a steady zigzagging swim toward Ireland—some 2,000 miles away. It was now going only about five miles an hour. Just about nightfall the sea began to make in a southwest wind. It got sloppy. The spray was heavy. I had to bail every once in a while. There was no let-up in the whale's power, but it kept changing its course.

A long and ugly shark paddled by my boat. Its dorsal fin was about a foot above water. It gave me a grin as it passed. The whale was bleeding from the harpoon wound. The shark, following the trail of blood, passed on up ahead toward the whale. In another few minutes another big shark put in an appearance. It too looked me over. Its dorsal fin appeared to be about a foot and a half high. Either it was a lot larger than the first shark, or the phosphorescent wake made it seem longer. Soon along came another. As it grew darker, and I became more lonesome, those fins got bigger!

I did not like the situation. Those hungry lads looked very much longer than my little dory; and they took too much interest in me and my whale.

One's imagination gets to working when one finds oneself alone, way out in an indifferent ocean—and hooked to a sea monster, with other monsters hovering about, seemingly awaiting eventualities. As yet, I had no idea of what that whale would decide to do, once it became bored with me and my dory. By 10 o'clock that night I could hardly see Ironbound Light. The whale seemed as fresh as ever. The ocean sparkled with eerie flashes of phosphorescence, made by those darned sharks—or I thought it did.

My enthusiasm for towing a whale into port dwindled. I was getting a long way from home. I was tired of talking to the whale, and of cursing the sharks.

At this point the towline went slack. The boat lost headway and wallowed in the sea. What now? Had the line parted? Was the whale doubling back to look me over? I soon got the answer. Almost alongside the sea erupted once more.

The dory gave a dangerous lurch. There was a whoosh! The top wave came into my lap; I could see a mass like a vast dark tidal wave almost over my head.

By some magic the dory slid out and away from this menace. There was a jerk of the line, and the dory tilted, all but buried her bow, then went swishing through those seas like a runaway torpedo! Then again the line went slack. Meantime I had started bailing as fast as I could, for the dory had shipped a lot of water.

Again the whale—or maybe a different one—leaped clear of the water. It was but a short distance ahead. I caught its huge menacing bulk against the sky as we settled in the trough. The thought raced through my mind that the monster was acting up the way a salmon sometimes does when, finding

The line came at last to its end, the boat was yanked sharply ahead, and I speeded up the engine to relieve the strain.

itself tired and unable to break away from the line, it will rush madly about and jump repeatedly in an effort to shake the hook.

But there was this difference: I could hold on and laugh at the salmon, whereas all the whale need do was give me just one good bump, or a slap with its flukes, and it would be good night for the fisherman—and no foolin'!

The line gave a jerk and again the whale went racing away, my dory hanging on and keeping on top as best it might. I bailed and cursed and prayed . . .and bailed and bailed.

Another whale whooshed right alongside; that did it. Too many whales!

The sea was choppy—and wet. I was fatigued with bailing, wearied with whales. I picked up the hatchet, went forward and cut the line, then gave the engine a spin and headed back for Chester. The wind was astern and the binnacle aglow.

In thirty minutes I again picked up Ironbound Light. It was a welcome sight. The dory spun along like the great craft she is, tossing the spray aside with the disdain of a first-class boat. She would wallow between two waves, take a breath, shoulder into the crest, then shoot like a rocket as she ran the rollers toward the home port. It took three hours to make the Chester landing, and I figured I had cut loose from Mister Whale and chums when some forty-five miles from home.

Yes sir, I now know exactly how it feels to navigate impudently up to a whale and practically stick my finger in its starboard eye! So what? Well, if you are looking for excitement, go out alone and try it. In the night.

And my wife? I switched on the light in the boudoir.

"Did you get the iron into it?" she yawned, one eye peeking from beneath the blankets.

I nodded.

"You decided not to bring it home with you, eh?"

"Right," I agreed.

"That's good," she sighed, and went back to sleep.

Phil A. Moore

A LION MANGLED ME by John Kingsley-Heath

The author of this story, John Kingsley-Heath, is no stranger to readers of Outdoor Life. *A professional white hunter in Nairobi, he guided Jack O'Connor on his 1959 African safari, and has been mentioned in a number of O'Connor's stories, including "Big as an Ox," in August, 1961.*

Kingsley-Heath has held a professional hunter's license since 1951, barring a brief interruption during the Mau Mau emergency, and is rated among the top white hunters of Africa. Up to the episode he describes here, he had been attacked by an animal only once.

That happened at the very start, when he was training under an old hunter. He approached too close to an elephant he was stalking. The bull knew he was there, waited until he was within reach, grabbed him up in its trunk. and sent him flying into a swamp tangle. By good fortune he escaped unhurt, except for a sight stiffness in the right shoulder. In this lion encounter, he was far less lucky.—The Editor (1963)

Our leopard bait was an impala we had shot and hung in an acacia tree on the edge of a dry river bed. It had ripened in the hot sun for three days, long enough so that we were sure if there were leopards in the country they could not resist it. We had hung a number of baits, including zebra, gazelle and impala, but for some reason Bud Lindus and I both felt that this was the one that would get us what we hoped for.

The time was August of 1961. I was on safari with Lindus, his wife Pamela, and their 14-year-old son Roger, along the Ruaha River in the semiarid desert country of central Tanganyika. A retired oil salesman from Honolulu, Bud rates African hunting very high, and Pam and the boy share his enthusiasm for it. Bud and his wife were old clients of mine.

The foremost object of this hunt was a really good trophy lion. Two years earlier Bud and I had been led up the garden by a big-maned male, in the Kajiado district of Kenya. That one seemed to have the uncanny ability of disappearing at exactly the crucial minute, whether we approached him on foot or by car. He hid in the day, ate our baits at night, and, try as we did, Bud never got his sights on him.

He had come back to Africa this time determined to do better. Buffalo and kudu also were on his list, he wanted a good leopard for his wife, and if we came across an elephant with satisfactory ivory we didn't mean to turn it down.

We had sharpened our hunting senses on buffalo in the thick bush country of northern Tanganyika before moving down to the Ruaha River. Two buffaloes had got within a yard of us before going down permanently. After that we felt we were ready to take on most anything, including the biggest lion in Tanganyika if we could find him.

Our camp had been made on the bank of the Ruaha, under acacia trees that spread like huge green umbrellas. Thousands of sand grouse watered in front of the tents every morning. The wingshooting was wonderful.

Alvin Adams, a friend of Bud's from the States, had come out to join us for a fortnight, wanting a big leopard, and was hunting with Kevin Torrens, the second white hunter on the safari. Our numerous leopard baits were hung partly in the hope of helping Al get his wish.

Bud and I hunted lions, elephants, and kudu for days with no success. Tracks and signs were plentiful but we couldn't come across anything of the sort we were looking for. Leopards refused to touch our baits, and we began to wonder whether our luck was in or out. But when we hung the impala in the tree at the edge of the river two or three miles from camp, I had a hunch we were going to get action.

Bud, Pam, Roger, and I came into camp for a late lunch the afternoon of the third day after that, and when we finished our sandwiches and tea I suggested we go have a look at the bait. It was time for things to be happening if they were going to.

We drove out in the hunting car, taking along two gunbearers and trackers, Kiebe and Ndaka. Halfway to the leopard bait, however, I sent them off to follow some elephant tracks, with instructions to rejoin us near the bait tree.

We drove the hunting car to within 600 yards of the tree, then walked carefully the rest of the way. One peep around a large bush told us that a leopard had taken his fill. It was late afternoon now, almost time for him to return for his evening meal. There was not a minute to waste. We'd sit for him at once.

It was decided that Pam should have this first chance. Bud and Roger went back to the car to wait. Pam and I stole carefully up behind a thick bush and secreted ourselves in the bottom of it, first making a little hole for our guns.

Pam was carrying a rifle of European make, as light as the Tanganyika game laws permitted, for the sake of minimum recoil, mounted with a 4X scope. Mine was a Winchester Model 70 in .300 Magnum with a 6X Kollmorgen scope. Neither of the guns was right for what was going to happen, but there were good reasons for choosing them.

Sitting up for a leopard can be on the sticky side, especially if you are not used to it, since you know that if you fail to make a clean kill you have one of the most dangerous animals in Africa to deal with. Pam made no secret of the fact she was nervous. Unless the cat fell dead at her shot, she asked me to back her by putting another into him immediately.

That was why I had brought the scope-sighted Winchester. A 6X scope may seem unusual for a job of that kind, but it has its advantages. To begin with, it enables you to increase your distance from the bait, and often you can select a better spot by moving off a bit. Also, a leopard almost invariably comes on a bait late, when the light is failing fast, and the more powerful your scope the better its light-gathering ability.

Had my two gunbearers not been off following the elephant tracks, I'd have had one of them with us with my .470 Westley Richards double, but I couldn't very well manage to handle two guns by myself.

Pam and I made ourselves comfortable, with our rifles trained on the spot where we expected the leopard to appear. For 20 minutes nothing happened. The silence of late afternoon was settling over the bush. Puffs of wind blew through the acacias, stirring up little dust devils, but the breeze was from

the bait tree, so we had no worry on that score. Now and then a bird twittered, and the shrunken river whispered around its sand bars. Save for those small sounds, nothing broke the stillness.

It was an uneasy quiet, and as the minutes dragged on I began to be suspicious. Something wasn't quite right. Was the leopard approaching from behind us? Had he scented us and slunk away? We tried to keep a sharp watch all around, but there was no movement in the brush or grass. The time ticked off and my uneasiness grew. Then, suddenly aware of movement or noise behind my right shoulder, I turned my head ever so slowly and I was looking a huge maned lion in the face, just 20 feet away.

The whole situation was clear in a flash. The leopard had not come to the hanging bait because the lion had kept him away. The lion couldn't reach the impala himself. (A lion can get only about 12 feet off the ground on a very thick, sloping branch, but a leopard can run up one about three inches thick.) Now, hungry, disappointed, and angry, he had spotted us in our thick bush, had not seen or smelled enough of us to know what we were, and was stalking us for a kill. And he was close enough for that final, lightning-fast rush with which a lion takes his prey at the last second.

When I turned my head and we stared into each other's eyes, he recognized me for man, but it was too late for that to make any difference. I saw his expression change from the intent look of a stalking cat to one of rage. His face wrinkled in a snarl and he bunched his feet under him for the spring.

It all happened a great deal quicker than I can relate it. One second I was staring fixedly at the leopard bait. The next I was looking the lion in the face, he was gathering for his leap, and I was swiveling my rifle around from the hip.

The eyes of the big cats, I think more than those of any other animal, mirror what is going on behind them. At the instant of attack those of a lion seem to be on fire. The burning yellow orbs of this big male blazed into mine, and there was no misreading their message.

I did not wait to bring the rifle to my shoulder. I was sitting on my hunkers, and I whipped it across my knees and pulled off at him, all in a split second, trying for the thickness of his shoulder. The shot struck a little too far back, but he reacted to the 180-grain soft-nose as most lions do to a hit, whipping his great head around and biting savagely at the wound.

Pam and I were not conscious, then or afterward, of running through the six-foot bush where we were hidden, but we did it, and never got scratched. We got clear and raced for the car. In the thicket

Back in camp, Kiebe (left) and safari boy display fangs of lion that savaged me.

behind us bwana simba was roaring and thrashing in pain and anger. We ran until we were far enough away to be safe, then stopped to get our breath and congratulate ourselves on a very narrow escape.

"We have to get this chap," I told Bud when we finished panting out the story. "You and I will have a lion war."

My two gunbearers were not yet back from their elephant scout. We left Pam and Roger in the car, and Lindus and I took our heavy rifles and hurried off. Mine was the .470, Bud's a .450/400 double made by Manton & Co., a London firm. Both were good lion guns, but because we had not expected to encounter a lion and had thought we might get a chance at an elephant that afternoon, we had only solid ammunition along instead of the soft-nose loads we would have preferred.

The lion had left the place where I shot him, and it was plain from the blood that he was reasonably well hit. The blood spoor led down to the bottom of the dry river bed. There, although he was bleeding heavily, it had dried in the sand and lost its color, making it difficult to follow in the evening light.

He had run for a way under the river bank, climbed a small gully, and had gone into a thicket of mswaki bush, an evergreen that grows like thick weeping willow, with the outer branches draping right down to the ground, leaving a cavelike opening underneath. The lion had left little sign on the hard-baked sand, and we went down on our hands and knees to track him through gaps between the bushes.

We didn't crawl far before I pulled up short. "This is no good," I told Bud. "If we go ahead with our eyes on the ground, we'll walk right down his

throat. Kiebe and Ndaka should be back at the car by now. We'll get them and let them do the tracking while we watch over their heads."

Kiebe is a particularly good man to have along in a situation of this kind. A Kamba by tribe, he had hunted for 25 years, eight of them with me, and before that with Miles Turner, one of the most famous of East African white hunters. I had saved Kiebe's life a time or two, and he had saved mine. Tracking down a wounded lion is nothing new to him, and he is absolutely without fear. I knew I could count on him no matter what happened. The second tracker, Ndaka, was a stand-in, and he was willing and brave.

The two of them were at the car, and we hurried back to the place where we had left the lion track. It was lucky we had quit when we did, for 15 yards ahead we found the blood-stained bed where he had been lying.

He had moved about 30 yards into another thicket while we were gone, still bleeding. We tracked him foot by foot, with Kiebe in the lead. It was not a job any of us liked, but we had no choice. Once a hunter starts an affair of that kind it's up to him to finish it, no matter how sticky it gets.

Kiebe wiped warm blood off the leaves, and held up a hand to warn me we were getting close. Then the lion announced his presence with an angry growl from the mswaki just ahead, and we saw him shoot across a narrow opening into the next bush.

It was almost dark now and in a few minutes we'd have to give up. We left the track and circled, hoping to push him into the open, but nothing stirred and no sound came from the thicket. We wasted precious time, the light got worse, and at last I whispered to Kiebe in Swahili, "This is for tomorrow. We'll let him stiffen up and beat him out in the morning."

The tracker's reply was a finger jabbed sharply to the left. There, under a low bush 50 feet away, the lion lay broadside, breathing heavily, watching us. I could barely make out the shape of his heavy body in the dusk.

The range was close enough, but we were shooting with open sights in very bad light and had to be absolutely certain of a hit. I took Bud by the arm without saying a word, and we shortened the distance to 40 feet, moving warily to the nearest tree, where a leaning branch would give us a rest for the rifles.

The shot belonged to the client, and since Bud was a first-class rifleman I did not expect there'd be any need for me to fire. But I made one bad mistake. I overlooked the fact that in the half-darkness the flash of his rifle would blind me for that critical fraction of a second when the lion might come for us in case Bud failed to kill him where he lay.

Bud's 400-grain solid took him in the shoulder a bit high, but because the bullet was not a soft-nose it went all the way through without opening up, doing only slight damage to the lungs. And in the instant when I should have hammered another into him I could see neither lion, thicket, or anyting else.

He came in a rush the first few feet, then covered the rest of the distance in two great bounds. I had time only to yell at Bud to dodge behind me, when a huge ball of snarling fury landed at my feet.

I slammed a 500-grain solid into his head between the eyes, point blank, and, but for a fluke, that would have ended the affair. But, because he was badly wounded, when he hit the ground in front of me his head jerked forward and down, like a man who has jumped off a stool. My bullet struck him squarely between the eyes, as the hole in the skull showed later, but instead of going through his

brain and leaving him deader than mutton, it passed down between his lower jaw bones and out the side of his throat, hardly more than blinding him with the rifle flash.

He leaped past me within a foot and lit between Bud and me, headed for Bud. I saw that Bud's rifle was tangled in branches and he couldn't get it down. The quarters were too close for a second shot without endangering him. I took one step and clubbed the lion on the head with the barrels of my .470 as hard as I could. He grunted, shook his head, and wheeled around. Before I had time to pull my second barrel, he pounced.

A quarter of a ton of growling, raging cat hit me full length, and I went down as if I had been electrocuted. It felt about like that, too. There was no pain and I was not stunned, but the shock of the blow as the lion crashed into me, with his forepaws over my shoulders and his huge body bearing me to the ground, was beyond description. My gun went flying out of my hands, and then I was lying on my back with the lion on top of me, his front legs wrapped around me and his paws under my shoulder blades.

A lion, even wounded, often pauses for a second after his initial leap has knocked his victim down, and this one did just that. That tiny pause saved my life. I knew that within a second or two he would bite me through the head, and I smashed my right fist into his nose with every ounce of strength I had. I broke the bones of the hand, but he opened his mouth at the punch, I suppose to growl, and I followed through. I rammed my fist down his throat, and his teeth closed on my arm halfway to the elbow.

I heard the bones crunch, but in a strange detached way, not as a sound from outside, but as if I were hearing the arm break from inside my body.

So long as I kept my fist down his gullet he could not get at my head or throat. I could feel his claws under me, ripping my sheepskin hunting jacket to shreds and my back with it. I knew that if he got his hind feet on my belly he'd tear my guts out with one rake. I twisted on my left side, drew my legs up to protect myself, and concentrated on trying to keep my arm in his mouth.

The statement has been made more than once that a man attacked by one of the big carnivores is overcome with a merciful numbness, so that he feels little or no pain or fright at the time, perhaps because the shock overwhelms his nervous system. I think the part about being benumbed is true, but for a different reason. The victim of such an attack is fighting for his life and knows it, and a man in that situation has little sense of feeling. Certainly, in my case, I felt very little pain through the whole mauling. When it was all over my back looked as if I'd been flogged with a cat-o'-nine-tails, but it didn't hurt while it was happening.

Nor did I smell the lion's breath or have any sensation of feeling his mane against my face, although I know it was there. I did have a bad bit of nightmare in the hospital later, when I felt his saliva all over my fingers and woke up in a cold sweat trying to get my mangled arm out of his jaws.

Actually, he took care of that for me. He shook me as a terrier shakes a rat, rolling me back and forth, and freed himself of my fist and arm as a big fish gets rid of a bait.

It takes far longer to describe such an experi-ence than to live through it. Everything was hap-ing at once. "Get my gun!" I yelled at Kiebe in li. "Kamata bunduki yangu! Piga the bloody iga means hit, but in this case I meant shoot cker knew it.

aw Bud come into sight over the lion's his .450 bellowed twice. But because he cat he could only shoot far back. t he broke a hind leg, but the neither flinching nor turning growling and mauling me, Kiebe, or Ndaka. That is ba gets his victim down rd will rush from one at the first man he fresh victim, only lion, however,

swiftly to ved the his ute

ian McShane looks on as I start trip to hospital.

wrist, and once more I heard my own bones break like match sticks, not as I would have heard another man's but as a noise coming from inside me.

At this point, Ndaka did a very brave thing. He threw himself on the lion and stabbed it again and again in the ribs and throat with a six-inch knife. Then Bud, who had been stuffing fresh shells into the breech of his double while Kiebe got in his shot, stepped close and sent two more solids crashing into the lion. The great body jerked and sagged and rolled off me.

As I struggled to my knees, half helpless from my broken arms, I jabbed my left foot into his face to kick myself away from him. That was the wrong thing to do, even with a lion breathing his last. His jaws closed on my shoe and he bit down, and for the third time I heard the crunch of breaking bones, in my foot and ankle now. And this time it hurt like hell! I wrenched my foot free, but the lion died with my shoe in his mouth.

We left him where he lay. We'd have to run the risk of hyenas tearing him up before morning. Bud and the natives carried me to the car and wrapped me in the rain curtains to keep me warm. Then we set off in the darkness for camp. There was no moon and we couldn't follow our tire tracks, so rather than get lost we stopped, made a fire, and let off a shot every 10 minutes. It's a rule on safari that if anyone fails to return to camp by an hour after dark, the search-and-rescue operation gets under way at once. We knew that by now Kevin Torrens, our other white hunter, was out looking for us.

My wounds had clotted well and I was bleed-ing only a little, but I drank water like a mad thing. Kiebe and Ndaka left us to try to find the way to camp, and shortly after that we heard the hum of a motor and then the lights of Kevin's Landrover appeared.

It was 2 a.m. by the time we found our way back to camp. Torrens cleaned my wounds, poured disinfectant into them, and I swallowed three times the normal dose of antibiotic tablets, washing them down with hot tea. Next, I got down two cups of up and began to feel quite comfortable. But about time I suppose I went into shock, for I started ble violently from head to foot and kept it ours.

ad a radio telephone in camp, but now it morning (the lion had attacked me on ing) and the government radio in d down, so Kevin left for the nearest 120 miles away, 30 of it rough h, to call for a plane. We had irstrip near camp earlier. gh to Peter Whitehead, manag-airobi safari firm, at 6:15 on Sunday d 45 minutes later Dr. Brian McShane, my physician and good friend, was air-borne and on the way with a supply of blood and the other things he needed to fix me up temporarily. Bill Ryan, another professional hunter from Nairobi and also an old friend, came along to take over the safari in my place. It was a 2½-hour flight. They touched down at camp at 9:30 that morning.

By that time I had sent our safari boys out and they had brought the lion to camp. The hyenas had not molested him. He was a magnificent brute, the biggest I had ever had a hand in killing, 10½ feet long and weighing 497 pounds. He must have weighed a bit above 500 alive, before he lost blood. There, in the Dodoma district, the lions live on buffaloes and the full-grown males are among the finest trophies in all of Africa. This one was paler than average, but not quite a blond, with a very heavy mane. As friends remarked later, at least I had been savaged by a decent lion, not one with just a ruff around its neck. Bud has the pelt, and I doubt he will ever take another trophy that will give him a more exciting time. He gave me a tooth and claw, which I have had mounted and use as paperweights.

Dr. McShane poured blood into me and set about patching me up for the flight back to Nairobi. I had two broken arms, a broken hand, a foot chewed and badly crushed, a horribly lacerated back, and a few deep holes in various parts of my body. As I was being carried into my tent after the attack, I had heard Kiebe tell the other safari boys, "Bwana ameliwa na simba" which is Swahili for the bwana was eaten by a lion. Maybe Kiebe exaggerated a little, but he was close enough to the truth so that I didn't feel like contradicting him.

I entered the Princess Elizabeth Hospital in Nairobi that afternoon, August 13, and stayed until October 2. I was on the danger list for a few days, but the surgeons repaired my broken bones and by great good fortune I escaped infection, which is very likely to follow an attack by one of the big cats because of their habit of feeding on putrid meat. The fact that I had been able to get down a massive dose of antibiotics a few hours after the accident probably accounted for my very good luck on that score.

The mauling proved far worse than the aftermath, and most of my stay in the hospital was not a bad ordeal, thanks in large measure to the efficient care of Dr. McShane. Bud and Pam were able to finish their hunt as they had planned, with Bill Ryan's help. They took a couple of fine kudu, and by the time they got back to Nairobi two weeks later, I was able to sit up and drink champagne with them, by way of celebrating my escape. I was well enough to leave on an easy safari the day I got out of the hospital, too.

For the courage he had shown, Kiebe receive the Queen's Commendation for Brave Conduct few months later. Asked what his thoughts wer the time, he replied matter of factly, "Do you pose I am going to do nothing when a lion is

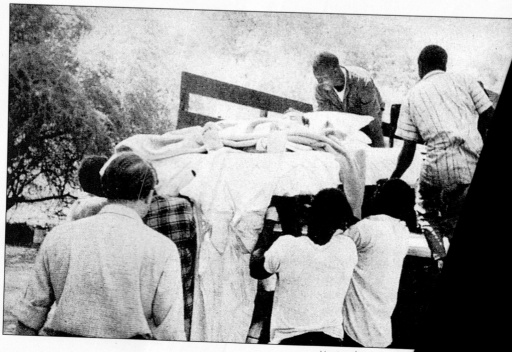

Morning after mauling, Dr.

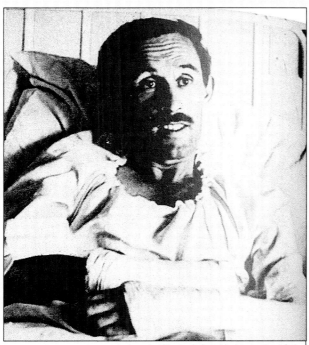
Two weeks later, I look worse than I feel.

to kill my bwana? What would we do without him? We would have no safaris." And the only reward he wanted was corrugated iron to roof his house.

The following February I had the satisfaction of helping to whack another good lion in Kenya. I'm all for a lion war any time now, and I suppose I shall be the rest of my life.

There's an interesting sequel to the story. On August 12, 1962, a year to the day from the time the lion mauled me, I sat up for a leopard at that same tree and at the same hour. I had a lady client again, and we sat in the same bush where Pam and I had waited. The leopard put in an appearance as the light was starting to fade, my client fired, and the cat tumbled, hit hard but not dead. In the twinkling of an eye I now found myself in exactly the same predicament I had faced on that fateful evening a year earlier, except that this time I was dealing with a leopard rather than a lion. Not that that is much to be preferred.

It was too dark for tracking, so we went back to camp and returned the next morning. The blood spoor led into a bush nearby, and to my great relief the leopard lay dead there. So if there was any jinx connected with that tree it has been laid to rest. And one thing is sure. In all of Africa there is not another tree that I shall remember so vividly and long.

John Kingsley-Heath

THIS HAPPENED TO US!

by The Editors of *Outdoor Life*

"This Happened To Me" is the most popular department in Outdoor Life. *We receive literally hundreds of stories each year from readers detailing their close calls while hunting and fishing. Some are humorous; some are absolutely terrifying. That's part of what makes venturing into the outdoors so exciting. There are no rules, other than those you set for yourself, and no boundaries. That's why all of us feel so free when we're out there. But don't get complacent: Nature has a funny way of putting each of us in our place. Bad luck or a simple twist of fate has cost many a seasoned woodsman his life. That's why I thought it would be fun to poll our staff to see which stories come back to haunt them in the dead of night—the ones that bring them bolt upright in their beds staring wild-eyed into the darkness with a cold sweat running down their backs. They didn't disappoint.—The Editor (1997)*

Jim Carmichel
POINT-BLANK LION

Scariest thing that's happened to me? Not much I can think of except the odd times I've almost gone over cliffs, been caught in avalanches, nearly frozen on mountaintops, gotten lost in dark caves, been chased by moose, bears, elephants, buffalo, lions and revolutionaries, had deadly snakes, spiders and scorpions visit me in my tents, huts and sleeping bags, or watched a boat sink under me in crocodile-infested water. Not to mention the charming fevers, skin eruptions and bowel corruptions I've collected, like trophies, in faraway rivers and jungles and deserts. Or the time insane tribesmen in northern Iran took me ibex poaching on a Soviet artillery range. And the bush plane crashes and near crashes too numerous to remember.

One incident that sticks in my memory, however, happened on a cool morning in Central Africa a few years back. We were hunting giant eland and picked up the tracks of a couple of lions. The prints were fresh and promising so we followed for a mile or so and spotted two big males across an opening in the scrubby forest. They spotted us at the same time and, for some reason, it was murderous hatred at first sight. The bigger of the two lions didn't hesitate, he simply set his sights and came at me like a rocket. My professional hunter got off one wild shot and the front sight flew off his ancient .375, rendering him hors de combat and leaving me to fend for myself. (Our trackers were already enjoying the view from the tops of local trees.)

About then a pint or two of adrenaline hit my veins and everything switched to slow motion. The lion seemed to be swimming in molasses and I had hours to shoot. My first bullet went into his chest but the lion didn't notice. He didn't seem to mind the second bullet, either, and was getting close when I closed the bolt on my last round and put the crosshairs on his nose. Then, suddenly, his fight was gone and he stopped, a gun-barrel length away.

We searched deep in each other's eyes for a moment, trying to understand what had happened, and in another moment he was dead on his feet.

"There's another lion," I suddenly remembered, and swung to meet his charge. He was crouching, head and tail low, eyes aimed at my guts. He was coming too and there was only one cartridge in my rifle...

But that's another story....

Todd Smith
SNAKES IN THE BATHROOM
"I hate snakes!"

Indiana Jones's fateful words whirled through my head as I started back to my hut. My Zambian safari had gone great— great that is until one of the camp staff beat the stuffing out of a five-foot mamba that had taken a shine to hanging out around the propane freezer where we kept the cocktail ice.

Our skinner brought the still-wriggling body to us over lunch. The snake was as gray as the dirt floor of the dining hut and my first thought was, "My God, you'd never see one of the buggers until it was too late." You see, the black mamba has a rather impressive batting average. Only a handful of people have ever survived a mamba bite, owing to the snake's frighteningly powerful venom, which sends bitees into a convulsive, frothing death the likes of which I had no mind to see (or experience) firsthand.

"Probably another one lurking about," my professional said casually, his voice sounding more British than South African as he calmly examined the coffin-shaped head of the deceased. "Not uncommon for them to travel in pairs. Best take a bright torch when you head off to bed tonight."

"A bright torch?" I thought. "How about aircraft landing lights?"

"And mind that you give your duffel a good bash before you go rummaging around inside it. They do love dark places."

"Wonderful," I thought, as I headed for my cot and a noontime siesta, picking up a four-foot branch along the way.

The Zambian locals do fabulous things with thatch. My hut was more like a house, with a bedroom in front and a shower and latrine area built off the back. You had to step through the shower area to get to the latrine, which I had just finished doing when something came flying out of the shower outlet. The something moved liked lightning, was pencil-thin and as gray as the charcoal ground, but oh that coffin-shaped head.

"Mamba!" I thought, and I felt my body go stiff as stone. The snake whipped around like a snapped cable and rose up on its tail, its eyes locked on the bare legs below my bush shorts, only three feet away from it.

"Don't move or you're dead," I told myself, eyeing the useless stick that lay propped against the wall just out of reach.

Time stopped. The trilling noise of the crickets outside ceased. And in the nanosecond that followed I could hear the blood hiss through my veins. The snake moved first: In between heartbeats, he swapped ends and flew back out the drain hole like he owned the place.

My shouts brought the entire camp staff running. I blurted out my story, and our trackers started beating the grass behind my hut with long sticks. Sure enough, my old friend surfaced and was quickly thrashed into pulp. (We later discovered that he'd been living in the filled-in remains of a latrine that had been built off the back of a hut that had stood where mine was a few years before.)

"Probably came in to feed on the field mice nesting in the thatch," my professional said. My stomach did a back flip.

"What's the matter with you, man? Looks like you've seen a ghost."

"I have," I gasped.

Back in the dining hut, over four fingers of Dewars, I related how I had been awakened the night before by the sound of a mouse screeching from one end of my hut to the other and then back again.

"I've never heard a mouse scream before," I said.

"And you probably never will again," my professional answered. "Odds are that bloody snake was in there chasing him around."

I took a deep gulp of air and drained my glass, feeling the whiskey burn all the way down.

Bob Brown
TRAPPED ON THE NISSEQUOGUE

Had I read the tide tables I would have known how much time I had left to live.

More to the point, had I read the tide tables I wouldn't be in this fix.

The fix being up to my crotch in sucking, viscous muck. Stuck firm. Each move of my legs to free myself causing me to sink an inch or more into the water.

The rising water. As the tide had turned and the current was now rushing into the Nissequogue River, an estuary into Long Island Sound.

De dum, de dum...de dum, de dum. The theme from *The Twilight Zone* began to play ominously in my head as the incoming tide recalled the one about the wayward husband being playfully buried up to his neck in sand and left there by his knowing wife as the tide rolls in. I had always considered it one of Rod Serling's most terrifying episodes.

And for me, the cause of death would be a fishing spoon. It had gotten hung up on a submerged branch to which I had been casting, thinking it would be a good lie for sea-run brown trout. This was new water to me, running through a mile-wide marsh. It was late fall and the eight-foot high flagellum that surrounded the meander where I fished had already turned to a wall of thatch.

When I waded deeper, hoping to retrieve the ultralight spoon given to me by a Welsh coworker a few years earlier, the sandy bottom abruptly ended and my left leg plunged into bottomless muck. Quicksand.

I lurched, pile-driving my leg deep into the mud and, worse, reflexively causing myself to step forward with my right leg to keep balance—ramming it even deeper into the quicksand than my left leg.

Now, entombed up to my hips as the tide rose on my torso, I fought with panic, the only possible

"When I waded deeper, hoping to retrieve the spoon, the sandy bottom abruptly ended and my left leg plunged into bottomless muck. Quicksand."

witnesses to my predicament the snapping turtles whose nests pockmarked the riverbank. Any effort to free myself simply drove me deeper into the muck. I could safely move only my hands and arms.

I could still see the spoon fluttering from the snag about 20 feet downstream. *S-l-o-w-l-y*, I started to reel in line. I had no idea how big the entire branch might be, but if I could work it toward me, I might be able to brace it on the bottom and push myself out of this mess before the now fast-rising tide was over my head.

I felt the branch begin to lift, and I could see that it was crowned by a tangle of branches that would offer the widebased support that might allow me to pry myself loose. But it was all attached to a substantial branch, one that probably weighed 30 pounds. Inch by agonizing inch, line came back on the reel and the branch rose farther off the muck bottom.

The speed with which it wrenched free and then was caught by the current took me by surprise. Desperately I lunged as the branch drifted by. My legs drove deeper with the violence of the effort.

I had the branch. Cautiously, trying not to put too much downward force into my legs, I wrestled the branch into position, even as the current tried to rip this only hope from my hands. But I had to work quickly, too, as the water was now trickling over the top of my waders. In ultra-slow motion it all came together. I strained—evenly, methodically—as I used just my arms to lever loose my legs. Finally my front foot gained a slight hold on a stone or branch (I'll never know which) buried deep in the muck that held me. From this small and unexpected platform, I could carefully rock forward and back, working my lower body upward against the cloying quicksand.

Unlike the branch, I did not pop free. Anything but. It was a slow-motion race with the incoming tide. Finally, sweat-drenched and shaking, I was able to reach to the side and grab a heavy root exposed in the undercut riverbank. I could pull myself free.

Exhausted, with black mud coating me to my armpits, I looked at my watch. It had taken more than 35 minutes to work myself free. When I looked in the newspaper that evening, I saw that the tide would have continued rising for another 50 minutes. It would have risen another foot and a half in that time. *De dum, de dum...de dum, de dum.*

Jerry Gibbs
BAD NEWS BEAR

It was a bad time to be on the Brooks. The old alpha bear called Scar had lost his first battle and was in a vile mood. Across his forelegs, gashes from the fight gaped like slashes in whale blubber. He had killed a cub that had wandered into his fish-

ing territory, and for a time the mother sow raged down the riverbanks. The bear of my trouble, however, was a teenager pumping more testosterone than was good for himself or anyone around him. His shtick was false-charging anglers. So far, the charges had been bluffs.

It was sockeye time on the little river in Alaska's Katmai National Park. The great bears were fishing, tolerating (under stress) the nearness to one another as well as to humans. When a bear came down the bank you moved from the river to the opposite shore. Fixed on the fish, they usually ignored you—except for the teenage male coming toward us now. My guide, Ron, was into a fish.

Seeing a good photo opportunity, I dropped my rod on a midstream bar and grabbed my camera. "Go right," I said, directing. Suddenly both Ron and the bear were sharp as tacks in the viewfinder. "Right, hell," he sputtered, breaking off the fish. I looked up. The bear was too close and still coming. It had not committed to one bank, and was quartering like a hunting dog across the river, his head swinging.

Ron gambled on the left bank. I stayed in the water, grabbing my rod as I passed the bar. I was last in line now, the straggler in the school—the appetizer. Then Ron slid fast off the bank into the river, heading right, and over my shoulder I saw that the bear had changed course. Farther upstream, anglers were swinging in a bizarre conga line as the bear switched banks. My wife, Judy, was in that line, and I thought this might be ugly for her. I glanced over my shoulder and knew I would not turn again.

The water had gone from calf deep to crotch deep. Wading fast against it reminded me of the slow-motion flight from faceless horror in a childhood nightmare. I thought I ought to talk, yell at this bear, tell it something. In those slow-mo nightmares you always wake up just as the thing catches you, or just before, and you're okay even if you do have the sweats. But this wasn't dreamtime.

"Left," Ron screamed. "Go left!"

I did, panting hard, and saw the bear an awfully easy cast away as it ghosted by in the water. It looked at me, eyes devoid of expression, then cut to the far bank, moving on.

We clustered with the others then, everyone talking in the nervous relief that comes after a close

one. "I really thought you might be eaten," my wife told me seriously. "What could I have told the boys?"

"That the insurance is paid up," I said, "and that the rubber waders probably gave the bear worse heartburn than your spareribs could." She hit me with something, but I couldn't feel it.

Pat McManus
GRAZED BY A GATOR
September 1983. Mac Beatty and I are fishing the Cuiabá River deep in the interior of Brazil. Our boat resembles a very long and skinny canoe, except it is powered and steered by what looks like a Chevy engine on a stick. The craft gives the sense of being highly unstable, as does the guide.

His attention occupied by a search for signs of baitfish, the guide suddenly swerves the boat straight toward a high bank. Sunning itself atop this bank and directly ahead of us is the largest alligator I've ever seen. Mac, sitting with his back to the bow, is totally unaware of what only the alligator and I know is about to occur. Then the boat hits the bank. The situation couldn't be worse—unless, of course, I was the one sitting in the bow.

The alligator launches itself right over the top of Mac, missing him by a good two or three inches. I judged from Mac's reaction that he'd never before had an alligator leap over the top of him. Odd. Shucks, that sort of thing happens to me all the time.

Larry Mueller
SURFING THE LEVEE
For several years, until the flooded brush died and rotted away, our mostly shallow Brush Lake was a dog man's duck-hunting paradise. An L-shaped levee impounded 40 acres of overgrown, frequently flooded Silver Creek bottoms. One spring, however, an especially high flood threatened to destroy our paradise. It crested over a low spot in the levee, and the spillway couldn't handle the volume, so the water cut another exit.

My brother, Willie, and I inspected the levee cut and concluded it wasn't terribly deep and could be sandbagged. I presented a carefully engineered plan. We would use the small johnboat with the little motor that could be turned around to face backwards. A sandbag would be placed on the bow seat, Willie would sit in the center and I would idle the motor, letting the current carry us to the cut. Then I would rev up the engine to hold us in place while Willie deposited the sandbag.

We did a careful test run—in and back out—to get a feel for motor speeds. I instructed my crew to stand by for the first drop as we eased back to the cut. I could see Dad watching from the spillway. I smiled with satisfaction. You know fathers, forever expecting sons to unconsciously neglect important details. But this was working.

Willie moved forward. Suddenly the bow dipped to the gunwale under his extra weight, the stern rose, and the motor's prop was spinning in thin air. In a blink, the current shot us through the cut on a gush of water that drenched us, filled the boat and carried us out into the unknown depths of the flooded timber. The bow slammed into a tree. We could feel the flooded boat sinking. Could we swim in this current? The boat hit bottom.

"Hey! The water's only a couple of feet deep," I said. "We can walk out of here." I could see Dad coming across the narrow plank that spanned the spillway. His hipboots were flapping, the plank was bouncing under him like a diving board and his lately acquired bay-window belly was flopping in alternating rhythm with the plank. I almost wished we had to be rescued. You know fathers. After finding us safe, he'd be mad as hell.

Vin T. Sparano
MAY DAY
My most terrifying day came about a decade ago when my son Matt and I were fishing in a tournament from my 24-foot boat. We left Little Egg Inlet in New Jersey at daybreak and headed southeast in search of fish. At about 1 p.m. and more than 20 miles offshore, we heard a loud boom and my single 175-horsepower engine quit. We made

all the obvious engine checks, but it was a major lower-unit breakdown. We were dead in the water.

There were no other boats in sight and it would be dark in about four hours. Worse yet, the previously calm sea was now becoming a mass of whitecaps with the winds building. To my horror, I discovered that the fuse connector on the VHF radio was corroded. I could only contact the Coast Guard sporadically, if I squeezed the connector tightly in my fist. Water was coming over the transom, the fish boxes on deck were now full of water and the bilge pump was running continuously, draining the battery and our only source of power for the VHF radio.

The Coast Guard asked for my position. I said southeast of the inlet when, in fact, we had drifted northeast of the inlet. I had a new Loran unit but it had yet to be programmed and the manual was back at the car, so we couldn't give them a Loran position.

The Coast Guard began using triangulation to pick up our position and I was instructed to shoot flares when they thought they were close enough for visual contact. I had only two flares left.

Matt and I were now in life jackets, the wind was still increasing and it was getting dark. How much power was left in the battery? What if we lost contact with the Coast Guard? It was too deep to anchor and we were being blown out to sea. How long would we last in the cold fall water?

Just when I thought that prayer was our only salvation, the Coast Guard asked me to fire one of my two remaining flares. Within seconds, a voice came over the radio: "We have you in sight." As darkness approached, a Coast Guard cutter arrived and towed us back home. Winds reached gale force that night and a Northeaster blew for three days.

I sometimes joke about that day at sea, but it's always a very shallow cover-up for a truly terrifying experience.

Jim Zumbo
FLAMEOUT

"Doug, your truck is on fire!" I shouted.

That statement galvanized my pal and me into action, and together we raced wildly for the pickup. Black smoke was rising from underneath it, and flames licked along the driveshaft and around the oil pan. The gas tank was inches away.

Desperately we scooped up handfuls of sand and tossed them at the fire, but the flames grew larger. We worked like madmen for a few seconds, and then prudently decided to get the hell out of there.

Backing off 20 yards, we assessed the predicament. A whole lot of things go through your mind when your truck is on fire, you're in a desert wilderness, the temperature is 110 degrees, camp is 23 miles away and your only water is in the burning vehicle.

My rifle was in the truck, too—my beloved .30/06 that I had hunted with for 20 years. Doug and I knew that we had to get the water out, so we dashed to the vehicle and grabbed canteens, coolers, gear and everything of value, including my rifle. The flames grew stronger, and we quickly placed the recovered equipment as far from the truck as possible. I expected it to blow at any second.

Suddenly Doug raced back to the truck, yelling something about a handgun his grandfather had given him that was still in the glove compartment. The heat was too intense and he turned away. The flames were now 30 feet high and the truck was engulfed in a furious fire.

My Utah desert sheep hunt was over. Facing us was a long hike to camp, and then a horrible drive down a rockstrewn hillside in my vehicle to collect our gear. We were whipped when we got the job done, but there was even worse news to come.

Another hunter camped near us had killed a ram, and a companion ram had been laid down close by. A member of the party drove hurriedly to fetch me, but Doug and I had already left, headed home in defeat. Only two of 17 hunters took rams in that unit. I wasn't one of them.

FAMOUS
PEOPLE

GOV. ROOSEVELT'S
COLORADO LION HUNT by J.A. McGuire

Theodore Roosevelt is not only a natural man of the people, and an unassuming, honest, fearless and intrepid fighter for what he considers just, but he is as deep a lover of the hills and streams, and the free and unconventional life of the frontier as Nimrod, Izaak Walton or "Nessmuk." To meet Roosevelt as a sportsman is to meet him upon the foothold of man to man. There certainly never lived a more rigid follower of the ethics of true sportsmanship than he, and certainly none more inclined to cast off conventional manners and social dignity while in the hills.

Like my brethren of Colorado, I had learned during the past fall of his intended trip to Colorado with pleasure and pride. I concluded immediately that he would get his share of game, and get it in the ordinary way, for he has killed lots of big game before, including animals requiring more prowess and skill than mountain lions. But, no sooner did our vice-president-elect invade the borders of our game fields than there was immediately set a-going the grandest pyrotechnic display of camp lies imaginable. Reporters were hurried to Meeker, while others ventured as far into the borders of Coyote Basin as their time permitted, only to return to Meeker and concoct such an agglomerated mess of missfit stories as was never before heralded to an American public. This feature of the hunt was certainly no credit to Colorado.

The governor's trip was a success from start to finish. He killed twelve lions and five lynx during the five weeks that he was hunting, a record certainly to be proud of. Everything possible conducive to his comfort and pleasure was done, and hospitality was lavished on him as profusely by the residents of the towns and cities of the state through which he passed as by the ranchmen and farmers of Routt and Rio Blanco counties. He had what I consider the best guide in this country, a man with whom I have hunted over the deer and elk country of the White River—a sportsman from the soles of his feet to the crown of his head, and a man who has probably had more experience hunting big game than any other in America—John B. Goff of Meeker, Colo.

Governor Roosevelt arrived in Colorado Springs on January 10, where he was met by

John B. Goff, Gov. Roosevelt's guide.

P. B. Stewart and Dr. Webb, who accompanied him to Meeker, going by rail to Rifle, and thence forty-five miles by stage to Meeker. Here they were met on the 12th by John B. Goff, the guide, and were immediately piloted to the Keystone Ranch, twenty-seven miles from Meeker, where they remained a great deal of the time. Dr. Webb and Mr. Stewart returned home after a stay of three weeks, but Mr. Roosevelt remained with Goff, changing the location of their hunting grounds from ranch to ranch, according to the advantages offered, until February 15. Then they returned to Meeker, where the governor took the stage to Rifle and the train from there to Colorado Springs, arriving at the latter point on February 18. On the morning of the 18th he was accompanied by a coterie of Colorado Springs sportsmen on a coyote hunt, on which thirty-five miles were covered, but without success, although three coyotes and a wolf were sighted. On the morning of the 19th they arose early and started in quest of the same game, taking their lunches and intending this time to remain all day if it were necessary in order to "hang a hide." But, although they did not return to the Springs until 4 p. m. on the 19th, after covering over forty miles on horseback, they were unable to reverse the luck of the previous day. The governor departed on a special at 6:45 on the same

Meditation.

evening over the Colorado & Southern railway, to Denver, from which point he left direct for his home at Oyster Bay, Long Island, N. Y.

I was one of the few who were fortunate enough to meet Governor Roosevelt while in Colorado. When he boarded his "special" at Colorado Springs on the evening of his departure I mounted the platform, pulled out a card, asked for "a five-minute talk," handed the card to the porter, and was pleased when the latter returned with a pleasant "Come right in, sah." I was agreeably surprised to learn on meeting Mr. Roosevelt that an introduction was out of the question. He grasped my hand warmly, insisted on my sitting down and visiting with him, and remarked immediately in the language and tone known to all sportsmen: "Mr. McGuire, I do not want you to be formal with me, I won't have it. I have read and admired your magazine for a long time. In fact, I can heartily say that it was one of the most pleasant companions I had on my hunt. For, you know, there are lots of dull days, as well as exciting ones, on a trip into the hills, and I like to read sportsman litera-ture at such times. I particularly enjoyed your article on Dall DeWeese in your January number, and I want to say right here that he is a man after my own heart—a typical sportsman and an ideal hunter. One of my keenest regrets on leaving Colorado is to go away without having had the pleasure of becoming personally acquainted with him."

At this point I pulled from my pocket a note-book, but his hand went up like a flash and he said: "Please do not make this a formal interview. I detest them and would rather talk to you as one sportsman to another."

I assured him that the honor was appreciated, and said that my reason for being brief was a fear of keeping him from retiring early, as I knew he was very tired after his long hunt; but as this seemed no obstacle we settled down to a good old-fashioned

talk that was only interrupted by the noise of the train or the balancing motion necessary to get an equilibrium as the coach sped around the curves at a rate of sixty miles an hour.

During the train ride to Denver we talked of many things connected with the hunt; of arms and ammunition, of the daring and gentlemanly demeanor of John Goff, the guide, of the kindness of the Colorado people, of the greatness of the state as a game and scenic country and many other things. During our chat he pulled down his rifle, took it from its leather case, and showed it to me with evi-dent pride. It was a 30:30 Winchester, with heavy stock and open sights. "I have given the gun much usage," he said, and it looked it, for aside from the general appearance of having had much handling, it had four or five teeth imprints in the stock, large enough to place a pea in, made by a lion which showed fight when the governor went to stab it with a knife. "It is a good gun," he remarked, "and I believe the 30:30 is plenty big and powerful enough to use on all the ordinary big game." He entered into the caliber question with much earnestness, the above being his conclusions.

I received a fund of information from Governor Roosevelt on that ride, and while I did not "take notes," yet I will attempt to epitomize some of the information in as brief a form as possible, believing that it will be of interest to the readers of *Outdoor Life*:

Governor Roosevelt has been fond of hunting and of the life of the frontier ever since his youth. He has written many interesting books on outdoor life, including "Hunting Trips of a Ranchman," and "The Wilderness Hunter."

Big game hunting is his favorite sport, and bear and lion hunting he especially delights in. He has killed many bear, lions, wolves, coyotes, bobcats, etc., as well as antelope, black and white-tailed deer, elk, sheep, white goats and, in fact, all the game indige-nous to the temperate zones. He has hunted in all the Western game fields, but never in Colorado before.

He always dresses in a buckskin suit while in the hills, and is one of the greatest admirers of good horseflesh in the country. He knows how to ride, too, as well as any cowboy of the plains, and has the endurance of one who is in the saddle every day.

All his game on his last hunt was weighed with a steelyards when killed. One lion weighed 227

Wildcat treed—killed by Gov. Roosevelt.

pounds, another 164 and another 160. These were the three largest killed. The skins of all the game killed will be mounted in the best of shape for Governor Roosevelt's den.

Governor Roosevelt is one of the most congenial, whole-souled men imaginable, and he makes one feel at home in his presence immediately. He dislikes formality, and loves earnestness and sincerity. His grasp is that of a warm-hearted sportsman, and his conversation and manner unusually friendly and pleasant. Our meeting afforded me one of the most delightful pleasures of my life.

Believing that a personal letter received immediately after the hunt from John B. Goff, Governor Roosevelt's guide, may be of much interest to the readers of *Outdoor Life*, I take the liberty of appending it herewith:

Meeker, Colo., Feb. 15, 1901.

Mr. J. A. McGuire, Editor *Outdoor Life*, Denver, Colo.

Dear Sir,—Governor Roosevelt has just left Meeker, having come in with me from the hunting grounds to-day. I believe he has had the most enjoyable hunt of his life, and I certainly shared in the pleasure.

I am sending you to-day some snapshots taken on the hunt, and a little later will send you some more, also an article for publication, giving a full account of the trip.

Governor Roosevelt killed twelve lions and five lynx on the trip. Four of the lions he stabbed with his knife while the dogs were holding them. Some of the newspaper people seem much excited over such "daring feats." They seem to think this a favorite form of sport, but it is only done as the best practical method of quickly dispatching the animals, as it would be dangerous to shoot a lion while down and surrounded by half a dozen dogs, as one or more of the latter might be killed. Of course the animals are shot when possible, but often they jump from a tree and are surrounded by the dogs so quickly that it is hard to get in a shot.

One of the lions killed was the largest ever killed in this country, measuring eight feet in length and weighing 227 pounds. One of the photos sent shows him stretched on the ground.

On the arrival of the governor and party in Meeker on January 12, we started for the Keystone Ranch, where we hunted some weeks. The foreman of this ranch, William Wilson, treated us with every courtesy and kindness. From there we went to the Mathes ranch, where we stayed two weeks and got three lions. Bob Clarence and Zack Mathes have fine ranches, and showed us what true hospitality is.

From the Mathes ranch we went to Judge Foreman's ranch, and spent a few pleasant nights with the kind and agreeable judge and his son, who soon made us feel perfectly at home.

Governor Roosevelt took the measurements and weights of all the game killed on the trip. He has some of the finest specimens of mountain lion ever seen in any country.

I will say in conclusion that I have hunted with a great many sportsmen, but found Governor Roosevelt one of the most thorough hunters and courageous sportsmen I have ever had the pleasure of hunting with. The five weeks I was with him was one long period of delights and pleasures.

Very truly yours, John B. Goff.

J. A. McGuire

AN ELK HUNT

AT TWO-OCEAN PASS, WYO.

by Theodore Roosevelt

During September, 1891, with my ranch-partner, Ferguson, I made an elk hunt in northwestern Wyoming among the Shoshone Mountains, where they join the Hoodoo and Absoraka ranges. There is no more beautiful game country in the United States. It is a park land, where glades, meadows, and high mountain pastures break the evergreen forest; a forest which is open compared to the tangled density of the woodland farther north. It is a high, cold region of many lakes and clear rushing streams. The steep mountains are generally of the rounded form so often seen in the ranges of the Cordilleras of the United States; but the Hoodoos, or Goblins, are carved in fantastic and extraordinary shapes, while the Tetons, a group of isolated rock peaks, show a striking boldness in their lofty outlines.

This one was one of the pleasantest hunts I ever made. As always in the mountains, save where the country is so rough and densely wooded that one must go a-foot, we had a pack-train, and we took a more complete outfit than we had ever before taken on such a hunt, and so traveled in much comfort. Usually when in the mountains I have merely had one companion, or at most a couple, and two or three pack ponies, each of us doing his share of the packing, cooking, fetching water, and pitching the small square of canvas which served as a tent. In itself packing is both an art and a mystery, and a skillful professional packer, versed in the intricacies of the "diamond hitch," packs with a speed which no non-professional can hope to rival, and fixes the side packs and top packs with such scientific nicety, and adjusts the doubles and turns of the lash-rope so accurately, that everything stays in place under any

but the most adverse conditions. Of course like most hunters, I can myself in case of need throw a "diamond hitch" after a fashion, and pack on either the off or near side. Indeed, unless a man can pack it is not possible to make a really hard hunt in the mountains, if alone, or only with a single companion. The mere fair-weather hunter, who trusts entirely to the exertion of others, and does nothing more than ride or walk about under favorable circumstances, and shoot at what somebody else shows him, is a hunter in name only. Whoever would really deserve the title must be able at a pinch to shift for himself, to grapple with the difficulties and hardships of wilderness life unaided, and not only to hunt, but at times to travel for days, whether on foot or on horseback, alone. However, after one has passed one's novitiate, it is pleasant to be comfortable when the comfort does not interfere with the sport, and although a man sometimes likes to hunt alone, yet often it is well to be with some old mountain hunter, a master of woodcraft, who is a first-rate hand at finding game, creeping up on it, and tracking it when wounded. With such a companion one gets much more game, and learns many things by observation instead of by painful experience.

On this trip we had with us two hunters, Tazewell Woody and Elwood Hofer, a packer who acted as cook, and a boy to herd the horses. Of the latter, there were twenty, six saddle animals and fourteen for the packs—two or three being spare horses, to be used later in carrying the elk-antlers, sheep-horns, and other trophies.

Starting a day's journey south of Heart Lake, we traveled and hunted on the eastern edge of the great basin, wooded and mountainous, wherein rise the headwaters of the mighty Snake river. There was not so much as a spotted line—that series of blazes made with the axe, man's first highway through the hoary forest—but this we did not mind, as for most of the distance we followed well worn elk trails. The train traveled in Indian file. At the head, to pick the path, rode tall, silent old Woody, a true type of the fast vanishing race of game hunters and Indian fighters, a man who had been one of the California forty-niners, and who ever since had lived the restless, reckless life of the wilderness. Then came Ferguson and myself, then the pack animals strung out in line, while from the rear arose the varied oaths of our three companions, whose miserable duty it was to urge forward the beasts of burden.

For two days our journey was uneventful, save that we came on the camp of a squaw-man—one Beaver Dick—an old mountain hunter, living in a skin tepee, where dwelt his comely Indian wife and half-breed children. He had quite a herd of horses, many of them mares and colts; they had evidently been well treated and came up to us fearlessly.

The morning of the third day of our journey was gray and lowering. Gusts of rain blew in my face as I rode at the head of the train. It still lacked an hour of noon, as we were plodding up a valley beside a rapid brook running through narrow willow flats, the daro forest crowding down on either hand from the low foothills of the mountains. Suddenly the call of bull elk came echoing down through the wet woodland on our right, beyond the brook, seemingly less than half a mile off, and was answered by a faint, far-off call from a rival on the mountain beyond. Instantly halting the train, Woody and I slipped off our horses, crossed the brook, and started to still-hunt the first bull.

It was very exciting as we crept toward the great bull, and the challenge sounded nearer and nearer. While we were still at some distance the pealing notes were like those of a bugle, delivered in two bars, first rising, then abruptly falling; as we drew nearer they took on a harsh squealing sound. Each call made our veins thrill; it sounded like the cry of some huge beast of prey. At last we heard the roar of the challenger not eighty yards off. Stealing forward three or four yards, I saw the tips of the horns through a mass of dead timber and young growth, and I slipped to one side to get a clean shot. Seeing us, but not making out what we were, and full of fierce and insolent excitement, the wapiti bull stepped boldly toward us with a stately, swinging gait. Then he stood motionless, facing us, barely fifty yards away, his handsome twelve-tined antlers tossed aloft, as he held his head with the lordly grace of his kind. I fired into his chest, and as he turned I raced forward and shot him in the flank; but the second bullet was not needed, for the first wound was mortal, and he fell before going fifty yards.

The dead elk lay among the young evergreens. The huge, shapely body was set on legs that were as strong as steel rods, and yet slender, clean, and smooth; they were in color a beautiful dark brown, contrasting well with the yellowish color of the body. The neck and throat were garnished with a mane of long hair; the symmetry of the great horns

Cow elk in Jackson Hole, Wyo.

set off the fine, delicate lines of the noble head. He had been wallowing, as elk are fond of doing, and the dried mud clung in patches to his flanks; a stab in the haunch showed that he had been overcome in battle by some master bull who had turned him out of the herd.

We cut off the head, and bore it down to the train. The horses crowded together, snorting, with their ears pricked forward, as they smelt blood. We also took the loins with us, as we were out of meat, though bull elk in the rutting season is not very good. The rain had changed to a steady downpour when we again got under way. Two or three miles farther we pitched camp in a clump of pines on a hillock in the bottom of the valley, starting hot fires of pitchy stumps before the tents, to dry our wet things.—From "The Wilderness Hunter," published by G. P. Putnam's Sons.

Theodore Roosevelt

FORESTRY
AND FORESTERS by Theodore Roosevelt

I believe that there is no body of men who have it in their power today to do a greater service to the country than those engaged in the scientific study of, and practical application of, approved methods of forestry for the preservation of the woods of the United States.

And now, first and foremost, you can never afford to forget for one moment what is the object of our forest policy. That object is not to preserve the forests because they are beautiful, though that is good in itself, nor because they are refuges for the wild creatures of the wilderness, though that, too, is good in itself; but the primary object of our forest policy, as of the land policy of the United States, is the making of prosperous homes. It is part of the traditional policy of home-making of our country. Every other consideration comes as secondary. The whole effort of the government in dealing with the forests must be directed to this end, keeping in view the fact that it is not only necessary to start the homes as prosperous, but to keep them so. That is why the forests have got to be kept. You can start a prosperous home by destroying the forests, but you can not keep it prosperous that way.

And you are going to be able to make that policy permanently the policy of the country only in so far as you are able to make the people at large, and,

Forest planting on mountain sides denuded by fire, southern California.

above all, the people concretely interested in the results in the different localities, appreciative of what it means. Impress upon them the full recognition of the value of its policy, and make them earnest and zealous adherents of it. Keep in mind the fact that in a government such as ours it is out of the question to impose a policy like this from without. The policy, as a permanent policy, can come only from the intelligent conviction of the people themselves that it is wise and useful; nay, indispensable. We shall decide, in the long run, whether or not we are to preserve or destroy the forests of the Rocky mountains accordingly as we are or are not able to make the people of the mountain states hearty believers in the policy of forest preservation.

That is the only way in which this policy can be made a permanent success. You must convince the people of the truth—and it is the truth—that the success of homemakers depends in the long run upon the wisdom with which the nation takes care of its forests. That seems a strong statement, but it is none too strong.

You have got to keep this practical object before your mind; to remember that a forest which contributes nothing to the wealth, progress, or safety of the country is of no interest to the government and should be of little interest to the forester. Your attention must be directed to the preservation of the forests, not as an end in itself, but as a means of preserving and increasing the prosperity of the nation.

"Forestry is the preservation of forests by wise use," to quote a phrase I used in my first message to congress. Keep before your minds that definition. Forestry does not mean abbreviating that use; it means making the forest useful, not only to the settler, the rancher, the miner, the man who lives in the

Minneopa Lake and Tent Mountain, Montana.

neighborhood, but, indirectly, to the man who may live hundreds of miles off down the course of some great river which has had its rise among the forest-bearing mountains.

The forest problem is in many ways the most vital internal problem in the United States. The more closely this statement is examined the more evident its truth becomes. In the arid region of the West agriculture depends first of all upon the available water supply. In such a region forest protection alone can maintain the stream flow necessary for irrigation, and can prevent the great and destructive floods so ruinous to communities farther down the same streams that head in the arid regions.

The relation between the forests and the whole mineral industry is an extremely intimate one; for, as every man who has had experience in the West knows, mines cannot be developed without timber—usually not without timber close at hand. In many regions throughout the arid country ore is more abundant than wood, and this means that if the ore is of low grade, the transportation of timber from any distance being out of the question, the use of the mine is limited by the amount of timber available.

The very existence of lumbering, of course—and lumbering is the fourth great industry of the United States—depends upon the success of our work as a nation in putting practical forestry into effective operation.

As it is with mining and lumbering, so it is in only a less degree with transportation, manufactures, commerce in general. The relation of all of these industries to forestry is of the most intimate and dependent kind.

Nowhere else is the development of a country more closely bound up with the creation and execution of a judicious forest policy. This is, of course, especially true of the West, but it is true of the East, also. Fortunately in the West we have been able, relatively to the growth of the country, to begin at an earlier day, so that we have been able to establish great forest reserves in the Rocky mountains instead of having to wait and attempt to get congress to pay large sums for their creation, as we are now endeavoring to do in the Southern Appalachians.

The United States is exhausting its forest supplies far more rapidly than they are being produced. The situation is grave, and there is only one remedy. That remedy is the introduction of practical forestry on a large scale, and, of course, that is impossible without trained men, men trained in the closet, and also by actual field work under practical conditions.

Theodore Roosevelt

IN THE HEART OF
THE ROCKIES WITH CODY

by Irving R. Bacon

As I read from the diary before me the above quoted words, my thoughts go back to November, 1903. There, in northwestern Wyoming, on the headwaters of the Shoshone river, at an altitude of 7,000 feet, I see a group of teepees and a little log cabin nestling under the somber shadow of a great snow-capped mountain. I see hunters and prospectors with their sure-footed pack animals; and all the thrilling experiences of a never-to-be-forgotten trip with that old frontiersman, "Buffalo Bill" (Col. W. F. Cody).

The millions of Americans and foreigners who have seen this distinguished man galloping at a headlong pace—a Centaur incarnate—around the arena at the head of his whirlwind of rough riders; who have heard him responding to toasts in the society of the great men of this and other countries; who have learned to look upon him as the typical representative of the fast disappearing pioneers and state builders, and who have associated him with all that is wild, dashing and intrepid; know little of the real man. Others have told of his daring deeds, which first brought him before the public; but to

the writer remains the pleasant task of telling the world some things about this man Cody, that it does not know.

To begin with, this man, who has many times braved death with a smiling face and has often been so near its door that he could gaze through its portals into the great beyond, has another side to his nature, which best manifests itself when far away from civilization with a few chosen friends, resting and at ease, and oblivious to the bustle of business and the turmoil of money-getting.

Fresh from a brilliant season with his show in England, Cody arrived in Chicago in record-breaking time. He has from childhood been a transient, ever striving to race with time since the days of the wonderful Pony Express. Now his faculty for rapid itineracy has become one of his most dexterous feats. The expedition with which he moves his mammoth show from town to town astonishes Europeans. Great military powers have detailed their officers from time to time to study his methods. He yearns to be on the move as the roving bison he once hunted,

"I see a group of teepees and a little log cabin nestling under the shadow of a snow-capped mountain."

and no foible of mortal man roils his nature so much as dawdling, dilatory action.

In the lobby of the "Annex," his friends and admirers gathered to greet him. They marvelled at his healthfulness. He seemed ten years younger than but one short year before. Such men as General Nelson A. Miles, Colonel Finerty, General Newberry, "Pony Bob" Haslam, and others, made his brief stop-over pass delightfully. In all such gatherings, hovering around a popular idol, certain mediocre people presume to force themselves to the front, but there are few men who can let an officious person down to his proper level in the graceful style of Colonel Cody.

Among the farewell words of General Miles to Cody were these: "How is your grandson Will?"

"Oh, he's the finest little chap in all the world," returned Cody.

"When he is old enough, let me know. I want to send him to West Point."

"My boy? Yes—he's there—six-foot three tall now. Why, he's away up here," said the proud general, holding his hand above his head in delight.

The next forenoon was spent with the dear old pals of Omaha and vicinity. Dr. Frank Powell, called "White Beaver" by the Indians, now joined the party en route to the mountains. A score or more, including Jules Lombard, W. A. Allen, Denis Cuningham, Klein and others, gathered around the colonel, which title was now dropped and plain "Bill" used for awhile. What a treat it was to see the affection reciprocated between these plainsmen, now grown gray and aged, but still big, rugged fellows. For two hours the "old boys" rehearsed all over again the by-gone days of frontier life.

"Bill" joined in the boisterousness of the celebration with the best of them in all but one respect, and no one urged his reasons.

"'Tanglefoot' and I don't get along well together; it poisons my whole system," I heard him say. It is several years now since split-apollinaris has been his limit.

Stories and reminiscences were swapped in hearty accord, and some were choice, I tell you. When introduced to the hoary-headed old Jules Lombard, I ventured to remark: "You are a remarkably well preserved man, Mr. Lombard."

"Yep, just got out of pickle last spring," was the reply I got for my flattery.

Great big Klein in a shocked tone of voice shouted: "Well, I'll be darned; look at Jim thar drinkin' pop."

"Why you old hide-bound cuss," growled back the indignant Jim, "if you don't shet up I'll jest grab holt o' that breath o' yourn and yank you inside out."

On westward the growing party traveled. In Wyoming we would meet Col. John Bell, Professor Lehnen and others. Arriving at the station of Cody, Wyo., the party all made for the big Concord coach. The stage coach ride is a feature of the town, and Colonel Cody employs it to treat his patrons to a smack of the old way of traveling, just enough to raise the hair of the tenderfoot a little and let him know that he is not riding in a city omnibus. The click of the unloosed brakes, and the report of the long cracking whip, announced the start, and the lumbering stage craddled forward and swayed on its great leathern springs. Four fractious horses, well in hand by the old-time stage driver, trotted us smartly away. A moment later the steep grade of the 200-foot river bank was reached, and with brakes all set, down we slid and lurched. It was a breathholding moment for many; especially those clinging to the sky-scraping perches on top, for such they seemed, until we struck the bridge crossing the fretting waters of the Shoshone river, and rumbled across to the opposite steep ascent.

A thousand cheering Codyites, reinforced by the Cowboy Band, welcomed the colonel's return, the ovation bringing tears of joy to the eyes of the man who had fostered this country so lavishly. He has made it inhabitable by building great irrigation ditches and changing vast barren flats into fertile homesteads, where now grow waving fields of grain and green alfalfa. As a nucleus to this Big Horn basin country he has established the promising town of Cody, an Elysium for a thousand enterprising people. From Toluca he has had a railroad built to it, a very costly undertaking. Now big stores and trading companies, a lumber yard, a school house, churches, a bank, a brick yard, three newspapers and several hotels thrive there. That visitors might enjoy their accustomed comforts of the East, he has built the Irma, a beautiful $100,000 hotel, and the finest in the state. In this palace of these mountain fastnesses Cody and his friends assembled.

All day long natives poured into the town until by night the city was "chuck full" of all those characters which make this country so picturesque. Long-haired and bearded giants, like the trappers of the past decades, swaggered around; and cowboys frisked their "bronks" before the crowds on Main street. By 8 o'clock the town was whooping with excitement, and celebrators and their partners choked the Irma in readiness for the ball. Dress suits with starched white vests and low-necked gowns were "rustled" from the sage brush somewhere. When the orchestra struck up an exquisite waltz the dancing commenced and the floor of the ball room vanished in the dizzy maze.

High-heeled boots click clacked the time with gliding enameled pumps and ranch wives' ginghams blended with the rustling silks. Mind and manners

Powell and Cody ready for a ride.

class you here and not soft clothes. To this festive celebration some had ridden in sixty miles and more. All kinds of stunts were rendered, from cake walks to soprano solos. Of course it is difficult on these occasions to restrain the exuberant spirits of "cow punchers" and the like; but all the antics they cut up here were innocent and wholesome and only gave the affair the proper local coloring. One untutored giant, who had seldom been in touch with the city doings, almost fell down in fright, when a lady soloist launched forth with proper vim into a jolly song.

Recovering from his surprise, he innocently cried out, "What's she shoutin' fer? What's she shoutin' fer?"

When the appreciative audience responded with a large, vociferous encore he yelled again above the crowd, "What's them blame fools clappin' thar heads off fer?"

The colonel's head cowpuncher felt hilarious, too, a usual condition on his rare visits to the town. He went around, not dodging Cody either, telling in strenuous tones, "The colonel said he'd fire me if I got drunk, but he'd hire me in the mornin'."

Who could refrain from smiling at such incidents as these?

Thus, with dancing and feasting, the evening passed in pleasure, another page of honor to Cody's fame.

The following morning, all dressed in furs and proper clothing, the party bade adieu to town, pre-pared to sever ties with conventional affairs, and plunge into the mountainous reigns to the west, a hundred miles from telegraph or railroad. Escort wagons preceded some hours before the party, which was distributed in several buggies. At noon we paused for a rest at Carter ranch. Here at the base of the Shoshone mountains, lives a bachelor outfit tending Cody's herds of cattle and horses. On resuming our journey snowflakes were falling softly, dimming the faintly-marked trail. We must yet drive twenty-five long miles without a stop. Winter was now setting in in earnest, the thermometer registering below zero.

Big Horn basin, high mountain-walled on every side, has a climate all its own. Snow may pile in monstrous drifts on outside mountain faces, while within all is serene. Yet, once a year, through some freak chance or other, old "Jack Frost" finds entrance through the mountain barriers. Then he does freeze things up lively for a few days. This annual cold snap, a little earlier than usual, was what the Cody party was now encountering. Now and then a glimpse of grand mountains on either side was had. So strange it seemed to gaze far up and see great opaque chunks of rocky mountains resting seemingly on air, storm clouds far below their summits hid their base.

Some time after 4 p.m. the party reached the outer gate of grand old "T. E."—Colonel Cody's favorite ranch. Smoke curled up through the tops of giant leaf-bare cottonwoods, and, presently, through the gray trunks gleamed the white ranch buildings.

Never do I expect to see again such another enchanting scene. The storm had ceased and all around great mountains towered, soft and blue. Meadows and timbered bottoms lay from base to base across. Long undulating shadows blued the lowlands into quiet that snow-capped peaks might shine in splendor. Brawling streams from far-off springs and mountain nooks coursed noisily across to augment the river and gold-yellow alfalfa stubble peeped above the vast meadow's robe of snow. Weaned calves and yearlings stared stupidly at our approach, then scampered aside through the brush. Past long cattle sheds and big feed stacks we rode, not seen nor heard except by inquisitive magpies. Noiselessly on the snowy road, up to the great swing gate we drove. As the barking dogs and neighing horses announced our arrival, ranch hands and friends appeared from all directions to greet with welcome we tired travelers.

But the kind of welcome we most longed for was found inside the house. There big fires blazed fiercely in yawning grates and close to the blistering warmth all crowded. For weeks the hands had been hard at work on the ranch house, remodeling and decorating. The results made the old scout's face glow with happiness. At the tolling of the ranch bell out in front, the hungry party left off chatting and made their way to the spacious dining room. The inmates of the bunk house filed in, too, all washed and dressed for company. Twenty men gathered around the table, piled with the feast. Flavored roasts of elk and venison, hot coffee, jugs of sweet cream, toppling piles of new bread, home-made butter, fruits and sweet alfalfa honey, all dared our appetites. The air was burdened with an appetizing fragrance. Like chivalrous knights of old, these bronzed mountaineers sat around to banquet with their chieftain, and, "Well, boys, take a hold," was the signal to begin.

About this time far off on the back trail a lone buckboard and team were coming. A trusted man was driving our mining expert through the darkness over the precarious trail from Cody to T. E. Down in a flat, miles away, a wolf loped past the team and stampeded them. The driver lost a rein in the excitement and the runaways dashed in terror over the rough country. The buckboard careened and jolted against rocks and in holes, behind the mad team's flight. Clinging in terror to his seat, the professor awaited his uncertain fate, while again and again the driver tried in vain to grab the flapping rein. The horses galloped and fairly flew, traveling in large, looping circles to the force of one rein, until from sheer exhaustion they quieted down.

A shout and "hello" after supper brought the inmates of snug T. E. to its feet. "Why, that must be the professor, boys. Hurry and bring him in," sang out Cody. The door was flung wide open and

the light from the warm room flooded out into the cold darkness and on to the stamping professor. In he came, hungry, to be sure, but none the worse for his trying experience.

Cody adheres religiously to the old adage, "Early to bed and early to rise." By breakfast time his correspondence for the day is written. On the following morning while his companions were still deep in sleep he was up and around dispensing gifts he had brought for the ranch folk. I later found the ranch superintendent fondling a new fur overcoat, cap and gauntlets—his present. His eyes told of a gratitude he was unable to express in words.

This day a general inspection of all the interesting features of a great cattle ranch was made. Enfenced hay mows and stacked alfalfa backed the barns. The henery was found most depleted of inmates, sixty-five good hens having fallen to the ravages of a glutinous bob-cat that paid with his life for his crime. In the blacksmith shop the ingenious Carl sounded his ringing anvil. Granaries filled to the roof, defied famine for the stock; but it was the store house, however, that caught Cody's eye. Here, from the rafters hung quarters of beef, hogs, elk and

A sentimental moment in the house.

several carcasses of black-tailed deer with the hide and antlered heads still whole.

"Well," exclaimed Cony in delight, "I reckon we aren't going to starve, aye, people? There's shore meat enough there to keep us from want for some time to come."

The next occasion was a grand review of the "round-up" to take place in the great meadow. For days the cowboys had been gleaning every accessible nook of the mountain ranges surrounding. Every one mounted a horse and took part in the drive. Cody, astride gaited "Tony," whirled after truant calves in dashing chase, emulating his cowboys in their reckless calling. Hundreds of lowing cattle and neighing horses moved restlessly before the drivers, lifting their weird noise to the welkin above. Ah! such an entrancing sight beggars description. Picturesque "cow punchers" racing back and forth and shouting their cow language, enhanced the bedlam scene. This wild herd was driven into the corral and there, so crowded you could have walked across their backs. Cody rode amongst them, and their slick sides and sea of white upturned faces, showing their Herford breeding, formed a unique background for their proud owner. Here we will leave them for the cowboys and their work. How cruel it seemed to throw the little unmarred calves down, fry a great scar into their shrinking sides, ear trim them and all. But, alas, such conditions are necessary here, where cattle range at will; else who would know his own and prove it? All the fascinating life of cowboyism was here enacted, from lassoing and riding wild broncos, to playing stud poker in the bunk house.

To continue with our trip, already a few hardy prospectors were ahead in the mining district, drilling and blasting at the rich croppings showing. One of their number, "Major General John Reckless" Davis, so nicknamed by Cody in a facetious moment, was to guide the party and pack train through the mountains to their little cabin. Wagons were to be used as far as Cabin creek; beyond a wagon road was impossible. On the evening before the departure, a baggage wagon drawn by two teams came in from Cody, but without my trunk containing photographic materials. It was no welcome task to allow the party to proceed and back-track twenty-five miles to Carter Ranch in twenty-below-zero weather. Though I started early in the morning, it was 5 o'clock that afternoon when the poor team, fagged with the fifty-mile drive, drew me into T. E. Ranch. With my big reflex camera tied on my back, I mounted an "onery," dull-eyed "bronk" called "Sleepy Dick." He surprised me later with antics very unbecoming such a title. He was to carry me to the Cody party through the unknown country intervening. It was after 9 o'clock that night when

"Reckless" Davis bringing along the stray horses.

a very tired stranger, who had been lost on the way, was made welcome in a hunter's cabin, where my guide for the morrow was stopping.

Not until the following noon did we catch up with Cody's outfit. His cavalcade clattered on up the rocky river bottoms until it narrowed. At this juncture the long string of saddle horses and loose pack animals forded the stream and scrambled up the left side of the canon, mounting higher and higher. At one place a mountain cascade crossed the trail, the tumbling torrents changed to crystal ice. To walk the horses across the glary, slanting surface, a fearful risk, confronted us. All reached the other side in safety but a pack horse. This horse timidly felt his way across, sprawling his limbs out table-leg fashion, his very caution bringing him to disaster. Down the glazed surface he slowly sagged, then fell. Like a helpless mass he slid, struggling in vain to stop. But for an interceding snag forty feet below the crossing, his finish would have been a 300-foot drop over the precipice. Thompson "cussed" some in an undertone, and carefully roped the beast, undoing the diamond hitches and removing the pack just where he lay. Then we dragged him to the bank.

How happy Colonel Cody appeared, back at his old vocation again. He was always in the lead. Thus over the whole trail he rode, without dismounting, but always solicitous for the safety of his charge. Across side hills of loose shale, which descended at appalling pitches from dizzy heights above, down to the chasm's brink below, the surefooted mountain horses stepped their way.

Up we zig-zagged on the old game trail until progress forward could be made only along a narrow ledge, notched in the perpendicular wall rock by queer nature. All dismounted but Cody, whose faith in horseflesh was stronger than even the oldest mountaineer's. We hung close to the inside of that path and led our horses behind. Here, if one dared to look across the abyss and follow with his eyes from top to bottom of the opposite cliff, the aweing sight brought on a frightful sensation, as if a magnet drew him to it. On the summit of the route we were treated to a wonderful view. The silvery glistening of far-down stream, hemmed in by painted cliffs, approached and vanished behind our path. Circling swiftly above, two eagles screamed in searching flight; and stones rolled down, loosened by the fleeting feet of mountain sheep. Miles beyond our camping ground was pointed out, a verdant pit walled in by mountains. We passed on where cloud-bursts had left their havoc, and where avalanches of snow had swept the mountain clean of timber, and left its disastrous cuttings of shattered trunks, hundreds of feet above the stream on opposite slopes, whose barren sides had never grown a tree. And then we descended to the river and crossed and recrossed through the ice and tumbling waters, several times before we reached the margin of the park to be our shelter.

From timber line down to the encircling fringe of quaking asps the dense, dark tracts of pines were a setting for this jewel of a park, a dreamy snow-covered dell "In the Very Heart of the Rockies." Far to the westward towered the great Tetons, those landmarks of the early explorers, to the north banked up the high divide, walling in the National Park, to the east followed along the Shoshones and to the south lay the Greybull country. The mountains swept steeply upward, how far above I can only guess, from this open spot a half mile square. Elk and deer tracks literally cross-hatched it, and in the streams on every side but one, teemed shoals of speckled trout. Bursting through the fringing thickets, on such a scene as this we came. Teepees were already up and camp fires burning. Welcome rest begged us to dismount.

One day after the hunters had returned and the venison was beginning to send its aroma in delicious incense to the God of Nature, I sat sketching Saddle mountain, with the ever snow-capped Baldy in the distance. While there I heard the following conversation between Cody and his bosom friend, Dr. Powell. They were smoking their pipes a few feet away by the glowing fire-place inside.

"Yes," I heard Cody say, "I have met the great men of all countries. I have seen them at their best and at their worst. I have hobnobbed with royalty, have eaten salmon with his lordship and 'stirabout' with Paddy and the pig. Everything that money could buy has been mine. But, when I sit here looking out of this cabin window at Needle mountain and the gray range beyond and see the clouds passing over those peaks, never to return; when I hear the wind sighing through the pine tops, moaning as if loathe to leave this enchanted amphitheater of mountains;

when I listen to the rushing waters of the creek passing the cabin door; when I arise at night and see the myriads of stars shining on the bosom of heaven and see the contour of the rocky cliffs and lofty peaks on all sides and by the moon's bright light catch a glimpse of that scarcely a foot wide trail meandering over precipice and steep-sided canon, where a false step means death, I wonder whether we all would not be happier were nature to suddenly obliterate that one path leading to the outside world and force us to remain here forever."

"I fully realize how environment makes you feel as you speak," replied Dr. Powell, "But how about the loved ones far beyond those crags and gorges, from whom we would be shut off forever?"

"Aye, there's the rub, as Shakespeare says," replied Cody. "'Tis said that home is where the heart is and I believe that heaven is where our loved ones are. Ah, well, I guess we will have to hang onto that path to civilization for a while longer. But if we could have the beloved here I believe that you or I would never care to leave the home of Nature's God in His resting place."

Quietly arising, I peeped through the cabin door and saw a sight never to be forgotten. There sat the two men clasping each other's hands and within their hearts ratifying the brotherhood beginning forty years ago. Long association with western men has taught me that nearly all of them are really tender hearted and under an assumed sterneness or graveness most of them hide the romance and sentimentality of a loving woman. As I saw them in the glow of the firelight, Cody's head suggested to me that of a

Fording the frozen Shoshone.

Greek god, while all that Powell needed to make him resemble an old Roman emperor was the toga.

"Well, old pard," said Cody, suddenly arising and slapping Powell on the shoulder, "this artist here will think we are growing sentimental in our old age, eh Frank?"

"I guess the young man understands us pretty well, Will," replied the doctor. "Undoubtedly he is still having his day dreams and will not begrudge us ours of the evening."

Just then a loud voice was heard shouting from the cook shanty, "Come in and get it." This was the way that "Reckless" had of calling us to our meals. Well we "didn't do a thing" to the elk and venison steaks and mountain trout, with potatoes, hot biscuits and coffee that were piled on the split log table.

In every crowd of this kind there is always some one person good naturedly selected for all the nonsensical things that the others can suggest. On this trip it was an eastern millionaire's son who had never been west of Hoboken before in his life, I believe, but who, nevertheless, thought himself the great man of the party.

He was the veriest snob that ever crossed the "Big Muddy," conceited, purseproud and overbearing. When he returned home he must have realized what an insignificant being he was, compared with the sturdy, saturine westerners, with whom he had been associated.

Said Gus, with a wink, "Did any of you fellows hear them bob-cats around last night?" Of course we had all heard them except the "Dude," as the boys had dubbed him. He had not heard them.

"W-all, I'll be hanged," said Gus. "You must sleep heap sound. Why them bob-cats tore all th' bark offen th' logs o' this cabin tryin' to get in last night. Some of 'em was on the roof and one would shore have got in down the chimney, but I heard him comin' an' stirred up the fire just in time to singe him out."

The "Dude" was becoming deeply interested and wanted to know if there wasn't some way he could secure a bob-cat, without danger to himself, of course, and take it back East.

"Why, certainly," said Gus, and "certainly" said we all.

The "Dude" did want to get one badly, so Gus took a gunny sack, attached it to the end of a forked sapling and put a green bough in the mouth to keep it open. When we all got ready to turn in for the night the "Dude" was assisted to the limb of a tree about ten feet from the ground. He was told to remain there quietly and when the bob-cats began playing around the roots of the tree, where some meat was left, to throw the net over one and yell. Then the boys were to come out and help secure him. One by one the

boys slipped out of the cabin and hid in the brush around. Soon snarling began on all sides. The two dogs left inside of the cabin now added to the racket with their barking and for awhile it seemed as if a pandemonium had broken loose. In the meantime the "Dude" in the tree behind the cabin had become thoroughly frightened. At a preconcerted signal the writer, carrying a big stone, added his snarls to the deafening din and managed to pitch the rock into the net. The unexpected weight of the stone jerked the "Dude" from his perch, but he managed to catch himself on a limb below, and began begging in agonizing cries to be rescued. We all reached the cabin in the meantime. As we entered the dogs rushed out and began paying their undivided attention to the victim.

Gus now went partially around the cabin and sleepily inquired, "What's yer fussin' about?"

"Oh!" cried the terrified "Dude," "I have a bob-cat in my net, but I'm afraid to come down after him for fear of the dogs. For mercy sake, call them off!"

"I dasn't," said Gus. "Them's bob-cat dogs. If I go to monkeyin' with 'em they'll eat my hide off. You'll have to hang thar till mornin'."

As it was becoming pretty cold out, Cody whispered to the giggling crowd inside, "Say, boys, you'd better let up; the poor cuss will freeze to death."

So we collared the inoffensive dogs at the risk of our lives and led them into the cabin. In the meantime someone removed the rock from the bag and the victim was assisted to the ground. He made a dash for the cabin and fell in a heap on a bundle of blankets in a corner, saying: "That beastly bob-cat is in the bag yet. 'Reckless,' won't you bring him in?"

"I'm afeared to go alone, but if you'll go with the rest of we-all, we'll shore get him," he said. After some persuasion the "Dude" went out with us and grabbed the end of the sapling and made a rush for the cabin, but, of course, the bob-cat had escaped.

How we all did enjoy the discussions between Professor Lehnen and old John Donovan, a celebrated western character. Both were skilled mineralogists, one a learned chemist and the other a practical miner. Donovan had very decided views on rock. On one occasion he attended a lecture given by an eminent mining expert to an assembly of students. As the lecturer was endeavoring to explain to his spellbound listeners bow easily it was to locate where rich quartz lay, old John Donovan felt compelled to interrupt him.

So he blurted out, "Now yo're goin' too fast. If yez knows so much about rock and how to foind ut, phwat's preventin' ye from goin' out yerself an lo-ka-tin a claim? Yere knows as well as Oi ther's lots o' ore a waitin' t' be dug. Oi says if yez ken foind ut, yez ken moike more money in a mointh than tachen skule a century."

While our party would sit before the cabin fire at night Cody would quietly prepare for bed. Once in his bunk he would light a fresh cigar and take part in our discussions. Once, someone mentioned the changed attitude of the people toward the theater in the last decade.

"Well," said Cody, in answer to the question, "the theater, circus and other classes of amusement have distinct places in the education of the masses. To illustrate: the 'Wild West' exhibition is nothing more than local western history of today exemplified in the arena. Every play placed on the stage depicts the past realistically. Actors are history's illustrators."

Speaking of evolution, Cody talked as one who had made the obstruse sciences a life-long study.

"Nature hides her secrets carefully," he said, "and few of them can be learned. Now if Dr. Loeb can prove that he can develop new life in his laboratory and if that French chemist and his wife succeed in revolutionizing physics with their radium compounds, I reckon we'll have to study natural philosophy all over again. I wonder if we will be laughed at for having lived before the year 2003 by those who will know all about these things?"

And so he would dwell on one subject after another, astonishing all by his resources of general information.

In these happy days of rest amongst the towering mountain peaks Cody was wont to mount his horse and ride away into the solitude the environment here afforded. I have seen him pass by some mountain clearing all alone, whistling the happy tunes of youth and feasting his eyes on Nature's handiwork so beautifully pictured on every side. He is a child of Nature; he loves to commune with her alone. His long association with red men and their ways has imbued their sacred religion into his soul. He loves the beautiful; he seeks the beautiful.

Perhaps his character can not be better delineated than in the simple words of one of his good neighbors on the Shoshone, who said to me one day:

"Cody has a long head an' a big heart. Some people set him down as easy 'cause he's sometimes taken a hand in a game of kyards and dropped a hundred or so. He stacks that money in to boom the town. Others think him foolish 'cause he spends money so free-like. That's his way of advertisin' his business. He may be a cinch to get donations from, but when it comes to a heap big deal you can't get the edge on him then. That old boy is as keen as they make 'em. He knows, too, when a man's needin' help, and he gives without bein' asked. That man Cody's shore got a big heart—too big for his own good."

Irving R. Bacon

"He's a child of Nature and loves to commune with her alone."

HEMINGWAY ON

MUTILATED FISH by Ernest Hemingway

I believe rod-and-reel records should be of two classes—those that show the largest fish caught on rod and reel—regardless of whether the angler had assistance or not—and those in which no one touched the rod or the line from the time the angler hooked the fish until the leader was in the boatman's hands. In this way the first records show the size of fish which can be taken on rod and reel; the second show the prowess of the individual angler.

A case in point is the 119½-lb. Atlantic sailfish which was hooked and fought for a few minutes by T. J. S. McGrath, and then fought and landed by me. Neither McGrath nor I would enter this fish as a record for ourselves since neither of us hooked, fought, or landed the fish without assistance. But the unusual size of the fish for the Atlantic Ocean is certainly worthy of record. It is the largest sailfish, to date, caught in the Atlantic, but neither angler can claim it as a record. McGrath had an arm crippled with arthritis and, while an enthusiastic fisherman, did not want to hook into a big fish because of his condition. In spite of this, he had just hooked and lost a sailfish that a shark attacked after the fish had made 14 jumps. He had just slacked out a line to hold it, while I prepared another bait, when the big sailfish struck. His arm was so crippled from the work on the previous fish that he turned the big fish over to me to fight, under my protest. Now, neither of us would claim the fish as a record, but the fact remains that it is the largest caught on rod and reel in the Atlantic, and should be so listed, together with the fact that it was hooked by one man and fought and landed by another.

I understand that very large tuna have been taken on rod and reel after the fish have been fought by several different people. If these fish are larger than any other that has been caught on rod and reel, why not list them, asking the men who caught them to give their weight and measurements and the names of the various people who handled the rods, and exact details of the catch? Such fish would be listed in the records for size of fish, rather than in those in which the angler received no assistance.

I have frequently seen fish lost or eaten by sharks through the utter exhaustion of the angler. If the man

who hooks a fish turns the rod over to another angler, he should so state when reporting the capture of the fish, and, if the fish is larger than any other ever caught by rod and reel, it should be recorded in a separate list with the names of the men who fought it. If the fish were hand-lined, or harpooned, or shot, it should not be listed as caught by rod and reel, but, if it is of extraordinary size, would come under the list of fish taken by any means, such as commercial fishing, nets, harpooning, etc.

In that way there would be three just classifications of record fish:

First—Size and weight of fish taken by any means. Useful to science and to the fisherman as showing to what size his quarry are known to grow. This has nothing to do with sportsmanship.

Second—Size and weight of the largest fish taken on rod and reel as the catch of any individual angler, if the fish were disqualified because another

Ernest Hemingway, center, accepts the congratulations of Michael Lerner on a 540-pound marlin.

angler gave assistance, with a note in parenthesis to this effect, with the names of the men aiding in the fighting of the fish. This list would be of value to the angler as showing the size and weight of fish he could hope to capture on rod and reel by himself, without assistance, provided he had the necessary physical condition and stamina.

Third—Size and weight of largest fish taken on rod and reel by individual anglers without assistance in the hooking or fighting of the fish. This list should give details of the tackle and the time taken to bring the fish to gaff.

Now about mutilation. If a fish is killed by sharks, certainly the angler should not receive credit for killing him. But, if a fish is attacked by sharks after he is gaffed or when the fish is whipped by the angler and the boatman is holding the leader, I believe the angler should receive full credit for catching him as he will be penalized in the recording of the fish by the blood and weight lost.

Take this instance: Say three men are fishing in a launch off the north coast of Cuba. There is the angler, the man at the wheel, and the mate. The day is very rough. Say the angler hooks, fights, and brings to gaff a marlin weighing 1,200 lb. As soon as the fish is gaffed, he bleeds. As soon as he bleeds, sharks show up. There will be at least 14 ft. of that fish in the water. If a shark takes a bite out of him while he is being made fast alongside is he to be disqualified as a record fish?

Who is going to do the disqualifying? If any three of the disqualifiers were there in a heavy sea such as you get off Cuba in the afternoon, do they think they could put that fish in the cockpit or guarantee to keep sharks away from him while making him fast?

Here is another practical side of the shark business. You whip a marlin completely and have him coming to the boat, his fin and tail out of water ready to gaff. A shark shows up and your fish, which has given up the fight, starts out again with the shark after him. You have a choice of letting him run free, which usually would mean having the shark hit him 'way out, since he is exhausted, or of rough-housing him and holding him tighter than you should, and possibly breaking him off. Say you land him either way, and the shark has hit him perhaps once, in the first rush he made. Do you think the shark helped the angler land that fish?

What does mutilation consist of? Is any wound a mutilation, or does it imply a crippling of the fish? If you catch a fish that is so big that he has to be cut in two or three pieces to be weighed, is that mutilation?

The world's record marlin as recognized by *Outdoor Life* was cut into pieces to be weighed. Yet a bigger fish, which had some of his tail meat torn

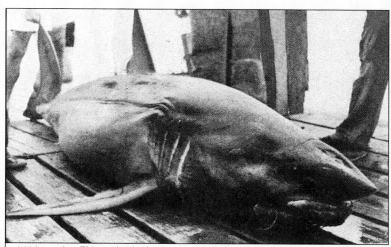

A Mako weighing 786 pounds, taken by Hemingway. It stood as a North American record till a month ago.

away while at gaff, according to the man who caught him, is not recognized. Let us clear this up. What is mutilation? I would certainly recognize both of the above fish.

I take no sides in this, because I fish for fun, not for records. I can tell when I whip a fish or when he whips me. The only thing is that he has a hook in his mouth so that he can whip me several times, sometimes, and I can still bring him in. But I wish that instead of having a bitter fight about mutilated or unmutilated fish, fishermen could try to see each other's standpoint, and, without jealousy or bitterness, get together on a set of three different records which would mean something. If a fish has been hit by sharks when he was actually caught, let a note be made of that in the record, in parenthesis. The fisherman is going to feel like hell that his fish lost weight. Nobody is going to put in fish that are half eaten, and then dragged up out of the ocean, as records. In the first place they will not weigh enough to be records; in the second place the fish should be disqualified unless he was at the boat and whipped when the shark hit him. That's how it seems to me, anyway. But I'm speaking as an individual fisherman and not for any organization.

Ernest Hemingway

ANOTHER GRAND SLAM
FOR BOBBY JONES by Charles Elliott

Watching the wind catch the bass lure that Bob Jones powered out over the lake, I remembered other years when I, along with a thousand spectators around me, would have groaned aloud to see one of his shots plunk into the water.

Now I grunted approval. The Emperor, as sports writers called him, had dropped his silver spoon in perfect position along the best shoreline we'd fished all morning.

I slid my paddle into the boat and picked up my own spinning rod just as Bob started his retrieve. His spoon, digging across a narrow underwater shelf that skirted the deeper run of the impounded river, took a jolting wallop. Bob sat back on the six-foot glass wand until it bucked in his hands and a coppery largemouth bass erupted into the sun. My fishing partner glanced back at me and laughed aloud.

"Close your mouth, boy," he said. "If this fish jumps your way he'll have a hole in one."

I didn't realize it until then, but I was holding my breath as if the fishing championship of the universe depended on landing that bass. As I started to relax, the largemouth waltzed again, the silver spoon flashing in one corner of his tremendous maw.

"This is it!" I said.

I dropped my rod and reached for the net, but the bass had other ideas. Shaking his head, he bored for depth and the skeleton of a submerged tree, leaving my boatmate with a fouled line and an empty hook.

"Sometimes," Bob philosophized, "it's almost enough to make a man seriously take up golf."

I couldn't have been nearly as disappointed if I'd lost that bass myself. A week before, I sat in Bob's office and promised him that this would be the finest fishing trip we'd ever made together. Bob had cocked his head and looked at me like he was lining up a putt.

"By what stretch of the imagination," he asked, "do you think you and I could ever snag anything but a lost week-end, if we were fishing out of the same boat?"

"At Clark Hill Lake," I said, "we can't miss. Even the bent-pinners are knocking off their limits of four and five-pound bass. Every day, too."

Bob sighed. "All fishermen are half nuts," he declared. "They'll believe any story with scales on it. And I'm as bad as the worst."

Bob and I have fished and played golf together for many years. On the fairways and greens, we made an undisputed champ-and-dub combination, with him shooting in the 60's and me being trolled along a dozen strokes in the rear. That was during the years just after he retired from competitive golf. I hadn't known him when he won his sensational first major championship at the age of 15, or when he'd gone on from there to take 15 of golfdom's most coveted crowns.

He made his final grand slam winning both the American and British amateur and open championships in 1930, at the age of 28.

Those days of playing golf with him in the 1930's and '40's have been memorable ones for me, but not a whit more unforgettable than our fishing trips. It seems just as difficult to beat him with a casting rod as it has been to top him with one of his own blunt instruments.

I'm sure we must have been the ones who first established the fact that bass always hit the day before you get there, and again give themselves up in wholesale numbers the day after you go home. Take the trip to Lake Chatuge, in northern Georgia. The Maestro and I drove the 100 miles from Atlanta before dawn, packing along a dozen live minnows to bolster our load of artificial lures. The minnows didn't take to auto riding too well, and long before we arrived at the lake some had turned belly up. Shortly after sunup we anchored off a rocky point a couple of miles from the dock and sank two of the livelier baits in the blue lake. To keep the others fresh, I tied our minnow bucket at the stern of the boat.

When the bass didn't bite after an hour, I cranked the outboard to change locations. Only the snapping of the cord made me remember the metal bucket, and I looked back to see it going down in 30 feet of water. That was the end of our minnow fishing for the day, and when we got back to the dock that night Bob let his eyes range from me to the empty stringer before he began to gather up his tackle.

"You're the only fellow I ever fished with," he said, "who carried out more fish than we brought in."

That had been one of many trips we'd made together, both before and after an injured vertebra had removed the greatest champion of them all from the golfing scene. Sometimes we caught a few fish and sometimes we didn't, but that makes little difference in the success of a trip with Bobby Jones.

Fishing has become a very large part of his life, and he does it with the same brand of sportsmanship that marked his golfing career. If he wasn't a champion of anything else, he'd be a champion of men. He goes out of his way to do things for others, and I never heard him speak a bad word toward anybody.

Bob says there aren't many bad breaks a guy can't make up, one way or another, and that's the way he dismissed the loss of his lunker bass. After he had wound in his line and examined it for abrasions, we both cast back to the bank again and dragged our lures over the underwater shelf. We kept casting as the wind turned us slowly around and blew us deeper into the cove. On his third cast, Bob hooked and boated a two-pound largemouth.

"You're tossing that spoon pretty accurately," I observed. He chuckled. "Maybe it's because this shoreline looks just like the row of shrubbery in my front yard. I've thrown so many practice plugs at it that I've worn off all the grass."

I hooked another small bass in the cove, and then we moved to a long point at the junction of Soap Creek and the river. On this 20-foot bar between the channels, we caught two bass and I lost one which felt like a lunker. Since neither Bob nor I got a glimpse of him, my claim went unchallenged.

That was all for the day, and for the next couple of days, too, with the exception of a few yearlings which Bob refused to keep. As hard as we tried, we simply couldn't find that picture bass.

"I'm glad fishing is supposed to be fun," the Maestro said, while we were wrapping ourselves around one of Jack Burdett's brag steaks. "If it wasn't, think what a couple of miserable dubs we'd be."

"I marked it off my fun list this afternoon," I replied.

"You don't mean," Bob said, "that after almost 50 years, you're getting serious?"

"I know the bass are in this lake," I grumbled, "and I intend to find where they are and what they'll hit. It may be this autumn or the next, but when I do, I'll come looking for you again."

"I'll be easy to find," Bob said.

Next morning, when Bob left for Atlanta, I cornered Bear Elam and started to pry some information out of him. Elam owns a Soap Creek camp near Lincolnton, on the Georgia side of the impoundment.

"Clark Hill Dam," Bear told me, "backs up the Savannah River for 40 miles along the Georgia-South Carolina border. With its creeks and rivers, its shoreline is longer'n from here to Hudson Bay— around 1,100 miles all together. You'll find bass all right, but where they are, it's might' nigh impossible to fish for 'em. Wait," he said, "I'll get a map."

I found it fascinating, for with all its coves, sloughs, and ragged islands, Clark Hill Lake resembles a scrambled jigsaw puzzle. Its waters spread over 72,000 acres of land in the two states. The land was cleared a year before the water was impounded, but before the water rose in its basin, brush from five to 15 feet high grew back as sprouts, in places thicker than the wool on a cat's rump. Bob and I had found that out the hard way, when we tried to troll deep-running lures through the submarine forest.

A fellow with a handful of rods and a beat-up tackle box ambled through while Bear and I studied the map. The stranger and I looked at each other like a couple of strange dogs and he and Bear exchanged nods.

"Who's that?" I asked later.

"Buck Perry. Thought ever'body knew him. Only man I ever saw who could catch fish on dry land."

Buck was out on the dock stowing gear in his boat. Lanky, sunburned, bespeckled—he looked like a cross between a Tarheel mountaineer and a Cracker farmer.

"One of your guides?" I asked.

Bear gave me an amused glance. "Nope. Now as I was saying, this lake is new. Water's been up less

Bob Jones beams over two of the big bass he caught when we anchored near Dry Fork.

than four years. But there's some tackle-bustin' bass in it already. Fellow caught an 8½ pounder right by the bridge, day before you and Bob Jones came."

"I'd like to meet Buck Perry," I said.

"Might pay you," Bear grunted. "He knows a durn sight more about fishin' than you do."

"Bear tells me you've got a formula for catching fish," I said, when Buck and I had shaken hands.

"Catching is easy," Buck replied. "The tough part is finding them."

"Last week he took 31 out of a hole with 31 casts," Elam put in, "and brought in 10—prettiest string I've seen come out of this lake."

"How do you find them?" I asked Buck. "Is it a secret?"

"How about going with me today?" Buck invited. "I can't guarantee a single scale, but I'd like to have you."

Now I'm a sucker for new methods, especially after such luck as Jones and I had, so I changed my rods, tackle box, and camera to Buck's boat.

Before we pulled away from the dock, Buck laid out a number of trolling spoons of assorted sizes and colors.

"Spoon-plugging," he explained, "is really a method of fishing, rather than the use of one particular lure. Any number of baits which can be trolled fast in the shallows, or that will run deep, can be used. Personally I prefer the spoon-plug; I know what it will do."

For a while after we left the dock I just watched Buck Perry in action. The first pass at a long point sticking out into the lake was made with his smallest spoon. The water under our boat wasn't more than four feet deep and we cut it with his five-horse motor practically open, several times faster than the most eager troller I'd ever seen. I must have had a question mark in my eye, because Buck passed his stiff rod and reel, loaded with 30-pound-test monofilament, back to me. At the end of the line the small spoon was singing through the shallows with a high-pitched hum. I could feel its vibration all the way into my shoulders.

"We'll soon know," he said, "if any fish are feeding in the shallows. If not, we can move to deeper water."

He put out another line for himself and we covered a mile of shore in a matter of minutes before we reeled in and changed to slightly larger spoons. We tried these in deeper water for a mile before we graduated to a third and even larger size. During this process Buck swapped colors constantly, both on his rod and mine from a red-head to a silver, then to gold, bronze, and even a silver-speckled lure which would have passed for a Christmas-tree ornament. He also shifted speeds, trying both large and small

spoons from fast to slow. I was becoming skeptical and I suppose Buck must have sensed my attitude.

"When you catch bass in shallow water," he explained, "you can load the boat. So it's always best to try the shoreline first."

We had stopped to change lures again and I pointed out one of the creek runs where Bob and I had taken several bass out of deep water. Here a couple of creeks had flowed together, and five points of land jutted into the lake.

"Chances are," Buck declared, "that if any bass are around, we'll find them near one of those points, where any disturbance can send them off into deep water."

We were working across one of the points when we were both hit at the same instant.

"There they are!" Buck barked.

On the second jump his bass threw its spoon, and while I was landing mine, he turned back and dropped anchor just off the point. I got the fish—about a 2½-pounder—where buck could net it, and while he was snapping it on the stringer I picked up my spinning rod and threw back into the hole.

I let the lure flutter all the way to the bottom and rest there a minute before I picked it up for the retrieve. A bass hit it instantly, the line curved upward for the jump, and I brought him in. He was about the same size as the first. Buck insisted on stringing the catch, so I cast again and hooked my third fish before the spoon touched bottom.

"Best feature about spoon-plugging is that it finds the concentrations," Buck said. "You're doing O.K."

I had my fourth bass on before he finished stringing the third. Buck looked up from where he was rattling the brass at the back of the boat.

"Wait a minute," he said. "Gimme one chance to soak a plug before you fish it out completely!"

We hooked more than 40 bass in that hole and, of course, lost the largest—one that made my reel drag screech before it went into an underwater tree and fouled the line. We brought our limit of 20 good bass into the clubhouse at dark.

That night I called Bob. "The bass are hitting at Clark Hill," I said. "We got the limit."

The Maestro let off steam as if someone had punctured him with a pin. "Got that broken record on again?"

"Look Bob," I said. "I couldn't find 'em, but I've found the guy who can. I promised you a mess of bass out of this lake, and this time it's for sure."

I must have been as convincing as I was convinced, for the next afternoon Bob joined us at Soap Creek. I paired Bob and Buck and tagged along in my boat to take pictures, as well as to team with them to troll both shores of Soap Creek out to the main lake. We crisscrossed points and shorelines diligently, but I was able to pick up only a pair of two-pound strays. Bob hooked into one whopper that stripped out monofilament despite his 20-pound star drag. Then the hooks tore out.

It was not until late afternoon that Buck located a school of largemouths at the end of Dry Fork, a long slough flowing into the upper reaches of Soap Creek. Soon after anchoring beside an old roadbed he tied into a largemouth that ripped line out, jumped, and tossed his spoon into the air.

Bob let the silver sliver wobble again toward the bottom, and another bass snagged it on the way down, so he hauled on his rod tip with authority. After a brief skirmish with the metal the fish made a long circle and came to Buck's net.

I was anchored about a dozen yards away, and I got into the game, bumping my lure off the bottom just once before it connected. I sunk the hook with a heavy hand and glanced at the other boat to see if I had a gallery. But its occupants were busy on their own. Bob was playing a bass and Buck had a deuce—two largemouths on separate hooks of the same plug. He almost got his double in, when one hook tore loose and the escapee took off across the surface like a skipjack.

For an hour we sat in that one spot, almost duplicating the feat that Buck and I had pulled a couple of days before. It was as Buck said—"Find them, and the rest is easy."

We caught and released the chunky fighters until my arms began to weary under the pressure. Buck called attention to several of his bass, which had such small heads and mouths, in proportion to the rest of the body, that they looked like some exotic species.

Bob's big moment of the day came just before sundown. With his light casting rod, he overshot his spoon—to a place where he knew the bottom was bristling with trees. So as his lure touched the water, he reeled vigorously to get it back to the fairway.

This old lunker must have been just cruising by. Bob's fast retrieve struck his fancy just right, for he hit the spoon with a wallop that swung the bow of the boat on its anchor. From where I sat I heard Buck sharply suck in his breath, just before the bass went into a series of top-water convulsions that reminded me of a roped alligator I had once seen.

Buck declared the fish weighed six pounds. To me, he looked twice that size. And he had no intention of staying on anyone's line. The first sprig of vegetation he tried to wrap up was brittle and Bob pulled him free. He jumped twice and rushed the boat, with Bob cranking furiously, then went under it, almost fouling the anchor rope.

As Bob strained to turn him from the stern toward the bow, he veered straight away. Then,

Bob's got one and Buck has left off casting to grab the net.

50 feet out, he reversed directions so sharply that he caught the line under one of his stiff dorsal spines and threw a gallon of water with his tail. Bob strained the nylon to its breaking point before he turned the bass and unfouled the line.

There were other hazards, too, in that vegetation-matted slough. The inevitable had to happen, for Bob's lie was simply unplayable. When the lunker finally decided to sound, the game was all over except for working the lure loose from the log where the charging fish had stuck it.

The Emperor examined the sprung hook on his spoon in silence for a moment. Then he began to laugh, and I felt that at least a portion of my promise had been paid.

I hope to keep on fishing with Bob as much in the future as I have in the past. I wasn't on hand to see him make sports history on the fairways and greens but—the red gods willing—I'll be there when he makes that grand slam in bass.

Charles Elliott

GRANCEL FITZ'S
LAST TROPHY by Grancel Fitz

This is the story of Grancel Fitz's last trophy, written on assignment for Outdoor Life. *The author numbered among his trophies all 25 legal species of North American big game—the first man to achieve this distinction—as well as heads from South America and Asia, but had never hunted in Africa until this time. Modestly, he originally entitled the story "Tenderfoot in Tanganyika." Unknown to us, as well as to most others, he had suffered several heart attacks, the first some years ago on a grizzly hunt. Characteristically, he kept his ailment to himself and refused to let it interfere with his activities as hunter, writer, and authority on big-game scoring until his death in May of this year.—The Editor (1963)*

My first safari day in Africa brought me two notable experiences in one minute. After our start from Arusha, Frank Miller had headed the Land Rover west through the parched-looking Tanganyika countryside. Close behind us followed the big lorry loaded with camp gear. A couple of hours before sunset we took a narrow road that led into much higher country, and we seemed to be traveling just under the crest of a long ridge when Frank stopped the car.

"Bring your camera and binoculars," he said. "We can get a good view from here."

To me, that landscape was hardly remarkable. The long, forested slope below us showed a number of open glades. Some dense brush covered the nearby skyline on the uphill side of the road, and while I'd known that Frank planned to show me something special along our way, I had no idea we had reached it as I followed him up the little rise. But we'd hardly started into those screening bushes at the top when I stopped in sheer amazement. We were on the edge— and I mean the edge—of Ngorongoro, the long-extinct volcanic crater that is 12 miles from rim to rim. Only a step in front of us, the side of this colossal bowl swooped down at a dizzy angle for 2,000 feet.

With the binoculars, I could see a distant lake in the comparatively level bottom, along with forests and open plains dotted with herds of animals. The crater is so ancient that its floor shows little sign of being volcanic. Erosion has made it ideal game coun-

try, and this was recognized years ago when the bowl and its surrounding areas were made into a sanctuary for the many species of game which drift in and out. I know that the vastness of any such spectacle can rarely be captured in a photograph, but I made a few, anyhow.

Then, in less than a minute, we walked down to the road. The four natives in back of the Land Rover were talking in Swahili. Frank pointed down the mountainside. In one of those open glades, a short way below us, I saw my first Cape buffalo. And that was another experience to be vividly remembered.

Like everyone else interested in these matters, I'd read dozens of accounts of the buffalo's vindictive thoroughness in working over his victims until there was almost nothing left, and knew he'd often been described as the most dangerous of all game. So while this one stood broadside, staring at us, I welcomed the chance to size up the kind of animal I wanted to hunt more than any other in Africa. The short-legged, stubby-faced, helmet-horned beast bulged all over with muscle, and I guessed he'd weigh a ton. At last, leaving him standing in his sanctuary like a dark statue, we went back to the car.

"What's your opinion of the buffalo as a dangerous animal?" I asked Frank as we started away.

"A man can get too reckless with any of the big five," he said, "but you can often turn a rhino, a lion, an elephant, or a leopard with a punishing shot. You can't turn a charging bull. You've got to kill him, or you've had it."

"How often do they charge before you shoot at them?"

"Very rarely," he replied. "But you can never count on it. You might meet one that some poacher has shot up."

He also explained that cows with young calves are sometimes aggressive, and that a bull may attack with no provocation after a fight with another. Sick bulls, he said, are especially unpredictable. Aside from the periodic epidemics of rinderpest, a few herds get this malady every year. An infected herd may run like any other when first alarmed. But when you follow those buffaloes into cover, knowing nothing about their illness, you are likely to be ambushed by one or two bulls and charged without warning.

On the drive to our first camping place—an overnight location—we didn't even bother to put up tents. There I began to get better acquainted with Frank Miller, at age 40 a senior professional hunter for Tanganyika Tours and Safaris, Ltd., the company in Arusha I'd chosen in booking my safari. Before my trip was half over, this Tanganyika-born Englishman proved to be one of the finest and hardest-working guides I've ever known. I believe he'd rank very close to the top among the really gifted white hunters in Africa. Particularly, on that first day, we talked about the unusual sort of hunt I had in mind.

Most men on their first safaris want general bags, with as many kinds of trophies as they can get. I didn't. I'd crowded my home in New York with North American, South American, and Asiatic heads. In 35 years of serious big-game hunting, I'd been fortunate enough to bag trophies of all 25 legal species of North American big game. With no room left to hang more than a couple of African specimens, I hoped to shoot only a trophy buffalo and—on the outside chance that we might be lucky enough to see one—an exceptionally fine lion. So I hadn't bought supplementary licenses for elephant, greater or lesser kudu, oryx, or sable antelope.

"We'll find plenty of buffaloes," Frank assured me. "I'll show you some lions, too. Trouble is that almost all the big-maned lions are in the preserves."

The following morning our lorry crew went on to pitch camp near a game-department station called Kimali. Frank and I drove to the little town of Maswa, where the district commissioner had promised him permits for both lion and buffalo in the Maswa Controlled Area. All of Kenya and much of north-ern Tanganyika is now divided into controlled areas similar to the "shooting blocks" of India, reserved for one safari at a time. While baiting for lion is no longer permitted in any of them, there was some possibility we might see a good one on our buffalo hunt. The Maswa region borders the west side of the famous Serengeti preserve, which contains some of the finest lions in the world.

We were given the buffalo permit at once. When the D. C. found no lion permits in his quota, he wired a request for one to the head game ranger of the district, but as this official might be away in the field, we had no assurance of a prompt answer.

"He'll send it to Kimali when it comes through," Frank said as we drove to camp. "The country south of there is uncontrolled, so we can put out some lion baits while we're waiting. We just might be lucky."

As things turned out, more than a week passed before we learned that our Maswa lion permit was unobtainable. The area had been recently closed for lion, so we didn't get back to the Maswa region for 16 days.

But what an eventful interlude that was!

We saw more than 20 different species of game in widely varying terrain, and I could have collected heads of practically all of them. Shooting only to get lion baits and camp meat for ourselves and the 10 natives in our outfit, I clobbered zebras, wilde-beeste, and warthogs, along with a Thomson's gazelle, an eland, a reedbuck, and a hartebeeste.

Oddly, the four zebras the law allows gave me the most trouble. When we didn't want one, lots of them were usually standing around at close range. If we needed a lion bait in a hurry, though, we had to drive all over the country to find zebras, and they were wild as hawks. In scrubby brush country, they soon proved I wasn't so hot on 250-yard running shots; I missed more often than I connected.

While this region had no buffaloes, it had a few rhinos, which are now protected completely in Tanganyika. One gave us a tense minute when he chased the Land Rover across rock-studded ground; Frank had to do some fancy driving to get away. Also, on eight different days, we found elephants without looking for them. A hunter after a general bag would have been happy with the biggest bull we saw. His tusks would have weighed about 60 pounds each, and as he never knew we were there, we could hardly have failed to get a shot at him after a short stalk.

On another day, we were following a trail across a heavily forested hillside when Frank suddenly stopped. He was far more excited than I'd ever seen him.

"Up there is a greater kudu with fantastic horns," he said. "Fantastic."

In a small opening in the cover, not over 200 yards up the hill, I saw two kudu bulls together. Frank hadn't bothered to mention one with a fair head, and I understood why as soon as I turned my binoculars on his companion. This giant stood facing us, not even twitching his big ears, with nothing to obstruct our view of him.

How good was he? I had carefully studied a beautiful head with 58-inch horns in the Tanganyika Tours and Safaris office in Arusha, and this one was bigger in every way. His wide-flaring horns may not have been many inches longer (their more open spirals made them hard for me to judge), but they were much heavier, and when Frank said they had a 40-inch spread, I couldn't doubt it.

For a full two minutes the gorgeous bull faced us, his broad chest offering a perfect mark for a scope-sighted rifle. Then, as if he understood perfectly that I had no kudu license, he turned broadside and watched us for two or three minutes more. With him in that position, the shot would have been a cinch. I had always thought of a greater-kudu head as one of the world's handsomest trophies, but even when I had wall space left to hang one, I'd never dreamed of a specimen as fine as this. It was maddening.

"If we could have a bit of luck like that with a lion..." Frank began, and left the sentence unfinished. He turned away, shaking his head.

This started a new train of thought. I was a raw tenderfoot in Africa. Many times I studied clear footprints without being able to identify the animals that made them. To make things worse, I had only some book knowledge of the local game species, and the strange shapes and colors of those beasts in the unfamiliar cover made them hard for me to see.

But I was beginning to understand how a present-day East African safari compares with hunts on other continents.

While everyone now knows that the amount of game left in Africa is a fast-dwindllng fraction of what it was a generation ago, the quantity we saw surprised me. I couldn't think of another country where you can run across a dozen kinds of shootable animals in a single day, as we did occasionally. It is also still possible to get some trophies of superb quality, like the kudu we'd just met and a fabulous roan antelope I saw later, and I knew about the successful safari Frank had taken out just before mine. His client, Jim Codding of California, had bagged a huge leopard, as well as one of the best sable antelope ever shot in Tanganyika, with massive horns more than 45 inches long. And that was on an 18-day, general-bag hunt.

Furthermore, even old-timers concede that a few kinds of game are as plentiful as ever. We saw impala constantly. I never tired of watching their grasshopper leaps when they were alarmed. Elephants are so destructive that government hunters must take out about 4,000 a year, and many white residents make their own annual hunts for ivory, just as an Alaska settler hunts his moose for winter meat. Right now elephants in Tanganyika are both numerous and increasing.

On the other hand, lions have taken a beating, as I learned almost as soon as I landed in Africa. They used to be considered pests and shot on sight, regardless of age or sex. Sometimes this view was undoubtedly justified. Forty years ago, when man-eaters were common in the Tabora region, Frank Miller's father killed more than 200 lions in 30 months, hunting at night with a motor bike and an acetylene lamp. More recently, I believe that lions are the only African species which has been seriously reduced by sport shooting. The others, particularly rhinos, have suffered mainly through native poaching and the settlement of new land, and many thousands of hoofed animals were needlessly slaughtered in programs for tsetse-fly control, which didn't work. But safari outfitting grew into really big business after World War II, and every visiting sportsman wanted to shoot a lion.

Today, only great luck can turn up a big-maned specimen where they aren't protected. It is much like hoping to see a record-class whitetail deer where the hunting pressure limits a buck's life expectancy to less than three years. About the only time to bag an old male is when he has temporarily strayed out of a preserve, for in areas where lions can be baited, they have almost no chance of living long enough to grow manes of trophy quality. Females, fortunately, are now illegal game. So while Frank's best efforts brought 11 lions to our baits, I wasn't surprised none tempted me.

"How long has it been since a man could be fairly sure of finding one with a full mane growing back to his shoulders, in maybe a month of hunting?" I once asked.

"They weren't too scarce right after the war," Frank said. "The war years gave them a rest. But those old lions didn't last long after that."

Some other aspects showed me how times have changed. The greatest change is in the speed, ease, and comfort with which a safari can be made.

With a minimum of red tape, I'd handed my rifles to a shipping agent at home, and found them waiting for me in Arusha, where my shooting licenses were bought. Instead of making the long and more expensive sea voyage of the old days, I had traveled on sumptuous Alitalia jet planes which took me from New York to Rome in less than eight hours, and then—after I'd enjoyed a few days in Italy—on down to Nairobi in an incredible 5½ hours. There is also fast air service between Nairobi and Arusha, but I preferred seeing Africa by bus.

Other things impressed me after the hunting began. The luxury of standard African outfitting is too well known to need description, but I'd been wondering about the attitude of the natives. In Tanganyika I found no slightest sign of trouble. Our crew couldn't have been more pleasant, and their smooth efficiency, in everything from pitching camp to preparing trophies, had come from long and careful training.

Only the weather caused us any concern. A severe drought that had afflicted much of East Africa for nearly three years was broken by unprecedented rains. In Kenya, where the Tana River overflowed its banks for as much as 30 miles, decent hunting for some safaris was literally washed out. While we didn't have many showers where we were, we could see them falling in the Maswa country north of us, and Frank postponed our buffalo hunt there for about a week. He wanted to give that area a chance to dry out, for the soil can bog down any motorized transport when it gets wet. When we did go, we left our heavy lorry behind, to avoid getting stuck, but there was one incident before we quit the country below Kimali that deserves mention.

As I'd shot leopards in India, I wanted no more of those, though there seemed to be many around. We saw five while driving to camp after dark, and ran across another in the daytime. Then one evening when we were heading back through brushy country, a black leopard crossed the trail in front of us. Seeing it clearly in the beams of the headlights, Frank and I were astonished. This color phase is said to be common in parts of Ethiopia, but it's the greatest of rarities elsewhere in Africa. That "black panther" might have made a unique trophy under different circumstances, but all shooting is illegal in East Africa between sunset and sunrise.

At last came the sunny morning when Frank thought the Maswa could be safely invaded. If we found it dry enough, he planned to get the lorry in later, but we started with the usual four helpers in the back of the Land Rover and a sketchy but adequate outfit. The indispensable native was Maté, a hard-bitten, middle-aged gunbearer of the M'tende tribe, who is also an excellent tracker.

"We'll stop in at Gavin Anderson's diamond camp," Frank said. "Those boys can tell us how things are."

I knew that a lot of prospecting is being done by Williamson Diamonds, Ltd., owned jointly by DeBeers and the Tanganyika Government.

Heading into the controlled area on one of the diamond company's new roads, we had driven for not more than an hour when Maté stopped us by slapping the top of the car. As usual, that eagle-eyed character had been standing with his head out of the roof hatch, and he'd spotted some buffaloes among the scrubby trees to our left. They were several hundred yards away. The noise of our approach hadn't bothered them; doubtless they were used to hearing the Williamson trucks. So we slipped out to see what kinds of heads they carried.

The wind was in our faces as we walked into the thin forest, and soon we found ourselves dealing with an uncommonly big herd. Along with those in front of us, there were others as far to both sides as the trees would let us see, so we had to avoid passing some that might get our scent. I understood that a bull with a 40-inch spread was considered a trophy specimen. A spread of 45 inches or better is a prize. I saw several that looked at least that big, though the cover made it hard to judge.

"Look at the spread on that one," I whispered.

"Cow," Frank replied as we silently moved on.

A moment later I spotted an unmistakable bull with another wide-spreading head. But again Frank vetoed it.

"Too young. Horn bosses are narrow, and they don't come close to meeting in the center," he explained, and he pointed to a much heavier buffalo that had just appeared. "Now, there is a heavy-headed old one, but his horns are short. The tips are worn off too much."

This was the kind of hunting I thoroughly enjoyed. There seemed every reason to hold out for an especially fine trophy, with so many to choose from, and I was getting a quick education in what a buffalo head should be. Following me like a shadow, Maté carried my .375 Magnum, a Model

70 Winchester. This is the lightest caliber now legal for dangerous East African game. Frank carried his own .458, a caliber he highly recommends, and he managed the stalking so well that we inspected several other promising bulls in the next hour.

The big-bodied, old bulls with the wide, thick horn bosses impressed me most. It seemed logical that one of those would represent a better trophy, and taking them would surely be better conservation than shooting the younger herd bulls, no matter what spreads they carried. The problem was to find a massive-headed old bull with long enough horns and good conformation.

In the end, of course, we alarmed them to the point where we couldn't hope to get close again without giving them a long rest. The scattered bands had joined up when we saw them last, and as they streamed out of the scrub into an open place half a mile away, we learned that there were at least 250 animals in the herd.

Turning back toward the car, I reflected that the scoring system for buffaloes used by the Conseil International de la Chasse makes a lot more sense than the British method of ranking them by spread alone. It gives an old bull the credit he deserves by measuring the massiveness of each horn at three places, to offset the length he has worn away. Some cows and young bulls showed wider spreads and

longer horns than any I'd seen in that whole bunch, and this, Frank told me, was very often so.

We drove on to the diamond camp, and there we stopped for a chat. When the prospectors reported more buffaloes a dozen miles farther up the road, we kept right on going. The scrub-covered terrain gave way to open plains, and on them we saw topi and bands of Grant's gazelles as well as Thomson's gazelles and many hartebeeste.

Early that afternoon, when the road topped a little rise, we saw buffaloes scattered out to the left of us a quarter of a mile away. There were about 150. To my surprise—for they couldn't scent us—they promptly took off on a course that brought them gradually closer to the road ahead. I soon learned that their gait, a rocking, lumbering kind of gallop, was a lot faster than it looked. Our speedometer showed about 25 miles an hour, and the whole herd was keeping up with us. We slowed down, looking for big heads. In another minute they were crossing the road, and as we watched the parade go by, a bull toward the rear struck me as a stand-out.

"I'll never try to outrun one of those beasts," I said as they raced away. "The whole bunch was going faster than any human sprinter ever ran on an Olympic track."

"They can keep it up for miles, too," Frank told me. "I've seen them run to the tops of high, steep-sided ridges without slowing down. We'll let them alone for an hour; then we'll try to sneak up on that wide-horned bull."

The buffaloes kept going until they reached a big patch of cover nearly a mile away, but they slackened their pace as they entered. We stayed put. After finishing lunch, we drove off in a new direction, making the stalk against the wind when we left the car.

Half an hour later, the bull I'd wanted to see again stood calmly looking at me, hardly 65 yards from us. The spread of his horns must have been 48 inches, maybe 50, and they curved out and turned inward in beautiful conformation. But there was a five-inch gap between the rather narrow bases of his horns, and the Cape buffalo heads I like best have those wide, rugged-looking bosses that almost jam against each other. That is one feature which sets them apart from all other buffaloes in the world. I turned to Frank with an unspoken question. He shook his head. Then the usually silent Maté ended my temptation with a single comment.

"Bura," he said in Swahili. "Nothing."

We quietly retreated to the car and turned toward the road, but we soon saw something that stopped us. Off across a narrow plain to the north was a half-a-mile strip of low, sparse brush alive with traveling game. A seemingly endless column of wildbeeste, zebras, and kongoni kept coming out of heavier

A stop for local information. Note Maté in the roof hatch.

growth to the northwest and moving through the strip to where all these animals disappeared into some fairly dense cover to the east. While I gave up trying to count them, we surely saw 1,000 in the minutes we watched.

"They've been over near Lake Victoria since the drought burned up the feed in the Serengeti preserve," Frank said. "Now that the rains have started, they're going back."

In the rest of the afternoon we saw no other notable heads, though we found some small bunches of buffaloes, which brought our count to more than 500 of them since we'd entered the Maswa area that morning. But we also ran into difficult traveling after a drenching rain. At two places on the road, the Land Rover sank so far into the mud we had to use a winch to haul out. When we finally turned back toward camp, we were barely able to cross a little brook with steep, high banks that had turned slippery. The place had given us no trouble on the earlier crossing, and there was no reason to suspect the part this brook would play before our hunt was over.

Gavin Anderson and his men had invited us to stay at the diamond camp. We spent a most interesting evening there, and that night I went to bed thinking that the day had been as memorable as any I'd ever spent in game country, though I hadn't fired a shot. We had seen more than 1,500 animals. The figure might easily have been doubled if we'd watched that migrating horde a little longer. With so many buffaloes in the area, I felt sure I'd soon have an outstanding trophy.

At dawn we drove out to locate the first big herd of the day before. It had rained hard again in the night, washing out a lot of tracks. The lower parts of the country off the road were too soft to cross, so we decided to let them dry out for a few hours in the hot sun. Having seen nothing unusual except the first cheetah of the trip—the 26th kind of large animal I'd noted since our hunt began—we headed north again for the open plains.

We spotted less game than usual on the way. When we came to the brook with the high, sloping

banks, my hopes of finding a trophy bull that morning dropped considerably. The little stream had become an uncrossable torrent.

"One of Gavin's lads mentioned a higher trail east of here," Frank said. "We might walk that way for a bit and see the lay of the land."

When Maté loaded our rifles, the three of us scrambled up the little slope to the right of the road.

Directly ahead we saw a fairly sizable expanse in which the low, thorny silale trees reminded me of a long-abandoned orchard. The underbrush was mainly "singing thorn," named for the noise a high wind makes when it blows through them. Perhaps 1½ miles away, this growth ended in a small plain. But the visibility in the nearby cover wasn't bad, and after we'd gone only 200 yards we began to find more game than we'd seen in all that bright, sunny morning. Many kongoni were there, along with a few warthogs, zebras, roans, elands, wildebeestes, and ostriches. Before long we added steinboks, dikdiks, Tommies, and Grant's gazelles to this list.

We also saw something else that wasn't nearly so welcome. Off to the northeast, some dark clouds were dropping a curtain of rain. Worse yet, a bigger storm had started between us and the diamond camp, roughly 15 miles from where we stood. Frank began to look worried.

"I'm afraid we'll have to leave the Maswa this afternoon," he said. "With the road no worse than it is now, our lorry couldn't possibly come in. And if we have more of these storms, we might not get the Land Rover out for a month."

We'd gone about a mile from the car when Maté spotted buffaloes. They were fairly close, on the windward side of a trail we'd been following. We hadn't been discovered. The herd was moving slowly; we could see little except some dark patches shifting among the trees. We'd commented on how quickly the whole region turned green after the rains had come, but I hadn't realized how many new leaves had sprouted until I tried to pick out a bull.

Here was a real problem. More than any other animals I can think of, buffaloes rely almost equally on eyes, ears, and nose, and all those senses seem excellent. We didn't know the number in this herd. Along with the risk of stampeding them all by spooking an unseen one, we had to think about the other game, for even a startled dikdik could spoil the whole show.

As the herd worked through half a mile of, cover to the edge of the plain, we learned there were 30 to 40 buffaloes in it. The biggest was an old, huge-bodied bull, but we hadn't been able to tell much about his head except that the bosses seemed very wide. Then I saw them all start out into the open. I'd taken my rifle from Maté, and when we made

Fitz (right) shown with white hunter Frank Miller and craggy-horned Maswa Cape buffalo author dropped with .375 Magnum.

a hurried approach to the last screen of thornbush, I had my first clear sight of the bull's massive, helmetlike horns. He was well under 100 yards away.

"The spread is nothing to brag about," Frank whispered. "It's around 40. The bosses are fine."

"Hang the spread. He has character," I answered, trying to slip into a more open place to shoot without scaring him. But I must have botched that job; I moved, and the whole herd bolted.

The bull was angling toward my left when I shot first, the bullet hitting ahead of that flank as I aimed to drive it through to his far shoulder. It didn't stop him, but he slowed so much that I missed in front of him when he turned almost broadside, and the next shot wasn't so accurate, either. I tried for the spine, about 14 inches below his withers. Instead of connecting there, I tagged the center of his shoulder. And that 300-grain Silvertip bullet killed him, not 20 yards from where he'd been when my first shot was fired.

When we walked over and examined the old bull's head, even Maté was jubilant about it. The massive, rough-hewn bosses were as wide and closely set as I'd thought, and the deep dips of the symmetrical horns gave them good length for a trophy of that age and compact type.

So, while admirers of extreme spreads may think I made a tenderfoot's choice, I liked this buf-falo better than any other we'd seen—and better than any we found in the Lolkisale region a week later, when we were far away from the threat of Maswa mud. Maybe his picture shows why I was so contented with him.

Grancel Fitz

FOR TED WILLIAMS-
A NEW TRIPLE CROWN

by H. Lea Lawrence
with Pat Smith

In a feat as remarkable as his baseball triple crown, Ted Williams has just hooked his 1,000th salmon, adding to the 1,000 bonefish and 1,000 tarpon he's taken on a fly. A profile...
—*The Editor (1978)*

The Lord made Ted Williams to excel in at least four things. The first, of course was hitting baseballs. From 1939 to 1960, Williams hit baseballs better than anyone in the Majors, ending his career for the Boston Red Sox by hitting a home run in his last time at bat. The second thing he did so well was fly a fighter plane in World War II and the Korean conflict; accounts of his combat exploits are still being told in the flight shacks of Marine Air Wing bases from Cherry Point to Atsugi. Third, Ted was a superlative hunter. Whether it was woodcock and grouse in Maine, waterfowl on Currituck Sound, or water buffalo in Kenya, Williams was perfection afield. But beyond these accomplishments, it is the fourth activity that has given Williams more joy than all the others combined. Ted is one of the world's finest flycasters.

And today, at 60, Ted Williams has laid down his other tools of excellence and taken up the fly rod exclusively, living what many of us would regard as the impossible dream. With the exception of a four-year stretch as manager of the Washington Senators and the Texas Rangers, Williams has been following the seasons with the responsiveness of a wild goose. His year begins in the spring, in May, when he travels north to his hideaway on the Miramichi, a highly productive salmon river that flows into the Gulf of St. Lawrence out of New Brunswick. There Ted stays through the summer, fishing for what he believes to be the greatest gamefish in the world. Before the snow flies in October, Ted heads south to his comfortable home on the gulf side of Islamorada, where he ties bonefish flies and tarpon streamers when he isn't chasing the phantom speedsters across the flats of the Florida Keys in his shallow-draft, no-frills sneakboat that, like all else he owns, is symbolic of its master—trim, durable, and made for action.

Ted is not quite so trim as he was during his playing days. His eyes, which once were compared to Clark Kent's, aren't as sharp as they were in 1941 when he hit .406. His reflexes have no doubt slowed a bit since he was carving up the skies over North Korea in a Fury jet back in 1952. And one is fairly certain that his strength has diminished somewhat since that late summer day in 1964 off Rhode Island when he boated a 550-pound bluefin tuna in less than an hour without using the boat to his advantage. If the parts are not quite so perfect anymore, the man has ripened and mellowed over the years and now he pursues his last love with an almost monkish dedication.

Like all baseball men, Ted measures his life in statistics. When he won the triple crown in 1947 his 32 home runs, 114 runs batted in, and .343 batting average were duly set forth in record books forever. But this past summer, Ted accomplished another triple crown that holds a more private meaning. He already had 1,000 bonefish on flies and 1,000 tarpon on flyrods; and last August, Ted sunk a feathered hook into the lip of his 1,000th Atlantic salmon. No flycaster in the world has duplicated the feat.

When Ted was 950 or so along the way, I and some friends visited him up at the Miramichi. Since everyone was acquainted, Ted hardly hesitated before plunging headlong into the moment. "Look at this fly," he demanded, brandishing a colorful number he had just finished tying. "Be absolutely honest now. Isn't it the most beautiful creation you've ever seen?" When Karl Smith, who flew with Ted during WWII, muttered something about modesty, Williams shook his head and smiled mischievously. "Great hands," he said, as though to himself. "Great eyes. I should have been a surgeon."

We moved out of his living room to the front porch that overlooks the home pool, slightly ruffled now by a soft breeze blowing upriver. There on the porch, in the shade of a copse of birches, we talked, each of the four visitors bringing Ted up to date on his life. Williams listened intently until we were done. Then, with his face alive and his body moving to the rhythm of his words, he paid daily homage to his best and truest friend. "I consider it a privilege to fish for the Atlantic salmon," he said at full volume. "It has character and if a fish can be called regal, then it deserves credit for that as well." Then he stood and looked across the pool to the sinking sun and noted it was time we went fishing.

Ted's camp consists of a one-story house and two guest cottages. It is perched on a high bank of the Miramichi, above one of three pools he owns on the river, which curls eastward for perhaps 60 miles before spilling into the Atlantic above Prince Edward Island. Ted first went salmon fishing in 1955 while making a film, and he came away indifferent to the sport. But two years later he returned and caught a 20-pounder and he was instantly hooked.

Before the season was over in 1958, Williams had purchased a mile stretch of the Miramichi, and ever since, this small slice of paradise has been home to Ted for a third of every year. He shares it with his guide and good friend Roy Curtis. Each dawn the two leave camp and while Edna, Roy's wife, keeps house and cooks, Ted fishes with the same dedication that has made him a champion hitter, pilot, and hunter.

Using an 8½-foot graphite rod he designed specifically for his seasons on the Miramichi, Williams takes a position in one of his pools and begins shooting holes in the wind. With the same effortless grace he once swung a baseball bat, the great left-hander sends cast after cast out over the waters with a precision that can only be appreciated firsthand. Each cast ranges between 78 and 82 feet. Each cast is a moment of flyrodding perfection. With his phenomenal eyesight he searches the sliding black ceiling of the river, looking for signs of active salmon— a winking flash, a tail or just a swirl that shouldn't be there.

He stops only to drink tea or to talk to a local fisherman who has waded out to a pile of rocks called "Hawk's Point." The rockpile was so dubbed by Curtis, who for 18 years has watched Williams perch there to study the stream or, on the rare occasions when he has guests, to observe the casting prowess of a companion. Like the rockpile's namesake, Williams seldom misses a trick.

When the sun is high and hot on the water, Williams and Curtis return to camp, where they eat the main meal of the day. Then they rest until the sun drops behind the treeline, which is the signal to return to the river and fish until night closes in. And so it goes, day after day, week after week, year after year. For some, it would seem a monotonous existence. But for a man who has lived in a fishbowl all his life, it is the sweetest form of pleasure and peace left in all the world.

So on this first day of our visit with Ted, I sat at streamside and watched the great man work the "swinging bridge" pool, so named for such a structure that was washed out by a flood years ago. As Williams cast, he delivered a lecture on the finer points of the art. He showed me various hand grips he uses; showed me how to retrieve line and hold the coils; how to check a fly with the least effort and loss of time, how to get that extra distance we all look for. All the while he was sending his fly on 80-foot flights with no more effort than it takes to play catch with a small boy.

"I can get lots more distance on a cast if I want to," he said. "But this is the right amount of line for this particular pool. And there's no use working harder just for the hell of it. This is a comfortable cast and I can handle it for hours without tiring."

Then as if to remove any doubt he picked up the line, double-hauled and sent the fly well out over the pool. "Now that's over 90 feet," he said. "Probably 95 feet. But I seldom have reason to reach that far. But sometimes with a strong wind I have to work that hard on every cast to get normal length."

While the others continued to fish, Ted and I moved to a shanty that stood by the pool. As we drank some tea, Ted talked of his beloved Miramichi and its future. Since the Danes have stopped taking salmon in the high seas and strict netting restrictions have been imposed on most of the New Brunswick rivers, the salmon fishing in the Miramichi is better than it has been in 30 years.

Ted, quite naturally, wants to see it stay that way.

"Every consideration regarding the Atlantic salmon in this country," he said, "must be made in favor of the fish and the fisherman. Season lengths, limits, special regulations, and license fees—all these things should be designed to benefit the fish and its future. The resource of the Atlantic salmon is too valuable from an economic and aesthetic viewpoint to play politics with. Take the license fee, for example. A lot of people complain that it is too high ($35 for seven days) for visiting anglers. I hope they set it

Using an 8½-foot graphite rod he designed himself, Williams casts on the Miramichi.

higher, as high as the traffic will bear. Sure I know I have my own water and that I have more money than the average guy. But the point is the money is used for Atlantic salmon research, protection, and preservation. So it benefits all fishermen in the end. If it aids the perpetuation of a truly great sport, who's to complain. Look, something like the cost of a fishing license is incidental to the amount of money a fisherman from the states has to cough up to come here and fish for salmon. If he can afford the trip, he can afford the license. It's that simple."

One of the guests, Tom Smith, who is the son of Karl, began working the pool directly in front of us. When Ted noticed him, he dropped the conversation like a spent match, stood up and began telling Tom to bring his fly off the water with greater speed and not to pause so long on his backcast. Ted's expressions and gestures were exaggerated, like those of a drama coach. When Tom was performing to the master's satisfaction, he returned to his tea and talk.

I asked him to compare the Atlantic salmon with bonefish and tarpon.

"There really isn't any comparison," he said. "The Atlantic salmon has all other gamefish beat hands down. I wouldn't want to diminish the qualities of either the bonefish or the tarpon, but the salmon is so much more. The salmon attacks the angler's mind, challenging him to lay the right fly in precisely the right place and retrieve it in exactly the right way. He's more fun to fish for than to catch. There are so many things about the sport I find satisfying that it's almost impossible to think of them all. Flytying is one. I get so engrossed in it that I lose track of everything. To create a fly that has perfect balance in the water, a fly that exhibits that something extra—call it life—that every flytyer thinks he can instill in his creation. It's a minor art form. Then there is casting. There's a kind of discipline in it that I like. I can't do things imperfectly, it's got to be right. Every day I try to add a little more polish to my casts, just a hair more efficiency. Compared to these aspects of the sport I find the actual catching of the fish a minor consequence,

an anticlimax. Hooking them is important since it proves that the fly was tied right and the cast laid down properly. But as far as I'm concerned I would just as well hand the rod to someone else after the fish is hooked and sit back and enjoy the fight from the stands."

I'd heard much the same words from other individuals and I never quite believed them. But coming from a man who was closing in on 1,000 salmon, a man who had already caught 1,000 tarpon and 1,000 bonefish on flies, coming from Ted Williams, who speaks the truth like a sharp spear, I believed. Williams put down his tea cup, stretched his 6 feet 4 inches to the fullest and proceeded upstream to the farthest of his three pools. We fished until dark with only small success. But that afternoon on the Miramichi had been made permanent in my memory by the large and vivid presence of Ted Williams, the man and the fisherman.

H. Lea Lawrence with Pat Smith

FRED BEAR AT 80:

THE MAN WHO MADE MODERN BOWHUNTING POSSIBLE by Clare Conley

In the early 1940s a seemingly insignificant event took place. A man from New York, who worked for the Corning Glass Company, walked into a small archery company in Detroit, Michigan. In his hand he had a piece of fabric woven from tiny fibers of glass. It was a novelty—cloth made of glass—and the owner of the company saw it that way until the New York man mentioned that glass in this form was slightly elastic. It would stretch about 3 percent.

That remark combined instantly with another piece of knowledge that the bow maker had in his mental catalog of information. And this was the moment the birth of modem archery and bowhunting took place. That unknown bow maker had two pieces of information and the common sense to combine them. This was the cornerstone of the $150 million-a-year business archery is today.

That bow maker was Fred Bear. And what he also knew was that a glue recently had been invented by Chrysler Corporation that would hold rubber to metal under extreme conditions. That glue, called 5509, was the first epoxy.

Bear wondered. Could 5509 be combined with glass cloth to create a new material that could be bonded to the front and back of bows making them stronger, lighter and certainly more durable than the yew, hickory and osage wood bows dominant at that time? The chief chemist of Chrysler, Don Swazey, agreed to saturate several layers of the cloth with the epoxy, then put it in a press and cure it at 325°.

Bear found that the new fiberglass and epoxy material worked well on the outside, or back, of bows, but not on the inside, or belly. The woven glass on the inside kinked and crushed under the compression. A different material would have to be used on the inside—aluminum. With more help from Chrysler, Bear was able to make the first bow using fiberglass. It had a fiberglass back and aluminum belly.

But unlike other bows of the time, its limbs were wide and flat like a leaf from a car spring. Also, the limbs were light and would spring forward quickly.

"The first one I made I covered with masking tape so no one could see how it was built. And when archers would come into the office I would hand it to them and ask them what they thought of it," recalls Bear.

"The bow looked like it might pull twenty pounds. The archers were amazed at how strong the bow was for its size. Then when they shot it they were more amazed at the arrow speed. Later developments didn't do a whole lot more than that. That first bow was the breakthrough with glass."

Soon after that, Bear developed a way of making glass in which strands only ran lengthwise on the bow limb. Fiberglass could then be used on the inside of the limbs as well as the outside. Bow making has virtually stayed the same since.

For the first time a person could walk into a sporting-goods store and buy the best bow that could be built right off the shelf. Fiberglass made possible the mass production of bows. The lone artisan in his shop shaving out a single bow at a time from a stave of wood was a thing of the past.

Fred Bear in one step had advanced bow design from the long bow that the English took on the Crusades in the 10th and 11th centuries up to the 20th century. Actually, laminated bows with recurving limbs were an ancient Turkish design. Sinew was used on the outside and horn on the inside, but no waterproof adhesive was known, and when the bows got wet they came apart. Bear had eliminated the weight and slowness of the English bow and the structural defects of the Turkish design.

Fred Bear was born the son of a toolmaker in Carlisle, Pennsylvania, on March 5, 1902. From his father, who lived to be 85, he acquired a love of working with tools and building things. From his rural surroundings he gained a love of the outdoors, and in particular, a love of horses.

The first joint of the third finger of Fred Bear's right hand is missing as a permanent reminder of that farm life. His sister cut it off with a hand-operated hay chopper. Young Fred and his sister were cutting hay to prepare a mixture of horse feed. The first step required chopping the hay into short lengths in a trough-like cutter with a shear handle, like a paper cutter.

Fred fed the hay and his sister chopped. Soon it developed into a game. Fred would put the hay in and pull it back before his sister could cut it. With a little experience she began to plan ahead, and Fred's hand didn't quite clear the chopper.

Fred rushed to the house where his two Mennonite aunts treated the remainder of the finger with lily leaves and rosewater while they took the time to clean the boy up before going to see the doctor. Even the tips of his sox, which were sticking out of holes in his shoes, were summarily snipped off with scissors.

Bear in later years became a left-handed archer, which meant he could draw the bowstring with his left hand. This may be a result of his childhood accident, because he shoots both a rifle and shotgun right-handed.

In his late 20s Fred Bear moved to Detroit where he worked in a company that subcontracted work from the major car companies. Bear worked up to managing the operations—but a problem soon became apparent. The Great Depression was on and the owner of the company needed cash. Twice he tried to set the place on fire, but each time Fred discovered it in time. The third time, he didn't.

Out of work and with no jobs around, Fred teamed up with a man who had connections that could get them subcontracting work from Chrysler. In 1933 these two men, with a total of $1,200 in tools and cash, opened up shop in a large garage. They did silk-screen work for the car companies on such things as tire covers. But in one corner of the building, Bear started another tiny venture. It couldn't pay its own way, but Fred wanted it. The company was called Bear Archery.

Fred knew how to make bows but he soon realized he would have to create a market for them.

First came the Detroit Archery Club, but Fred noticed another possibility.

"I found that the newspapers would run the scores from archery tournaments we had but it didn't mean anything. However, if you gave them a picture of a deer or a bear that some archer shot, that might make the front page. So I got in the promotion business."

Bear has been promoting archery and bowhunting ever since.

By 1939 both companies had grown and the partners split it up. Bear took the archery company and continued with it in Detroit through World War II. But he wanted to move out of town, so Bear Archery was incorporated with three stock holders. His original partner sold his business and bought stock, a friend put in $20,000, and Bear's holdings, the majority, were the remainder making the total about $100,000. In 1947 they moved the company

to Grayling, Michigan. Calamity was waiting for them there.

The small corporation was short of money. Just at the moment when it needed to do some business and make money, an all-aluminum bow came on the market. For a year, until problems in it began to show up, the aluminum bow captured the market and nearly broke Bear Archery. For two years during the warm months, Fred Bear and his wife lived in a tent along the Manastee River to keep costs down.

Though the fiberglass laminated bow was a revolutionary breakthrough, it still hadn't taken a major share of the small bow market. But by 1950-51, Bear had worked out a way to make uni-directional glass that eliminated the cross threads, so the material could be used on the inside of the bow as well. Fiberglass bows were on their way. Nothing would ever stop them.

In 1960 a mysterious increase in bow breakage occurred, and put the company on the ropes again. Bear was determined to replace every bow that broke and about one out of five did. The reason, which took two years to discover, was in the face of two of the heated presses in which bows were made. The face had warped and would not properly bond the laminations.

Another problem was winters in Grayling. The very dry winter air in northern Michigan caused the wood in the bows to dry out. Bows made in winter and later used in humid climates absorbed moisture in the wood and broke the laminations.

In 1960-61 Bear Archery was in serious trouble. It had lost $180,000 through breakage. The company was making television cabinets for Admiral for extra income, but they still owed the IRS about $15,000,

"The IRS came to Grayling and picked up a state policeman. They were going to lock the place up."

Fred was out in the plant when his financial man came out with the news. "It looks like we've had it. The IRS is here and we haven't any money in the bank. What are we going to do?"

And Bear replied, "Well, I'm just going to keep on working, and you're going back in there and sell them some kind of a bill of goods."

What he did was give the IRS a bad check for $500 and convinced them to take it. When the check returned, the Grayling bank was supposed to warn Fred, but this time they missed. The check was bounced. But Bear had friends who believed in him. He explained the desperate situation to one of them

and ended by saying he needed $500 for 30 days. The man turned to his wife and asked her for his checkbook.

People seemed to want to help Fred Bear. One of his employees, a bachelor, realized things were tough for the company. He took his paychecks, but refused to cash them for six to eight months.

For another 10 years of amazing growth, Bear Archery continued as an independent company. But offers to buy were frequent and attractive. Finally the corporation sold to Victor, and Victor a few years later was taken over by Kidde, the present parent company of Bear Archery. Also, in the late 1970s the company moved to Gainesville, Florida.

Fred Bear is one of the few people alive today who was a personal friend of Art Young—the Young of Pope and Young, the recognized trophy-record keeping organizaton of bowhunting. In fact, Bear's first interest in the sport came from seeing Art Young put on a demonstration of shooting at a Rotary Club in Detroit. Young made his living putting on such shows, although he had gained fame through films on bowhunting in Africa and Alaska. Bear did not know Dr. Saxton Pope, a medical professor at the University of California who teamed up with Young on several hunts. Young was 10 years older than Bear, but he died when he was 45 of a ruptured appendix.

"He was my hero. Anything he said was gospel," Fred remembers. "He was a great, clean-living fellow. Big guy, good looking, no bad habits. I was kind of amazed I could keep up with this guy in roving." (A type of shooting in which archers roam, picking targets and seeing who can come the closest.) Young never shot in tournaments.

"At that time archers had different ways of measuring how good they were. One was to see how many arrows they could keep in the air at a time. Young used a Mongolian release that lends itself to fast shooting because it combines nocking the arrow and pulling the string. He could shoot fast."

However, few people know that Fred Bear about this time was the Michigan State Target Champion.

Fred Bear in his own way became a much greater advocate of bowhunting than either Pope or Young ever dreamed of. For one thing, by the time Bear began to make promotional films of his adventures and to appear on television on "The American Sportsman" and "Arthur Godfrey" shows, bows of quality were readily available to anyone who wanted to try the sport. So there was much more potential to bring people into bowhunting. Bear also made many more films and through television reached millions more people.

Bear's hunting trips to India, Africa, South America, Alaska and the Arctic had as their reason the promotion of bowhunting and Bear Archery.

But Fred loves to hunt, too. At one time, Bear held five Pope and Young trophy records. He still holds two, brown bear and stone sheep.

Although the first big game he bagged with a bow was a deer in northern Michigan in 1935, Fred Bear's favorite animal to hunt is—naturally—bear. Once on a hunt in British Columbia he saw 62 grizzlies in 25 days. Some of his tightest moments have also come on bear hunts.

On a grizzly hunt to make a television film for ABC, he was charged by a sow grizzly that put him up a tree and kept him there from late one afternoon to 8:30 a.m. the next day.

He was charged by polar bears twice. The second charge came instantly after Fred had hit it with an arrow at 30 yards. At 20 yards the guide dropped the bear with a rifle. Fred walked over to it to pull out his arrow. At that moment the bear stood up, and Fred had to kill it with a .44 Magnum handgun. The rifle shot had only creased the bear's head, stunning it.

In Africa, Bear along with his white hunter and natives were pinned in a small brush blind for half a night by a lion that could have jumped in on them at any second.

But sometimes his hunts resulted in amazing twists. When I was hunting with him in Alaska he shot a bull moose at 15 feet. And then there was his Indian tiger.

Perched in the top of a palm tree, Fred was waiting for the beaters to drive the tiger past. This was in a small canyon. Suddenly Bear saw the cat about 90 or 100 yards away. It was pacing back and forth at the base of the rimrock that formed the side of the canyon. It was apparently trying to find a way to go over the side.

"Finally I decided that maybe if I shot an arrow beyond the tiger, he might turn back my way. So I picked my poorest arrow and shot it. I hit the tiger right through the lungs and killed him."

Innovating, designing, promoting, hunting, Fred Bear has led the way. During the interviews for this article, I tried to encourage Fred Bear to describe his role in the development of American bowhunting particularly in relation to Pope and Young. Politely, he dodged the question.

It took a while, but eventually I figured why. Without Fred Bear, there is a chance that the modern fiberglass laminated bow would either not have been invented or would have been invented much later. Without Fred Bear but even with the fiberglass laminated bow, the promotion of bowhunting might never have taken place.

So what does it all boil down to? Well for one thing, without Fred Bear there probably wouldn't have been a Pope and Young Club. Think about it. Bear made the sport that created the organization. I'll bet that Saxton Pope and Art Young would welcome having a name like Fred Bear alongside theirs. Pope, Young and Bear. And at 80 years old, the only one left to enjoy the honor.

Clare Conley

CONSERVATION

THE PROTECTION
OF ALASKAN GAME by Dall DeWeese

The above is a subject that appeals to every "true blue sportsman," every lover of animal life and all those who see beauty in nature, embracing forests, plains and mountains throughout our entire country; and while the woods, plains and mountains are naturally beautiful, we all agree that they are much more grand and life like when the wild animals and birds are present. While there are now several organizations doing good work toward the preservation of wild animal and bird life, there is much yet for us to do; to resolve is to act, so let us be up and at it.

For twenty-seven years of my life, I have taken fall outings in territory embracing the greater part of North America. I have made trips in recent years to various parts of our mountains where I hunted eighteen to twenty years ago, and it is appalling to note how rapidly the wild animals are disappearing. While I am but forty-three years of age, I have seen in this short period the extermination of our buffalo. At the time of my first trip west there were millions of them. The antelope at that time were seen by thousands; they are now reduced to dozens, here and there. There were also elk upon the plains—now there are none. There were bison in our mountains within twenty-five miles of the place in which I am writing. I doubt if there are twenty bison (wild), now in the United States. I have seen thousands of deer in Montana, Wyoming, Idaho, Utah, Mexico and Colorado, where these numbers are now, comparatively, reduced to one, three, five and twenties. The "big horn" mountain sheep (Ovis Montana) that were then found in hundreds, are now reduced in comparative ratio to the rest.

When I was hunting in New Brunswick in 1896 I was told by good authority that these conditions were not quite so bad there, and that the enforcement of their laws was the safeguard there as well as in Maine.

During my four seasons' hunting in Alaska, my observations from past experience, points to the prediction that, without stringent laws and their rigid enforcement, the big game of Alaska is doomed to as rapid an extermination as it was upon the plains and mountains of Colorado. I will narrate one instance: When in the Kenai Mountains, Alaska, on the 23rd day of August, 1897 (from my diary), Mr. Berg and myself, while sitting together on a mountain side, with the aid of a field glass counted five hundred wild white sheep ("Ovis Dalli"), all within a radius of six to eight miles, ten here, six there, then twenty to thirty in another locality. Can a true hunter or a lover of nature imagine a more beautiful sight? Here and there were grand old towering mountains, all snow capped, some furrowed with gaping canyons, some separated with a mighty glacier, others with a gradual slope carpeted with nutritious grasses, upon which these beautiful denizens of the snowy mountains of the North loitered about in groups, either feeding or resting.

I was in these same mountains again in 1898. My wife accompanied me there again in 1899. I wanted her to see what had never before been woman's pleasure.

I was in these same mountains again last season, 1901, and there is no question about the "Ovis Dalli" perceptibly decreasing in numbers. If mineral should be discovered in these mountains, and with no laws to protect these animals, they would be exterminated in a very short time. In 1899, when passing through a section where a so-called sportsman had been hunting, four carcasses were lying on one small hill, nothing having been touched, the heads and horns being too small and the work of skinning and preserving too great to suit his—I was going to say his "sport"-ship—but will make it "devil"-ship.

In 1899 myself, wife and party killed but four sheep—two killed by her. We could have killed a hundred. This season (1901) we killed but one, needing it for meat; also one bull caribou.

The natives are very destructive to sheep. I have seen them, in parties of their own, shoot sheep and if these ran off wounded or fell over a low cliff they never went after them, "too much work—shoot more." In my parties I never allowed a native to carry a gun. The conditions I have mentioned regarding sheep extermination apply also to moose and caribou.

Now then, dear reader, if all I have said about this transformation of game from plenty to almost extinction is so preceptible in one man's short life, we all can see its finish in a very few years unless we act quickly while there is yet time.

Alaska is a new country and a good portion of it is uninhabitable for man; in this respect it is more suitable for game and there is less excuse for its being slaughtered on account of the country not being desirable for the use of "homeseekers." I am sorry to say although it is true, that where the climatic conditions are favorable for the advancement of civilization and the "tiller" of the soil, just so sure is the doom of the game in that land—remote and inaccessible localities and game preserves that extend to winter feeding grounds excepted.

It is not necessary that big game be slaughtered to furnish the "meat-stuff" in Alaska, for where a man can go a pack train can go also; pack trails are soon made possible for wagons, then railroads. Neither is it necessary that game be slaughtered for the native food supply, yet let them kill what they will actually use and if our government would thoroughly instruct the missionaries and priests of Alaska to intercede with the natives on behalf of the game, much good could be done. Teach them the wrong in killing the female and the young of any and all animals. I have talked this over with natives in my camp and noticed it was hard for them to conceive, yet by constant teaching, it will have its effect. I believe that some such laws as I hereafter mention would be effective in Alaska, if enforced.

My twenty-seven years of experience in hunting has convinced me that the market meat hunter is the most destructive to big game. Where mining localities are remote from railroads or steamship transportation "meat stuff" is correspondingly expensive, hence if game abound the meat hunter finds a profitable business and he is always on hand. Make and enforce a law making it a penal offense coupled with a fine of one hundred dollars for each offense, where a party or parties offer for sale or barter the flesh of any game animal or bird at any spot or place in Alaskan Territory. The same law to apply to any and every company or individual attempting to illegally ship or transport game flesh of any kind out of the territory. Make a non-resident license law requiring every sportsman hunting in Alaska to pay fifty dollars for that privilege, and that this sum allows him to take out of the territory only one specimen of each species killed by him, the same law to provide a license fee of $100 which would give the sportsman or hunter taking out that license the right to kill and transport two specimens of each species of animal killed by him, and that he be not allowed to take out more than this quoto. The money thus paid to the district game commissioners, who may be the nearest postmasters where the hunting is done, to be used first for the prosecution of any person or persons violating this law, and any surplus that might accumulate in one year over $800 to go to the native school fund of that district.

Make a law that gives an open season only on game from August 15th to November 1st, with a fine of one hundred dollars for its violation. This law should apply to natives, also, as well as non-residents except where the animal is shot absolutely for immediate food necessity.

Make a law that prohibits sportsmen or other persons from employing natives or other men from killing big game animals or birds, for in so doing most of the meat is wasted and the heads shipped out and sold.

Make a law prohibiting the killing of the big brown bear ("Ursus Middendorffi") on Kodiak Island for a period of five years; this will in no way be an injustice to the natives as this island now contains so few of this animal that hunting them is no longer profitable and neither do the natives depend on this for support.

Negotiations should be commenced with Great Britain to induce them to pass such laws as would coincide with ours for the government of that part of the Yukon Territory in British Columbia that joins Alaska.

I know full well what objections will be made to such laws by fur traders and hide and head hunters; but is it right that the grand old bull moose or bull caribou or the great old ram "Ovis Dalli" be shot down by a native paid for so doing by a so-called "sportsman" and only the head taken from the carcass and that shipped out and sold?

I say, is it right that this should be permitted for the gain of a few individuals at the expense of all the big game of that country, as well as to the lovers of nature and the "true blue sportsman" not yet born, to all of whom we are responsible?

Let us act now and use our influence to have some protective measures properly brought before the coming session of Congress, with an earnest appeal for their enactment.

I have talked several times with the governor of Alaska, Hon. J. G. Brady, regarding this subject, and he urged me to formulate some practical measure and he would give it his support.

Dall DeWeese

THE LACEY ACT

Editorial by J.A. McGuire

We have had so many inquiries during the past couple of years concerning the Lacey law and its provisions that we have decided to publish the whole text this month. We hope that every exponent of bird protection will cut this out and either pin it in their hat or some place else where it will be read and re-read until the provisions of the measure are indelibly stamped in the memory.

This act (of May 25, 1900), which is commonly known as the Lacey act, (1) places the preservation, distribution, introduction and restoration of game and other birds under the Department of Agriculture; (2) regulates the importation of foreign birds and animals, prohibiting absolutely the introduction of certain injurious species; and (3) prohibits interstate traffic in birds or game killed in violation of state laws. The act reads as follows:

An act to enlarge the powers of the Department of Agriculture, prohibit the transportation by interstate commerce of game killed in violation of local laws, and for other purposes.

Be it enacted by the Senate and House of Representatives of the United States of America in Congress assembled, that the duties and powers of the Department of Agriculture are hereby enlarged so as to include the preservation, distribution, introduction and restoration of game birds and other wild birds. The Secretary of Agriculture is hereby authorized to adopt such measures as may be necessary to carry out the purposes of this act and to purchase such game birds and other wild birds as may be required therefor, subject, however, to the laws of the various states and territories. The object and purpose of this act is to aid in the restoration of such birds in those parts of the United States adapted there to, where the same have become scarce or extinct, and also to regulate the introduction of American or foreign birds or animals in localities where they have not heretofore existed.

The Secretary of Agriculture shall from time to time collect and publish useful information as to the propagation, uses, and preservation of such birds.

And the Secretary of Agriculture shall make and publish all needful rules and regulations for carrying out the purposes of this act, and shall expend for said purposes such sums as Congress may appropriate therefor.

Sec. 2. That it shall be unlawful for any person or persons to import into the United States any foreign wild animal or bird except under special permit from the United States Department of Agriculture; provided, that nothing in this section shall restrict the importation of natural history specimens for museums or scientific collections or the importation of certain cage birds, such as domesticated canaries, parrots, or such other species as the Secretary of Agriculture may designate.

The importation of the mongoose, the so-called "flying foxes" or fruit bats, the English sparrow, the starling, or such other birds or animals as the Secretary of Agriculture may from time to time declare injurious to the interest of agriculture or horticulture, is hereby prohibited; and such species, upon arrival at any of the ports of the United States, shall be destroyed or returned at the expense of the owner. The Secretary of the Treasury is hereby authorized to make regulations for carrying into effect the provisions of this section.

Sec. 3. That it shall be unlawful for any person or persons to deliver to any common carrier, or for any common carrier to transport from one state or territory to another state or territory, or from the District of Columbia or Alaska to any state or territory, or from any state or territory to the District of Columbia or Alaska, any foreign animals or birds the importation of which is prohibited, or the dead bodies or parts thereof of any wild animals or birds, where such animals or birds have been killed in violation of the laws of the state, territory or district in which the same were killed; provided, that nothing herein shall prevent the transportation of any dead birds or animals killed during the season when the same may be lawfully captured, and the export of which is not prohibited by law in the state, territory or district in which the same are killed.

Sec. 4. That all packages containing such dead animals, birds or parts thereof, when shipped by interstate commerce, as provided in section 1 of this act, shall be plainly and clearly marked, so that the name and address of the shipper and the nature of the contents may be readily ascertained on inspection of the outside of such packages. For each evasion or violation of this act the shipper shall, upon conviction, pay a fine of not exceeding two hundred dollars; and the consignee knowingly receiving such articles so shipped and transported in violation of this act shall, upon conviction, pay a fine of not exceeding two hundred dollars; and the carrier knowingly carrying or transporting the same shall, upon conviction, pay a fine of not exceeding two hundred dollars.

Sec. 5. That all dead bodies, or parts thereof, of any foreign game animals, or game or song birds, the importation of which is prohibited, or the dead bodies, or parts thereof, of any wild game animals, or game or song birds transported into any state or territory, or remaining therein for use, consumption sale or storage therein shall upon arrival in such state or territory be subject to the operation and effect of the laws of such state or territory enacted in the exercise of its police powers, to the same extent and in the same manner as though such animals and birds had been produced in such state or territory, and shall not be exempt therefrom by reason of being introduced therein in original packages or otherwise. This act shall not prevent the importation, transportation or sale of birds or bird plumage manufactured from the feathers of barnyard fowl.

The object of placing this work in charge of the executive department of the federal government was merely to supplement and not to hamper or replace the work hitherto done by state commissions and organizations; in other words, to co-ordinate and direct individual efforts, and thus insure more uniform and more satisfactory results than could otherwise be obtained. Greater uniformity in state legislation and better enforcement of existing laws can be secured only by the most complete co-operation between the various forces now at work in the cause of bird protection.

The act authorizes but does not provide an appropriation for the purchase and distribution of birds. The Department of Agriculture, therefore, has no quail, pheasants or other game birds for distribution.

The department issues no permits for shipping birds from one state to another. In some states, as in California, the Board of Fish and Game Commissioners, is authorized to issue permits for shipping birds for propagating purposes, and a few states, such as Michigan and New Jersey, make exceptions in their game laws in the case of birds captured for breeding purposes; but when a state forbids the exportation of birds without exception, interstate commerce in birds from that state is in violation of the Lacey act, whether the birds are captured during open seasons or whether they are intended for propagation or not.

The attention of sportsmen, commission merchants, shippers and express agents is especially called to sections 3, 4 and 5, which make it unlawful to ship from one state to another animals or birds which have been killed or captured in violation of local laws. In referring to these sections, the House Committee on Interstate Commerce reported as follows: "The killing or carrying of game within the limits of a state is a matter wholly within the jurisdiction of the state, but when the fruits of the violation of state law are carried beyond the state, the nation alone has the power to forbid the transit and to punish those engaged in the traffic. This bill will give the game wardens the very power that they now lack, and which will be the most effective for the purpose of breaking up this commerce. * * * In some of the states the sale of certain game is forbidden at all seasons without regard to the place where the game was killed. The purpose of these laws is to prevent the sale of game shipped into the state from being used as a cloak for the sale of game killed within the state in violation of local laws." Section 5 of the act is intended to meet this difficulty by subjecting imported animals, birds or game, whether introduced in original packages or otherwise, to the laws of the state in which imported.

J.A. McGuire

THE GENTLE ART
OF CONSERVATION by El Comancho

Within the last years—a very few years, too—some far-sighted men, notably Jas. J. Hill, of the Great Northern Railway, have looked into the future and seen impending calamity in the wastefull, reckless way that America handles her natural resources. Two hundred years ago America was one of the richest, best adapted countries in all the world for the welfare and enjoyment of millions of people, for it had everything ready at hand that humanity needed—all that was necessary was to use them intelligently. Let us ask ourselves for an accounting of our stewardship of these two hundred years—what have we done with our country and its natural resources?

First off, we wiped out the buffalo—millions of them, huge animals that roamed a half-desert that we have not improved much over its natural conditions. We killed off the finest herd of free wild beef that humanity has any knowledge of and we got nothing out of it but hides and a few bags of un-needed fertilizer! The herd is gone, the herd that I saw blacken the prairie for miles and miles, that shook the ground with its tread, that turned miles of dry desert into a beef-producing country, that made the sweetest, juiciest, best beef in all the the world, as I know, for I helped to eat that herd!

The old buffalo range today is semidesert country that the government is spending millions on to try and remake into an agricultural country, to half-sole it, so to speak, and they are succeeding to some extent. It would have been a better thing and a bet-

ter investment if the government had reserved eastern Montana, the Dakotas, Wyoming, western Nebraska and Kansas and eastern Colorado, New Mexico, Arizona and west Texas for a buffalo range and raised the buffalo for beef, each year only killing the increase of the herds as the Indians did before the white men came.

All of the country contains much waste land and the buffalo waxed fat on what is now and always will be more or less useless country—therefore as a business proposition the buffalo herds would have produced more value than the land will under present conditions or those to come—but we thoughtlessly killed off that herd so that now we have to spend money to make the country over into a habitable land.

Then there is the Great North Woods, the vast pineries that covered the country bordering the great lakes—a forest that was supposed to be inexhaustible—that, too, is gone—as utterly wiped out as though it had never existed. The same story covers the woods of Maine, the Pennsylvania Hemlock forests and today is the beginning of the end of the yellow pine forests of the South with the great Pacific Coast forests already going the same way before the saw.

As I write this I can look out of my window and see five forest fires right here on Puget Sound, fires that are eating up acres of valuable timber. That is wicked carelessness, for a tree once burned is gone, uselessly, for all time, and every man should remember that never a tree grew that was not made in the leaf, a slow, slow process that means one hundred or five hundred years to grow one single

Shipment of 1,000 China pheasants from Simpson's Pheasant Farm, Corvallis, Ore., to the state of Idaho, Sept. 13, 1909. Gene M. Simpson, the shipper, is shown in car door at the left; B.T. Livingston, chief deputy game warden of Idaho, at the right, pointing to the word, "Idaho."

tree—and the civilization of today demands thousands of trees every day!

Look at the very soil itself—plowed on side hills and not looked after so that millions of tons of the finest surface soil in America goes into the Mississippi, Missouri and Ohio Rivers and their branches every year to fill the streams, spoil the water and drift south, where it finally blocks the river until it has to be dredged and the surplus goes out to sea where it is slowly filling up the Gulf of Mexico!

Many other resources are going just as fast—just as little heeded, and most of this tremendous waste is due to the carelessness of the American people, who have a fixed habit of taking only the cream and leaving the milk as worthless.

It is about time we planted two trees for every one we cut down. It is time we put in catch basins to hold the flood silt from going into the gulf. It is time we plowed crosswise across the face of a hill rather than have furrows running up and down to wash into gullies when a rain has dug away the soil.

We can't bring back the buffalo, but we can save the terrible waste of natural resources from now on and we can teach our children to waste nothing of the bountiful store of resources that the Creator put here and intended us to use.

It is as important to educate the children in these matters as it is to save the waste ourselves; therefore if you have a son show him and teach him why he should plant two trees when he cuts down one, for

it is a good investment for the world. It means that waste should stop and that saving should be enforced and if this is properly done your son's great grandson will have a wilderness where he may shoot and fish—otherwise he must attend pink teas and lady's day for all his life.

El Comancho

166

BULLETIN- AMERICAN GAME PROTECTIVE ASSOCIATION

"MORE GAME!" Editorial by E.A. Quarles

With this issue there is started a new department of this publication, edited by the American Game Protective Association. While most of our readers doubtless know this organization, a word regarding its history and activities is fitting.

The Association is the sportsmen's national organization, having affiliated with it thirty-eight state sportsmen's associations, with a combined membership in excess of 250,000.

For more than six years now the Association has been conducting a vigorous national campaign for more game. It has coordinated the efforts of the country's sportsmen to that end with an efficiency hitherto unknown. Its first efforts were concerned with the federal law for the protection of migratory birds, the campaign for which it organized largely and led to a successful conclusion. Its activities were next extended to the successful movement for the treaty whereby birds that migrate between this country and Canada are given adequate protection. The setting aside of Mount McKinley Park as a game refuge was another activity in which it joined with other well-known sportsmen's organizations.

Aid has been given most of the states of the Union, in co-operation with state officials, along the following lines:

1. In securing adequate game laws.

2. In effecting efficient enforcement of those laws.

The Association has been particularly active in stimulating game breeding and preserving and has published authoritative books and pamphlets on this subject relating to quail, mallard and wood ducks, pheasants and Virginia deer.

Very recently it secured the establishment of an experimental game farm at Cornell University, Ithaca, New York, by act of Legislature. Game breeding and the conservation of wild life will be taught at Cornell in regular courses.

This constitutes a brief outline of the Association's work. Readers of this magazine will be enabled to follow it in detail from now on thru this department.

Many sportsmen in sympathy with this sort of work wish to aid it but end by doing nothing, because they do not know just how to set about joining the Association. Such as these will no longer be able to plead a valid excuse. A simple, inexpensive plan whereby each may do his bit has been evolved.

E.A. Quarles

A PLEA FOR WILDERNESS
HUNTING GROUNDS by Aldo Leopold

(The United States Forest Service has not formally adopted a policy in respect to wilderness hunting grounds. Consequently this article reflects the writer's personal views rather than the official views of the Forest Service.—Aldo Leopold)

This article is a plea for establishing in each of the Rocky Mountain states at least one area in which there shall be a permanent closed season on roads.

It would, of course, be an absurdity to ask whether we need more and better roads in any state. Obviously we do. But where we need them is another question. We need them almost but not quite everywhere. I believe that every state needs a factory-less park, every community a clubless fishing water, and every summer playground a cottageless camping ground. Factories, fishing clubs, and summer cottages are good things—to those that profit by them—but that is no reason why they should be allowed to exclude other good things incompatible with them.

The practical point is that good roads are being pushed into the western mountains so rapidly that in some states at least there will soon be no place left for the wilderness hunter whose recreation comes from getting out into a wild roadless area. It seems to me just as important (and infinitely less expensive), to provide the wilderness hunter with his roadless playground, as it is to provide the motor tourist with his surfaced highways and free public camps.

As long as there remained a roadless frontier, the wilderness hunter was of course "well heeled." But the roadless frontier is just about gone. The well-to-do sportsman is already going to British Columbia, Alaska, Africa, and Siberia instead of to the Mogollons or Jackson's Hole. But the expense of such trips puts them out of the question for the citizen of moderate means, and he is the man I am talking about. I am trying to make it clear that a wilderness hunting trip is by way of becoming a rich man's privilege, whereas it has always been a poor man's right. Are we prepared to accept the consequences of the change? Do we really realize its possible effect on the nation's character and happiness?

Now, if our remaining frontier consisted of $200 corn land there would not be much except theory to argue about. The point is that it consists mostly of the national forests—rough mountain lands embracing

At every point where roads might enter is set a rugged mountain.

here and there particular areas of such crumpled topography and high altitude as to make the customary development of roads, Fords, and summer boarders of very questionable practicability. One would think that the ordinary laws of economics would automatically tend to exclude roads from such areas. But mark this well: the laws of economics are the last thing the roads booster is thinking about. Roads are going to continue to be built into such areas, unless the public at large thinks it is best not to, and unless the public says what it thinks.

To illustrate: ten years ago there were six big areas of exclusively "pack" country in the two states of Arizona and New Mexico. Let us see what has happened.

First, there was the White Mountain and Blue Range country of Arizona, the cream of the Southwest. The Forest Service, in co-operation with the local counties, is about to complete the Clifton-Springerville road right thru the heart of this magnificent region. Stub roads to develop the various recreational facilities will undoubtedly follow. There is a good deal of logic in "sacrificing" this area, since the big copper-mining centers in the hot valleys to the southward need the timber and the opportunity to escape from the summer heat for week-ends in the cool mountains.

Second, there was the Jemez division of the Santa Fe National Forest of northern New Mexico —a splendid wilderness but with too much valuable timber and range and of too smooth topography to justify exclusion of roads. A railroad is now tapping the timber, and the Forest Service—wisely I think —is building the trans-Jemez road which will open it to motor recreationists.

Third, there was the Pecos division of the same National Forest. Its foothills contain many Spanish-American villages which make very intensive use of the higher mountains for grazing. It would have been impracticable to avoid the road which the Forest Service has recently built up the Pecos River. Moreover, the surrounding cities needed summer home facilities on the Pecos, and the only way to provide them was to build a road up the Pecos River.

Fourth, there was the Tonto Basin of Arizona, famous in cowboy song and story. Into the crumpled hills of the Tonto are set many little green valleys, which filled up with settlers away back in covered-wagon days. Obviously these existing settlements could not be kept locked up by lack of roads, which the several counties and the Forest Service are trying to build as rapidly and as well as the crumpled hills will let them.

Fifth, there was and is—the Kaibab. Obviously the Kaibab contains two predominant values, the scenery of the north rim of the Grand Canyon and

Wherever a foaming trout stream has cut its way thru the mountain wall, a jagged box canyon says, "They shall not pass."

the Kaibab deer herd. It so happens that both need at least a limited amount of roads. In the case of the scenic values of the canyon, the reason is plain. In the case of the deer herd, the reason is this: the Kaibab is a country of limited water-holes. Apparently it will require somewhere around 2,000 hunters each year to utilize the natural increase of the deer (would this were true elsewhere!). To camp 2,000 hunters on a couple of dozen water-holes would entirely destroy the recreational value of the hunting. These hunters will have to camp dry; dry camps are practicable on such a scale only with motors; and motor camps mean at least some roads. Hence the Kaibab is not adapted by nature to be a roadless hunting ground.

Sixth, there was—and is—the head of the Gila, in the Gila National Forest. The Creator must have foreseen the present plight of the wilderness hunter, for in this precious remnant of the old frontier he piled up the hills "high, wide, and handsome." At every point where roads might enter is set a rugged mountain. Wherever a foaming trout-stream has cut its way thru the mountain wall a jagged box canyon says, "They shall not pass." Agricultural valleys are few, and these the merest shoe-strings, from which prescient floods have torn out the little fields as if to say, "This is the last stand—these hills are meant to play in, not to live in." There are three or four frontier cow-ranches tucked away in the Gila hills— but somehow they decorate the wilderness rather than detract from it. The dedication of the Gila headwaters as a wilderness hunting ground need in no wise interfere with the continuance of their grazing privileges.

To sum up: our six big wilderness areas of a decade ago have been, for good and sufficient reasons, reduced to one. Are those reasons good and sufficient to "develop" that one also? I say no reason is good enough to justify opening up the Gila. I say that to open up the Gila wilderness is not development, but blindness. The very fact that it is the last wilderness is in itself proof that its highest use is to remain so.

What I am trying to make clear is that if in a city we had six vacant lots available to the youngsters of a certain neighborhood for playing ball, it might be "development" to build houses on the first, and the second, and the third, and the fourth, and even the fifth, but when we build houses on the last

Who shall say that the diamond hitch and the tumpline are not worth conserving?

one, we forget what houses are for. The sixth house would not be development at all, but rather it would be mere short-sighted stupidity. "Development" is like Shakespeare's virtue, "which grown into a pleurisy, dies of its own too-much."

In objection to the dedication of the Gila as a permanent wilderness hunting ground, it has been truly said that a part of the area which would be "locked up" bears valuable stands of timber. I admit that this is true. Likewise might our sixth lot be a corner lot, and hence very valuable for a grocery store or a filling station. I still insist *it is the last lot* for a needed playground, and this being the case, I am not interested in grocery stores or filling stations, of which we have a fair to middling supply elsewhere.

It has been likewise objected that to keep roads out of the Gila would cripple the fire control system. The Gila fire fighting organization was put to a pretty severe test in the big fires of 1922, and the result would seem to indicate that the present system of Forest Service trails, telephone lines, and lookout towers will handle the fire situation, even in a bad year. In fact, to build roads into this kind of country might introduce quite as much new fire risk as they would help combat.

Now, the question is this: Why should not the Gila area, and other similar areas, if possible one in each western state, be declared permanently roadless, and dedicated to that particular form of public recreation beloved by the wilderness hunter? The necessary authority would seem already to exist, the Forest Service now having discretionary power to determine what constitutes the highest use of each resource in the National Forest, and if any area has its highest use in wilderness hunting, the Service should dedicate it to that purpose, just as it dedicates particular areas for millsites, summer-home sites, and public camping grounds. It certainly would require no additional appropriations; the wilderness is the one thing on earth which was furnished us complete and perfect.

The one thing required is a sufficient expression of public sentiment to assure the Forest Service that the thinking citizens of the country would back up such a policy when subjected to the acid test. The acid test would surely come, even on an area of as low economic value as the Gila. Some day somebody will promote a railroad into the Gila timber, and the tangible benefits of exploiting it will have to be weighed against the intangible benefits of keeping it. For unnumbered centuries of human history the wilderness has given way. The priority of industry has become dogma. Are we as yet sufficiently enlightened to realize that we must now challenge that dogma, or do without our wilderness? Do we realize that industry, which has been our good servant,

Roads are being pushed into the western mountains so rapidly that in some states at least there will soon be no place left for the wilderness hunter.

might make a poor master? Let no man expect that one lone government bureau is able—even tho it be willing—to thrash out this question alone.

It so happens that an agency suitable for expressing public opinion on such questions has now been established; namely, the President Commission on Outdoor Recreation. If the public wants wilderness areas established in the rougher, less valuable parts of the national forests, the commission is the agency thru which to express the want.

It should require no explanation that this proposal of wilderness areas is not, primarily, a game conservation measure. Certainly 99 per cent, figuratively speaking, of our country should and must have roads. We must learn to raise game and build roads on the same ground, or go gameless. It so happens, however, that the establishment of wilderness areas would provide an opportunity to produce and hunt certain kinds of game, such as elk, sheep, and bears, which do not always "mix well" with settlement, but the majority of game species can and must be produced on all the grounds suitable for them.

Wilderness areas are primarily a proposal to conserve at least a sample of a certain kind of recreational environment, of which game and hunting is an essential part but nevertheless only a part. Who shall say that the diamond hitch and the tumpline are not as much worth conserving as the black-tail buck or the moose? Who shall say that the opportunity to disappear into the trackless wild is not as valuable as the opportunity to hang up a trophy? Who shall say that we have not room enough in this huge country to earn a living without destroying the opportunity to enjoy it after it is earned, each after his own taste?

Some centuries ago that conqueror of the wilderness, Sir Humphrey Gilbert, naively remarked: "The countries lying North of Florida God hath reserved to be reduced into Christian civility by the English Nation." But even old Sir Humphrey might turn uneasily in his grave if he could know at what rate they have been "reduced," and with what profligate waste of their beauty and their resources. The question now is not whether they will be "reduced," but what constitutes that "Christian civility" for which "God hath reserved" them. There are some of us who challenge the prevalent assumption that Christian civility is to be measured wholly by the roar of industry, and the assumption that the destruction of the wild places is the objective of civilization, rather than merely a means providing it with a livelihood. Our remnants of wilderness will yield bigger values to the nation's character and health than they will to its pocketbook, and to destroy them will be to admit that the latter are the only values that interest us.

Aldo Leopold

FEDERAL AID

FOR WILDLIFE

Editorial by Raymond J. Brown

State conservation officials are now engaged in studying closely the federal Wildlife Restoration Act, recently enacted, to determine how their states can benefit to the fullest under the provisions of the act. The new law provides that nearly $3,000,000 annually be granted to the states to carry on conservation work. It becomes effective July 1 next year.

The act has been endorsed by the country's important conservation groups, as well as by women's clubs, garden clubs, and other organizations and individuals interested in restoring wildlife.

At the moment, no information is available as to the number of states eligible to receive federal aid. Only those states will be eligible, the act says, that shall have passed laws "for the conservation of wildlife which meet the minimum requirements of the Secretary of Agriculture, which requirements shall include a prohibition against the diversion of license fees paid by hunters for any other purpose than the administration of said state fish and game departments." Such is the wording of the act.

Funds allocated by the federal government to the state are to be used for the selection, acquisition, rehabilitation, and improvement of land and water adaptable as feeding, resting, or breeding places for wildlife. Land may be leased if necessary. No federal funds are to be used to maintain these restoration projects, which work is to be carried out by the states themselves. All proposals for refuges or other conservation work must be submitted to the Secretary of Agriculture for approval. Before federal funds are allocated, the state applying for them must be prepared to contribute 25 percent of the total cost of the proposed work.

The funds to be allocated by the federal government will be appropriated by Congress to an amount equal to the taxes derived from the levy on firearms, shells, and cartridges, imposed by the Revenue Act of 1932. Previously, the taxes collected went into general treasury funds, and were appropriated along with other funds for general purposes. About $240,000 will be deducted for administering the act.

Allocation of the funds will be made, first, according to the area of the states, and, second, according to the number of hunting licenses issued, half of the available money being ear-marked for each class of distribution. On the basis of area alone, many thinly populated states would get a lion's share of the funds, although they might have few hunters to pay the tax or to hunt the game to be restored. If hunting licenses alone were the basis of the distribution, the thickly populated states would get the bulk of the money, despite the fact that their land, suitable for restoration projects, might be comparatively limited. Even under the act, some of the larger states would share too largely in the federal funds as would some populous ones, so a minimum of $15,000 is set upon allotments, and a maximum of $150,000.

According to figures compiled by the Wildlife Institute, one of the most ardent supporters of the act, only two states—New York and Pennsylvania—could qualify for the maximum amount. Three states—Connecticut, Delaware, and Rhode Island—would receive the minimum of $15,000, although on the basis of hunting licenses and area they would receive far less.

Some states, observers have pointed out, may find it inadvisable to qualify for their full share of federal funds. Arizona, for example, issues only slightly more than 20,000 hunting licenses a year, yet, because of its great area, would be entitled, if it qualified otherwise, to $56,710.95. To obtain this, however, it would have to set aside $18,903.65 of the State hunting-license income for new conservation projects, an amount equal to about 90 cents a hunter, and one that would leave little for normal State conservation activities and game-law enforcement. The money needed to qualify for the full amount of federal funds would, in such a case, have to be raised by taxing hunters more or by appropriations from the general State funds.

Pennsylvania, on the other hand, would find it easy to qualify for the maximum of $150,000. The State in 1935 led the country by issuing 606,107 hunting licenses. Since it would have to put up only $53,813.23 to get the full $150,000 from the federal government, it would have to set aside only about nine cents a hunter.

Any funds remaining unexpended at the end of each year, through failure of any state to qualify for its full share, are, the act provides, to be expended by the Secretary of Agriculture to carry out the provisions of the Migratory Bird Conservation Act.

Under the act, the Secretary of Agriculture has until November 2 to notify each state fish and game department of the sum he has apportioned each state for the fiscal year ending June 30, 1938. Within the next two months, or before January 2, 1938, states must notify the Secretary of intention to avail themselves of the benefits of the act if they expect to share in the appropriations.

Raymond J. Brown

THE CANADA GOOSE

CAN BE BROUGHT BACK

by Ben East

The Canada goose—ace of North American waterfowl, but now in lamentably short supply—can be brought back to abundance by artificial management!

This has been proved beyond question by an experiment carried on in the last thirteen years at the Seney Migratory Wildfowl Refuge, operated by the U.S. Fish and Wildlife Service near Germfask, in the upper peninsula of Michigan.

The Seney project has been so successful in a country where wild geese were never before produced in substantial numbers—that farmers in the neighborhood actually filed depredation complaints a year ago because of crop damage by big flocks of refuge-hatched geese.

What has been done at Seney can be duplicated any place in the northern United States or Canada where suitable habitat is available. That is big news, since it comes at a time when the Canada-goose population has shrunk alarmingly. This shortage has been reflected in reduced bag limits, brief or even closed seasons, and other restrictions. Wildfowl experts have been saying that the dwindling Canadas face a precarious future.

Thus it is highly encouraging to know that burned-out goose marshes can be put back to work, that a native population of Canadas can be established almost at will, and that new flights can be built up in areas that never before have produced geese.

The formula, as it was worked out in the Seney Refuge experiment, is not complicated. And a goose-restoration project is close to ideal for sportsmen's clubs, other conservation groups, game farms, state game departments, and prison and country farms. It's a natural, in fact, for just about anybody interested in tackling a practical problem in game managment and wanting to help provide better waterfowl hunting.

The Seney story had its beginning in 1934, when the refuge was established by the United States Bureau of Biological Survey, which later became the Fish and Wildlife Service. That year the survey began buying up 96,000 acres of dry marsh some thirty miles inland from Lake Superior. It aimed to produce ducks in the area; geese, as we shall see, were added starters.

The country had been logged and burned, drainage ditches had been cut through it, and a land boom had run its course. The drained land had failed to produce crops, beavers had taken over the neglected ditches, and the whole area lay abandoned and

First step at Seney was the erection of sand dikes to put 12,000 acres of dried-out and burned-over marsh under water.

idle. It was the old story of misuse and abuse, ax and fires and exploitation, and it would have been hard to find more hopeless-looking marshes.

It Looked Anything But Hopeful. They weren't even promising for waterfowl. For many years, at least, there had been too little water and too little food to attract or hold ducks, either migrant or local. There was no flight through the Seney country, or if there was it went through without stopping. Some duck experts said the refuge would never be worth a dime as a waterfowl factory. And there were local "sportsmen" who violently opposed it, simply because the dry marshes afforded prairie-chicken shooting, and they were more interested in harvesting today's chickens than in producing tomorrow's ducks.

But executives in the Biological Survey were convinced that the Seney marshes could be made to yield ducks in numbers. The Michigan Department of Conservation and the sportsmen of the state backed them.

And so Uncle Sam's waterfowl custodians acquired the 96,000 acres of dry marshland. The following spring, CCC crews started throwing up sand dikes that would create duck ponds with the waters of a number of rivers flowing through the tract. When the job was done, 12,000 acres of the Seney lay under water, affording more and better waterfowl habitat than that part of the country had ever seen before. The refuge has paid good, sound dividends in duck production, and is getting better year by year, but that is not part of this story.

The year that work was started on the pond system the geese entered the picture. On a farm in southern Michigan, fifty miles west of Detroit, a sportsman and conservationist named Henry Wallace (not the 1948 Presidential candidate) had built up a flock of 300 pinioned Canadas as part of his hobby of breeding upland game birds and water-fowl. In 1935 he offered them to the Seney Refuge authorities as an outright gift.

The geese arrived in two trucks in January, 1936, on a bitter, windy day when the temp was 22 below zero. The Canadas had made the 300-mile trip without mishap, in crates protected from the weather by straw and burlap. They were turned into a small enclosure that had been prepared for them. And the Seney duck refuge—so far, without ducks—had a flock of 300 wild geese.

The goose experiment was born then and there. Here was a golden opportunity to learn the answers to several questions the waterfowl experts had been wondering about.

The region around the refuge was goose country, with big tracts of uncultivated land and plenty of lakes, streams, marshes, and swamps for nesting places. But it had no geese. A few scattered pairs of Canadas had once nested there, but they were long gone.

Could a resident population be built up by holding a captive breeding flock as an anchor and leaving their offspring full-winged, free to migrate as they pleased? Would the young geese go south in autumn and come back in spring to their native marshes to nest and rear young of their own? Could this region, formerly as gooseless as the Mojave Desert, be made to send Canadas down the flyway by the thousands each fall? Could a whole new flight be manufactured in this newly established waterfowl factory?

If that could be done, the way would be open for increasing the annual goose crop in many other places, and the rather dim future of one of America's greatest wildfowl would look far more rosy. Certainly the experiment was worth trying.

Many a disappointment, many a setback, lay in the years ahead. When the geese arrived, management of the refuge was in the hands of C. S. Johnson

These Birds on the Seney (Mich.) Migratory Wildfowl Refuge prove honkers can be induced to nest in any suitable area.

(who died in a plane crash last summer at the Lower Souris Refuge, North Dakota). The project was his baby from the start.

First Years Were the Hardest. And for a long while it was a touch-and-go affair. When Johnson talked to me about the early years of the experiment he recalled the bitter winters, when it was a daily chore to chop water holes through the ice for 300 geese, and the winter nights when lanterns were hung on trees to keep coyotes and foxes away, and the time when the birds ate themselves out of house and home in midsummer and had to be moved hurriedly to a bigger enclosure, built with four miles of snow fence borrowed from the Michigan Highway Department.

Then there was the night when plow crews battled a marsh fire from dusk to dawn to save the geese. Once, spring floods carried out a section of the pen fence, and eighty precious birds went floating down the Manistique River, traveling with the current. And because they were pinioned geese, there was no way that they could get back.

Production of young birds was discouragingly slow in the beginning. With the first nesting season at hand, twenty-two of the geese escaped through a small hole in the fence. Five pairs of them scattered over the refuge, nested, and succeeded in hatching nineteen goslings. The flock in the pen failed to hatch any, and so the nineteen represented the first year's total crop. Not exactly a rousing start.

The hatch was better the second year, and still better the third. In the spring of 1940, a 400-acre permanent goose pen went into operation, and production spurted. By 1942 the geese were hatching some 200 young annually.

But in spite of successful nesting, the goose project still faced a major crisis. Following the original plan, almost all of the young birds had been left full-winged, able to come and go as they wished.

Each year the original pinioned flock dwindled smaller and smaller, as the geese died of old age and other causes. With family ties broken, more and more of the full-winged geese were going south each fall. One vital link was still missing to complete the chain and make the project a success. Few of the geese that departed in autumn returned the following spring.

By 1945, the pinioned anchor flock had dropped to forty-odd, and the experiment reached a critical stage. The refuge harbored some 900 geese, most of them flyers capable of migration. And in November of that year all but 200 of this group left for the south.

Would they come back? Up to that time, the return in spring had never been more than a trickle. But now there had been a mass exodus. Would there be a mass home-coming? If not, the goose experiment was doomed. The pinioned birds were dying

range. Just as the beaver, opossum, porcupine, and black bear have moved into areas from which they had long been absent or in which they had never occurred before, so the coyote has been gradually infiltrating the Northeastern United States over the past 50 years.

Coyotes made their first known appearance in this general area in New York State in 1912. Having expanded their range eastward from Ontario along the Canadian border, they then crossed the ice-bound St. Lawrence River. This was Canis latrans thamnos, largest of the species, which ranged eastward from Minnesota and western Ontario and is now known as the Northeastern coyote. It is about the size of, and somewhat resembles, a German shepherd dog.

It was not until 1925 that the first of these animals was shot in New York by a hunter at the town of Belmont Center in Franklin County, about 14 miles south of the Quebec border. Who was this hunter? What were the circumstances under which he shot the coyote? No one seems to recall, although there must have been quite a to-do in the town when he came home lugging this strange trophy.

Little more was heard from New York's coyotes until the 1930's when another specimen was shot at Belmont Center, this time by a game protector. By the 30's coyotes had also been reported some 200 miles south around the Luther Forest Preserve below Saratoga and at Vischer Ferry on the Mohawk River. Here we can begin to name names. The first coyote shot in this area was bagged by a Jack Hallren of Wayville, and it was taken to the Saratoga County Court House where the late Fred Streever, outdoor writer and hound man, was called in to help identify it.

Later Streever recalled, "It needed only the briefest examination to show that this was no dog, nor fox, but in all surface appearances had the same general appearance of coyotes which I had shot during big-game hunts in the West and Mexico."

During the next several years, Streever and his companions killed over a dozen coyotes ahead of hounds in the Saratoga region and, later, over a dozen more in the Stony Creek area in Warren County. Meanwhile, reports came in with increasing frequency of coyotes in widely separated parts of the state—from the Adirondacks and the Catskills, from Jefferson, Clinton, and St. Lawrence counties. These crafty and prolific immigrants from farther West flourished in their new homes. It is also said that these early settlers were given an assist by coyotes brought in as pets from the West, and later set free or allowed to escape. More and more hunters began to see coyotes and more and more coyotes were shot.

From the first, there was confusion. For a time, some wildlife authorites stubbornly insisted that these animals were not coyotes but wild dogs. Some hunters

Mating of coyote and dog produces coydog. Vermonter Robert Vaughn shot this one.

as stubbornly maintained they were timber wolves. Eventually, the weight of proof became so overwhelming that both game men and most hunters agreed that coyotes had become a definite part of the New York outdoor scene. But even today some confusion still exists.

One reason for this may be the variations in color phases from gray to brown and from dark to light which exist between individuals of different areas. In a restaurant near Northville, I even saw a mounted cream-colored coyote which had been shot in the vicinity a few years ago.

"A fellow over in Broadalbin got this one's mate," the counter man told me, "and he's as dark as she is light."

Another factor is the size of these animals, which are considerably larger than their Western cousins. They were always the largest of the 19 species and subspecies of Canis latrans, and they have grown even larger here in the Northeast on an abundant diet of snowshoe hares and deer. Out West, coyotes average from 25 to 30 pounds but Eastern specimens weighing up to 50 pounds or more are not uncommon.

Still another source of confusion is terminology. In the West, coyotes are often called prairie wolves and in the Midwest brush wolves. This latter name has caught on to some extent in the East, and to many hunters a wolf is a wolf is a wolf.

By the late 1940's, coyotes had become well established in New York and had spread throughout the northern half of the state from the Hudson River to Lake Ontario. Biologists and game-management personnel now had ample opportunity to study this new resident and to learn much about his adaptation to Eastern ways.

The coniferous northern forests, and the wooded stream valleys and sub-marginal farmlands of fringe areas, have all proved to be ideal habitat for these former dwellers of the plains. Their diet consists of all kinds of fish, flesh, and fowl—dead or alive—as well as fruits in season. The chief food is rabbits—which coyotes can catch easily. They also eat a few deer and birds, and occasionally a pig, turkey, lamb, or chicken.

Coyotes can and do kill deer, especially in winter when they can run their victims down in the snow and hamstring them just as wolves do. But many of the deer they eat are dead or starving, or crippled by hunters and would have died anyway. Sometimes coyotes hunt alone or in pairs, sometimes in small packs.

Through the years, coyotes have learned to live with man and have increased in numbers. Actually, it was civilization which paved the way for the expansion of coyote range. Loggers and farmers, opening up the country, created the sort of habitat these one-time plains animals like best, and the extermination of their chief enemy, the timber wolf, from portions of its range set the stage for their spread into the Northeast.

Coyotes are full of guile but are not as crafty as the wolf, according to veteran trappers. They are, however, adept in avoiding snares and steel traps and one state trapper, Ed Maunton, figured that it took about 30 man-hours of hard work to trap one coyote.

"They cover a lot of territory in their hunting," Maunton declared, "and it may be days or even a week before they return to a certain area. You've got to wait 'em out, and even then you won't get 'em all. The ones you don't catch smarten up fast."

Trapping is probably the best way to control coyotes, although it is a losing battle. A good example of this is the average of 20 coyotes a month trapped for some years within the city limits of Los Angeles without noticeably reducing the population.

Coyotes mate in February and their five to seven pups are born in April in a den excavated by the parents or in an abandoned fox burrow. The male helps feed the young when they are weaned at about six weeks. The family stays together until fall when the young pups leave home. Their chief enemies during this growing-up period are eagles and horned owls. Grown coyotes will not attack man but they will fight viciously if disturbed by other animals, and there are records of their slugging it out on equal terms with the Canada lynx and the bobcat.

That coyotes are not very destructive to deer herds is proved by the fact that there are many more deer today in the Adirondacks than there were before the brush wolves appeared upon the scene. But even before coyotes gained a foothold in New York, sportsmen demanded that a bounty be placed upon them—in spite of the fact that the bounty system has never been successful in controlling any animal anywhere in the country. Many states have placed bounties on coyotes since Missouri initiated the program in 1825. Millions of dollars have been paid out, but there are probably more coyotes today than ever before. From 1936 to 1946, for example, Michigan paid over $300,000 in bounties on 23,000 coyotes, only to find that these animals had increased one and a half times during this period. But bounties seem to be the first idea which comes to laymen's minds, and sometimes for criminal reasons, as we shall see.

In any event, a bounty of $100 was set in New York. In the late 1920's the bounty was raised to $300, with the result that three coyotes killed in Orleans County brought their captors the tidy sum of $900. These animals were sent to the late Professor A. A. Allen at Cornell University.

As soon as news of this profitable venture spread, large numbers of persons, including a detachment of State Police, took up coyote hunting practically as a business. Because Dr. Allen feared that unscrupulous bounty hunters might import coyotes into the state, he sponsored a bill making it unlawful to own or import destructive wild animals without a permit. This bill was introduced into the legislature, passed, and signed into law by Gov. Alfred E. Smith just a month after the three Orleans coyotes arrived in Professor Allen's laboratory.

The good professor had reason for being suspicious. In a Midwestern state, a small but steady income accrued to one enterprising individual who for several years staked out his shepherd bitch in coyote country and then brought the resulting pups in for a bounty of $25 a head. A Far Western state learned that it had paid bounties on hundreds of coyotes killed in a neighboring state where the bounty was lower. Other similar cases of fraud are numerous.

As time went by, bounties in New York were lowered and eventually discarded over much of the state, but even today several counties continue to pay bounties averaging $25. Biologists, as a group, oppose bounties, but the system persists.

Poisoning as a control measure has proved even less successful than trapping, and much more dangerous. Strychnine was the agent originally employed, and it resulted in the death of valuable wildlife. Today its place has been taken by 1080, a far deadlier poison. Indiscriminate use of it has destroyed deer, birds, dogs, sheep, and cattle—but not many coyotes, which early learned to avoid it.

Meanwhile, despite hunting, trapping, and poison, coyotes continued to flourish in New York and gradually began to spread into neighboring states. The first specimen seen in Vermont was shot in the mid-1940's at Orleans. During the 1950's they increased considerably but now, according to Commissioner George W. Davis, the coyote population appears to have become stabilized.

"We don't feel that coyotes pose any threat to our deer herd," he states. "Sure, they take an occasional fawn or snowbound deer, but they'd much rather kill rabbits."

There is no bounty on coyotes in Vermont.

A coyote was shot at Holden, New Hampshire, some years ago but they are still not plentiful in the state. In 1937 a coyote was trapped near Edinburg in Penobscot County, Maine, and since then several others have been killed in various parts of the Pine Tree State, the latest in a place known as Lower Enchanted Township in Somerset County. A coyote was shot in Massachusetts in 1957 and another in Connecticut in 1958. Recently there have been other sightings in both states.

In 1958, Laurence Pringle, a graduate student at the University of Massachusetts, carried on a special predator study during which he trapped three female coyotes on the Quabbin Reservation. He reported that there were two others that he did not catch, and that there were several sightings of coyotes on the reservation during the spring and summer of 1959. A 31-pound female was shot near Grafton that year and another coyote was shot at Leyden in 1961.

The brush wolves made their first appearance in Pennsylvania in the early 1960's, and several are said to have been shot by deer hunters in the northern part of the state in recent years. From the fore-going it can be seen that coyotes have definitely established themselves in New York and Vermont and are gradually extending their range throughout New England and other parts of the Northeast. In some localities they are common enough to have become old hat; in others they are still rare enough to cause confusion and inspire letters to the editor.

In some cases, mystery beasts are coydogs, a cross between coyotes and dogs. These two animals are not naturally compatible, and the brush wolves will frequently kill domestic dogs, except females in heat. At one time there was scientific disagreement on whether or not coyotes and dogs could breed, but it has now been proved that they can and do. The various mixtures of coyote and dog resulting from these matings further confuse the identification process.

Henry S. Carson, Maine game biologist, says, "Even with the best of reference materials, it is not possible to make positive identifications in all cases. A simple technique that will work 100 percent of the time has yet to be devised."

In 1960 an event occurred which may well have significant results in this search for better techniques. In that year a group of hunters tracking down deer-killing predators in Corbin Park near Newport, New Hampshire, came upon fresh gravel scattered upon the snow at the entrance to an old fox den. The hunters heard whimpering cries and dug into the den, where they found five recently born puppies. This litter was turned over to the State Fish and Game Department, which still has three of the animals. The mother, incidentally, was never caught and apparently left the area.

Studies of these specimens have been conducted via funds supplied by Harvard University, the National Academy of Science, and Sigma XI. In 1963 the National Science Foundation approved a $38,000 grant to Miss Barbara Lawrence, Curator of Mammals,

Museum of Comparative Zoology at Harvard University, to continue these studies for three more years. Miss Lawrence will make chromosome comparisons of bone marrow from the specimens with dogs, wolves, coyotes, and coydogs. Her results will be checked against those of Dr. Murray L. Johnson, Puget Sound University, Washington, who—under a separate grant—is working on species identification through variations in blood proteins.

At the same time, Walter and Helenette Silver, New Hampshire Fish and Game Department biologists, will continue to conduct growth and behavior studies and breeding experiments with these animals. To date they have raised three litters from the original stock—two from a brother-sister mating, and one from a cross with a wild female dog. Neither Miss Lawrence nor the Silvers have published any findings as yet, but these studies should advance identification techniques.

Meanwhile an interesting pattern has already emerged which shows a definite relationship between coyote populations and the incidence of coydogs. This pattern has been seen in New York and Vermont and is emerging in other New England states.

A study made by Greenleaf Chase and Earl Westervelt, of the New York Conservation Department, shows that in the Adirondack region, where coyotes are most abundant, practically all wild canids trapped or shot are either wild dogs or full-blooded coyotes. Very few coydogs are found. This was not true in

the 1940's, when coyotes were establishing themselves. Then coydogs were present in greater numbers.

The same situation holds true in Vermont. According to state biologist Roger Seamans, during the 1950's both coyotes and coydogs were killed in the northern section of the state. But today coyotes dominate in remote areas where they are most plentiful. This pattern is also developing in Maine and New Hampshire.

To Seamans and several other authorities, this pattern indicates that coyotes infiltrating a new area will settle for dogs as mates as long as there are not enough coyotes of the opposite sex. When a sufficient number of coyotes is present to provide mates, they prefer to breed with their own kind. When coyotes mate with dogs, incidentally, they are likely to select those breeds which most nearly resemble themselves—shepherds and mongrels with shepherd blood.

One thing these mystery beasts almost surely are not is timber wolves, despite a great deal of popular fancy to the contrary. Dr. William J. Hamilton, Emeritus Professor of Zoology at Cornell University, states flatly, "There are no timber wolves in the Northeast."

There are several reasons for the persistence of the wolf myth. One, as I have pointed out, stems from nomenclature—prairie wolf and brush wolf as alternative names for the coyote. In fact, in Mexican Indian language coyote means "little yellow wolf." Another reason, also mentioned, is the undeniably wolfish appearance of large coyotes, coydogs, and wild dogs. And, finally, part of the persistence of the myth is wishful thinking.

From earliest times, wolves have been surrounded by an aura of romantic legend. We are a pioneering people, and while wolves remain, the frontier is not dead. Illusion dies hard, and it is somehow reassuring to populate our wilderness areas with elemental things like wolves as an antidote to our atomic civilization. And so the hopeful rumor of wolves in our forests persists. Some hunters will even hint darkly that state conservation department officials are fully aware that wolf packs are aprowl in local woodlands, but that they are keeping the information to themselves to prevent unfavorable publicity. Parents wouldn't allow children to attend summer camps, vacationists would shun the area, and the recreation business would go to pot.

Others demand defiantly, "If there are coyotes in the Northeastern United States, why not wolves?"

The answer is that for the past 50 years or so our Northeastern terrain has been entirely unsuitable to support these animals. It is a simple matter of ecology, the relation of a species to its environment. A century ago the great pine forests of Maine and New York were being cut down by the westward-moving loggers, and when they disappeared the

This tame timber wolf shows relative size of species.

wolves disappeared with them. Not all at once, but gradually. They had already been driven from Massachusetts, New Hampshire, and Vermont by encroaching civilization. Unlike the coyote, wolves have been unable to adapt themselves to life with man.

While the country remains primitive, inhabited by only a few settlers, wolves can survive by depredations upon sheep and cattle. But as soon as land is cleared and towns spring up, wolves are forced to leave. They have always thrived best where food was superabundant—near the great caribou herds of the North, the vast bison concentrations of the plains, and the cattle ranges of the West. Everywhere today these natural food supplies are decreasing and everywhere wolves are becoming scarcer. There are no wolf packs left in southern Quebec and southern Ontario to expand into New York and New England as the coyote has done. Instead, their Canadian range has been constricted to ever-shrinking areas of the far north where remnants of the once numerous packs are struggling for survival.

Wolves are much larger animals than coyotes. A king-size coyote might weigh up to 60 pounds, but wolves average from 75 to 110 pounds. However, it is true that coydogs and some dogs may tip the beam at 90 pounds or more, so size is not always a significant factor in distinguishing wolves from their wild cousins. Neither is color. Wolves vary from black through gray to brownish white, but so do coydogs, dogs, and, to a lesser extent, coyotes. These factors also confuse the issue and lead to the false label wolf being pinned on other wild canids. The important point, however, is the fact that wolves cannot and do not live in the Northeastern United States. Only trained biologists can make accurate identifications of the dogs, coyotes, and hybrids which do inhabit this area, and sometimes even they are wrong.

To sum up, coyotes in considerable numbers are present in the Northeast and are continuing to expand their range. However, in time their populations become stablized in each new area. They pose no serious threat to the region's deer herds and may even be beneficial in helping to maintain nature's balance. Where there are coyotes there will be coydogs, especially in fringe areas, but their numbers will never be great and their effect upon deer populations will also be negligible. Most numerous and most dangerous of all are wild dogs, which continue to take a sickening toll of deer annually.

These are the mystery beasts of the Northeast. The only wolves in this region are the ones who walk on two legs.

Ted Janes

CLASSICS

A LOST SOUL by Dan De Foe

The Marie du Chien Valley is one of the most fruitful and enchanting in the southwest part of Missouri, and Jethro Cushman owned one of the most fruitful and enchanting plantations to be found within its limits. Brother Cushman was a Presbyterian of the old school, one who insisted, always, that his children should obey his behests, even as he tried to obey those of the Almighty. His pride and the pride of his family was the youngest daughter, Marie, a tall, handsome girl of sixteen, precociously developed, whose brown hair, blue eyes and sprightly mien were known and admired by scores of the young gentry of the region.

It is sad, but true, that self-willed fathers frequently find themselves confronted with problems offered by the incorrigible caprices of self-willed girls, and that was precisely the predicament in which Mr. Jethro Cushman found himself in attempting to outline and to prescribe proper paths of conduct for the 16-year-old baby. He very much desired that Marie should be a Presbyterian; she preferred to be an Episcopalian, and when the father objected to this she at once decided that she would be nothing, and thereafter strenuously adhered to the determination. The old gentleman's ideal girl was one who was demure, retiring and quiet, and he indiscreetly insisted upon the adoption of such a demeanor by a girl to whom such a task was simply a physical impossibility. As a consequence, in her determination to be natural, the daughter went to the other extreme, with the result that she was hoydenish, capricious, and a tomboy. Being, however, a young person of good impulses and warm affections it is likely that her intense pride and her devotion to an indulgent mother would have restrained her from anything more rash than occasional outbursts of temper, to be followed by reluctant obedience to her father's wishes, but for a blind and unreasoning love affair in which she became involved, and which the father determined, by an arbitrary assumption of parental authority, to crush and obliterate, entirely regardless of consequences.

It is but justice to Brother Cushman to admit that, though he had definite matrimonial ambitions with regard to his daughter, they never were declared. She was only made to understand that she ought to look for her company among the people of her father's church, and that chief among the qualifications most desirable in lover and prospective husband were respectability and wealth. In the abstract the advice could hardly have been better, but the girl shrewdly believed, and it was true, although the father had never ventured an open statement of the fact, that he would have been glad if she had encouraged the attentions of a very worthy and very wealthy young neighbor, of mediocre abilities but excellent prospects, who was educating himself for, and was expected to make his mark in, the ministry. But, as generally happens in such cases, even if the young lady had not been (which she declared in her heart of hearts that she was) madly, hopelessly, irreclaimably in love with handsome Clarence Woodruff, she decided, off-hand, that the young minister was positively the last man on her entire list of acquaintances that she would select for a husband. What encouragement has a father to do the best he can for a daughter in such a behalf?

Clarence Woodruff was not wealthy, hardly well-to-do. Worse than that, he was inclined to be wild. He attended dances and horse races; and, though not a drinker or a gambler, he was worldly minded and had the force and dash and steam of youth that plunged him ahead in conformity with his own sweet will, in utter defiance of the opinions of older and wiser heads, and this, of course, placed him under the ban of Mr. Cushman's unqualified disapproval.

When the daughter was forbidden to meet or encourage, or even think of young Woodruff, she, of course, clandestinely did all three. And when the father, in his exasperation and rage, prescribed the same terms to the lover, that worthy, in a manner characteristic of him, had the hardihood to defy him to his face. The war waxed warm, with the result that while the lovers were planning an elopement Miss Marie was suddenly and secretly conveyed by her father to a denominational school at St. Louis,

"A covered wagon, drawn by a span of large but bony horses."

where she was for some weeks held prisoner, and a prisoner who could not even send or receive a letter except under the espionage of the strictest tutors, made more strict by the peremptory directions of the girl's irascible father.

The girl's resentment was natural, but it burned in her bosom with a fierceness and intensity little suspected by her devoted parent. Regardless of the consequences, and declaring to herself that she cared nothing for the future, she planned an escape, and was so successful in executing it that while detectives were systematically searching the city she was in the private car of a wealthy but lecherous railway magnate, speeding toward the city of Chicago.

Of her life there little is known, but in a reproachful letter to her father she admitted that she had adopted an abandoned life and declared that it was her intention at once to take the jewels and finery which her official admirer had lavished upon her and escape to parts unknown.

Rumors crept back to the little community in which she had lived that she had drifted to the West, to Denver, to Leadville and other mining camps; but at home she was mourned as one dead, and the hardiest gossipers did not dare utter her name in the presence of the heartbroken father or the members of the sorrowing family.

Glenwood Springs, Colorado, was a nondescript sort of health resort in 1884, but one extensively patronized for all that. Though there was not a railroad within a hundred miles, news of the miraculous cures wrought by its wonderful hot springs had gone abroad and had attracted thither the sick and afflicted, the lame and the blind, not only from neighboring regions, but from points some times located in the most distant parts of the Union.

A large portion of the "town" was composed of tents, not only used as temporary tenements but as temporary offices and places of business. Saloons, gambling houses and maisons de joie were plentiful, and there was abroad that indescribable free-and-easy atmosphere, since entirely obliterated, that marks the inception of the "boom" town of the mountains, whether it be a prospective health resort, commercial mart or mining camp.

It was on a mellow, dreamy, autumn afternoon, such as are the boast and the glory of the western slope of Colorado, because they seem especially designed by an indulgent Creator for pleasant excursions along the adjacent trout streams, or for more exciting experiences among the different species of game that abounds among the mountain parks of that favored region. A corps of surveyors were chaining and driving stakes down in the center of the principal streets; real estate dealers were hurrying here and there disposing of choice lots to newcomers who were anxious to buy; a crowd of loafers were enjoying themselves trying the courage of a formidable looking bulldog by attempting to lead him within reach of the chains of a pair of full-grown mountain lions, the pets of a gambler at the Senate saloon. Men and women, in vehicles and on foot, with crutches and without, were passing and repassing on their way to and from the mammoth hot springs or the natural steam cave in the side of the hill above the town, as their predilections and preferences happened to lead them. Crowds poured in and out of the saloons and gambling places; and among them were women from "on the hill"—privileged in every new-born mountain town, at first, to drink and smoke and joke and swagger, the same as other loafers, and afterward, by advancing civilization, forced to retire from view and confine their operations to the houses that they occupy.

On this September morning the loafers on "Grand avenue," principally an avenue of tents, saw, entering the town from the Roaring Fork Valley, on the south, a covered wagon. It attracted attention because it was a dusty and worn-looking veteran, drawn by a span of large but bony horses, whose jaded, discouraged look told plainly that their lack of flesh was due to days of weary toiling over sandy plains and precipitous mountain passes.

When the vehicle had stopped in front of a large tent that displayed upon its flaring front the badly painted sign, "Groceries and Provisions," the clusters of loiterers saw that it contained a young man of 30, or thereabout, who occupied the spring seat in company with a woman of 25 years, presumably his wife. Two flaxen-haired girls of tender years sat upon a bundle behind the seat, while upon a bed made down in the middle of the wagon lay a woman of 50, whose thin hands, contracted joints, pale face and heavy eyes bore unmistakable evidence of the ravaging waste of disease and suffering. The driver himself, but for travel stain and a stubby growth of beard, was a man whose face and manner would have been a favorable introduction among honest men anywhere. He was large, quick spoken and with a mien that was neither bold nor shy. As he stopped he spoke confidently and respectfully to Doc McCabe, as the first man whose attention he attracted, a man, by the way, well known to many of the earlier settlers in the Grand Valley.

"Are you acquainted here?" he asked.

"Yes; as well as anybody, I guess."

"Well, stranger, I'm about broke, and —"

"Haven't got any the best o' me," answered Doc, with a careless chuckle.

"What I was goin' to say is, I've got a sick mother here, that I've hauled all the way from Bates County, Missouri. Bad luck on the road has run us short of money and I want to get into a house, the first thing, an' some teamin' or some kind of work to do right away afterward. What do you think's the show?"

"You won't be able to get a house, that's sure, thout you build it. You can get all the work you want—more, too."

"No house, eh?"

"Not a house."

"That'll be bad."

"I dunno; what's the matter with your mother? Consumption?"

"No. The doctors can't tell us. It's the drawin' up of the joints an' a wastin' away of the muscles. I brought her here because an old friend of ours by the name of Porter—lives in El Paso now—he had the same thing and these springs cured him, sound and well. Guess they're all right, ain't they?"

"I guess they are. If there's anything they won't cure we ain't found it out yet. I came here a year ago so full of sores that they wouldn't let me stay in a boarding house in this town—nor even at a hospital. I had to take blankets and sleep under those cedars

over there on the side of the hill. I've taken the baths all the time since, and today I'm as healthy as anybody, am a deputy sheriff and doin' the most of the work of the office. Tell you what you do."

"I'm sure I'll be much obliged," said the stranger.

"You rig up a camp with your wagon sheet some place handy to the springs, so you can get your mother to 'em—'tain't gon' to be anything but nice weather like this till about Christmas, it always is—give your mother the baths once a day to start with and go on with your teamin', there's plenty of it to be done. You'll be all right there until you can get a house. Everybody is buildin' houses to rent and in a month there'll be houses to spare."

The stranger thanked him, gave the lines to his wife, inquired as to the present needs of their commissary and went into the tent store to make some unimportant purchases.

Hardly had he disappeared when McCabe, a master in verterinary matters, said to the wife:

"Madam, your husband's got a sick horse there."

One of the animals, indeed, showed sudden but unmistakable signs of distress, and McCabe at once summoned the husband and called his attention to the fact.

The animal was taken out of the harness immediately and the usual remedies applied, but apparently to no purpose. A boy was placed upon its back with instructions to gallop it up and down the street, the incident attracting the usual crowd of people, most of whom were, as usual, ready with suggestions and advice; but despite their efforts the animal lay down and could not again be coaxed or driven to rise. Other remedies were applied but to no effect. The beast, bloated to twice its normal proportions, groaned with pain, and when it was suggested that it would be humane to kill it, and thus end its misery, the owner declared that its death would ruin him; and the wife and children, until then silent spectators of the scene, begged the husband and father, with tears, which they made no attempt to conceal, not to allow the poor animal to be put to death.

While the crowd of sympathetic citizens were looking on, admittedly nonplussed, and the owner of the suffering horse was still drenching it with medicine, two women of the demi-monde came by, one smoking a cigarette with evident relish, the other chatting carelessly. As they drew nearer, attracted by the crowd, the taller one, with the brown hair and blue eyes, seeing the sick horse and distressed owner kneeling at its head, gasped:

"Oh, my God!"

She came near fainting, but rallied and, by the aid of the woman who was with her, succeeded in tottering into the "Palace" saloon (a pine board shanty), where she ordered a full glass of brandy,

"The beast, bloated to twice its normal size, groaned with pain."

which she hastily swallowed, then begged her companion to hurry with her to her home "on the hill."

As the two passed out the tall woman, keeping her own face from view, looked again at the stranger from Missouri, then at the worn and weary occupants of the wagon. She heard a gambler among the onlookers say:

"Guess his horse is dead."

"Yes," replied his comrade, another gambler, "and it's hard luck; broke, and with a sick family. We'll have to give him a benefit."

The tall woman immediately changed her purpose. Instead of going toward the row "on the hill" she turned and walked rapidly in the direction of the bank, a one-story structure, but an institution representing millions of money. She entered, came out, walked away again, and within five minutes a bank clerk elbowed his way through the crowd to the side of the stranger from Missouri. "What is your name?" he asked.

"Clarence B. Woodruff," answered the stranger with a puzzled expression on his sun-tanned face.

"Well, Mr. Woodruff, there's $100 up at the bank, to your credit, and more if you need it. Come in and get it whenever you're ready."

"Guess you're mistaken," declared the Missourian, candidly; "I'm a stranger here; just got in."

"No; there's no mistake, I think. You were the owner of this horse, weren't you?"

"Yes sir."

"Well, you are the man. It is all straight."

"Who done it?" asked the Missourian, still doubtingly.

"A friend; and that is all that I am at liberty to tell you."

"I need the money, God knows, an' ef I kin git it, I'll secure my note with a mor'gage on the wagon an' the other horse," he said, humbly and thankfully.

"We're not to take any note, or any mortgage," said the clerk. "You can call and get the money whenever it suits you."

The clerk hurried away, again, in the direction of the bank, leaving the Missourian standing there, dazed and dumbfounded.

His countenance was a study. Plainly he was struggling between a hope for help and the vague fear of a practical joke. His face was pale and with the lump in his throat and the conflicting emotions in his breast, he looked as though called upon to say something when to say anything was an utter impossibility. He looked appealingly at his wife, but the look his helpless partner returned him offered no clue to the mystery. He looked irreolutely at the crowd of astonished spectators, at his dead horse, at his wife again then tried twice before he could utter a word.

"I'm a-goin' up to the bank," he said, "an' ef that money is fer me, hyarafter I'll b'lieve in God and angels."

The money was for him; but he had to accept it without any explanation further than that already given. He bought a tent at once, and another horse. With plenty of work, for himself and his team, the man contrived to keep the mother and the wife and children in comparative comfort, and had the satisfaction of seeing the invalid improve from the first, and finally restored to the most perfect health.

Marie Cushman (not known by that name, however) departed immediately for Salt Lake City, and the first intimation her former lover had that he had been near her or that she was the mysterious bank depositor, was when he called at that institution to replace the sum obtained. She had left a note there to be delivered to him on that occasion, not before. It read:

Do not think of repaying any part of the money, Clarence, for my whereabouts will be unknown to the bank and I shall never get it. Do not ask about me, or try to find me, or ever think of me again. I am lost. Good-by, forever. MARIE.

Dan De Foe

LIFETIME BUCK by Allen Parsons

The children speak of that head as "Baa-baa." Indeed, it does somewhat suggest a sheep. The farmer-taxidermist who mounted it made the nose too pointed. The head, too, was set upon the maple shield with the full length of the neck behind it, so that it stands out from the wall in surprising fashion. It might well be an okapi or un unspotted giraffe, except for its antlers. They establish its identity. It's the head of a little three-point buck deer, that couldn't have weighed over 100 pounds. As a trophy it leaves much to be desired. But to me it's precious, for it was my first, and I shot it the night before my fifteenth birthday.

The emotions aroused by your first deer, or trout, or ruffed grouse shot on the wing, are so profound, your sense of triumph so exhilarating, that you can never forget them. But, when a beardless boy, unaided and alone, has brought down a wary deer, then sir, life has given him its richest triumph.

As a youngster in boarding school, I became a victim of too-rapid growth. I put on height but no breadth, weight, or muscle. The doctor was frank and wise. He told my father, "My medicines won't do that boy a bit of good. Outdoor air and exercise are what he needs. Get him out in the woods somewhere."

The end of June found me in an old lumber camp in southern Quebec. As companion and guardian I was given the camp cook, a French-Canadian with a name I could never make out. Two syllables in it sounded like Riley, so Riley he was to me. Riley spoke English that required an interpreter; my French was no better. With pathetic persistence, we tried constantly to converse in each other's language, and eventually we learned to catch the other's drift. When Riley said something like "Eet ees necessaire *poissons* we have *pour manger demain*," I guessed he was suggesting that I catch a mess of trout for the morrow's breakfast.

The lumber camp, in the office of which we made our home, was located in a narrow valley. Down this valley flowed a crystal stream, small, and icy cold, with a succession of miniature waterfalls and pools. It was filled with brook trout. In an hour or so before breakfast I could catch ten or a dozen, their average length being only seven or eight inches.

Its antlers prove it is the head of a deer.

Once in a while, I would proudly show Riley a noble fish at least ten inches long, and revel in his "Magnifique!" The largest I ever took there was about eleven inches long, and his hooked lower jaw and venerable appearance told me that he was truly one of the giants of that brook.

Unlike so many of his compatriots, Riley was no spiritual brother of the coureur de bois and the voyageur. He could never be persuaded to go fishing, and deer tracks left him cold. Though in the woods, he was not of them. Even his manner of dressing bore that out. He favored white, starched collars, laundered carefully by himself, and worn with a black string tie. The clerical aspect of this strange woods garb was completed by a low-crowned, black felt hat, without which one never saw him save when he took to his bunk at bedtime. Then, when he doffed it and hung it carefully on a peg, his round poll appeared indecently nude, for Riley was bald to his ears. But, if the forest, with its fish and game, were not his passion, music was. As soon as breakfast was finished, and I was off with my little fly rod, Riley would pick up his violin. He would seat himself in the wooden armchair outside, with a sigh of pleasure for the joys to come. Back he would tilt against the wall of the cabin, hook his heels into the chair rounds, close his eyes, and ply the bow. As I worked up the stream, putting the Parmachene Belle over likely little pools, I would hear that violin until it died away in the distance.

Before I had gone north, I had, through channels of boyish barter beginning with the capital of a bicycle, acquired a .32 Stevens rifle. I have never heard this caliber of rifle well spoken of for deer hunting, but to me, it was beyond all doubt the finest rifle that money could buy. I had plenty of cartridges, and almost every afternoon practiced shooting. My target was a sheet of wrapping paper, fastened with pitch to a big maple tree. The distance was fifty paces. At first I consistently missed even the tree. When I first put a bullet into the paper, I had to summon Riley to be a witness to the achievement.

Then, with practice, I hit the paper more often until, finally, I could get all my shots into it. True, some of them might cut the edges, but the bullets were there. I practiced standing, sitting, prone, and kneeling shots, and came to know the feel and the whimsies of that rifle.

So the summer passed pleasantly, and I picked up weight and strength amazingly. While doing my target shooting, there had been no thought that I would be able to do any hunting that season, but one day, toward the first of September, there came word that the opening of school had been delayed until the second week in October. Here was an opportunity long desired. There were many deer in those woods. Their tracks were all along the brook. Occasionally at dusk as I came pussy-footing along the stream in my moccasins, I would hear the sudden crash of the brush, and see the disappearing white flag of a doe, perhaps with a fawn.

About the middle of September the trout fishing, hitherto unvaryingly good, became poor. Pools that had never failed to yield a fat, little trout or two were barren, and I was hard put to it to get enough for our breakfasts. The thing was a mystery. I could not have caught them all. There were at least three miles of water that I fished, and the ten trout or so that I had taken daily surely could not have exhausted it. Thinking that they might have run upstream with the September rains, I decided to follow.

The lumber road followed the stream for perhaps two miles, crossing it again and again on rough log bridges. It came to an end in a big clearing where the tree tops were heaped in an impenetrable tangle. It was useless to try to walk across that clearing. I had to follow the brook bed. Here was wilderness

indeed. The ground was thick with pine needles, the air fragrant with their smell. There was a pleasant thrill to this exploration. Here was the home of the wildcat and the lynx, and once, in the soft earth by the stream side, I saw the footprint of a bear. I felt little chills as I thought that I might be watched by unfriendly eyes, but the slight uneasiness gave the final zest that my adventure needed.

Then, at last, I came to a sun-lit opening in the forest, a wild meadow thick with grass. There had been a beaver dam there, and, as the animals had departed or been trapped out, their dam had broken and left this meadow, rich with silt, as their monument. The brook here flowed silently over a bed of sand and gravel, the water perhaps six inches deep. I saw what appeared to be many sticks on the stream bed, but all were lying in the same direction facing up stream. Curious, I lay flat on my stomach in the lush grass and peered into the water. There were my missing trout! The water swarmed with little chaps of five or six inches, up to one or two lunkers over a foot long. They were spawning, and, in that clear water, the whole mystery of their reproduction was disclosed. With their fins and noses, they made little hollows in the gravel. The females took their positions over these hollows, the males swimming around them excitedly. The eggs were deposited, fertilized by the males, and the gravel fanned over them. I forgot fishing.

The long grass quite concealed me and, to avoid disturbing the trout, I was motionless. From across the brook came stealthy sounds. I raised my eyes. Not more than fifty feet away, a young buck was feeding at the edge of the woods. He would take a mouthful of grass, flip his white tail, raise his head, look around. Nose, ears, and eyes all were alert to warn him of danger. Never had I seen a wild deer so close. I trembled with excitement as I watched him. I was down wind from him, and he was unsuspecting. Then he threw his head into the air, ears and nose twitching, and faded into the forest. From that moment, I had an ambition, an object in life. As a successful hunter of big game, I felt I might attain the status of a school celebrity.

Downstream the meadow ended where the hills and the forest on both sides came almost together. The brook poured through this narrow defile, and became a wild, foaming torrent. Across this bottle neck lay the peeled trunk of a big tree, which had collected a mass of driftwood. Here was a perfect blind. Hidden behind it, I could command that meadow, and, given the chance, I felt that the little buck would be mine. From that day on I haunted the spot. Fishing forgot, I would take the rifle with me, steal up to the shelter of the fallen tree, peer eagerly through the tangle of driftwood, and settle down to wait for the buck. Day after day I lay in wait but, though each morning the meadow showed fresh tracks, I did not see their maker.

Then I concluded that he was feeding either early in the morning or in the evening. I tried getting there before sunrise, but was always too late. I waited until sundown, but had to leave too early, for I had no desire to come down that brook through the forest after dark.

Could any buck possibly be worth the terrors of a night alone in the woods? Riley refused to have any part of it. "What? Leave a bed so warm to shiver so foolishly in the wet woods? *Mais non, non!*" Riley snapped his fingers with a "Pouf!" I mentally did the same thing. Would I do it *alone? Mais non!*

The red and yellow leaves that had painted the maples were gone. Each night there was frost. Each morning we had to break the ice in the water pail. My vacation would soon be ended. In four more days I must say good-by to the amiable Riley and our snug log cabin. Let the little buck add more points to his horns. Perhaps he would still be there if I came up again. To show what I could do to him, I took the rifle, stuck a small envelope to the maple tree, and proceeded to puncture it with five successive shots. Never had I shot so well. If I could shoot like that, was not the buck as good as mine? Why wait till next year?

Eagerness to become a big game hunter now outweighed my fears of the wilderness in the dark. I oiled my rifle, dressed in my warmest clothing, told Riley not to expect me until some time after dark, took my little flash light and a blanket, and set off upstream. In my pocket were two sandwiches and a bar of chocolate. I trembled with nervous excitement. I was embarking upon the first big adventure of my life.

Arriving at the fallen tree I found a rest for the rifle among the stubs of the branches, and left it there so that there would be less motion to alarm the deer when it should come time to aim. Then I seated myself upon the blanket to wait the coming of the deer.

The afternoon ended with a wintry sunset, and, in spite my two heavy sweaters, I shivered. The meadow darkened. All that I could see was the steely reflection of the sky in the brook. From the hillside, a great horned owl hooted dismally, and my teeth began involuntarily to chatter. Far up the stream, from the blackness, came a long, savage, wavering cry. What it was I knew not, but I feared it was the howl of a wolf.

It was now between dusk and darkness. I heard new noises in the little meadow, such as a sheep makes when grazing. I strained my eyes to see. Surely there was a blacker shadow in the grass. Was it my imagination, or was there life in that shadow? I dared not fire at an uncertainty. I did not wish to experi-

The brook caught all the light of the sky. As the shadow came into it, I saw the outline of the proud head and branching horns.

ment upon a bear for my first big game shooting. Was my long, cold, and fearsome wait to end fruitlessly because it was too dark to see my mark? I sat frozen, not daring to move, except to clutch my rifle, finger on trigger, in the hope it would be my buck. The shadow moved toward the brook and seemed to flow into it. What fortune! The brook caught all the little light of the sky, and, as the shadow entered it, I saw its outline clearly. There was a head held high, and on the head were horns!

I do not remember sighting the rifle. The moment of pulling the trigger was lost in the shock of the rifle's awful sound in the silence of the woods. The shadow disappeared even as I looked at it. With my youthful nerves shocked into a state of collapse, I sat behind the windfall, and trembled. I tried to summon courage to go with my flash light and see what had happened, but I could not.

Probably it was but a few moments later when I finally arose, though it seemed that the night must be far gone. I turned on my little flash light, and waded upstream to where the deer had been. There he was, motionless, hind legs in the water, body on the bank. My bullet had entered his left shoulder, and by the most fortunate chance had hit the heart. I had been told that it was necessary to bleed a deer after shooting, and I shuddered at what I must do. I pulled out Riley's long carving knife, which I had thought to bring, stuck it in where neck and chest joined, turned away my eyes and gagged. I wouldn't be fifteen until sunrise.

In my nervousness, I dropped the little flash light. I pawed around desperately in the grass and

After a night of thrills Riley carried the little buck back to the cabin upon his shoulders, while I led with a lantern.

water trying to find it, but it had disappeared. I must go back to the camp through the darkness. I never can forget my frenzied dash downstream. It was a dash, too. I was frightened, and eager to get back to where there was light and human companionship. I took to the brook as offering the only certain road, and ran. I slammed into boulders, bounced from trees, went head-on into the log bridges, and fell on my face in the pools. My only comfort was that the noise I made would doubtless warn every bear and wildcat to get away.

Eventually, I panted into the lumber-camp clearing, and my heart bounded to see the windows aglow with light. I threw open the door. What my appearance was like I can guess, for Riley's eyes fairly popped from his head. "Come!" I gasped. "I've got him! Get the lantern, quick!"

Blessings upon that squat little Frenchman. He would have had reason to say, "Tomorrow is yet another day. We shall await it!" But, with rare under-standing and sympathy, he lighted the lantern, put on his coat, and started back with me.

He carried that little buck back to the cabin upon his shoulders, I going ahead with the lantern. When he had dumped his load upon the floor of the cook house, we stood side by side and gazed long and silently at my trophy. When Riley spoke it was with proper respect and awe.

"*Monsieur*"—never before had I been "*monsieur*" to Riley—"is a shooter the most skilled. *Quelle bête!* What antlers. Here is a *trophée* the most *magnifique!*"

"How much will he weigh, Riley?" I asked, expanding my narrow chest. Riley looked judicial. He hefted the buck, just as though he had not already packed him over three miles. He did not rush into a conclusion so momentous.

"Tree ondred pound!" declared Riley.

Allen Parsons

WOLF DOG by Charles Elliott

Lobo turned his black nose to the wind and loped into the twilight of the forest. The air currents, woven together by threads of scent and sound, brought to his primitive senses a picture of the mountain woods ahead. It set the scalp between his pointed ears to tingling. Here the world was new and strange. He tasted the wind with a fierce exhilaration born of freedom and adventure.

Then suddenly the woods, which had been so fresh and clean, were filled with the reek of man. Lobo spun from his swinging lope and froze into a furry statue beside the trail. He stood through a moment of indecision, then turned and drifted like a dark shadow away from the path. He crouched where an ancient, mossback log pressed against the earth.

The human scent grew stronger. Out of the purple gloom that deepened where the trees were thick, the man appeared. His long stride brought him directly toward the log where the big wolf dog lay as taut as the string of a drawn bow.

A murderous growl died in Lobo's throat. His bleak straw-colored eyes clung to the booted human. The stick in John Livingston's hand was a symbol of authority and supremacy. But Lobo was ready. If the man paused suddenly and raised that stick to strike at him, he'd tear a human throat out with his steel-trap jaws.

John Livingston, however, did not pause or turn his head. He wondered vaguely why the hackles on his neck should tingle unpleasantly, but he strode on and faded into the dusk. The sound of his boots on the rocky trail grew faint. Once more the air was clean of human stench.

Minutes after the man had gone, Lobo rose warily. He did not take the trail again, but turned into the mountain woods which sloped sharply up to Balsam Ridge. A game trail climbed the crest of the ridge to Eagle Point. He padded across the rocky pinnacle and stood on its barren tip. The wind blew full and hard against him. Beyond the point the earth fell into opaque darkness. The broad, deep valley at his feet glinted with spots of silver where Eagle River sliced through the hills. An amber globe of moon hung on the violet rim beyond the valley.

The blood raced wild through Lobo's body. Man had tamed his eager muscles and forced knowledge into his stubborn brain, but had not been able to conquer his spirit. From this night on, no man would ever be his master.

This exciting new life sprang from a dramatic clash between the wolf dog and his master. Behind him were centuries upon centuries of wildness and fierceness which transformed him into a raging killer. Through generations of carefully bred and highly trained champions, the brutal wolf strain had lain dormant, waiting for such a dog as Lobo.

He had been the largest in a litter of six Alsatians. He was whelped in the purple, a line-bred descendant of Hamilton Anne Von Kruger, the finest strain of German shepherd dogs in the world. But Lobo was not a dog. He was a wolf. He was a product of that phenomenon by which shepherd dogs occasionally bring forth a true wolf from which their breed originated.

John Livingston knew he had a wolf cub in the litter. He watched the young puppy stand on legs so wobbly that they would scarcely support his weight and hoist his tiny black muzzle into the wind, while the other puppies lay curled up, asleep. The wolf dog puppy strutted across the kennel yard and stuck his long mouth into the water pan. Instead of lapping like a dog, he sucked up the water just as any member of a wild pack would have done.

John pushed open the gate and stepped into the pen. Lobo backed into a corner, a ball of fur on buckling legs, and growled. The breeder laughed. He caught the puppy by the scruff of its neck and lifted it into his arms. He stroked the silky hair between the tiny ears.

"I have a weakness for outlaws," he said, "or you'd get the guillotine."

John Livingston's eyes glowed at his discovery. He'd known men who had found wolf cubs in a litter. He had never believed they could be trained. George Cuvier once wrote how a wolf raised in the Jardin des Plantes in Paris had become fanatically devoted to its master. John scoffed at that, too, but the experiment was worth a trial. If he could harness all the vibrant fire and courage in such an animal, he'd have the champion dog of the world.

From the moment his eyes opened on his thirteenth day, Lobo was a malicious little brute with an ugly temper. Before he could stand on his stubby legs, he tried to chew the foot off a sister puppy. His mother cuffed him into a corner of the pen. He did not cry or whine. Instead, he growled defiance.

Lobo was weaned two weeks before his litter mates quit suckling. John brought a piece of red meat into the kennel and held it down before the pups. Only Lobo scented it. He rushed forward, tore the meat from his master's hand, and dragged it to a corner of the pen where he crouched and ripped the steak apart with gusty greed.

Several months after he was born, Lobo almost lost his head. It was not exactly his own fault, but it helped contribute to his general delinquency.

John's five-year-old daughter, Mary, had been told never to enter the pen of the Alsatians, and that order from her father, of course, made the kennel the most intriguing spot in the yard. When no one was looking, she worked at the heavy hasp which held the gate shut while the dogs watched her in indolent curiosity.

One day she gave the hasp an extra twist and the gate came open in her hand. Half fearfully, Mary stepped inside. Janie, Lobo's huge, dark mother, rose slowly to her feet, stretched, and sniffed at the little girl. Then she went back to her straw bed in the corner.

The puppies surged toward her, tumbling around her feet; all except Lobo, who lay by the fence and never took his eyes away from the girl. Being a female, and human, the little girl waded through the furry shepherd pups to Lobo, the one who showed no sign of affection for her. She stooped to stroke the wolf dog's silky hair, and he snapped at her hand, his needle teeth scratching her chubby fingers.

Mary stumbled backward in surprise and lost her balance. She fell sprawling on the ground and instantly Lobo was upon her, growling and biting at her ankles. The other puppies, sensing some kind of a new game, tumbled over her and one of them

pushed Lobo away. Janie, who had watched John Livingston roll her progeny around affectionately, looked on with sleepy eyes.

The little girl, badly frightened, managed to scramble to her feet and run to the gate. She did not try to put the hasp back in place. John Livingston found her half hidden under the rose bush at the front steps, her face wet with tears. He picked her up in his arms.

"What's the matter, honey?" he asked.

She told him in broken sentences, pointing out Lobo and the half-closed gate. For a long minute the man studied Lobo with thoughtful eyes.

"When you bother the dogs," he said quietly to his daughter, "they might hurt you. I'd punish Lobo if he had tried to bite you without teasing, but it was your fault and not his."

"I hate him," said the little girl.

Lobo, sensing the spirit behind her words, growled softly. Some day he would find Mary alone. His yellow eyes grew red around the rims.

John Livingston spent hours with Lobo each day. He was so fascinated by the wolf dog that he neglected the other puppies. Against the wishes of the young savage, he taught him to heel and charge and fetch a thrown ball.

Lobo found one bright spot in his training. He looked forward to those times when his master carried him into the woods with their deep glades and sun-splotched forest floors. Once John lost him for an hour and found him stalking a big cottontail, almost as large as the pup. The rabbit bounced away when John appeared and picked Lobo up in his arms.

"You little pagan," he said. "If that had been a coon or an otter, I probably would have found you without a scalp."

They ranged together frequently in Cooper's Cove. This primitive upland forest lay in the big bend of Eagle River. There the oaks and hickories were huge and formed a canopy so thick that no sunlight ever touched the ground. The cove was a favorite haunt of the Russian wild boars, recently introduced into the Southern mountains. The extensive woods, carpeted with leaves and decaying vegetation, were similar to their home in the Old World and provided delicate tidbits of acorns and mushrooms and tender shoots.

John and the puppy stumbled upon the herd one day. Lobo hurtled down the slope and charged a huge black boar that stood almost three feet at the shoulder and weighed more than an eighth of a ton. The boar, more in amazement than antagonism, swung to face the gangling puppy. His head went down and before Lobo could side-step he caught the dog a glancing blow that bowled him ten feet into the leaves.

Ignoring the danger to himself, Livingston raced downhill and scooped the puppy up into his arms. While the boar hesitated, rumbling in its throat, the man clawed his way to safety in the granite cliffs with Lobo twisting in his arms to free himself and make another attack.

John Livingston sewed up the cut in the puppy's shoulder. Two inches either way and the stiletto tusk would have cut off the young life almost before it had begun. But the experience only served to instill in Lobo a hatred for any creature that smelled like a hog. He was certain that without his master's interference he could have put the clumsy boar back on its haunches. Out of his confidence grew a challenge to the whole pig tribe. His hackles rose like brown wires when he found a split track in the earth and the bitter smell of swine blew to his nose.

When he was locked in his pen, Lobo paced the sides like a caged wild beast, searching for some means of escape. His litter mates were content to lie in the sun. He tested the fence with his teeth, or tried to dig away the concrete floor. He worked periodically at a loose board under the gate. One day when he pushed at the plank trying to get his nose out, it came loose at one end. Lobo did not hesitate. Sensing freedom, he pushed through, leaving a tuft of hair on the sharp nail.

He half circled the pen, thinking of the mountain woods which lay across the meadow. Then he saw Mary, playing at her favorite spot under the rosebush. She was upwind and her smell brought back the memory of that day in the pen. He crouched on his belly, watching her. He slunk within a dozen yards of the girl, his yellow eyes gleaming. Then he lay motionless. It wasn't knowledge or experience that kept him from hurting the little girl. It was instinct, a thousand generations old, that told him death would be his penalty for an attack on this man child.

So taut were his muscles, so intent his concentration, that he did not hear John Livingston walk into the yard. He came alive when the heavy step was over him. He sprang forward, too late. The man's iron fist was in the scruff of his neck. He snarled and fought when John lifted him bodily off the ground and broke a switch from the apple tree in the yard. The lashes stung his sides and legs and back, but Lobo did not whine or cry out. He fought silently to free himself, but the man was too strong.

Beads of sweat stood on John's forehead when he opened the gate and dropped Lobo back into the pen. "If I could read your mind," he said, grimly, "I'd probably kill you. But, by gad, I'll break you if it makes an old man of me."

Lobo did not realize that those incidents had become a part of him. He did not know it months later when he lay flattened on the kennel floor. But the first taste of the autumn wind was like sweet

John caught the puppy by the scruff of its neck and lifted it bodily.

perfume to his nose, and every nerve and muscle was a-tingle when John Livingston opened the gate to put on his training collar.

Lobo suddenly changed from an apparently sleeping dog to a flash of gray. He was gone before the man could slam the gate again. The dog whistle shrilled. Lobo knew it was a command for him to return, and he stopped to look back, ears pointed the sky. Training was strong, but not so strong as his instinct for freedom. He swept over the brow of the low hill that bordered the Livingston fields and headed at a dead run up the river trail. Later he left the trail and cut across the pastured acres of Jeremiah Duke who owned the farm across the creek.

This morning Lobo was only in a playful mood. He intended to make a short circle of a few miles and return to the pen where his master would be waiting. During the months of kindness and patience he had almost forgotten the whipping he received for stalking little Mary in the front yard. He learned fast and John always rewarded him with a piece of meat when he was obedient. So he turned back toward the house.

He was running fast when he crossed the corner of the Duke pasture and his sensitive nostrils swelled with the hated smell of swine. He wheeled and cut back through a clump of trees, following that scent.

He was in the middle of the pigs almost before he saw them. The thicket exploded and bawling shoats took off toward all points of the pasture. In sheer exuberance, Lobo leaped after one of the terrified animals, slashing at its hamstrings, much as a member of a wild pack would have done. The pig went down, bellowing in mortal terror. Lobo lunged for its throat. His teeth cut the bellow to a gasp and hot blood splashed into his eyes.

He ran to earth and killed another shoat before he heard the pound of running feet and saw

For the first time Lobo could not restrain the wild freedom in his heart. He gave voice and his running cry swelled upward through the night.

Jeremiah Duke angling across the field. The big dog swung and sprinted for the protection of the trees. The roar behind him kicked up gravel that stung through his heavy coat.

Lobo gained the shelter of the woods before the farmer shot again. His native intelligence told him that he was in danger and the only protection he knew was in the Livingston kennel yard. He fled across the slopes and crept through the gate his master had left open.

Duke was with John Livingston when they found him there, crouched in a corner, his eyes blazing. The farmer's face was red. John Livingston's white knuckles were tight around a stick. He dragged Lobo out by the nape of the neck and rubbed hog hair against his nose. Then he struck the wolf dog with his stick. He rubbed the hated smell in the dog's nostrils a second time and belted him in the loins.

"I hate to do this, old man," he said, "but you've got to learn sometime."

The wolf dog lunged and twisted with all the power of his young shoulders to tear out of his master's hand, but the grip in those fingers was too firm.

John raised his stick a third time, but a vicious jerk of the young demon threw the man off balance and he went down, losing his hold. Lobo did not hesitate. He plunged at his sprawling master's throat. But Duke was quicker than the dog. He swung his broad boot. It caught Lobo full in the face and knocked him against the kennel fence. The wolf dog leaped again. John Livingston, staggering to his feet, struck with the stick. Lobo met it in his lunge and went down with the breath knocked out of his body. John jumped forward to catch the dog again, but Lobo bolted past him through the gate. He ran with

long, low strides toward the big woods that climbed the slope beyond the river.

"He's a killer," Jeremiah Duke said, his big hand propped against the kennel fence.

John Livingston did not reply. In all his years as a trainer, he had never seen such spirit in a dog. He had almost met sudden death under Lobo's teeth, and he should have been glad to have the young devil out of his kennel. But somehow, deep inside, he felt a curious loss, for he knew that Lobo would never come home again.

Now the moon was swinging clear into the blackened sky and stars were popping out in the dome that arched over Windy Mountain. Lobo picked his way down the rocky slope and struck the forest trail that led into the laurel canyons where he and his master had often ranged together. There was no regret and no fear in his heart.

Halfway across the slope he nosed through a thicket and jumped a rabbit. The cottontail tumbled down the mountain like a leaping rubber ball. Lobo could have caught it in two easy bounds, but instead he loped along at an easy gait, following the hot scent that spread along the sweet bosom of the earth. Life was full and overflowing, and for the first time Lobo could not restrain the wild freedom in his heart. He gave voice and his running cry swelled upward through the night.

Far down in the valley, John Livingston stood up with half an armload of firewood. He had heard wolves in the arctic wastes and knew the hunting cry of the pack. In that faint, trailing sound he could sense the spirit Lobo felt, a spirit not to be denied by chains and wire and leather collar bands. The wolf dog had gone back to the wilderness which was his own, but in which he was now an evil influence. He must be hunted down and killed.

Mid-fall had spread its myriad colors in the Southern mountains. Lobo was fully grown. He stood more than two feet high at the shoulders and weighed almost as much as a man. The puppy black had disappeared from his body. His nose sat like a lump of wet coal at the end of his light-gray muzzle. His belly fur was creamy white. His back was dusky brown that blended on his flanks to gray and copper.

He had the lean and narrow muzzle of a true wolf. It swelled into a broad forehead and powerful jaws. His oblique eyes had lightened to the straw color of dead winter grass.

Lobo's home was a rocky cave under the summit of Windy Mountain. Below his den the ridges and coves spread out like a wrinkled relief map. This vast, wild upland, cradled in the heart of the southern Appalachians, was the finest game country in the region. Deer, bears, and smaller game were abundant. In its heart, Uncle Sam's foresters and game men had created a 50,000-acre game refuge. They had established a control program for foxes and wildcats and set up plans to maintain nature's balance of all the forest creatures. The appearance of Lobo was a menace to their plans.

Each day the big wolf dog dozed on the granite stoop at the entrance to his den. At night, from dusk until dawn flamed in the sky, he ranged the forest for sport and food. Sometimes he hunted in late afternoon when the wind was cold and his muscles were restless and tired.

Lobo's greatest sport was with the bears. These big black animals had grown more plentiful in the protected refuge, year by year. His first encounter with one of them came early one morning as he loafed back from a hunt along the river. He was loping along a game trail that led under a precipice when he came face to face with the bear. It reared up and put its nose to the wind. It was the largest animal Lobo had ever met in the woods. Caution, not fear, rumbled softly in the wolf dog's chest. His full scent reached the bruin's nose, and the creature wheeled and fled back up the trail. Lobo smashed after it, giving excited tongue. He remained a safe distance behind because those hairy paws were huge and had the power of dealing sudden destruction.

They ran only a short distance and the bear treed in an oak with limbs close to the ground. Lobo sat at the foot of the tree and looked up curiously. He could not understand why so huge a creature was a coward. The bear, with one leg over a large branch, cocked its head and watched the wolf dog in a comical manner.

After an hour of circling the tree and barking spasmodically, Lobo grew tired of the sport and trotted on up the trail to his den. But from that moment on, he never failed to chase any of the bruins he met in the woods.

Of all the creatures in the mountain forest, Lobo despised only the boars. The spoor of pigs deep in the coves raised his hunting hackles and bared his rapier teeth.

One day at dusk he padded along a mountain trail that led him into Cooper Cove beyond where Eagle River thundered down its gorge. His nose discovered pig scent in the air. The herd was stomping along the forest floor, snuffling in the leaves for acorns and sweet roots.

The wolf circled a laurel clump and crouched there until they fed almost beneath him on the cove floor. One enormous bound carried him into the herd, snapping, snarling, roaring in his throat. The sows and shoats scampered to safety up the cove, and Lobo found himself surrounded by three of the ugliest pigs he had ever seen. They had little black eyes as wicked as his own and bright ivory tusks that curled up out of lower jaws. They had no idea of running away from a fight.

One of the wild hogs lowered his head and charged. Lobo twisted away and doubled back, catching the pig behind its ear, clamping down with jaws that brought a squall of pain. A sharp stab in the flank made him snap his head around. He set his teeth and ripped off an ear.

The other boars were at his rear, cutting his flanks to ribbons with dagger tusks. Lobo leapt away and fled up the mountain. It was not bravery or cowardice. The odds against him were too great. Some day he'd meet one of those big hogs alone, and then his debt would be paid in full.

He loped on up the cove. The sun had gone. The trees blazed iridescent in the twilight and the forest aisles were thick with falling autumn leaves. The thunder of Balsam Falls grew loud, then dim again against his ears. He came into the upper cove, a silent cathedral of pillared oaks and poplars.

Deer scent sweetened the air. Lobo slunk to his belly. Two does with half-grown fawns nosed along the game trail of the cove. He stalked them, silent as a shadow of the stars, upwind so they could not scent him. He sprang before the deer were aware of death. He dragged down a fawn. The other animals in the little herd bounced away on startled slender legs.

Lobo feasted well. He preferred the heart and lungs and liver to the hot rump steaks. Dawn found

Two men dressed in green forest-ranger uniforms stopped a few feet from Lobo. The wolf dog lay on his belly and waited, seemingly friendly and whining gently, but with every muscle like a steel spring.

him curled in a hollow tree, high on the ridge. There he languished through the day. When night came his nerves and muscles lost their listlessness. He circled the ridge and traveled back to the cove. He planned to make a second meal from the carcass of the deer, but as he approached the kill, his eager nose was stuffy with the bitter scent of humans.

Lobo stopped full in his stride. He circled warily, distrustful of all man-made smells. He found a spot where the leaves had been disturbed and then rearranged. Out of curiosity he pawed gently at the leaves with his big foot. The ground gleamed bright under the leaf layer. He stuck out his forepaw timidly to touch the silvery object, and it suddenly leaped at him, snapping tight shut on the end of his paw.

Lobo tumbled backward, but too late. He bit at the trap, but the bright steel was more savage than his own jaws. It cut his lips and teeth. He lunged again, twisting, turning, jerking, trying to tear his paw away, but the steel only snagged more viciously into his flesh.

Blood trickled down where he cut his jaws. The leaves and black earth were mutilated where he had braced himself and pulled until he howled from sheer anguish. Then suddenly the big dog lay down beside the trap and let his cunning take over the madness which flashed warning signals in his brain.

John Livingston would finally come for him. John had punished him before and the heavy stick against his hide would never be as terrible as trying to tear his foot away, as useless as wasting his strength on a lifeless and inexorable antagonist.

For the remainder of the night Lobo lay with his head on his free paw, fighting back the impulse to struggle against that gray steel which held him helpless. His blood ran sluggish and his woolly coat quivered from the cold. His foot, which had been hot with pain, grew numb with a slow dull throb. He moved it and the agony came again, so he lay

still against the cold earth and waited. The first lesson of the wild is patience, and he was to learn it well.

Twilight passed, dawn came, and the stars in the sky winked out one by one. The dead leaves around him stirred in the morning wind that rose with the sun. The sunlight was yellow and cold and made faint shadows against the earth. Then his quick ears caught the pad of human feet on the mountain.

Lobo beat back an impulse to spring to his feet and tear out of the trap. His first instinct was the instinct of life, and he had not lived by strength alone. The human steps came closer, but he did not recognize the gangling stride of John Livingston. There were two men instead of one. He lay on his belly and waited, seemingly at ease, but every muscle was like a coiled steel spring.

The two men stopped a few feet from him. They were dressed in green and wore wide-brimmed hats. Their eyes were staring in amazement.

"Why," one said, "it's just a big police dog."

"It may be that wolf," the other replied skeptically. "Better kill him.'

Some strength greater than his mad impulses made Lobo whine gently in his throat.

"It's nothing but a dog, Joe," the first ranger stated again.

He leaned his rifle against a tree and stood over Lobo. The wolf dog was breathing fast now, but somehow he knew that his very life depended on not tearing off the hand that stroked the fur between his ears, much as John Livingston had done.

Joe knelt beside his fellow ranger and together the two men pried apart the jaws of the trap. The pain was sharp once more when Joe lifted out the mangled paw and Lobo's whine was genuine. The ranger pulled the trap away and bent over to pick the dog up in his arms, but Lobo was not there. One moment he was a pitiable creature, the next a flash of fur threading the forest aisles. He was gone before the startled ranger could jump for his gun.

Joe took off his hat and rubbed his forehead. "Don't ever tell the chief about this," he said. "We'd be sunk."

Lobo made his tortuous way through the forest and climbed the ridge to his den. There he lay in the sunshine and brooded with his eyes watching the ridges and a pair of hawks that circled beyond the cliffs above their aerie.

In the days that followed, Lobo's foot healed slowly. The trap had left a permanent scar in the big foot, but he soon lost his limp and was running with his old stamina through the forest. His hatred for mankind was bitter, and he avoided all taint of human smells. He found fresh sheep liver laid carelessly in the woods and walked around it, even though he had not made his kill. Sometimes he almost walked into a trap in the trail, or where a set of three or four traps had been made. The sign left by man when setting the steel snares were as plain as the sunrise in the east.

One day he found such a string of traps set in front of his den. He never returned to the den. His instinct for survival told him that the men had found his home. He moved to another rocky crevice in the high cliffs above Cooper Cove.

The wolf dog killed when he wanted food and occasionally for the sport of killing. He became the terror of all the mountain forest. When his hunting bark rang down the coves, the forest creatures shuddered in their beds and den trees. He never went hungry. The woods were full of deer and rabbits and mice, and sometimes he treed a raccoon or an opossum for sport, much as a trained hunting dog would have done.

Spring came to the mountains and to the ridges that climbed up from the valleys. The buds of maple trees swelled and burst in fiery red. The poplars by the streams were amber green, and new leaves on the oak trees looked like squirrel ears. The warm winds and rains painted the forest with a bright new emerald, and hordes of flitting birds filled the woods with color and song.

Lobo stood at the door of his rocky den, his feet braced against the stone step that bulwarked the empty

space beyond. A ravenous desire, not born of appetite or hatred, burned in his deep chest. It puzzled him, annoyed him, gleamed in his amber eyes. Somewhere from far beyond the ridges, as straight and true as a swallow to its cliff nest, the call had come to him. It was mating time.

Before the sun went down, Lobo left the cove and traveled the ridge trail to the high knob above Eagle River. The sky grew black, and yellow lights appeared like pinpoints in the valley. The call was there, where she was waiting, somewhere in the bottom lands beyond the river.

He ran swiftly down the ridge to Eagle River. The water was fast and cold, but he scarcely felt the chill on his trembling hide. He was following a hunger not born of empty vitals. It led him to Jeremiah Duke's house beside the tumbling creek.

A yellow light burned in the window of the house and Lobo circled cautiously. The call was in a shed that sloped off from the big barn 100 feet beyond the kitchen steps. The wolf dog crept up on his belly and stuck his muzzle into one of the cracks that ran the length of the shed wall. The crack was wide enough for vision. Locked inside was a beautiful collie, the loveliest creature he had ever seen. She stepped timidly forward and touched his black nose with hers.

Lobo explored the three sides of the shed, examining the walls minutely. He dug into the hard earth, but the floor was concrete on stone foundation. The collie whined softly, eagerly, setting his blood on a wild sweep through his body. He found a shaky board and thrust the upper part of his jaw into the crack. He set his teeth and threw his raw-boned weight against the plank. The shed was old and the piece of timber tore away, snapping like a pistol.

In a savage shower of splinters the hole grew larger. The collie, her nose almost touching him, was crying now in her fervor and impatience. Lobo worked feverishly, tearing out mouthfuls of the hard wood, wrecking the shed in his throes of anticipation and desire.

Suddenly his eyes caught the flash of yellow light that flooded from the back door of the house. The farmer stood, looking out into the moonlight.

"Hand me my gun quick, Sarah," he said. "There's something trying to git in the shed. It's as big as that wolf dog."

He ran into the yard and Lobo whirled. With lust burning in his throat he half faced the man. But the fear of humans had become a deeply rooted part of him. He spun and took off through the yard. He leaped to clear the high fence that marked the garden.

The roar of the farmer's gun blasted in his ears and his shoulder was almost torn out of the socket. The bullet knocked him completely over in the air

Lobo's eyes caught the flash of yellow light that came from the back door of the house. The farmer stood there, peering out into the moonlight.

and threw him on his back beyond the garden fence. He rolled to his feet as the gun roared again. The lead ball pelted dirt into his face.

Lobo fled remarkably fast with one leg dangling uselessly. He raged inside. He stifled a mad desire to circle back and attack the farmer from behind. But he was powerless against guns and clubs and his desire for survival was the most impelling sense of all.

His leg pounded in agony. This injury obliterated the whippings and the steel trap. He stopped and licked at the dripping blood. The bullet had torn through flesh and ligaments, and when he threw his weight against the foot his eyes went black with pain. He circled the river trail and climbed the long ridge to the head of Cooper Cove. There he lay down and soothed the torn muscles with his tongue.

Jeremiah Duke stood in the Livingston back yard, his gun still under his arm.

"I busted that wolf hard when he went over my back fence," he said. "I found blood where he hit the ground. He can't travel very fast or very far."

"Then it's killing time for that son of a dog," John Livingston said. His words were hard and crisp, but the farmer thought he could detect a note of resignation in his neighbor's voice.

"You finish your supper," Livingston said, "and I'll go after Buck Simpson's hounds in the truck. If Lobo's bad wounded, we won't have trouble finding him or running him to earth on the mountain."

An hour later Lobo heard dogs bellowing far below in the fields. They found his blood on the forest leaves and announced their find in a ringing chorus. They trailed up the slope and Lobo pushed himself

erect on his three sound feet. The pain in his leg spread through his other muscles and left them tight.

Normally Lobo would have fled, giving the hounds the race of their lives before he left them far behind on a lost trail. But he was grim and wounded tonight. He limped painfully 200 yards along the ridge crest, then doubled back, crouched beside a granite boulder, and waited.

The dogs came on, singing their melodious song of the trail. They struck his fresh scent and leapt ahead with frenzied tongues. They approached the wolf dog's ambush by the cliff. Lobo struck hard and fast. His useless leg was more than compensated by savage anger. He swept out of the shadows, into the pack, snarling and slashing. The first hound died with a bellow still in its throat. A second Walker swung to face him. The wolf dog cut it to a mangled heap before the look of surprise went off its face.

The big, flop-eared dogs were not fighters. The remaining dog leaped away and then came back, yelling at the top of its voice, telling the humans down the ridge that it had treed. Lobo jumped at the dog but it sprang out of range. It turned and bayed again.

The sound of running human feet beat through the woods. Lobo turned to sprint away and the hound swept after him with triumphant tones. But the wolf dog did not run. He snapped around and seized the hound at the base of its throat. He swung his head just once and the dog rolled over, quivering in the agony of a violent death.

Lobo climbed the jumbled heap of rocks. He crouched on top of the cliff with his face toward the area he had left. He was safe here. Human eyes could not see him in the dark. Human noses could not follow his trail.

The light from the lantern in Jeremiah Duke's hand glinted on the bodies of the dead hounds. His gnarled hand tightened slowly around the gun.

"Gad!" said John Livingston softly, "what a brute."

He unsnapped the bloody collars from the dogs, and the men stalked back down the trail, the shadows of their legs like monstrous spiders against the earth.

When they had gone beyond the range of his ears, Lobo arose and limped a weary mile up the mountain, where he crawled into a laurel thicket and sank down on a mattress of drifted leaves. There he lay for the remainder of the night and throughout the next day, alternately sleeping and licking the bullet wound in his shoulder.

The afternoon was waning fast when Lobo crawled out of the laurel thicket and stood erect. He could not put his foot down without pain stabbing through his muscles and nerves into his very brain. His eyes were bloodshot and the broad muscles ached across his chest. He had no desire to hunt, but his insides were complaining loudly at the lack of food.

He nosed along a thicket and jumped a rabbit at the forks of the Eagle trail. He sprang, but with the injured foreleg, landed at an awkward angle and missed. He threw out his game foot to catch his weight. When it touched the ground, an explosion of pain burned through his body. The leg buckled under him and he rolled over into the leaves.

All the wolf dog's ill temper flared into flame. He was diabolic. He raged down the forest trail into Cooper Cove, traveling fast on three legs, his eyes bloodshot and mad with the terrible punishment of his wound. The cold river was somewhere below him. He would find the icy water and submerge himself in it to drive out the fevered torment.

Suddenly he stumbled in his stride. His nostrils were full of human scent and the scent of a bear, all mixed up in one foul odor. The flat crack of a gun and a muffled human yell filled the forest. Lobo stood suddenly on a low knoll that rose above the broad floor of the cove.

Before him John Livingston lay sprawled on the ground. It was the second time he had ever seen his old master down. His leg was twisted at an ugly angle, his gun half buried in the leaves where it had been knocked out of his hands. Standing almost over the man was a huge black bear, with blood flowing out of its side.

Lobo did not see the two cubs scrambling for safety up the broad beam of a white oak. He did not know that John had surprised the mother bear and startled her so that she charged instinctively to pro-

tect her cubs. He only saw man, his enemy, helpless on the ground. His feverish brain was beyond reason, with only the unquenchable desire to kill. He did not hesitate. He charged downhill as fast as his three good legs would keep him upright.

The bear heard his padded feet in the leaves and swung to face this new menace to her cubs. Lobo was suddenly conscious that she was not running away, as had the other bears he'd treed. The big, ungainly creature had the temerity to stand up to him.

Instinct and the knowledge of fight had been born in the wolf dog. Momentarily he forgot John Livingston. He held his ground until the bear had thundered down almost upon him, then hurtled aside. He snapped at the white patch on her throat and missed. She spun in her tracks and ripped Lobo with her long claws. The dog swerved, but his weak leg folded under him and he half fell. The bear ripped open a long gash in his hide and his ribs stood white and bare, then streaked with red.

The blow knocked Lobo around, his head close to the broad ham of his foe. He snapped his teeth shut on the black thigh where the hamstrings were, crushing through fur and flesh to the sinews. The bear squalled in pain.

Lobo's mighty jaws closed tighter until the broad haunch gave way. Then one of the bear's flailing paws sent him rolling. She whirled on her good legs to face the wolf dog.

Lobo saw John Livingston crawling toward the gun. He knew that he must finish this first battle quickly and reach the man before the gun was in his hands. He forgot everything but the certain knowledge that he was fighting for his life.

He lashed in savagely, thrusting his head right and left. With his injured leg he could not maneuver quickly, so he traded blow for blow, thrust for counterthrust. The bear was fighting a short, furious battle. Her own hindquarter was useless. The bullet wound in her side was gnawing at her life.

Lobo, himself, was bleeding to death. Salty blood was in his eyes and nose. Through the blur he saw

With all his reserve power Lobo charged, and his grip of death closed on the bear's thick throat while Livingston struggled to aim his rifle.

that John Livingston was trying to point the gun, but the conflict raged too fast in its whirl of flying bodies.

"Fight her, Lobo!" He heard the words through dimming senses. "Fight her!"

Lobo could not run now. With all his reserve power he feinted twice and charged. His grip of death closed on the thick throat and blood spurted in his face. The bear shook with tremendous power, but Lobo held. She beat at him with ham-like paws, but his grip was the grip of death. The big black bear sank slowly down upon her belly.

The wolf dog freed his jaws from her throat and turned on unsteady legs to face the man. He could not see through the red mist that closed his eyes. His head was spinning but he lunged toward the human voice for his second kill. The man's voice was far away.

"Lobo! Lobo! Here, boy!"

He staggered forward to lash out with bloody jaws. He collapsed and his outstretched head, grinning in its malevolent purpose, fell into John Livingston's hands. The life went out of him. His great body shuddered convulsively and relaxed into oblivion.

Tears streamed down John Livingston's face. He laid the big head across his knee and stroked it gently with his finger tips. Words flooded out of his heart, but he could not speak. Lobo had come back to him, had given his own life for his master. There could be no greater test of a champion, no greater sacrifice for a friend.

Charles Elliott

RAY BERGMAN
SAYS GOODBYE by Ray Bergman

More than a year ago, Ray Bergman told us of his desire to retire. Now the time has come, and the news will come as no greater blow to the multitudes of Bergman's fans than it did to us here at Outdoor Life. *We asked Ray to write his valediction, feeling that a final message from the greatest of all angling editors would mean more to our readers than anything we might say, however inspired. Here Ray Bergman says, "Goodbye—until I write again." With our greatest good wishes to you, Ray, goes the one that you will feel the urge to write again soon. The latchstring is always out to you.—The Editor (1960)*

My angling column has been in each issue of *Outdoor Life* for 26 years. I wrote monthly features and a column about fishing for 12 years before I became *Outdoor Life's* angling editor. I am getting along in years. The time has come when I need to take a rest from the steady demands of writing to meet deadlines each month. For this reason I have resigned as angling editor.

It was a tough decision to make. Since joining the *Outdoor Life* staff in March of 1934 I have written for it exclusively. The association has been a happy one. Hence, I want to make it plain that, while this is my last monthly angling column, it is not necessarily the last story I will write for the magazine. I merely want to be free from a regular schedule.

I started writing simply because I loved fishing and wanted to share what I learned from my endless experiments with fishing tackle and tactics. Rather like a person airing his ideas through a letter to the editor, I typed out my first fishing story in 1921 and mailed it to the old *Forest and Stream* magazine. The story was published, and I have been writing similar stories ever since. All my writing has followed the same basic concept: to give the reader factual information gained and tested by my own practical experience, and to make it as interesting as my writing ability would allow.

I have been fishing as long as I can remember. As a child I fished with my father on the Hudson River, which runs by my home town of Nyack, New York. By the time I was 10 years of age I was using a bicycle to pedal to lakes and streams near Nyack to fish for trout, bass, pickerel, and panfish. Eventually I was seeking more distant waters by train and in an early vintage automobile with blowout-prone tires mounted on those frustrating clincher rims.

Though fishing has been my main interest, I have also written a few articles about hunting. At the age of 10, I acquired a .22 rifle (a brass-bore Hamilton) by selling magazine subscriptions. I was in the woods and hills as much as I was on the water, and I brought many a squirrel and rabbit home to add to the family larder.

I have only one painful recollection of my days as a boy hunter. This happened when I was 11.

Father had a double-barreled, muzzle-loading, 12 gauge shotgun. He didn't object to my hunts with the .22 rifle, but he had forbidden me to use the shotgun. This created a desire in me to fire that gun the first chance I got.

Before long the opportunity came. Father was at work in the city and mother had taken a later train to go shopping there. Neither would be home until 6 p.m. It was a splendid setup.

That day I played hooky. I gathered up the shotgun, the powder horn, a bag of shot, and the necessary firing caps. Making sure that none of the neighbors saw me, I sneaked into the woods.

I charged the old muzzle-loader with powder and shot, and began scanning the trees for squirrels. I saw one, drew a bead on it, and pulled the trigger. The next thing I knew I was flat on my back. I had put in too big a powder charge and had held the gun too loosely. Besides, I was just a small child. The tremendous recoil bruised my armpit and badly injured my right hand.

I got the gun home and put it back where it belonged, but I knew I was in for some questioning.

I could get away with the bruised armpit, but I couldn't hide the injured hand.

I am sorry to say that I lied about the hand. I told my parents I'd hurt it by falling. I was guilty of further treachery at school, where I showed my injured hand and was excused from the laborious written work my classmates were doing. I represented myself as a partial invalid for as long as I could. Perhaps my punishment for these boyhood deceits came through a loss of solid enthusiasm for shotguns, which some outdoorsmen cherish as I do my fine fly rods.

I was also a trapper during my youth and early manhood. Trapping season came at a time when there wasn't any fishing. It gave me an extra excuse to explore the woods and waters. I always inspected the trout waters near my traplines regularly during the closed fishing season—just to spy on the brook trout. This helped a lot when the fishing season opened. I knew just where to fish and how to approach the good spots without frightening the trout.

I was the proprietor of a sporting-goods store in Nyack when I was in my early 20's, but I still ran a trapline in season. I often got up at 3 a.m. to run my lines before I opened the store. Routine haul from my traps at this time was a few muskrats and skunks each week, but one morning I made what I considered a bonanza catch on my eight-trap brook line. In one trap was a star-black skunk, a premium-pelt animal with only a small patch of white on its head. In another was a very dark and large northern mink, and in the last was the largest muskrat I'd ever caught. They were all bonus-price furs.

I delayed getting back to the store until the last minute before I should open it for the commuters to pick up their papers. I wanted people on the streets to admire my catch.

I stalked slowly and proudly into town at the right moment—and drove a stream of pedestrians off the sidewalk as if I'd been playing a fire hose ahead of me. Skunk trappers forget how skunks smell to persons unaccustomed to the odor. My trek through town disrupted Nyack so that incident was headlined on the front page of our local paper.

It took a serious illness to get me started writing seriously. In April my doctor recommended a six to eight-month recuperation period in the woods. We didn't have enough money to consider such a thing, but God and good fortune came to our aid. A friend connected us with a couple in the Adirondack mountains of northern New York who had a cabin for rent at a very low fee. A family rented our own home furnished, which carried the expenses of both, as well as supplying a moderate surplus.

It was a marvelous seven months. All I did was fish and hunt. I wrote a two-part article about it that was accepted by *Forest and Stream* with a request for more.

Following my wilderness recuperation, I took a job with the fine old fishing-tackle firm of William Mills & Son of New York. After some 10 years on that job I started a one-man tackle business of my own, doing most of my business through mail order. I have been in some phase of the fishing-tackle business all of my adult life.

Between fishing for sport and working with fishing tackle, I naturally acquired a large store of knowledge of fishing subjects. I drew on this information to write four successful books—*Just Fishing*, *Trout*, *Fresh Water Bass*, and *With Fly, Plug and Bait*. My book *Trout*, which went through 13 printings after its first publication in 1938, was later revised to include a section on spinning tackle.

I remember 1932 as a banner year. I had taken leave of absence from William Mills & Son. By that time I had been writing and selling stories and articles for about 10 years. My wife and I had saved enough to finance a long fishing trip.

We began our fishing in the Catskills of New York state, then to the Adirondacks in the same state—all familiar territory. Then we went to New Brunswick, Canada. All this fishing was mostly for trout and salmon, although we also took some bass and northern pike. Next we made a long trek west to Lake of the Woods in Ontario, Canada, for muskies. Ernie Calvert, now deceased, gave us expert instructions on how to catch these giant members of the pike family. We also got well acquainted with northern pike.

We went from Ontario to Wisconsin, getting a variety of fishing. Then we drove down to North Carolina, where we fished for channel bass off the island of Ocracoke. Later we spent considerable time fishing in the bayous of Mississippi and Louisiana. After that we headed north, expecting to fish the Ozarks in Arkansas and Missouri, but at Little Rock winter struck so suddenly and hard we started home.

An ice storm plagued us for miles. By the time we reached Virginia a blizzard had taken over. We decided to keep going. We didn't make many miles that day but we managed to reach a town in northern Virginia about dark where we spent the night.

Next morning we got up before daylight. It was bitter cold and the roads were snowy, icy, and slippery. Before we reached Harrisburg, Pennsylvania, in late afternoon we'd worn out two sets of tire chains. We bought another pair that didn't fit well. We had about 200 miles to go. Being young, we decided to make for home.

The road was treacherous, the cold intense, hovering around 10°. The car was a five-year-old Model A Ford. It had no heater. The new chains got messed up within 30 miles. I took them off and we made out better without them.

We just had to keep going on. There wasn't much else to do. This was before the days of motels scattered all along the highways. There were few cars on the road.

Our own home in Nyack had been closed for months, so we went to the home of my wife's parents. How wonderful were the warm greetings, the warm house, the hot tea and food. It was a perfect ending to our first long fishing adventure. Since then we have fished in all the good fishing states, as well as many of the Canadian provinces.

Throughout the years there have been some fishing experiences that I remember more vividly than others, and some friends who through their knowledge and helpfulness taught me many of the secrets of successful fishing.

One of the first was an Adirondack guide named Chan Wescott, long since deceased. He put me to many subtle tests before he decided I was worth helping. Then he started giving me advice on where and how to fish. He taught me much about wet-fly and bait fishing, and I was a proud young man when one day he told me I was a good fisherman. It was an honor to be accepted on even terms by those old-time Adirondack guides.

The late J. D. (Don) Bell, who was a lawyer in Hillsdale, N. Y., was the source of much inspiration and help in dry-fly fishing. Gruff, tender-hearted Don was older than I by about 18 years, yet he could wear me out on the stream until he reached the age of 70 and keep up with me until he became 80.

One of the English setters that was Don Bell's constant companion was forever exposing the brawny, thunderous man for the soft touch that he really was. It was common practice for this setter to splash into the trout pool Dan was stalking and swim nonchalantly through the hole before the lawyer could make his first cast. Don would bellow threats at the top of his great voice, promising punishments too terrible to relate. The dog, knowing full well that all would be forgiven, would swim till it tired of the game.

Don had a weakness for dogs and dry-fly fishing. He never fished for anything but trout, and to my

knowledge he never fished with anything but dry flies. I learned much of what I know about dry-fly fishing from him.

I must confess that to me the trouts are the most enjoyable fish to catch. I like them all; the rainbow as the best and most spectacular fighter, the brook trout for beauty and dogged battle, and the brown for its seeming intelligence and its first spirited runs when hooked.

I also love to catch black bass, and I must say that a smallmouth bass of equal size in the same type of water can put a rainbow in a questionable spot as to which is the better fighter.

In some waters I have found the largemouth bass a very good fighter, but as a rule it doesn't have the staying power of either the smallmouth or the rainbow trout. Largemouths make up for this by their gameness in striking surface lures.

Trout and bass have held first place in my heart all through the years, but that doesn't mean I haven't greatly enjoyed fishing for all the other freshwater fish. Muskies, steelheads, and salmon have all had a part in giving me plenty of thrills. I like fishing for pike and pickerel.

I have never been enthusiastic about walleyes (pike-perch) though I have fished for them plenty. If they run large, they'll give you a fair fight, but on the whole I think a yellow perch of equal size is as active as a walleye.

I believe the valiant fight of the common sunfish or its close relative the bluegill is as good a resistance as that shown by a trout or bass of comparable size and maturity. However, it seems to me that sunfish show less intelligence in trying to escape. They simply tug and pull hard, mostly in a circular movement, whereas a trout or bass will leap and roll and tangle your line in snags.

If I had a flair for fiction, I might claim that I was charged by a huge rainbow trout I hooked while wading the Ausable River of upstate New York about 25 years ago. The fish took a dry fly I cast to the Slide Rock Pool and made a powerful run upstream. I was using a light 3X leader and standing hip-deep in the strong current, so there was nothing I could do but let the trout run. I saw him for the first time as he raced downstream and leaped high in the air within five feet of me. There was no mistaking the identity or size of the fish. It was a rainbow trout that would certainly have weighed more than 15 pounds, probably as much as 20.

This great fish took my line far downstream then, and I thought I'd lost him when the line went slack. A second later he was curving the slack line toward me on a sizzling upstream run. This time he was headed straight for me, and he never changed course. He struck the leg I was awkwardly balanced on with such force that I was upended in the water. The trout's mouth must have been open, for my waders were slashed as if his teeth had hung in them momentarily. Perhaps he was trying to knock off the dry fly that was stuck in his jaw.

Needless to say, the monster rainbow broke off as I floundered in the water. I dropped the rod in the tumble and only managed to retrieve it because the loose line looped around my leg.

There have been many interesting experiences in my years of fishing. Once, for example, some disgruntled anglers at Cranberry Lake, New York, decided to have me arrested as a game hog.

We were fishing where Brandy Brook flows into Cranberry Lake. On this particular evening the brook trout there were exceptionally wary. Only those fly fishermen who knew all the tricks for this water were catching any. I was one of those in the know, having been well coached by an old guide of the area.

There were eight anglers at the inlet, and this made the short stretch of shore rather crowded. Among the anglers who couldn't catch any fish was a party of three generally disliked by the local residents and an old saw filer who was on the job of sharpening saws for the Syracuse University forestry students who had a camp at the flow of another brook.

I had caught all the fish I wanted and so had my partner. I was about ready to head for our nearby tent when it occurred to me that the saw filer fishing close to me hadn't caught a fish. He had mentioned that he'd promised the boys at the forestry camp a feed of trout.

I decided to teach him how to get these "flow" trout. It was difficult because of the darkness (night fishing was legal then) but he finally got the knack. Eventually the old saw filer got his limit of brook trout.

In the meantime the three disliked big shots from the village had heard my voice in the dark and all the splashing of the saw filer's catch. They hadn't caught a fish.

Irritated by the sounds of our success, the three luckless men decided to send one of their party to town to get the game warden. They were sure I was exceeding the bag limit.

The game warden was routed out of bed and hauled six miles by boat to investigate. Our catch was strictly legal, but the sleepless warden arrested one of the three soreheads for fishing without a license. I must confess that this amused me.

Before a dam put an end to long float trips on the White River in the Ozarks, my wife and I enjoyed many wonderful days on that river. We fished it so much that Jim Owen of Branson, Missouri, included our home town on a sign post in one of the restaurants. The sign showed the mileage to St. Louis, Tulsa, and other large towns within a reasonable distance

of the river. Jim added Nyack—over 1,200 miles distant—to the list. Jim Owen introduced me to the Ozarks, something for which I have ever been grateful.

My wife and I have had many excellent guides. We remember them all with fondness. We have also had a few poor ones.

There is one thing I wish to press home to you about this guiding business. When a man is hired as a guide his responsibility is to see that the angler he's guiding gets the best possible service. The guide should always place the angler in the best available spot for catching fish. If fishing from a boat or canoe, the craft should be anchored or held in a place that gives the advantage to the sportsman who's paying the bill. The guide should not fish at all unless the paying sportsman asks him to.

I have found the guides in the north country the most considerate of their clients. We have never had one of them who'd think of fishing himself without being coaxed to do so. In this respect the Canadian guides have been outstanding.

I recall with amusement the heroic struggle described by a fisherman who lugged a big northern pike into the lobby of a resort hotel on the Canadian shore of Lake Erie. It had taken every grain of this man's strength and cunning to subdue the whopper he displayed before admiring hotel guests.

I was dressed for dinner and substantially changed in appearance as I stood listening to this story. The talkative angler didn't recognize me. I had met him on the lake that day and given him the big pike to keep him from coming in fishless. I didn't bother to tell the crowd that the fish they were ogling had been boated after a rather dull tug o' war against the spring of my fly rod.

I have fished in some dangerous situations due to the weather, but somehow the most memorable was a windy day in Wisconsin. This wind was raging at 60 to 70 miles an hour. Trees were toppling all over the woods, some of them dropping dangerously close to the cabin where we were staying. My wife stayed indoors and so did the owners. I went out to enjoy the play of the wind and got a great kick out of watching three nearby trees gradually succumb and fall. Not that I wanted the trees to be destroyed, but nothing could be done about that and it was definitely exciting to be out in the blow and to see things happen. The entire lake looked like the froth on a glass of beer. One couldn't possibly fish it and any small boat on it would have been capsized instantly or blown against the shore.

In the middle afternoon I became a bit bored watching the play of the elements. I was about to go inside and read a book when I remembered a protected creek that ran into the lake close to our cabin. It was well guarded against the wind by banks and staunch trees. A state road culvert was at the upper end.

I decided to investigate. I took a spinning outfit and a small box of lures and was partially blown to the edge of the stream. The reasonably calm section was short, not more than 150 feet long.

The wind was strong there, too, but most of it whizzed over my head and didn't disturb the creek much. I hooked two small muskies in this stretch and was about to fish it again, having reached the culvert end. Then I heard a splash that seemed to come from the culvert.

My first cast sent the lure well inside the tunnel, perhaps a distance of 15 to 20 feet. Because the current was coming toward me and I hadn't seen the lure hit, I started reeling quickly. A few seconds later I had hooked a fair muskie, the only decent fish we caught during our stay.

One of the greatest changes I've noticed through the years has been the continually increasing number of anglers. After each war there has been a great increase. Not too many years ago one could fish famous places and not meet more than half a dozen fishermen. Today the same places have paths worn deep along the banks of the streams.

When I first fished the Tennessee River in Alabama with Willie Young we could go to a spot where the fish were and have it to ourselves. Today there are many boats in every good spot. Fishing waters are becoming crowded the same as our highways. Fishing has become big business.

I think too many anglers set out to catch and keep the legal limit. In some places the limit is more than one family can use. Sometimes the excess is simply wasted. Also, I've known of freezers being loaded with frozen fish, many of them being kept there so long that the taste is impaired.

In my opinion, fresh-water fish lose flavor and quality after being frozen. They are at their best when kept really cold, but not frozen, for a few days. When too fresh they're inclined to cook poorly.

Keeping the limit is fine if you can use the fish yourself or have someone who really wants them for food. If you have caught all that you know you can possibly use and still haven't taken your limit, then put back the rest of the fish you catch.

Be careful not to injure a fish you plan to release. If you simply take an injured fish off the hook and throw it back it will eventually bloat and float to the surface. If it drifts to shore before being spoiled, some animal may come along to get it, or some bird like a fish hawk may pick it up. The only birds I've ever seen feeding on bloated or spoiled fish are crows and buzzards. If nothing eats fish that drift ashore they rot and stink up the area.

I suggest that the best way to dispose of a badly injured fish that you don't wish to keep is to open up the belly so it will sink to the bottom. Then it will become food for minnows and other aquatic creatures on which gamefish feed. Many anglers have had the bad habit of tossing unwanted trash fish such as suckers up on the bank to rot in the sun.

I also suggest that when you give fish away you clean them first. Many folk who like fish don't care to do the cleaning. Often unprepared fish are put in the garbage pail.

The best place to clean fish is right on the shore or lake where you've caught them. Then the remains should be thrown into the water where they will feed other fish and aquatic life.

There's plenty of need for improvement in common courtesy in fishing. This was needed even when there were only a fraction of the anglers we have now.

Do not crowd any stream angler who has selected a place to fish and was there before you. Keep far enough away so that you do not spoil his fishing and perhaps yours too. When fishing from a boat, never get so close to another angler that your lines may cross and tangle. Always apply the golden rule. Do unto others as you would have them do unto you.

I wish I could name all of the fine folk who have helped in one way or another along the road to my retirement. I trust that they will accept my sincere thanks for their generous aid in this general way.

Some of you may wonder what I'm going to do now that I've resigned from *Outdoor Life*. Candidly, I'm going to rest and do nothing except exactly what I feel like doing. What I feel like doing is some more fishing in a lazy, indolent way. I also hope to assemble all the notes I've made through the years. Then I'll write again when the urge comes to do so. Farewell for the present. I wish you all health, long life, and many tight lines.

Ray Bergman

JACK O'CONNOR REMEMBERED:

CACTUS JACK by John Madson

For a week we had been hunting chukars above the Snake River in eastern Washington, my son Chris and I, laboring along those god-awful lava slopes each day and getting back to camp late, bone-tired and rock-sore. We were set up just across the river from Lewiston, Idaho, where Jack O'Connor lived. I'd meant to call him and let him know we were around. But as the week wore on and we wore with it, getting raunchier by the day, we didn't figure the O'Connor hearth would be much enhanced by our presence.

I should have known better. The next time we stopped at Paul Nolte's Lolo Gun Shop in Lewiston there was a message waiting: "Dammit, call me O'Connor."

By phone, Jack told me he didn't give a hoot how we looked. He'd seen dirty Levis before. "When you get in from hunting today, come on up to the house," he barked. "We'll have a libation and look at some stuffed animals. Then we'll eat beefsteaks someplace. Adios." Click.

The libations were waiting when we got there, and the stuffed-animal tour got under way. It was something, it really was, although I can't recall many details. Hides, horns and tusks, cases of superb custom rifles and shotguns that dreams are made of. Shelves of classic books bound in buckram and leather. And in the high-ceilinged trophy room, the big heads—the grand slam of sheep, the stately racks of elk, caribou, moose, mule deer, kudu, and orderly benches with reloading presses, and racks of dies and com-

ponents. Then back by a slightly different route, past more hides and oiled walnut and blued steel.

If I was dazed by all this, 19-year-old Chris was stunned. He hadn't said a word. When we got back to the living room, Jack asked:

"Tell me, Chris, have you ever seen anything like that before?"

"No, sir. I sure haven't."

"What do you think of it?"

"Well, sir," said Chris thoughtfully, "you don't fish much, do you?"

In the 20 years I knew Jack O'Connor, it was the only time I ever saw him at a loss for words.

As a matter of fact, Jack hated fishing. And for a gun editor, surprisingly, he wasn't exactly breathless about handguns, either. But when it came to the long guns, and applying rifle and shotgun to the taking of game, he was deeply experienced and expressed that experience in some of the best writing that's been done on the subject.

Jack was one of my guiding lights in the late 1930s, when I was beginning to shoot and hunt. He was one of a special band of dream-spinners called gun writers—men like Bob Nichols, Col. Townsend Whelen, Maurice Decker, Ned Crossman, Phil Sharpe and Elmer Keith. I savored their exploits on the target range and in the field, coveted the wonderful guns they pictured and praised, and tried my best to apply what they taught me to my old low-wall .22 and the local farm thickets.

I don't know how many of those old-time gun writers and editors really hunted. Some of them, like some of today's shooting writers and editors, probably hunted little or never. But there's no denying O'Connor's credentials in that department. His hunting skill went beyond basic shooting ability and coolness in the presence of game, although he had developed great measures of each. Jack also knew the game he hunted. He knew what it took to hunt and kill that game decently, and even more important, he knew what the game needed from the land if it was to withstand hunting pressure. He wasn't just a sometime shooter who could turn a clever phrase. He was a hunter who'd been there and done it, and it showed. It always shows.

Jack relied heavily on personal experience, but he was enough of a technician to distrust isolated examples and fluke occurrences. He preferred to test a bullet, cartridge or rifle in many ways before drawing a conclusion. I don't think he ever felt really familiar with a particular cartridge until he had hunted with it. Sure, he reported on new loads and rifles tested only on the bench, but his gilt-edge endorsement was generally reserved for guns and ammo proved under rigorous field conditions.

To the shooting public, Jack O'Connor's middle name was ".270 Win." He was the cartridge's official press agent—so outspoken in its praises that he had a sort of spiritual copyright on it. The .270 may have been Winchester's baby, but Jack was its adopted daddy. This got a bit wearisome in his later years. He was sometimes a little touchy about his public identification with the .270, but he brought it on himself with glowing anecdotes like this one from his story "Up to Our Necks in Deer":

"Whoopee!" said Zefarino. "That's the kind of rifle I like, one that has power. One shot and the buck doesn't move. How do you call it?"

"The .270," I said.

"The same you shot the ram with, no?"

"The same."

"With the .30 you shot a buck and it ran. Then the smaller boy shot a buck with the .25 and it ran. Now the large boy shoots a buck with this rifle and it is dead in its tracks. How good a rifle, this .270!"

"It shoots a good ball," I said. "A very fast ball."

So spoke O'Connor, and the .270 flourished apace. And characteristically, Jack knew whereof he spoke. He'd wrung out the .270 on three continents. He shot at least 36 species of big game with his cartridge. These included more that 30 rams (four grand slams of American mountain sheep and four Old World species), an even dozen moose, more than a dozen black bears, two grizzlies, at least 18 elk, 17 caribou and several species of deer. How many deer? I doubt if even Jack knew. He also used the .270 in Africa on such tough game as oryx and zebra, as well as ibex, gazelle and antelope in Iran and India.

In many ways, Jack was in the catbird seat as a gun writer. He developed during the 1920s and 1930s when great advances were being made in really modern rifles, sights and cartridges. It was a time when the bolt-action sporting rifle and its high-intensity cartridges began to really come into their own. New powders and primers and revolutionary bullet designs were appearing, telescopic sights and mounts were evolving rapidly, giant strides were being take in fitting rifle actions and barrels into one-piece stocks,

and men were revising what they'd known about accuracy. Jack O'Connor knew many rifles and shotguns, but he'll always be most closely identified with the superbly accurate, strongly breached, bolt-action rifle with 'scope sight and fast, jacketed bullet. After all, he was mainly a man of open country, of mountains and plains and deserts, and this showed in his interests and preferences.

As a gun writer who depended heavily on hunting mileage, he had plenty of grist for his mill. Born in Arizona Territory in 1902, he grew up in a hunter's paradise that still had overtones of the Old West, next door to the game-rich desert wilderness of Mexican Sonora. He'd begun writing during a period when new road systems and air travel were opening up many remote hunting ranges in the West, British Columbia, the Yukon and Alaska. He had

served his apprenticeship at the close of one era and the beginning of another.

I first met him in the fall of 1958, at the first Winchester Gun Writers' Seminar, at Nilo Farms in southwestern Illinois. Those were some fandangos, those early seminars, including such scribes as Warren Page, Pete Kuhloff, Larry Koller, John Amber, Pete Brown, Dave Wolfe, Elmer Keith, Les Bowman, Col. Charley Askins, Bill Edwards, Tom Siatos and such notable drop-ins as Col. Townsend Whelen, Nash Buckingham and Andy Devine.

I've never laughed harder, learned more, or had days and nights pass any faster than at those early Winchester seminars. Rich talk and wild tales, all leavened with deep experience and salty humor. How I wish we'd taped some of those sessions in the old Stratford Hotel! About half the guys were more or less deaf, of course. A conversation between Jack O'Connor, Lee Bowman, John Amber and Elmer Keith could be heard through most of the hotel. A stranger might get the idea they were violent antagonists yelling at each other. Not so. They were good friends just trying to hear each other after too many years of unshielded muzzle blasts. And later on, after dinner, we'd all convene for the main bullshoot with half of us sitting on the floor while actor Frank Ferguson, Pete Kuhloff, Andy Devine and other masters vied in round-robin story contests that would send us to bed at 3 a.m., completely laughed out.

Yet, I don't think I ever heard Jack O'Connor tell a joke at one of those shindigs. He just wasn't a joke-teller. His style of humor was anecdotal. You never belly-laughed at an O'Connor story; it was wry, dry and low key. His humor lay in the sardonic twist of real experience, and he often used it to make a point. For instance, this comment on rifle stock design:

"Sometimes very slight changes in curves and angles make the difference between a beautiful and graceful stock and a homely and ordinary one. I am thinking of two sisters I once knew. Both were blonde, witty and charming. But one (though she was a fine cook and had a heart of gold) was a rather ordinary-looking lass who got by on her good disposition and winning ways. The other was a tearing beauty, a creature so lovely that one look at her sent young men's blood pressure skyward and set them to uttering wild, hoarse cries and tearing telephone directories apart with the bare hands. Yet actually those two girls looked much alike. It was easy to see they were sisters. What made the difference was an angle here, a line there, small dimensional differences in eyes, noses, mouths. And so it is with stocks."

Jack was a great admirer of the late H. L. Mencken and shared many of that great man's views on the sad state of the English language and the world in general. Like Mencken's, even Jack's compliments could have a wire edge. I once spoke at a dinner meeting that Jack attended. I can't remember the subject now, but Jack came up afterward and said:

"Well, that wasn't quite as bad as I thought it would be. It was fairly tolerable—although as a rule I hate after-dinner speakers like God hates St. Louis!"

He spoke with authority, for his wife, Eleanor, was a St. Louis girl. Jack met her at the University of Missouri. Still, I couldn't let that slight to one of my favorite cities go unanswered. I loved to needle Jack.

A couple of years later, coming into Lewiston from Missoula, I passed a pulp mill whose sulfite stink tainted the air for 10 miles up the Clearwater. When I saw Jack, I gave it to him:

"O'Connor, don't you ever badmouth St. Louis again! Why, I can't wait to get back to the Mississippi and away from this west Idaho stench! Come home with me, Jack, and breathe some good air for a change!"

He gave me a long, level look through those wire-rimmed glasses of his. You could almost hear the gears meshing. He asked: "Madson, tell me something. How much does Remington pay you to work for Winchester?"

"Not enough!" I said without thinking.

"AGREED!" Jack yelled triumphantly. It made his whole day.

We had some good yarning sessions on guns and hunting, although near the end of his life it seemed that Jack was less disposed to talk about guns than other subjects. And a thing he never tired of discussing was writing.

Jack was a trained journalist with years of teaching at Arizona universities. All that showed, too. His work was disciplined, carefully controlled and structured. It wears well. Jack never used a heavy word when a light one would do, and he seldom used any word carelessly. He was a relentless self-editor who knew that simplicity and directness are the essences of good communication. His sentences were short, crisp and to the point. No—come to think of it, they weren't always short. As a fine double-gun seems lighter because it is well designed and balanced, so Jack's longer sentences usually seem shorter than they really are.

Jack was a durable man and well designed for his calling, seemingly made of slabs, laths, bits of wire and scraps of leather. He had to be named O'something. With that long upper lip and wire-framed specs, he was Paddy to the life—and the older he got the more Irish he looked. Now and then he'd wear a shapeless tweed hat that someone had given him; all he needed then was a blackthorn stick to be the image of a reformed Donegal poacher.

He was also inclined to be a dour man. He was outspoken and intolerant of those he considered fools, phonies or bores, and some of his bitterest opinions were reserved for writers who produced what he called "the vast amount of vague, windy, sloppy and sometimes dishonest writing that is put out about rifle accuracy."

Most of Jack's career was linked with *Outdoor Life*. He wrote his first piece for OL in 1934—a conservation story titled "Arizona's Antelope Problem." He did several more stories for the magazine during the mid-1930s, and late in 1936 editor Ray Brown asked him to write exclusively for OL. Jack accepted, and took a year's leave of absence from teaching journalism at the University of Arizona to write magazine stories and work on a book. Thus he entered the rarefied world of freelance writing.

He was back at the university full-time, and still doing articles for *Outdoor Life*, when shooting editor Ned Crossman committed suicide in 1939. Jack was asked to replace him, and began doing a regular department called "Getting the Range." In the June 1942 issue Jack was named arms and ammunition editor and continued in that position until 1972. During his years with *Outdoor Life* he wrote more than 200 articles for the front of the book; in addition to shooting columns that appeared almost monthly for about 43 years. No other gun writer has racked up that much mileage with one magazine.

Jack retired officially from *Outdoor Life* in 1972 although he served as shooting editor for another year after that. During those last years I hunted upland birds in level fields with him. He got along fine, but his mountain days were over. He'd been in a bad car wreck in 1957.

Jack died on January 20, 1978, aboard a cruise ship returning from Hawaii, just two days before his 76th birthday. His wonderful wife and favorite hunting companion, Eleanor, was with him at the end—and followed him within the year.

A few years before Jack left *Outdoor Life* we were yarning away on an autumn evening in Lewiston, talking about hunting in general and gun writing in particular. Jack had been reflecting on the old-timers—Whelen, Sharpe, Nichols, Crossman and the rest—when he suddenly turned to me and said: "John, how in hell can they ever replace me? Who can they find who's seen what I've seen, and can write about it?"

My first impulse was to land on him for such a typical O'Connor remark, but after a moment's reflection I understood. No one could really replace him. He was the product of a special time, and we'll not see his like again, for the country and experience that shaped Jack will never exist again. He couldn't be replaced; he could only be succeeded—and by a younger man who'd write for today's shooters, sharing their problems and hopes and not letting the rich memories of vanished places and long-ago hunts sour today's adventures. A successor like Jim Carmichel, who Jack approved as "a good writer and a very knowledgeable young man." Coming from O'Connor, that was about as good as anyone will get.

The epitaph of Western artist Frederic Remington is simply: "He knew the horse." If two generations of shooters and hunters were to rephrase that, Jack's stone would say: "He knew the rifle and loved the game."

Good hunting, old friend. See you in camp at sundown.

John Madson

A BUCK FOR JANETTE by Jim Zumbo

My two daughters and I stood on the ridge and looked down into the juniper forest across the canyon. My binoculars helped me spot a doe and two fawns lying under a tree, and I glassed intently for a buck that might be hidden nearby. After 10 minutes, I gave up and sat down on a ledge, and instructed Judi and Janette to do likewise. Perhaps a buck would become restless and move around.

"Can I use your binoculars, Dad?" 14-year-old Judi asked in a whisper.

I passed them to her and relaxed as she scanned the canyon below us. It was 10 a.m. and the weather was superb—too good for hunting. The temperature was about 60°, and there wasn't a cloud in the brilliant blue Utah sky.

"I see a deer, Dad," Judi suddenly announced, "and it's a buck!"

I looked down to where the binoculars were aimed and saw two deer—a forkhorn and a doe.

"Don't move," I instructed. "They don't see us and I want Janette to find a good rest."

I eased over to a nearby cornice and wadded my jacket into a ball, watching the deer as I moved. I motioned to Janette to slip over to the jacket and use it for a rifle rest, but the deer quickly disappeared in the high sagebrush. Assuming they bedded down, we stood motionless and waited.

I was nervous and excited, because I badly wanted Janette to kill a buck. It would be the first for my 20-year-old daughter, and I had been feeling like a failure as a father. A few weeks before hunting sea-

son, Janette told me she wanted to hunt deer. I was mildly surprised, because, in the past, she was content to just go along on the hunt and hike around, or read in camp. She and her brother, Dan, had accompanied me on deer and elk hunts since they were 10 years old. Many times they followed dutifully behind me as I slipped along a deer trail, and every now and then I had to turn and bawl them out for making too much noise, or fighting to see who walked directly behind me.

Janette never winced or showed displeasure as I field-dressed game, and always seemed interested in the process. More than once, I identified each vital organ to the children as I cleaned birds, rabbits, deer, and elk.

Although Janette passed her hunter safety test when she was 14, she had never hunted, and never expressed an interest in doing so. That's why I was surprised when she announced she wanted to kill a deer.

As we sat there on the ridgetop, waiting for the buck to appear, I recalled the conversation I'd had with Janette a month ago.

"You really want to hunt a deer?" I had said to her when she asked about going on a hunt.

"Yes," she answered. "I always wanted to hunt."

"You have?" I responded incredulously. "For how long?"

"Ever since I was old enough," she replied quietly, "but you always took Dan."

"Why didn't you tell me?" I said.

"Oh, I don't know," she answered. "I guess I thought I'd always be too much of a bother."

Janette must have sensed my feelings. I was upset with myself, frustrated because I never knew my daughter's desire to hunt.

"Don't feel badly, Dad," she smiled. "It's no big deal."

It was a big deal, though. I'd failed her, and it took far too long to find out. My daughter was a lovely woman now, talented, intelligent, and mature. For too many years, I had neglected her, always assuming she wasn't interested in actively participating in our hunts.

Although I don't consider myself a male chauvinist, I was painfully guilty of ignoring Janette in favor of Dan. As I perceived it, hunting was a man's sport and, in my mind, it was natural to expend all my time and effort with my son.

After Janette and I had that talk, I recalled several outings we'd had. When she was 14, I took her along on a Wyoming mule deer hunt. The two of us walked a dozen miles that day, but she never complained.

Another time, she and I stalked a buck deer in a Utah forest, crawling 100 yards on our bellies to do so. When I killed the buck she was as excited as I was.

It was Dan, however, who received all my attention. When he was 3, I carried him on my shoulders when I trained my German Shorthair over live pheasants. I gave him an air rifle when he was 10, a .22 at 12, a shotgun at 14, and a rifle at 16. When he turned 14, I took him deer hunting in neighboring Colorado because the Utah minimum age is 16. And so it went.

Now it was time to undo all those wrongs. I prayed for the buck to appear, and I fervently hoped Janette wouldn't miss if she got a shot. A miss might turn her off for good.

As I glassed the sagebrush-choked canyon bottom, I heard rocks falling from the steep slope just below us. We all heard the noise at the same time, and I turned to see the buck and doe slowly walking up the mountain toward us. The deer hadn't spotted us, but it would only be a matter of time. We were in a clump of sparse brush and weren't concealed very well.

Janette eased the rifle to her shoulder and looked at me quizzically. I knew what was on her mind. She'd accompanied me on too many hunts.

"No time to find a rifle rest," I whispered, "and we don't dare move. You'll have to shoot him off-hand. Let him get as close as possible."

The deer were only 75 yards away when an errant breeze apparently alerted them. The doe tossed her head up and stared directly at us. The buck stopped instantly and also spotted us.

Time seemed to stand still as Janette drew a bead through the scope. Several thoughts raced through my mind. She was using my .30/06 and I feared she would flinch as she squeezed the trigger. Or perhaps she'd suffer a case of buck fever and blow the shot. Or, worse yet, she might wound the buck, requiring a careful pursuit in the steep, dangerous canyons.

Several seconds passed, but Janette didn't fire. I was beside myself with anxiety, but I didn't say a word. Suddenly, the doe snorted and made a quick bound up the slope. The buck took a short, nervous step, and it was his final act.

The rifle cracked and the deer fell to the ground. He lay still, and I knew he belonged to my daughter.

Normally, I don't display much outward emotion when an animal is claimed, but I couldn't help myself this time. I jumped around like a fool and hugged

Despite her father's parental anxiety, Janette Zumbo successfully took a buck on her first try.

Janette as we hurried over to the fallen buck. Both girls were wide-eyed and excited as we approached the deer, and I fumbled with my camera, unable to compose myself for the ensuing photo session.

After instructing Janette to pose with the buck, I observed her carefully for some show of feelings. She was trembling and her eyes were a bit teary, but I detected no misgivings in her attitude.

"Do you feel badly about killing the deer?" I asked.

"No, Dad," she answered. "It's young and fat, and will be good eating. Besides, there's no easy way for a deer to die. It could starve, get hit by a car, die from a horrible disease, or be killed by a cougar or coyotes."

I was relieved that my daughter had no regrets. Her philosophy about taking an animal's life was an intelligent one, but it wasn't an attitude that she'd come up with herself. I taught the children about the natural world—the real natural world, not the one portrayed in absurd movies and TV shows.

Our family lived in New York state for a period of time while the children were growing up. Each year I managed to hang a whitetail buck from the maple tree alongside our house, and occasionally some neighborhood children made comments to my youngsters about me killing deer. I explained hunting to Dan and Janette, and they were satisfied with my viewpoint. Because they accompanied me on hunts when they were young, they had a first-hand look at the sport.

Unfortunately, most kids these days have no opportunity to go hunting. Worse, boys are almost exclusively initiated into the hunting fraternity.

When girls do hunt with their fathers, it's usually because that particular family has no sons. Plenty of men have told me, "I don't have any boys, so my daughter is my hunting buddy."

That's too bad, but I understand the attitude. I was guilty of it myself until Janette finally told me she wanted to hunt.

I won't make the same mistake with Judi. She passed her hunter safety test and hunted cottontails with me last year.

Like Janette, Judi expressed no remorse when she killed her first animal. She ran over to the fatally hit but still-kicking rabbit, plucked it out of the snow, and proudly hoisted it up for me to see. She killed two more that day, and she helped me skin and dress them when the hunt was over.

To be sure, daughters require more understanding and patience than sons, when is it comes to hunting. Girls are expected to play with dolls; boys play with soldiers and toy guns.

They're programmed that way from an early age. It's easy and natural for a boy to make the transition from toy guns to real guns, but it's more of an effort to introduce girls to firearms if they haven't been exposed to them during pre-adolescence.

It's wrong to think that girls and women are automatically turned off by hunting. A good pal of mine recently took his wife on a Wyoming antelope hunt. He was apprehensive, because this was her first hunt. She had never fired a gun in her life until he prepared her for the trip. Born in Philadelphia, she was raised a city girl and had no outdoor experience. My pal's worries were in vain. His wife not only killed a buck antelope with a well-placed shot, but she bemoaned the fact that she didn't have a deer tag as well.

Another friend moved to the West a few years ago, and took his Connecticut-reared wife along on an antelope hunt. She was impressed, and quickly learned how to shoot. Now she's his constant hunting companion.

Hunting has long been thought to be solely a man's sport. It isn't. It's important to recognize that women, no matter what age, have many of the same outdoor interests as men. You might have to nudge your daughter, wife, or girlfriend to develop a latent urge that would never surface without your encouragement, but it's worth it.

As for me, Janette and Judi will be my regular hunting pals, as well as Dan and my wife, Lois, and I'm all the more happier for it.

And then there's 5-year-old Angela, who has just recently helped me carry cottontails back to the truck during a hunting trip. In a few short years, she'll be ready to shoulder a rifle and hunt with me.

I can't wait.

Jim Zumbo

"ADVENTURER"

IN THE SHARK TRADE by Jerry Gibbs

I've always taken sinister delight in the line from Bobby Darin's classic tune "Mack the Knife" about the shark having such pretty teeth, dear. That the shark keeps them pearly white is good stuff, too, both for the fierce imagery it conjures up and, in a practical sense, for anyone crafting the fish's distinctive dental work into nautical baubles. Which is exactly what Gloria Patience does after she's conquered the beasts with the ivory teeth.

On one such occasion, though, the item most noticeably pearly white was Gloria's blood-drained face.

Anchored in 250 feet of water, fishing down 1,500 feet at the edge of the continental shelf off Exuma, Bahamas, she and her brother were hand-lining red snappers. They'd been at it successfully for a while, and the cobalt-blue water was rich with bait and scent, and probably a little blood. That's when a middling-size mako shark, about seven feet long, exploded through the silky slick surface and smashed her brother in the neck, sending him to the deck unconscious. Gloria pitched over the side of her Boston Whaler in the continuing pandemonium. The free-jumping shark then disappeared.

"I taught my butt to walk on water in the next two seconds," says Gloria, affectionately known around Exuma as The Shark Lady. "The nearest thing was the boat's bow. Never thought I could climb over it, but I scurried right up like a damned crab." That was some years ago. Her brother still has neck problems. But Gloria's battle-seasoned 13-foot Whaler, *The Nut Cracker*, tooth-scarred and once stolen, is none the worse for the wear in the shark-catching trade. The same goes for Gloria Patience.

She may not fish as often these days, but that's OK. A cadre of international pals—adventurers, artists,

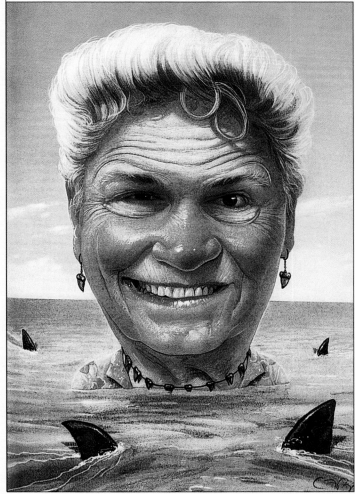

What does a 77-year-old grandmother do for fun? She tangles with 500-pound sharks, my dear.

The Shark Lady subdues a still-living shark after hauling it in with her unique fishing outfit. "I do it right, I do it big, I do it with class," is her motto.

thongs. She wears no shoes. Never. Not here, not on the mainland nor on the streets of London. "Not for the Queen—even if I had been invited for tea, which I wasn't when I visited there," she says. She fluffs her short silver hair and refocuses those bright, flinty blue eyes that click from mirthful to icicle sharp when the talk slides over to sharks.

For The Shark Lady there is no dark preoccupation with the predators themselves, the infinite brute power of them as nature's ultimate instruments of dissolution. No pathological Captain Quint-like thirst for revenge. No delicious titillative fear of being devoured alive. No thrill for the piston-thump of the 18-inch-barrel marine shotgun (used to quiet the sharks) and its spawn of havoc.

Shark collecting to Gloria is the same today as when she was a young girl: utilitarian, a way to make a living, with the added bonus of extreme adventure. And in the early years, possibly as a means of establishing equal footing with male siblings.

"My father showed me—once—how to wade out from the beach with a home-woven line made of silvertops [palmettos] and a brass hook he'd made and baited with a fish head. I learned to tie the line to a buttonwood tree to help me fight the sharks.

"That's how I made my money as a girl. I skinned my sharks and sold the salted skin to the Ocean Leather Company [still going strong in Newark, New Jersey]. I used to call myself an adventuress until I looked it up. Honest to God, it means a woman who uses men to get what she wants. I should have used 'adventurer.' I wanted to do everything my father and brothers did."

The Shark Lady did just about that. Straight out of the chute she needed no Equal Rights Amendment for common ground in the true dark ages of male jingoism. Equality Gloria grabbed by the, ahem, ears and made it hers. Over the years came the fellowship, respect and love of men from an odd mixture of worlds that spanned academic, military, art and sports disciplines.

Growing up on her Scots-Irish parents' farm on Hog Cay south of Exuma, she ran the hills like a colt and told the world what she was not about early on. "At age 3 I was kicked out of my first school for beating up a guy and throwing him into a prickly pear tree. They sent me to Sacred Heart [school] in Nassau where I lasted six months and was booted out at age 4½. My father brought me back to Hog Cay where he had hired a tutor I wouldn't listen to. I learned to read and write from a book called the *Mavis Spelling Book*. I cannot be taught, I have to do it myself."

Her approach to sharks is the same.

This is handline stuff. Then again, forget line. She uses 150 feet of braided polyester rope;

scientific types—donate the odd tooth-studded jaw or shark vertebrae, which she pieces-down into necklaces and bracelets. When she does go in pursuit of sharks, Gloria takes a local boat boy with her now to help truss captive, still-living sharks to the boat, but that's her only concession to the years. At 77, she handles a 60-pound grapnel with little more effort than a flower pot, and you would not want to challenge her to a quick bout of arm wrestling.

Four of her nine children, moved in recent years back to Great Exuma Island, constantly worry over her. "They call me up, tell me I shouldn't be chasing sharks, running the damn boat at my age. But I have confidence in my abilities, my dear. If I want to get up and wiggle my butt [she does so], or dance with a drink on my head [she does this also, without spilling a drop], I will."

We are just now at a beach house party on Little Exuma, and Gloria's demonstrations are eye-catching. The explosive yellow of her dress is echoed by the gold necklace and ring she wears against deeply, permanently tanned skin, a mockery of conventional wisdom—as is her style—about the terrors of UV exposure.

Strings of gold beads encircle her ankles and thread between her first two toes, forming faux sandal who knows how strong. To the rope is shackled a six-foot length of chain "leader" and a hook bigger than a big man's foot. A whole grouper head is impaled from the top, the hook point emerging below the jaw. The rig is dropped, the boat moved and anchored so that the line is tight. Sharks up to 10 feet long Gloria simply hauls in. The Shark Lady says she can tell instantly the size of the beasts and you don't doubt it; not from someone who can feel the brush of a red snapper against her baited line 1,500 or 2,000 feet down.

Big things more than 10 feet get the treatment. With the hooked shark going away, Gloria grabs the line and deftly knots to it a short rope attached to a preassembled buoy rig. From the buoy streams an additional 30 to 40 feet of rope tied to a 60-pound grapnel anchor. She heaves the whole works overboard. The rig is now free of the boat. She has yet to hook a shark that has trucked off with her gear. Does she let the creature fight the grapnel and buoy a bit?

"And let some other shark take the fruit of my labor? Oh no, my dear. I go right to it and haul his tail up. It's a neat system."

Alongside *The Nut Cracker's* gunnels, Gloria's methods have come full circle. There was a time when she owned a bang stick that made things simple. "It got their attention; it put a four-inch hole in their heads. But someone stole the thing and now I'm back to tying the suckers up." Which means that, to the amazement of most shark sport fishermen, Gloria snout-ties and tail-ties her 10-foot-and-less catches, heaving them aboard and lashing them down. The bigger fellows are likewise trussed but towed to a nearby beach.

She is fastidious about cleaning her catch. Dragging a shark up the sand, its tail is severed, no blood going back into the water. "In no time he's gone," she says. "It's the quickest way." The back vertebrae and teeth are removed, the body steaked for human consumption or turned into fertilizer. There is nothing wasted.

In 1934, when Gloria was 16, architect and civil engineer James Lewless anchored at Hog Cay

on an intended round-the-world cruise. "We fell in love," she says. "I married my first boyfriend. We raised nine children and lived in Nassau where his business was." They were married 27 years, the last 10 of which James, quite considerably her senior, was ill. Gloria turned to other professions to support the family. In her self-taught way, she became a physiotherapist, masseuse and nurse, sometimes working 18-hour days.

She's lived with her second husband, George Patience, for 33 years. Moving back to Exuma in 1970, she transformed the old post office into a cottage, naming it "Tara" ostensibly after the O'Hara homestead in *Gone With The Wind*, but perhaps subliminally for its original reference to the home of ancient Irish kings. "I've always been a romantic," she tells you.

But that truth is intermixed with the gritty realities of making a living. Knowing her childhood waters around Exuma intimately, and finding a ready market with no competition, she began supplying local resorts with fresh fish, handlining 300 pounds of snappers in a morning and simultaneously rekindling her old relationship with sharks. That relationship became all-consuming.

The shark-fighting grandmother's exploits were soon bannered from such widely ranging publications as London's *Tattler* tabloid and *National Geographic* magazine. She has appeared in books, prestigious travel periodicals and on "The American Sportsman" television series. She became pals with *Jaws* author Peter Benchley and a varied cast of visiting sports figures and writers. For R & R she competitively captained a sailing dinghy with a crew of topless women until a rules committee disallowed the team for unfair diversionary tactics.

With sharks, though, Gloria now takes a self-described diplomatic approach. The predators are hunted in channels and in the mouths of creeks back into the mangroves rather than in the open ocean.

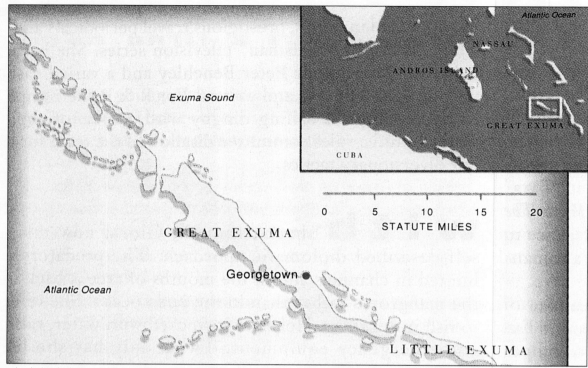

The Shark Lady's home in Great Exuma, Bahamas, is about 300 miles off the Florida coast, 150 miles from Cuba. And the surrounding waters are thick with sharks.

She refuses to fish in darkness. Her boat is stocked with water, rations and emergency equipment. Twice only has she been forced to overnight aboard the Whaler because of equipment failure. Such inconveniences and inherent risks of the game she accepts almost cavalierly. She has never considered herself in peril, although there was the thing with the tiger sharks once.

Gloria had trussed a 10-foot male tiger to the boat. Some tattered bait remained on the hook, which was thrown back in. "Male tigers are the only shark that lacerate the females with their teeth before they mate, and that's what must have been going on," says Gloria. "We suddenly hooked up again. It was a nine-foot female, her body cut from head to tail. She must have been in a terrible mood from it because she charged the boat and grabbed the gunnel in her jaws. We had to pry her off. The front row of teeth was left in the fiberglass. We got her, though."

The excitement resounds in her voice as she remembers other big fish, and her largest of all: "I had a mean seven-foot lemon shark on when this big mother of a shark came up and swallowed it—all except for the head.

"She came again, a tiger, 18 feet of her, and took the head and was hooked. When I finally beat her she was too big to tow in and I had to kill her there. She had that lemon shark in her stomach plus a hundred-pound turtle."

Gloria's eyes affect that characteristic flinty-sharp stare as she connects past remembrances with present-day experience. Her enthusiasm continues. "The other day we were fishing a creek for grunts and snappers and there were five lemon sharks there, one of them pretty big. They took some of our fish, our larger fish. I didn't have my shark gear or I would have got them. I still know every worthwhile fishing drop around here, my dear—for dinner fish or for sharks—and I can run right to them without any fancy equipment. I take my bearings and I know exactly where I'm going."

No one would doubt it.

Jerry Gibbs

THE BEST THE
WORLD NEVER KNEW
by Jeff Murray

Paul Schafer inched to within spitting distance of a pair of impressive pronghorns ... but they didn't quite measure up to his standard. Not after what he'd seen an hour earlier. A massive antelope—a potential state record—had filled the Montana bowhunter's binoculars, and he just couldn't shake the memory. But now the day was nearly over. A low sun glared in his eyes as he belly-crawled up a narrow rock ledge, hoping to catch one last glimpse of that monster. At the ridge, he put the glasses to his eyes—and there it was, a distant speck on the horizon. Tears running down his cheeks, Schafer squinted at the most magnificent pronghorn he'd ever seen.

Somehow, he managed to scratch and claw to within bow range for one last shot. Coolly, he nocked an arrow and focused on the buck's chest cavity. But just as his arrow was about to find its mark, the graceful animal whirled, causing the broadhead to glance off a back leg. The antelope of many lifetimes loped out of sight, Schafer scrambling behind ... but darkness ended the chase before it had begun.

For many hunters, an important question now must be answered: How long should a conscientious bowhunter pursue an animal with a superficial wound? Five miles the next morning? Ten miles or 10 hours, whichever comes first?

"TRY THREE DAYS AND MORE THAN 40 MILES," says eyewitness Tom Sander, noted wildlife artist and a longtime Schafer friend. "Paul got that antelope, which was a state record at the time, because both as a marksman and as a principled hunter, he was in a class by himself."

Like many legends, Paul Schafer's story could not be told while he lived. Shy, sensitive and ever humble, he shunned publicity, and only a loyal fraternity of close friends knew of his incredible legacy. But perhaps it's time, now that Schafer rests in peace, to share him with the world.

This Montana custom-bow maker extraordinaire succumbed to a tragic skiing accident on January 18, 1993, at the age of 44. While negotiating an icy slope on Big Mountain near his home in Kalispell, Montana, Schafer lost control at full speed and slid headfirst into a tree, breaking his neck and rupturing his aorta. He died instantly.

At 5 feet 10 inches and 190 pounds, the burly Schafer possessed the strength of three men. One time, while bear hunting with friend Scott Koelzer, a flat tire and broken jack threatened to strand the two in the middle of nowhere. No problem. "I'll lift the car," Schafer said to Koelzer, "while you change the tire." Which is exactly what he did!

"Schafe's upper body strength was amazing," buddy Gene Wensel says. "He was fanatical about his nocking point, so he'd continually draw his 85-pound recurve, then hold it out in front of him, arms spread apart, to eyeball the angle of the arrow shaft. And we still talk about the time he downed a nice bighorn sheep that threatened to tumble hundreds of feet over a cliff. He dove for the sheep, putting a

death-lock on one of its legs and holding his position by gripping a nearby tree with his other hand. Slow but sure, he wrestled that 250-pound sheep back on top of the ledge."

This sheep was one of many trophies that fell to an arrow driven by his own make of bow, the graceful, powerful Schafer Silvertip recurve. His other personal trophies include: world-class Canadian moose, bighorn sheep, mountain goat and likely the largest African Cape buffalo taken by a modern bowhunter; a trio of Montana bowhunting records for bighorn sheep, pronghorn and mule deer, a string of Pope and Young Club-class mountain goats, whitetails and blacktails, elk, grizzlies and black bears. On top of this, Schafer's Grand Slam of the four species of wild sheep—Dall, bighorn, desert bighorn, Stone's—is considered the best of the best.

Superhuman physical strength alone did not qualify Schafer for greatness; a sturdy inner strength propelled his uncompromising pursuit of excellence. Take the day that, as a star running back, he set the all-time Montana State University record for rushes in a single game, 58. That afternoon, he won the game in the waning seconds by carrying the ball eight times in a row, scoring the winning touchdown despite playing the entire second half with a broken collarbone, sprained knee and twisted ankle. Dennis Erickson, coach of the University of Miami Hurricanes, who was Montana State University's quarterback at the time, says, "Paul Schafer was the toughest man I've ever met on or off a football field."

An equally riveting testimony to this man's heart is a 1989 Zimbabwe hunt. M.R. James, Schafer's neighbor and editor of *Bowhunter* magazine, had encouraged the soft-spoken bowhunter to share a written narrative about the hunt. Schafer wrote:

"I inch across burning sands, pushing my bow ahead to belly-crawl [toward a herd of about 100 bedded Cape buffalo] less than 70 yards away. A suspicious cow at 10 yards, the whites of her red-rimmed eyes showing, threatens to stampede. My throat is dry, I try swallowing and must fight back the urge to cough. A good bull, alerted by the cow's action, circles closer ... a tempting target at under 10 yards—but the thought of the huge bull [in the distance] kept me motionless.

"... the cow whirled and pounded away. Buffalo rose from their beds all around me, milling about. The bull I wanted remained bedded [but] quartering away. I wanted a broadside shot or nothing, fearing heavy ribs could deflect anything but a perfectly placed arrow. Then he was on his feet, swinging his heavy head from side to side, facing directly away from me. I rose to my knees. As the buffalo started to turn broadside, I came to full draw. Smack! My arrow took him right behind the shoulder and disap-

A bighorn from Paul Schafer's grand slam.

peared to its fletching. Grunting, he thundered off, taking the herd with him. In an instant, he was lost in a cloud of choking dust. I knelt there, unmoving, awe-struck. I knew I had a good hit ... but it seemed almost too good to be true.

"Suddenly, from out of the clouds of dust, I could see dozens of dark shapes materializing shoulder to shoulder, moving my way. I had a fleeting sense of how Custer must have felt on that June day on the eastern Montana plains. I scarcely breathed. One cow, apparently catching our scent, abruptly lumbered our way menacingly, only to spin at 12 yards and pound away. [Eventually] the herd dispersed and we took up the trail of the stricken bull. He had only made it 80 yards. The stalk was incredible! The clean killing shot was a bonus."

On the same African hunt he felled a 350-pound lioness with his bow as she was about to maul the party's .375 Holland & Holland-armed professional hunter, who had been caught off-guard and was pinned against a tree by the animal. The lioness withdrew, and the next day, with the professional hunter patched up and on his feet, they returned to the site to find the lioness dead 150 yards from the attack scene.

African adventures notwithstanding, Schafer loved the mountainous terrain of North America—especially when sheep were the target. "I couldn't understand what was so great about sheep," he said back in 1986. "Well, I really fell in love with the North and its high, rugged mountain ranges. Sheep were different; and I was hooked."

Schafer's forte was glassing with 10X40 binoculars, and he developed an uncanny ability to

Schafer's record mountain goat.

steal within range of wary game. Yet despite his exceptional skills, he was quick to give others credit. On a Mexican hunt, hoping to complete his Grand Slam, he said, "I figured I was pretty good at spotting game. I might as well have left my binoculars at home. These [guides] put me to shame."

Schafer's modesty constantly concealed how great he really was. "He'd never let on," close friend Matt Riley says. "If you'd bump into him on the streets of Kalispell, he'd say something like, 'Yeah, I got into a few smaller bulls, but nothing outstanding; I'm still looking for a good bull.' But I'll never forget the day I stopped by his house and watched some video footage he'd just shot. I couldn't believe it—he had 5x5 and 6x6 bulls bugling their heads off within 15 yards! Any of us would go bonkers over something like this, but for Paul, it was just another day afield."

Schafer's inner strength—and his firm resolve not to settle for second best—was never more evident than on a Montana mountain goat hunt. Gene Wensel's twin brother, Barry, a friend and also an official Pope and Young Club measurer, wrote: "Video cameras recorded Paul passing up big billy after big billy. Late in the hunt, his cameraman filmed him easing to within nine yards of a huge bedded billy. At ultraclose range, Schafer pulled his binoculars from his shirt, checked the billy over and then slipped an arrow into its chest.

"Two months later, I put a tape to those horns. Checking my figures twice, I learned [that] the goat was not only a new Montana state record, but if entered in the records, [it] would rank number two

in the world. When I [gave] Paul the news, I'll never forget his reaction. He said, 'Huh? Good for him.' 'Good for who?' I asked. 'Good for the goat,' Paul said. 'He's the one that grew the horns, not me.'"

That goat and many of Schafer's other trophies won't be found in any record book. Matt Riley explains: "Paul worried that putting a number or a ranking on an animal might detract from its inherent worth. He believed in his heart that every bow-kill is a trophy. Although he entered a few head to help out some of the outfitters he hunted with, he was extremely sensitive about giving due respect to the animal instead of the hunter."

Schafer's respect for wild game drove him to perfect his shooting accuracy. He was an exceptional shot at twice the distance of most modern bow-hunters—as video footage amply proves—but he was particularly discreet about mentioning how far his longer shots were for fear of encouraging novices to shoot beyond their range.

Once, however, on a $10 bet, he shot an arrow at his own camera from 90 yards. "He nailed the lens dead-center, winning the bet," says Paul Brunner, who dedicated his book, *Tree Stand Hunting*, to Schafer, "but ruining a $400 camera."

Schafer had no shortage of friends, and it was rightly said at his funeral that if his best friend was asked to stand up, the entire congregation would rise. "Paul loved deeply," close friend Bob Windauer says. "He did an incredible amount of fathering to my two sons. When I could not get through to [them], I would talk to Paul [and] he would find a way to deliver what they needed to know. Paul was the world's best hunter but still had time to teach his niece, Jenny, how to hunt."

Windauer's son, Dave, who spent a four-year apprenticeship learning the craft of bow making from Schafer, says, "Paul was more like a father than a boss—it wasn't at all like work."

Just as Schafer gave, he occasionally got back. Forever short of cash, a hunt for desert sheep to complete his Grand Slam seemed out of reach. But then Tom Sander, with help from Rick Schmidt and Paul Brunner, hatched a plan to launch the hunt. Here's Schafer's own account:

"Out of the blue, [Sander] said, 'Well, let's get something going and send you to Mexico for your desert sheep!' I just sat back and laughed. There was no way I had that kind of money. But Tom said he would do a limited-edition print and donate it to me, and that I should match it with a limited-edition bow.

"As we continued our conversation, I realized that Tom really wanted to do this for me—and that I really wanted to take him up on his offer."

With the help of Schmidt, a custom-knife maker from Whitefish, Montana, a collector's set of 50 prints, bows and knives were sold to finance Schafer's 10-day sheep hunt, which would cost about $12,000. The sale went nicely, but while Schafer was in the Northwest Territories filming a bowhunting movie, he learned that the Mexican officials required the full amount to reserve the hunt. Frantically, Schafer called Brunner and Sander by radio-phone to see if they had the balance, but they were still $3,000 short. So Brunner promptly borrowed the money and wired it. Schafer later wrote, "Here's a guy who lacks only the desert sheep to fill his Grand Slam, and he borrows $3,000 so his friend has a chance to complete his!"

Without a doubt, the love of Schafer's life was his young son, Hunter. "A bitter custody battle for the child really hurt Paul," Bob Windauer says. "Paul was very sensitive and perhaps too trusting— his conscience was right where it belonged." In his will, Schafer wrote, "As usual, things are a mess I leave you with, but that's kinda the way my life has been (good but hard)."

"Like everybody else, Paul had struggles," says Joan Simonetti, Schafer's older sister, "but I must say nobody ever worked harder for what he got than Paul."

Indeed, Schafer would gladly go to what others might consider outlandish extremes in instances when the three major elements in his life—a love for hunting, bow crafting and youngsters—were present. At Christmastime two winters ago, a woman came into his bow shop to inquire about a "nice" bow for her young son. Not having a clue about the work that went into a $600-plus Schafer Silvertip recurve, she said, I've got about $35 to spend on his Christmas."

"Oh, I'm sure I can build him a really fine bow, ma'am," Schafer replied. And he did—for $35. To this day, the woman probably has no idea of her gift's true worth ... just as few bowhunters know how much the sport is diminished by the loss of Paul Schafer.

Jeff Murray

The great hunter and the little Hunter — Paul Schafer with his very favorite wild creature, his son.

MY FAVORITE
HUNTING RIFLES by Jim Carmichel

The two questions I'm most often asked are: "How did you become a gun writer?" and "What is your favorite gun?"

There seems to be a widespread notion that gun writers are anointed by Diana, Goddess of the Hunt, and dwell thereafter in a magic kingdom filled with luscious firearms, like a fat Sultan surrounded by a harem of delicious maidens. The fact of the matter is that if I gave honest answers to either of these two questions I'd be accused of inventing stories or pulling my questioner's leg. That's why I usually render a modest response that suits the occasion or simply leave the subject hanging in the air, especially when it comes to the matter of favorite guns. Who would believe me if I tried to explain that I have torrid-but-fickle love affairs with shotguns, and that last season's undying passion now reposes on the dark side of my gun rack?

In any event, like wives and mistresses, "favorite" guns are usually a matter of personal taste. The guy down the street may think the .30/30 he inherited from Dear Old Granddaddy is the sweetest thing in the deer woods, while you wonder why he bothers to take the clunker hunting. So with advance warning of these caveats, and since someone asked, I have a few favorites worth mentioning. My current favorite shotgun, like all properly conducted love affairs, shall remain secret. Rifles, on the other hand, tend to be more honest and businesslike and, unlike svelte smoothbores that blind you with coy promises, can be ranked according to how well they do their job, and why. But even then, as we shall see, reason sometimes gives way to sentiment.

From the standpoint of unrivaled hunting perfection, my favorite has to be a .338 Winchester Magnum built by the David Miller Company. If you're an aficionado of hand-built rifles you know that the "economy" model Miller rifle now sells for something in the neighborhood of eight grand, with deluxe grades having gone for over $200,000 on the auction block...which probably makes you wonder how an impoverished gun writer comes by such pricey hardware. The simple explanation is that I got my Miller rifle about 20 years ago, before wealthy sheikhs and oil tycoons discovered the remarkable talents of David Miller and Curt Crum, his stock-building partner.

Miller had developed a scope-mounting system that he was proud of and asked me to give it a try.

Carmichel's number-one rifle for all seasons is this David Miller-built custom .338 Win. Mag. Miller's unique scope-mounting system is so strong that Jim has never had to re-zero this rifle in nearly two decades of hard hunting for everything from Alaska brown bear to this Botswana buffalo. The rifle features an English-style "drop box" magazine that adds an extra round to the gun's capacity.

Though his friends laughed at him when he built his "do-it-yourself" elephant rifle, Carmichel used the customized Mauser in .458 Win. Mag. years later to fulfill his dream of hunting elephant when he took this northern Botswana tusker.

During our conversation, I learned about his budding rifle company and the upshot was that I had him build a rifle in .338 Mag., complete with the new Miller mount. The funny thing, however, was that I somehow got the idea that Miller's mounts were a quick-detachable system, so I figured that a set of English-style express sights would round out the rifle to perfection. I was doing a lot of jetting back and forth between Alaska and Africa in those days, and a .338 Win. Mag. would be good medicine for just about anything that roamed the veld or tundra, especially if fitted with some fast-pointing express sights for those tedious and aggravating moments when lions come roaring out of the yellow grass.

So that's why the Miller rifle came complete with stylish express sights fitted. The quarter rib on which the rear sight is dovetailed is not simply soldered to the barrel in the usual way, but actually machined from the barrel blank so that they are one integral unit. But alas, as it turns out, this tour de force of metalworking is of no practical purpose, because I have yet to squint across the elegant express sights, the reason being that the Miller system gives whole new meaning to the phrase "permanent mounting."

The base and lower half of the rings are machined from a single block of steel and form a rigid cradle that supports and protects the scope for almost the entire length of the tube. Before building his scope mount, Miller needs exact information about the customer's shooting stance and eye positioning, because once the base is machined to interlock with the scope turret, any fore or aft movement is impossible. And to further reduce the likelihood of scope movement, the rifle's receiver ring is notched to form a recoil lug-type union with the scope base. The one-piece scope cradle is then mated to the action so precisely that they appear to be a single unit.

When Miller introduced this super-strong, scope-mounting system the price was $300—a staggering sum back then considering that ordinary mounts could be had for about 10 bucks. But big-ticket hunters who'd lost trophies because of inferior mounts considered the Miller system a bargain. In time, the price for a Miller mount climbed to $900, and if that makes you gulp, consider that it now sells tor $1,500! But the only way you can get one is by ordering an entire David Miller rifle.

Is it worth it? All I can say is that for nearly two decades of hard hunting in temperatures ranging from 20 below zero to 110 above, in rainstorms and desert dryness, the only time I've touched the adjustment knobs on the rig's 4X Leupold scope was the first time I sighted it in. Since then it has been spot on.

Don't get the idea that my David Miller .338 is a favorite only because of the foolproof scope mounts. Actually, the Miller mounts are just one element of a total hunting machine. Nothing has been left to chance, from the rebuilt Mauser action, to the Model 70-style safety, to the raised checkering on the bolt knob, to the hinged floorplate on the magazine that has been "dropped" English-style so that capacity is increased by an extra round, to the gracefully curved trigger so closely fitted in the guard slot that seeds and grit can't work their way into the mechanism. Then everything is perfectly fitted into a luscious piece of smoky-hued French walnut, with classic styling by Curt Crum and checkered with a delicate fleur-de-lis pattern.

The years and the miles have left their scars on my David Miller rifle—the blue is getting thin on some of the corners, and every hunting season I find more scratches on the stock. Miller has invited me to send the rig back for a touch-up, but I don't think so. There is honor in those dents and nicks—each with its own story to tell. When I grow too old to climb the hill and chase the plain, I want to touch those scars and hear the stories again.

Another favorite that has graced my rack for more than two decades is a custom flyweight built on a pre-1964 Model 70 Winchester action and chambered in .280 Remington. The slender barrel is by Douglas, and the exquisite Clayton Nelson stock is that amber-streaked kind of French walnut that we can no longer find. I've long since lost count of the deer, elk, sheep and African-plains game this lovely .280 has taken, but, for the record, it is the rifle I took to Iran back in the 1970s when my pal Fred Huntington and I went there to collect the Iranian "Grand Slam" of ibex, red and urial sheep and the petite Armenian sheep.

One sad day, when I was hunting elk in Idaho, I left my horse tied to a tree while I glassed a canyon. Another horse, tied nearby, spied the unprotected French walnut butt of my rifle jutting from the scabbard and, being an ugly and unprincipled beast, figured it would be a handy thing on which to rub his chin. That chin, of course, was wearing a steel bridle bit that cut long gashes in my lovely rifle.

My tears were a long time drying, and after that tragic event the rifle was hunted with only once more—when I took it to Alaska for white sheep. Guns, like good hunting dogs, deserve a graceful retirement, and after having the stock repaired and refinished to its former radiance, I retired the faithful rifle to a place of honor in my rack.

Its replacement, a .280 Remington built by Ultra Light Arms, rates about a 2 out of 10 on the beauty scale but earns its keep—and a place in my heart—because it can cut three overlapping holes in a 100-yard target and (even better) because it weighs *less than six pounds*, scope and all. This little Ultra Light isn't really a favorite yet, but it will be, wait and see.

For sheer handling joy, I like a 7x57 built on a Mauser action by Al Bieson, a living legend in the custom-gun world because of his exquisite styling and craftsmanship. Though the Bieson rifle is gorgeous to look at, its real beauty comes to life when you snap it to your shoulder. I like to hand it to guys who think they know all about guns and watch their eyes light up when they experience for the first time the feel of a truly great hunting rifle. When you close your hand around the gracefully slender grip

the rifle seems to find the target with a will of its own. This is a difficult quality to describe. British gunmakers often call it "hand"—the way a gun becomes a living part of the shooter—but usually in reference only to shotguns. A rifle with hand is a rare treasure, and everyone who takes this jewel in hand instantly understands why.

If you'll excuse a moment of sentiment, one more favorite is a mildly battered and not particularly handsome .458 Winchester Magnum that was custom-made from a $30 surplus Mauser. Actually, a real maker of custom rifles would call it an amateur's do-it-yourself project, and I suppose that's all it is. I'm the amateur and it really was a do-it-yourself project from my college days. I'd found the slick Mauser in a junk store and, since I fancied myself something of a gunsmith back then, elected to convert it into something useful in the way of a big-game rifle. I mean *really* big game: elephants for example. My school chums hooted at the idea because they figured the chances of my going to Africa and bagging an elephant were about the same as Marilyn Monroe calling me for a date. Not that I was all that convinced myself, but the more they chuckled the more determined I became to at least *own* an elephant rifle.

To that end, I opened up the Mauser bolt face for the larger Magnum rim, had a .458 barrel fitted and laid out some $60 (big money in those days) for a classic-styled, semi-finished stock. After a couple of months of whittling and sanding and hand-rubbing stock oil, I had what I thought to be a rather elegant custom .458 and I promised myself that someday, somehow, I'd take that rifle to Africa and bag elephants, Cape buffalo, lions and other deadly beasts. It was a promise kept a decade later in a mopane thicket along the southern edge of Botswana's mysterious Okavango Swamp, when I put the crosshairs just below the ear on an old bull elephant carrying thick, heavy ivory. On that and other safaris the do-it-yourself "elephant rifle" my school chums had laughed at tallied not just elephants and lions, but scores of Cape buffalo. Now it is hunted with no longer and rests in a special rack on the wall of my den, serving as a daily reminder that dreams *will* come true if you dream hard enough. It was the first rifle in my big-game battery . . . and the last I'll ever part with.

Jim Carmichel

A LIFE WELL SPENT by Vin T. Sparano

Charles Newton Elliott was hired as a field editor for *Outdoor Life* in 1950. Today, at the age of 90, Charlie is still on the masthead. No other OL editor can match Elliott's tenure or his influence on millions of sportsmen.

In 1995, the State of Georgia, where Charlie was the first director of the Game and Fish Commission, dedicated a 6,400-acre tract of land in his honor, the Charlie Elliott Wildlife Center. Next month–on November 29, 1997, Charlie's 91st birthday–Georgia will dedicate the Charlie Elliott Visitors' Center at the wildlife center. More than 40,000 students each year are expected to use the $1.5 million dollar facility, which will also house an Outdoor Learning Center to instruct educators in how to use the outdoors as a classroom.

One of the unique features of the Visitor's Center will be the recreation of Charlie's den, where he has spent a lifetime writing for *Outdoor Life*. Thousands of visitors every year will be able to see the Dall ram over his fireplace, the bear and wolf rugs on the floor, the huge mule deer over his old desk and typewriter and all the memorabilia of a lifetime of outdoor adventures.

Keeping things in the OL family, Georgia has also asked award-winning sculptor and former OL field editor Bruce Brady (Compass, April) to produce a life-size bronze of Charlie, complete with his old Winchester Model 12 shotgun. The cost of the bronze is $48,000, and the Wildlife Center is accepting donations. Checks may be sent to John R. Williams, Campaign Chairman for the Charlie Elliott Wildlife Center, P.O. Box 1585, Covington, GA 30210.

Vin T. Sparano

Charlie Elliott at home in Covington, Georgia.